Emerging Trends, Technologies and Programming Paradigms

National Conference

Editors:
Dr. S.K. Shrivastav
B.E. (Gold Med.), MBA, M.S., Ph.D.
Director
Rukmini Devi Institute of Advanced Studies

Rakesh Kr. Arora
M.Tech. (IT), MCA
Assit. Profesor
Rukmini Devi Institue of Advanced Studies

Manoj Kr. Gupta
M.Tech, (IT), MCA
Asstt. Professor
Rukmini Devi Institue of Advanced Studies

GPH BOOK®

असतो मा सद्गमय
RUKMINI DEVI INSTITUTE OF ADV. ST.
MADHUBAN CHOWK Rohini

RUKMINI DEVI
Institue of Advanced Studies

ज्योतिर्वृणीत तमसो विज्ञानम्
GURU GOBIND SINGH INDRAPRASTHA UNIVERSITY

Publisher's Note

Every possible effort has been made to ensure that the information contained in this book is accurate at the time of going to press, and the publisher and author cannot accept responsibility for any errors of omission, however caused. No responsibility for loss or damage occasioned to any person acting, or refraining from action, as a result of the material in this publication can be accepted by the editor, the publisher of the author.

Every effort has been made to trace the owners of copyright material used in this book. The author and the publisher will be grateful for any omission brought to their notice for acknowledgement in the future editions of the book.

First Published 2009

Price Rs. 500/-

ISBN: 978-93-81970-41-6

Gullybaba Publishing House Pvt. Ltd

2525/193, 1st Floor, Old Bus Stand,

Opposite Street of Asha Maternity Center,

Tri Nagar, Delhi-110035

Tel.: 27387998, e-mail: info@gullybaba.com

Website: www.GullyBaba.com

www.enhanceyourchild.com

Dedicated to

Late (Smt.) Rukmini Devi

Mother of Shri K.C. Garg, a visionary educationsist, philanthropist and Social worker

Shir K.C. Garg

Founder

Rukmini Devi Group of Institutions

Shir K.C. Garg

Co-Founder

Rukmini Devi Group of Institutions

Prof. Dilip K. Bandyopadhyay
Vice Chancellor

GURU GOBIND SINGH INDRAPRASTHA UNIVERSITY
Kashmere Gate, Delhi-110403, India
Phone 91-11-23869802, 23900104
Fax 91-11-23865941
E-mail: mail®ipu.edu

GGSIPU/VC 2009
March 17, 2009

MESSAGE

I am pleased to know that Rukmini Devi Institute of Advanced Studies is organizing a National Conference on " Emerging Trends, Technologies and Programming Paradigms" on 21st March, 2009.

Information Technology has revolutionized the life of each and very person. In all walks of life impact of IT enabled services can be felt.

The IT sector is not only fastest developing sector, but also changing very fast. New researches are making equipments and services obsolete even within a year. In such a scenario, it is very important for academia, corporate sector and students to keep abreast of latest technologies and researches. Under these circumstances, this conference assumes great importance. I congratulate RDIAS for conducting such an important conference. I wish this conference will prove to all concerned an extremely important event. I wish all success to this endeavour.

(Dilip K Bandyopathyay)

RUKMINI DEVI
Institue of Advanced Studies
Approved by AICTE, HRD Ministry,
Affiliated to G.G.S. I.P. University, Delhi

Massage From the Chairman

I am glad to know that Rukmini Devi Institute of Advanced Studies is organising a National Conference on 'Emerging Trends, Technologies and Programming Paradigms'. In the backdrop of worldwide importance of I.T. enabled services this is indeed very important topic which, in turn, would make this event extremely important one. I am sure rich expertise available in the conference would be a treasure of knowledge and would benefit all the participants.

My best wishes for the Conference.

K.C. Garg

RUKMINI DEVI
Institue of Advanced Studies
Approved by AICTE, HRD Ministry,
Affiliated to G.G.S. I.P. University, Delhi

Massage From the Director

I.T. sector is not only growing very fast but also changing fast due to research and innovation. It is, therefore,- a must for the academia, professionals and I.T. enabled service providers to keep abreast themselves with the latest developments. This Conference, organized by our institute on the topic 'Emerging Trends, Technologies and Programming Paradigms', will provide an ideal platform for accumulating and disseminating latest I.T. related trends and technologies.

I am sure this Conference will prove is landmark event for all the participants and I extend my best wishes for the same.

Dr. S.K. Shrivastav

Preface

The IT sector has recorded phenomenal growth worldwide during the last few years and IT enabled operations are fast replacing other options. An important new trend in the field of information technology is to identify information from the ocean of data. This research area has witnessed a proliferation of concepts, models and methods. However, the problem of the relative expressive power of the various programming concepts has not been addressed systematically. This conference aims to facilitate copious flow of knowledge, ideas and information and provide an ideal platform and form allowing innovating exchanges of ideas and thinking related to the emerging trends and techniques.

The Conference in nutshell would lead:

- To sensitize key policy and decision makers on the potentials of IT.
- To provide a forum for inventors and developers to share their experiences and facilitate exchange of ideas.
- To increase IT awareness and expose participants to emerging trends, products and services in IT.

The Conference focuses on two themes namely:

- Emerging Trends & Technologies
- Programming Paradigms

We would like to place on record our sincere gratitude to Shri Mangat Ram Singhal, Hob'ble Cabinet Minister, Govt. of NCT of Delhi, for giving consent to grace the conference as Chief Guest. We also thank Prof. R.K. Datta for gracing this conference as Keynote Speaker. We also express our gratitude to Shri K.C. Garg, Chairman, Rukmini Devi Group of Institutions for this constant inspiration and guidance for organizing this conference.

We are certainly indebted to Prof. Navin Rajpal, Professoer, USIT, GGSIP University and Dr. Puneet Kumar, Vice President, Sabisa Info Technologies who have consented for Chairing a session to share very high professional expertise of great value with the participants.

We are also extremely thankful to the contributors of the papers that appear in this book. We thank the faculty members and staff members of Rukmini Devi Institute of Advanced Studies for editing and compiling the articles in bringing this book. We shall fail in our duty if we do not express sincere thanks to M/s GullyBaba Publishing House for their efforts in bringing out this book in such a nice manner. It is happed that this book will be an asset to all the participants in particular and academia and corporate executives in general.

Delhi
March 21, 2009

Editors:
Dr. S.K. Shrivastav
Rakesh Kr. Arora
Manoj Kr. Gupta

CONTENTS

Design and Implementation of a Digital Signature Solution for (W^2DMS) on Enterprise Wide Area Network (E-WAN)

Jitender Chugh
Scientist E, DECS, DRDO Head Quarter
Dr. C S Rai
Reader, USIT, GGS Indraprastha University.

Abstract
Many traditional and newer businesses and applications have recently been carrying out enormous amounts of electronic transactions, which have led to a critical need for protecting the information from being maliciously altered, for ensuring the authenticity, and for supporting nonrepudiation. Just as signatures facilitate validation and verification of the authenticity of paper documents, digital signatures serve the purpose of validation and authentication of electronic documents. This paper presents a digital signature solution implementation for Web based Workflow and Document Management System (W^2DMS). The W^2DMS System provides the electronic movement of file, Digital Signature implementation and provides the provision for issuing of Digital Certificates across the DRDO Labs. To implement this system, an in-house developed framework has been utilized. This framework consists of seven chronological stages. An in-depth study of these stages for W^2DMS, including guidelines for implementation issues has been provided.

Keywords: - *Digital Signature, Digital Certificate, W^2DMS, E-WAN*

Introduction

DRDO is the premier Defence R&D Organisation in the country. The very nature of the responsibilities entrusted to it, sets limitation on its public interaction so the concept of E-governance in DRDO is viewed as a technological tool to enhance the efficiency and productivity of employees and to inculcate the habit of Knowledge Sharing and having less paper office in the organization.

DRDO Technological Architecture: DRDO has set-up a highly secured Intranet, connecting more than 56 laboratories spread in various parts of the country. On this Intranet, information exchange, knowledge sharing and wide range of employee-centric application systems to manage human and material resources in an efficient and effective manner by use of ICT (Information and Communication Technology) are being used. These web based application systems are based on latest Industry standard viz. n Tier architecture[9]. These application systems are being used across DRDO on 365*24*7 basis. These systems enable us to move towards higher level of egovernance implementation. In the existing application system, it only captures the basic details of the files but the actual files move physically. It is a dilatory process and quick online view of content of file for reference is not possible. The physical file approval is time consuming task and file movement status is not available online. It was decided to undertake a task "Implementation Electronic movement of the file" at DRDO with the following objectives: -

- Implementation of web based workflow and Document management System (W2DMS) for movement of file.
- Design and Implementation of Digital Signature to provide Authentication, Data Integrity and Non-repudiation.
- Establishment of Certifying Authority at DRDO HQ for issuing of Digital Certificates to all the DRDO labs. The facilities provide the provision for issuing of certificates which contains public key and identity of the owner.

To meet the aforesaid objectives and scope, a framework has been developed in-house and the same will be used for implementation. This framework is diverse, modular and flexible; hence it was used for implementation. The framework consists of seven chronological stages. However, the framework is flexible allowing reverting to a previous stage at any time during the implementation if needed. The brief description of these stages is as follows: -

Stage 1: Infrastructure appraisal: - The infrastructure evaluation is done to provide overview of the existing infrastructure. It consists of description of process such as system, structure, policy and strategy.

Stage 2 : Aspiration and Objectives: - The objective is to eliminate the manual signature with in DRDO. This will trust relationships with in stakeholders.

Stage 3: Functional pensiveness: - This stage recommends the prioritization of attributes of security by assigning priority levels in relation to their importance in organization.

Stage 4: Analysis phase: - This step studies and analyses the impact of the proposed Implementation on work process, stakeholders and existing systems & applications.

Stage 5: Elucidation scrutiny: - The time & cost component, interoperability and standards are analyzed and evaluation criteria for each requirement is specified according to the implementation requirements.

Stage 6: Implementation: In this phase, the objectives are implemented. Risk Management, Communication Management, Integration and change Management are considered.

Stage 7: Evaluate: Evaluation is done for continuous improvement, if there is need to monitor, it can go to any stage.

This paper is organized as follows.

The second section of the paper focuses on the Overview of Workflow and Document Management System (W2DMS). This briefly discussed the key objectives, architecture and its principal components.

The third section describes about Digital Signature technology and Certifying and explains the process of Digital Signature using PKI.

The forth section briefly discusses the implementation of in-house developed framework and its stages. It will continue with the analysis of the digital signature implementation by utilizing the aforementioned framework. The value addition by adopting this framework and key benefits are mentioned.

The last part of the paper discuss the conclusion and scope for the future work.

Overview of Enterprise System

W2DMS provides Document management, Workflow, Collaboration environment and Knowledge Management in an integrated fashion and delivers as Electronic Workplace that will result in productivity improvement in E WAN.

W2DMS is J2EE (Java 2 Enterprise Edition) (Java 1.4) based n-tier solution using Model view Controller (MVC) architecture.

The Key Objectives of W2DMS are:

- Create an Office Automation System
- Enhance Productivity
- Enable Prioritization of work.
- Use IT as an enabler to help in daily work
- Design an efficient workplace
- Enable policy based Processing
- Access Controls at all levels.
- Efficient & Transparent administration

The architecture of W2DMS is as follows :-

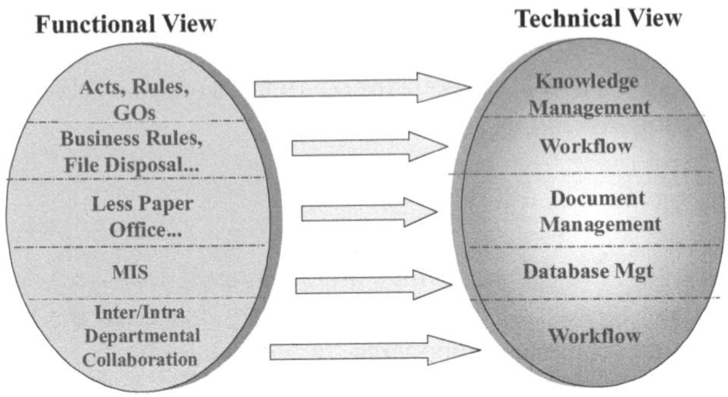

Figure 1: Architecture of W^{2}DMS

The Principal components of the System are:

- o Sub Systems such as
- o Knowledge Management System (KMS)
- o File Management system (FMS)
- o Dashboard
- o MIS

Digital Signature Technology

Digital Signature is a mechanism by which a message is authenticated i.e. proving that a message is effectively coming from a given sender, much like a signature on a paper document. For instance, suppose that A wants to digitally sign a message to B. To do so, he uses his private-key to encrypt the message; he then sends the message along his public key (typically, the public key is attached to the signed message), since A's public key is the only key that can decrypt the message, a successful decryption constitutes a Digital Signature Verification, meaning that there is no doubt that it is A's private key that encrypted the message.

For Digital Signature, another technique used is called hashing. Hashing produces a message digest that is small and unique representation (a bit like a sophisticated checksum) of the complete message. Hashing algorithm are a one-way encryption, i.e. it is impossible to derive the message from the digest. The main reasons for producing a message digest are:

1. The message integrity being sent is preserved; any message alteration will immediately be detected.

2. The digital signature will be applied to digest, which is usually considerably smaller than the message itself.
3. Hashing algorithms are much faster than any encryption algorithm (asymmetric or symmetric).

The following sections explains what really happens when encrypting and signing a message on one hand, and when decrypting a message and verifying its signature on the other hand.

Steps for Signing and encrypting a message

The following figure shows the set of operations required when A wants to send a signed and encrypted message to B.

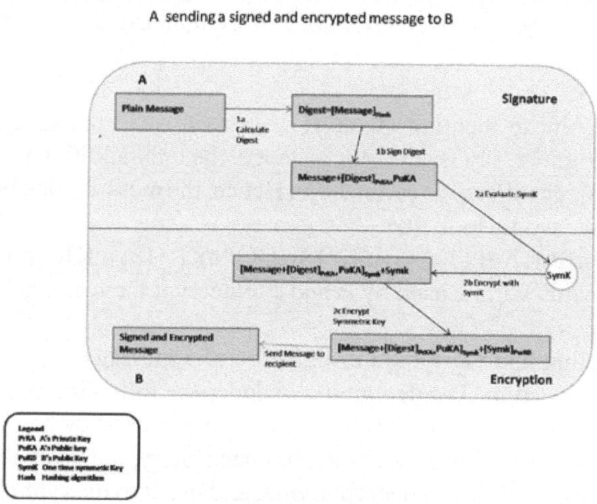

Figure 2: Signature and Encryption details with Keys

Message signature Digital Signature includes two steps:

a) Message digest evaluation: The main purpose for evaluating a digest is to ensure that the message is kept unaltered; this is called message integrity.
b) Digest signature A signature is in fact an encryption using the issue's (A in this case) private-key. Included in the signature is also the hashing algorithm name used by the issuer. The issue's public-key is also appended to the signature. Doing so lets anyone decrypt and verify the signature the issue's public-key and hashing algorithm. Given the properties of public-key encryption and hashing algorithms, the recipient has proof that:

i) The issuer's private-key has encrypted the digest;
ii) The message is protected against any alteration.

Message encryption. Encryption includes the following 3 steps:

a) Creation of a one-time symmetric encryption/decryption key. Remember that encryption and decryption algorithmic using asymmetric- keys are too slow to be used for long messages; symmetric-keys algorithm are very efficient and are therefore used.
b) Message encryption. The whole message (the message itself and the signature) is encrypted using SymK, the symmetric-key evaluated above.
c) Symmetric-key encryption. SymK is also used by the recipient to decrypt the message. SymK must therefore be available to the recipient(Bob) only. The way to hide the SymK from everybody except the recipient is to encrypt it using the recipient's public-key. Since SymK is a small piece of information compared to a message(that could be very long), the performance penalty associated with the relative inefficiency of asymmetric-key algorithms is acceptable.

One interesting point to mention is that if A wants to send the same message to more than one recipient, say B and J for instance, the only additional operation to be performed is to repeat 'step 2) c)' for John. Hence, the message that both Bob and John would receive would look like:
[Message+[Digest]PrKA+PuKA]SymK+[SymK]PuKB+[SymK]PuKJ . Notice that the exact same SymK will be used by B and J to decrypt the message.

Steps for Decrypting and verifying the signature of a message

1) **Message decryption**. The decryption includes the following steps:
a) Symmetric-Key decryption. The one time synmmetric-key has been used to encrypt the message. This key(SymK) has been encrypted using the recipient's (B) public-key. Only B can decrypt SymK and use it to decrypt the message.
b) Message decryption. The message (which includes the message itself and the signature) is decrypted using SymK.

2) **Signature verification**. The signature verification includes the following 3 steps:
a) Message digest decryption. The digest has been encryption using the issuer's (A) private-key. The digest is now decrypted using the issuer's public-key included in the message.
b) Digest evaluation. Since hashing is a one-way process i.e. the message cannot be derived from the digest itself, the recipient must re-evaluate the digest using the exact same hashing algorithm the issuer used.
c) Digest comparison. The digest decrypted in a) and the digest evaluated in b)

are compared. If there is a match, the signature has been verified, and the recipient can accept the message as coming unaltered from the issuer. If there is a mismatch this could mean that:

i) The message has not been signed by the issuer or
ii) The message has been altered.
iii) In both cases, the message should be rejected.

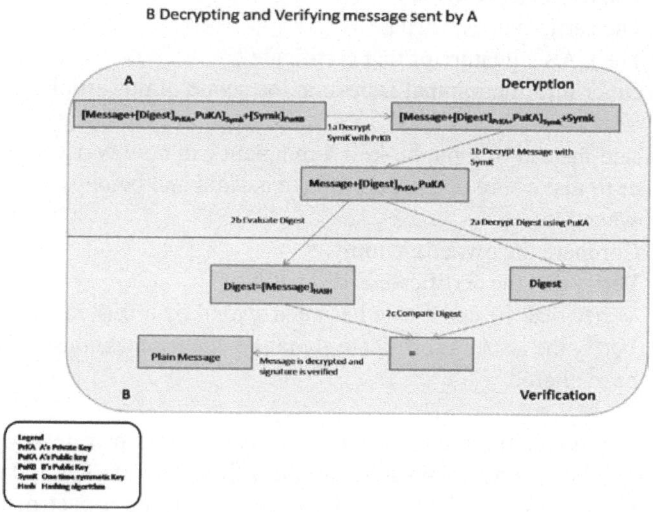

Figure 3: Decryption and Verification of the Signature of a Message

Identity and keys

Until now, we have taken for grated the keys being used for encryption/decryption and digital signature/verification belong to B and A. How can we be sure that A is really A? And, how can A be sure that only B will see what he encrypted? So far, the only thing we know is that the user of a given key pair has signed and encrypted the message. But, is he really the owner> G, for instance, may have sent a message to B pretending that he is A; B cannot tell whether or not it is A or G who is sending the message. The same applies to B's public-key.

Certifying Authority

A certificate is a place of information that proves the identity of a public-key's owner. Like a passport, a certificate provides recognized proof of a person's (or entity) identity. Certificates are signed and delivered securely by a trusted third party entity called a Certificate authority (CA). As long as Bob and Alice trust this third party, the CA, they can be assured that the keys belong to the persons they claim to be.

A certificate contains among other things:

i) The CA's identiy
ii) The owner's identity
iii) The owner's public-key
iv) The certificate expiry date
v) The CA's signature of that certificate
vi) Other information that is beyond the scope of this article.

With a certificate instead of a public-key, a recipient can now verify a few things about the issuer to make sure that the certificate is valid and belongs to the person claiming its ownership:

1) Compare the owner's identity.
2) Verify that the certificate is still valid
3) Verify that the certificate has been signad by a trusted CA
4) Verify the issuer's certificate signature , hence making sure it has not been altered.

B can now verify A's certificate and be assured that it is A's private-key that has been used to sign the message. A must be careful with her private-key and must not divulge how to get to it; by doing so, she is enforcing one aspect of the non-repudiation feature associated with her digital signature. There is more to consider for effective non-repudiation support.

Note that certificates are signed by a CA, which means that they cannot be altered. In turn, the CA signature can be verified using the CA's certificate.

Certification validation added to the process

When A encrypts a message from B, A uses B's certificate. Prior to using the public key included in B's Certificate, some additional steps are performed to validate B's certificate :

1) Validity period of B's certificate.
2) The Certificate belongs to B.
3) B's certificate has not been altered.
4) B's certificate has been signed by a trusted CA.

Additional steps would be required to validate the CA's certificate in the case where A does not trust B's CA. These steps are identical to the ones requires to validate B's certificate. In the example below, it is assumed that both B and A trust that CA.

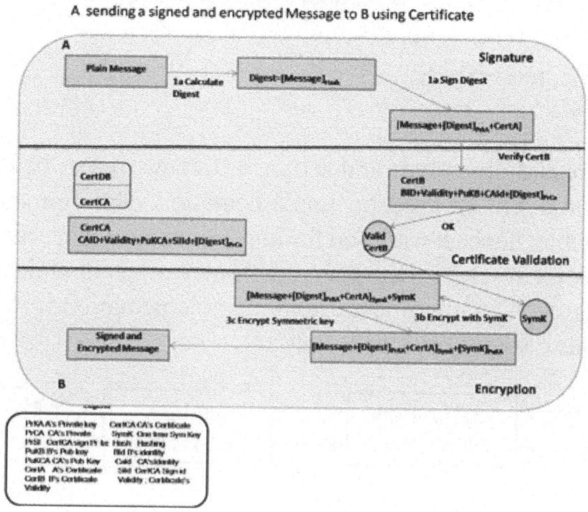

Figure 4: Message Encryption using Digital Certificate

In the figure above, a certificate validation step is added to what has been shown above. Only the fields required for the validation of a certificate are displayed.5 Our Model Architecture

Implementation of Framework

Security in health care information systems is among the highest priority research topics. Introduction of the Health Insurance Portability and Accountability Act of 1996 (HIPAA) increased the pressure on health careorganizations for implementing security. HIPAA proposes a techno-managerial framework that can aid planners of security systems as deployed within health care environment. Having a security framework will enable organizations to implement security standards more easily and quickly. As a result, wethepatientswill start seeing an increasing number of new health care services supported by the information technologies. HIPAA mandates rules to maintain the privacy of protected health information, to establish security requirements to protect that information, and to develop standard identifiers. Based on the HIPAA security rules (HIPAA.org, 2003), if a system or the communication between two systems was implemented using technology(s) meeting standards in a general security framework (Identification and Authentication; Authorization and Access Control; Accountability; Integrity and Availability; Security of Communication; and Security Administration.) then that system would be essentially secure. However, there is no single standards development organization (SDO) that is addressing all aspects of health care information security and confidentiality. As a result, HIPAA defines the security standard as a set of requirements with implementation features that providers, plans, and clearinghouses must include in their operations to assure that electronic health information pertaining to an individual remains secure [1].

To meet the aforesaid objectives and scope, a framework has been developed in-house and the same will be used for implementation. This framework is diverse, modular and flexible; hence it was used for implementation. The framework consists of seven chronological stages. However, the framework is flexible allowing revert ing to a previous stage at any time during the implementation if needed. The brief description of these stages is as follows:

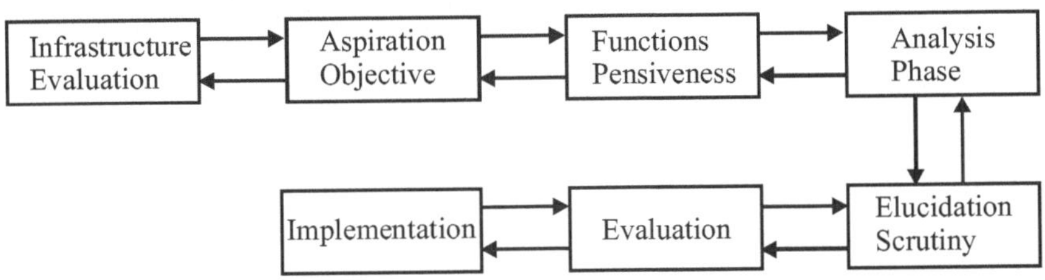

Figure 4: Stages of HIPAA Framework

The following subsections describe for implementation

Stage 1: Infrastructure appraisal
The infrastructure appraisal is intended to provide an overview of existing Infrastructure of W^2DMS. Table 1 below presents a brief summary.

Stage 2: Aspiration and Objectives
The main goal of the Digital Signature implementation is to eliminate the manual signature with in an organization using W^2DMS on E _ WAN and streamline the online process. Meanwhile, this will enable to implement a technology solution consistent with current and emerging standards and practices while satisfying the digital signature requirements. It will also establish a trust relationship with in stakeholders of W^2DMS.

Stage 3: Functional Pensiveness
This stage recommends an appraisal of the specific security requirements by rating them in importance of the operation for the enterprise. The basic security blocks are included in Table 2, which illustrates the results of this analysis specific to the W^2DMS. The values were derived from interaction with key personnel and security standards imposed

SYSTEM	Hardware: High End Servers, client machines Software : Redhat Linux, MS Windows OS, IE Explorer 5.5 or better, Mozilla etc. Applications: RDBMS,Application Server, Tomcat Jakarta web server, Struts, Hibernate, Network Security: HTTPS and SSL using Revising Server side certificates.
STRUCTURE	Work Process: Described as above Organizational Structure: The W^2DMS system is operational on E – WAN. It provides interfaces for different agencies, stakeholder at Corporate level and at Work center level. It provides the forms at work center level, so that using this interface, data can be entered into the system. Roles and Responsibilities: Information in W^2DMS is hierarchical in nature. Information is available on role basis and access control is through password. Geographic Spread: W^2DMS is based on E – WAN that connects more than fifty Six (56) work centers??
POLICY	Organizational Security Policy: The security policy that is used by W^2DMS is strictly controlled by various rules and regulations and is enforced by the notified agency. Management Support: The upper management is very supportive of technology use and aware of the security issues involved. Their mission is to be a pioneer in developing and implementing information technology to improve the effectiveness.
STRATEGY	A core competency of the organisation is bringing new technology to the field of disability evaluations. They have positioned themselves as pioneers and innovators in this field. In the case of this digital signature project, the organization is ahead of its clients which is introducing some new problems into their strategic decision making process. That is, they need to predict the behavior of their clients in order to implement a technology that will be compatible with future implementations.

Table 1: Existing Infrastructure

	Authentication	Authorization	Access Control	Integrity	Confidentiality	Privacy	Availability
Importance	High	High	High	High	High	High	High

Table 2: Functional Abstraction

Authentication is the process of determining whether someone or something is, in fact, who or what it is declared to be. Authorization is the process of deciding if someone or something is allowed to have access to a service or a resource. Access control is a much more general way of talking about controlling access to a resource. It is analogous to controlling entrance by some arbitrary condition which may or may not have anything to do with the attributes of the particular user (The Apache Software Foundation, 2003). Integrity is the process of preventing, deterring, and detecting improper modification of information during or after transit (Kleinsteiber, 2002). Confidentiality is the process of protecting against the disclosure of information to parties other than the intended recipient(s). Privacy is the ability and/or right to protect your personal secrets, privacy cannot extend to legal persons such as corporations (Anderson, 2001).

Stage 4: Analysis Phase

The digital signature standards that are accepted are Public Key Cryptography and the One-Way Hash function. Therefore, we should benefit from these digital signature standards. Preliminary analysis has indicated that the proposed solution would streamline the workflow process and eliminate the overhead on both officials and the organization. Impact analysis of the workflow process was mentioned in the previous subsection.

Stage 5: Elucidation Scrutiny

Meta Requirements	Implementation Requirements	Evaluation criteria
Legal compliance - This solution should be able to provide legal binding signatures.	E-SIGN	Match the requirements of E-SIGN and/or UTEA
	State laws	Match the state requirements
Client Requirements – The signature generated should be Digital Signature Standard (DSS) compatible with client requirements.	PKI based digital signature solution	Use one of the three algorithms provided by the Digital Signature Standard (DSS)
Special Industry Requirement- This solution should match the industry standard.	security matrix	Message integrity
		Non-repudiation
		User authentication
		Other Option Requirements
End user requirements – This solution should match the user requirement. The users include providers, clients, and the organisation.	Platform compatible	
	Integrated with current reporting system	Support Microsoft Windows Operating system, and Internet Information Server 5
		Support Microsoft Word documentation format
		Provide online signing and verification
	CA solution	No lock with single CA provider
	Manageability	Provide 3 management interface; audit trails; data storage solution for digitally signed documents.
	Customizable	Vendor provides standard APIs
	Easy to use	No special hardware and software requirements
	Cost	The cost should be minimum
		The implementation cost should be reasonable based on the fair market price

Table 3: Requirement Analysis

A complete requirements analysis will be necessary to formulate a solution. A digital signature solution, intended for internal use only, will mostly depend on the availability of technology and the preferences of internal users. In this case, however, the organisation and its clients will use the digital signature solution for authentication and verification. To evaluate the existing solutions, meta-requirements were first identified. Then, these meta-requirements were expanded to specify implementation requirements and standards. Finally, the evaluation criteria for each requirement were specified according to the implementation requirements. Table 3 illustrates the requirements and the evaluation criteria.

Table 4 illustrates the comparison of digital signature application solutions based on the five items listed in the framework as well as additional items that were identified during the requirements analysis phase. Pricing for a Signature/Certificate solutions analyzed for 100 users ranged from Rs.1,21,275/- to Rs.14,85,000/- The reason for the wide range in pricing was due to the one-time server fee requested by Provider2, which is Rs.11,02,500/- regardless of the number of users. However, if the number of users increases to 10,000, this solution becomes more cost effective whereas the suggested solution from Provider 1 becomes less cost effective. The price range for 10,000 users is Rs. 80,50,500/- to Rs.1,76,85,000/- . Here, the certificate cost is a higher proportion of the total annual cost.

Evaluation Criteria	Provider 1	Provider 2	Provider 3
Match the requirements of E-SIGN and/or UTEA Success case that work with government agents	Yes	Yes	Yes
Use one of the three algorithms in DSS	Yes	Yes	Yes
Message integrity	Yes	Yes	Yes
Non-repudiation	Yes	Yes	Yes
User authentication	Yes	Yes	Yes
Web based solutions	Yes	Yes	Custom
Support Windows-based application (IIS5, IE)	Yes	Yes	Yes
Support Microsoft Word format	Yes	Planned	Custom
Provide online signing and verification	Yes	Yes	Yes
	Yes	Yes	Yes
Friendly Management interface Audit trails Data storage solution for digital signed documents Vendor provides standard API or library No special hardware and software requirements	Yes (1)Transaction receipt (2) File management system Yes Yes	Yes Yes Yes	No demo for evaluation Yes Yes
The cost should be minimum	No cost, except the cost of certificate	No cost, except the cost of certificate	No cost, except the cost of certificate
The implementation cost should be reasonable based on the fair market price	N/A	N/A	N/A

Table 4: Solution Comparison

The study also compared different CA solutions based on the requirements and proposed three CA providers who are capable of satisfying all the requirements. The implementation strategy proposed was outsourcing the CA to a third-party CA provider so that the organisation can focus on the application side of the implementation. The organisation identified as a critical requirement that the application fits the office workflow as already defined. Pilot tests can help to reveal any issues related to the CA. Once the digital signature application is adopted, it will be easier for the organisation to identify any issues regarding the CA. After this experience, the organisation may decide to operate as their own CA. The size and geographic dispersion of the provider network will challenge the CA implementation. The number of CAs, how they will be placed, and what performances bottlenecks can appear are questions that should be addressed.

Stage 6: Implementation

The real value of digital Signatures is not in their application to transactions but in the level of security and trust they provide in a business process. They should be able to provide authentication of the sender and non-repudiation of the contents of a document. They should also be simple to use, secure, and meet all legal and regulatory requirements as laid down by legislation.

- Validating Digital Identities :- Since digital identities can expire or be revoked by Certificate Authorities, it is important that the verification process involves verification of the Digital ID used to sign the data in addition to verification of the integrity of the data content.
- Time Stamping :- There is need to consider signature validity with reference to time. For example, a document that is signed now should show as valid even if is verified years from now.
- Signing with valid digital identities :- Signing should not be allowed with a digital identity or certificate that has been revoked or has expired. This not only binds the sender to the contents of the document but ensures that the individual's digital identity is trusted and valid.

Value Addition:- Whether signatures are handwritten or digital, they are applied to achieve three security services :

- Authentication :- which is concerned with assurance of identity.
- Data Integrity :- Assurance that data has not been modified since the signature was applied. While a handwritten signature does not in itself provide data integrity services, the security practices traditionally surrounding handwritten signatures, including the use of indelible ink and tamper-evident paper, provide some measure of data integrity. Digital signatures provide excellent data integrity services by virtue of the digital signature value being a function of the message digest; even the slightest modification of digitally signed messages will always result in signature verification failure.
- Non-repudiation: - which is concerned with providing evidence to a third-party that a party participated in a transaction and thereby protect other parties in the transaction against false denials of participation.

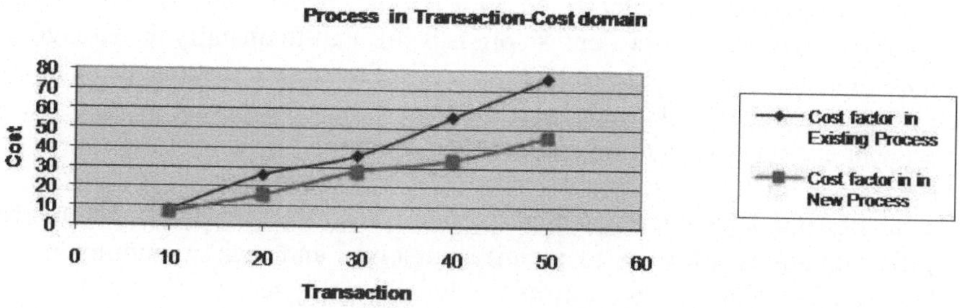

Figure 6: Graph drawn between Transaction-cost domain

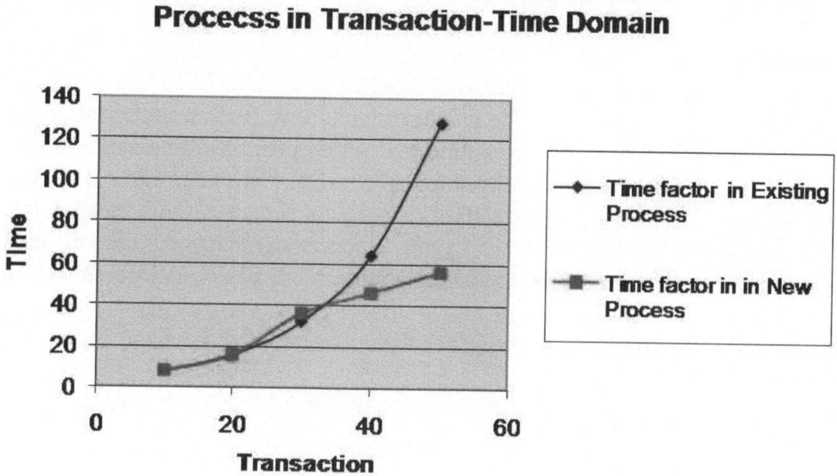

Figure 7: Graph drawn between Transaction-Time Domain

The Figure 6 & 7 shows the comparison of Existing process and New Process in Transaction-Cost and Transaction Time domain. It is clear from the figure that there is save of Time & Cost while adopting the new Process.

No security mechanism, whether manual or automated, provides absolute assurance. Modern forensic document examiners commonly compare a suspect signature with several examples of known valid signatures, and look for signs of forgery, which include

- Signatures written at a speed which is significantly slower than the genuine signatures
- Frequent change of the grasp of the writing implement
- Blunt line endings and beginnings
- Poor line quality with wavering and tremor of the line
- Retracing and patching
- Stops in places where the writing should be free.

These techniques are supplemented with ink and paper analysis, electrostatic detection of writing imprints, and so on. It is difficult to quantify the strength of handwritten signatures. It seems that the level of assurance that one can place in a handwritten signature depends largely on the technical expertise of the forensic document examiner used to investigate the signature.

Digital signatures have the potential to have the greatest impact on commerce. Digital signatures allow us to identify ourselves and make commitments in cyberspace in much the same way as we do in actual space.

Digital Signatures complement automation, bringing benefits that include faster, more efficient processing and reduced error rates and administrative costs.

Conclusion: -

The main goal is to eliminate the manual signature with in an organization using W^2DMS on E _ WAN and streamline the online process. Meanwhile, this will enable to implement a technology solution consistent with current and emerging standards and practices while satisfying the digital signature requirements. It will also establish a trust relationship having a security framework that will enable organizations to implement security standards more easily and quickly. It also ensures that the implementers and planners are aware of all the important information regarding the security needs and technologies, which they need to consider

References: -

- Tulu and Chatterjee. A New Security Framework for HIPAA-Compliant Health Information Systems. AMCIS 2003 Proceedings.
- David Fillingham. A Comparison of Digital and Handwritten Signatures. Ethics and Law on the Electronic Frontier, Fall 1997.
- William Stallings. Cryptography and Network Security. Prentice Hall of India.
- Kleinsteiber, J. (2002) Storage Networking Industry Association Technology Center, http://www.snia.org/apps/group_public/download.php/1634/ Authenicated_Infrastructures.pdf.
- PEC Solutions (2000) (Ed, Administration, U. S. D. o. J. D. E.) http:// www.deadiversion.usdoj.gov/ecomm/csos/cert_rea/section2/2 2.htm. :
- Policy and Communications Staff (2000) National Archives and Records Administration, Washington, DC.
- Polk, W. T. and Hastings, N. E. (2000) National Institute of Standards and Technology, Gaithersburg, MD, http:/ / csrc.nist.gov /pki/ documents/B2B-article.pdf. pdf.

- Schneier, B. (1996) Applied Cryptography, John Wiley & Sons.
- Lorenzo Rossi, Lorenzo Margola, Vania Manzelli : wHospital: a web-based application with digital signature for drugs dispensing management, Engineering in Medicine and Biology Society, 2006, Annual International Conference of the IEEE.

SQL Injection: A Threat to Database Security

Pramod Dhiman
Asst. Professor (IT),Institute of Technology & Science, Ghaziabad

Abstract

SQL Injection is an attack technique used to exploit web sites that construct SQL statements from user-supplied input. Structured Query Language (SQL) is a specialized programming language for sending queries to databases. Most small and industrial- strength database applications can be accessed using SQL statements. SQL is both an ANSI and an ISO standard. However, many database products supporting SQL do so with proprietary extensions to the standard language. Basically, SQL injection is a type of computer security exploit in which an attacker can gain access to remote database systems. Using a carefully-constructed value for a form field, such as a name or ***email*** *address, an attacker can fool the application into requesting* ***data*** *from a database which he would otherwise not have access to. SQL injection attacks are similar to* ***XSS attacks*** *in that the attacker is exploiting an application's regular input vectors. Also in common with XSS attacks, SQL injection attacks can be prevented by simple input filtering and validation before the data is passed on for storage or processing.*

Web applications may use user-supplied input to create custom SQL statements for dynamic web page requests. When a web application fails to properly sanitize user-supplied input, it is possible for an attacker to alter the construction of backend SQL statements. When an attacker is able to modify a SQL statement, the process will run with the same permissions as the component that executed the command. (e.g. Database server, Web application server, Web server, etc.). The impact of this attack can allow attackers to gain total control of the database or even execute commands on the system. The same advanced exploitation techniques available in LDAP Injection can also be similarly applied to SQL Injection.

Introduction

The visions of Internet applications (e.g., e-commerce) and pervasive computing not only push computations from a computer into everywhere, but also maximize our dependence

on networked computing systems. Quickly increased complexity, openness, inter-connection, and interdependence have made these systems more vulnerable and difficult to protect than ever. Intrusion-tolerant systems, with characteristics quite different from traditional secure systems [12, 3, 18, 40, 30], extend traditional secure systems to be able to *survive* or *operate through* attacks. The focus of intrusion-tolerant systems is the ability to continue delivering essential services in the face of attacks. New mechanisms of attack-resilient systems include but are not limited to intrusion detection, fragmentation, replication, migration, masking, isolation, containment, and recovery. Being a critical component of almost every mission critical information system, database products are today a multibillion dollar industry. Database systems motivated 32% of the hardware server volume in 1995 [41], and 39% of the server volume in 2000. Improving the intrusion tolerance of database systems has a direct positive impact on the technology that enables a variety of critical, trusted applications such as e-commerce, air traffic control, credit-card, telecommunication control, and electricity and water supply systems, that our everyday live depends on. However, existing database security mechanisms are very limited in tolerating intrusions. In particular, authentication and access control cannot prevent all attacks; integrity constraints are weak at prohibiting plausible but incorrect data; concurrency control and recovery mechanisms cannot distinguish legitimate transactions from malicious ones; and automatic replication facilities and active database triggers can even serve to spread the damage.

SQL Injection

SQL injection attacks expose sensitive database information by taking advantage of input validation vulnerabilities in Web site user interface software. In theory, Web sites validate all input, including character length and type, prior to sending queries to a backend database. However, if input validation is not carried out properly for each and every input (of which there may be thousands), an attacker may manipulate elements in a Web request to alter subsequent queries sent to a back-end database. The results of these unauthorized queries are then displayed as part of the HTML response generated by the Web site.

Consider the following simple example of a SQL Injection attack on a healthcare Web site.

A module in the healthcare site lists Social Security Numbers (SSNs) of family members

according to gender. The module is invoked with the following URL.

http://www.superhealth.com/show_members.asp?gender=m

The normal query subsequently sent to the database by the Web application looks like the following.

select SSN, NAME from PATIENTS where FAMILY = XXX and gender = 'm'

In this query, XXX represents the family identifier extracted from the database upon login. If the module is susceptible to SQL injection on the "gender" parameter, then the attacker may manipulate it by "injecting" additional characters as follows.

http://www.superhealth.com/show_members.asp?gender=m' or 1=1 or '1'='1

This URL effectively sends the following unauthorized query to the database.

select SSN, NAME from PATIENTS where FAMILY = XXX and gender = 'm' or 1=1 or '1'='1'

This query retrieves identification information for all patients in the entire database. The information is then displayed to the attacker by the Web application. Variations on this technique can display social security numbers even if the original query does not address a table containing this social security numbers. The ability of SQL injection to achieve bulk retrieval of thousands of user names at once makes it one of the most dangerous identity theft threats.

CATEGORIES OF SQL INJECTION ATTACKS

There are four main categories of SQL Injection attacks against Oracle databases

(i) SQL Manipulation
(ii) Code Injection
(iii) Function Call Injection
(iv) Buffer Overflows

The first two categories, SQL manipulation and code injection, should be well known to the reader, as these are the most commonly described attacks for all types of databases (including SQL Server, MySQL, PostgreSQL, and Oracle).

SQL manipulation typically involves modifying the SQL statement through set operations (e.g., UNION) or altering the WHERE clause to return a different result. Many documented SQL injection attacks are of this type. The most well known attack is to modify the WHERE clause of the user authentication statement so the WHERE clause always results in TRUE.

Code injection is when an attacker inserts new SQL statements or database commands into the SQL statement. The classic code injection attack is to append a SQL Server EXECUTE command to the vulnerable SQL statement. Code injection only works when multiple SQL statements per database request are supported. SQL Server and PostgreSQL have this capability and it is sometimes possible to inject multiple SQL statements with Oracle. Oracle code injection vulnerabilities involve the dynamic execution of SQL in PL/SQL.

The last two categories are more specific attacks against Oracle databases and are not well known or documented. In the vast majority of our application audits, we have found applications vulnerable to these two types of attacks.

Function call injection is the insertion of Oracle database functions or custom functions into a vulnerable SQL statement. These function calls can be used to make operating system calls or manipulate data in the database.

SQL injection of buffer overflows is a subset of function call injection. In several commercial and open-source databases, vulnerabilities exist in a few database functions that may result in a buffer overflow. Patches are available for most of these vulnerabilities, but many production databases remain un-patched.

(i) SQL MANIPULATION

The most common type of SQL Injection attack is SQL manipulation. The attacker attempts to modify the existing SQL statement by adding elements to the WHERE clause or extending the SQL statement with set operators like UNION, INTERSECT, or MINUS. There are other possible variations, but these are the most significant examples.

The classic SQL manipulation is during the login authentication. A simplistic web application may check user authentication by executing the following query and checking to see if any rows were returned –

SELECT * FROM users
WHERE username = 'bob' and PASSWORD = '*mypassword*'

The attacker attempts to manipulate the SQL statement to execute as –

SELECT * FROM users
WHERE username = 'bob' and PASSWORD = '*mypassword' or 'a' = 'a*'

Based on operator precedence, the WHERE clause is true for every row and the attacker has gained access to the application.

The set operator UNION is frequently used in SQL injection attacks. The goal is to manipulate a SQL statement into returning rows from another table. A web form may execute the following query to return a list of available products –

SELECT product_name FROM all_products
WHERE product_name like '%*Chairs*%'

The attacker attempts to manipulate the SQL statement to execute as –

SELECT product_name FROM all_products
WHERE product_name like '%*Chairs'*
UNION
SELECT username FROM dba_users
WHERE username like '%'

The list returned to the web form will include all the selected products, but also all the database users.

(ii) CODE INJECTION

Code injection attacks attempt to add additional SQL statements or commands to the existing SQL statement. This type of attack is frequently used against Microsoft SQL Server applications, but seldom works with an Oracle database. The EXECUTE statement in SQL Server is a frequent target of SQL injection attacks – there is no corresponding statement in Oracle.

In PL/SQL and Java, Oracle does not support multiple SQL statements per database request. Thus, the following common injection attack will not work against an Oracle database via a PL/SQL or Java application. This statement will result in an error

SELECT * FROM users WHERE username = 'bob' and PASSWORD = '*mypassword'; DELETE FROM users WHERE username = 'admin*';

However, some programming languages or APIs may allow multiple SQL statements to be executed.

PL/SQL and Java applications can dynamically execute anonymous PL/SQL blocks, which are vulnerable to code injection. The following is an example of a PL/SQL block executed in a web application –

BEGIN ENCRYPT PASSWORD('*bob*', '*mypassword*'); END;

The above example PL/SQL block executes an application stored procedure that encrypts and saves the user's password. An attacker will attempt to manipulate the PL/SQL block to execute as –

BEGIN ENCRYPT PASSWORD('bob', '*mypassword'); DELETE FROM users WHERE upper(username) = upper('admin*'); END;

(iii) FUNCTION CALL INJECTION

Function call injection is the insertion of Oracle database functions or custom functions into a vulnerable SQL statement. These function calls can be used to make operating system calls or manipulate data in the database.

The Oracle database allows functions or functions in packages to be executed as part of a SQL statement. By default, Oracle supplies over 1,000 functions in about 175 standard database packages, although only a fraction of these functions may be useful in a SQL injection attack. Some of these functions do perform network communication, which can be exploited. Any custom function or function residing in a custom package can also be executed in a SQL statement.

Functions executed as part of a SQL SELECT statement cannot make any changes to the database unless the function is marked as "PRAGMA TRANSACTION". Very few of the standard Oracle functions are executed as autonomous transactions. Functions executed in INSERT, UPDATE, or DELETE statements are able to modify data in the database. Using the standard Oracle functions, an attacker can send information from the database to a remote computer or execute other attacks from the database server. Many Oracle-based applications leverage database packages, which can be exploited by an attacker. These custom packages may include functions to change passwords or perform other sensitive application transactions. The issue with function call injection is that any dynamically generated SQL statement is vulnerable even the simplest SQL statements can be effectively exploited. The following example demonstrates even the most simple of SQL statements can be vulnerable. Application developers will sometimes use database functions instead of native code (e.g., Java) to perform common tasks. There is no direct equivalent of the TRANSLATE database function in Java, so the programmer decided to use a SQL statement.

SELECT TRANSLATE('*user input*',
'0123456789ABCDEFGHIJKLMNOPQRSTUVWXYZ',
'0123456789')
FROM dual;

This SQL statement is not vulnerable to other types of injection attacks, but is easily manipulated through a function injection attack. The attacker attempts to manipulate the SQL statement to execute as –

SELECT TRANSLATE(' *'|| UTL_HTTP.REQUEST('http://192.168.1.1/') ||* '',
'0123456789ABCDEFGHIJKLMNOPQRSTUVWXYZ',
'0123456789')
FROM dual;

The changed SQL statement will request a page from a web server. The attacker could manipulate the string and URL to include other functions in order to retrieve useful information from the database server and send it to the web server in the URL. Since the Oracle database server is most likely behind a firewall, it could also be used to attack other servers on the internal network.

Custom functions and functions in custom packages can also be executed. An example would be a custom application has the function ADDUSER in the custom package MYAPPADMIN. The developer marked the function as "PRAGMA TRANSACTION", so it could be executed under any special circumstances that the application might encounter. Since it is marked "PRAGMA TRANSACTION", it can write to the database even in a SELECT statement.

SELECT TRANSLATE(' *'|| myappadmin.adduser('admin', 'newpass') ||* '',
'0123456789ABCDEFGHIJKLMNOPQRSTUVWXYZ',
'0123456789')
FROM dual;

Executing the above SQL statement, the attacker is able to create new application users.

(iv) BUFFER OVERFLOWS

A number of standard Oracle database functions are susceptible to buffer overflows, which can be exploited through a SQL injection attack in an un-patched database. Known buffer overflows exist in the standard database packages as well as in standard database functions such as TZ_OFFSET, TO_TIMESTAMP_TZ, BFILENAME, FROM_TZ, NUMTOYMINTERVAL, and NUMTODSINTERVAL.

A buffer overflow attack using TZ_OFFSET, TO_TIMESTAMP_TZ, BFILENAME, FROM_TZ, NUMTOYMINTERVAL, or NUMTODSINTERVAL is executed using the function injection methods described previously. By exploiting the buffer overflow via a SQL injection attack, remote access to the operating system can be achieved. Additional information is widely available on executing and preventing buffer overflow attacks. In addition, some application and web servers do not gracefully handle the loss of a database connection due to a buffer overflow.

Usually, the web process will hang until the connection to the client is terminated, thus making this potentially an effective denial of service attack.

SQL Injection with PL/SQL

Oracle database stored procedures can be called directly from either the PL/SQL Gateway or using JDBC's ***callablestatement***. The PL/SQL Gateway (modplsql) is Oracle's Apache extension that allows web applications to be developed using database stored procedures. Modplsql is delivered with the Oracle Application Server and is used by some commercial applications. SQL injection vulnerabilities in database functions, procedures, and packages can also be exploited using a direct SQL*Net connect through SQL*Plus or other database tools. SQL statements can be executed four different ways in PL/SQL –

(i) Embedded SQL

(ii) ***execute immediate*** statements

(iii) DBMS_SQL package.

(iv) Dynamic Cursors

Embedded SQL statements and static cursors are compiled and only allow bind variables, however, dynamic cursors may be vulnerable to SQL injection attacks. ***Execute immediate*** and DBMS_SQL permit dynamic SQL, thus may be vulnerable to SQL injection attacks if bind variables are not used. From a SQL injection perspective, there is little difference between DBMS_SQL and ***execute immediate*** – both statements are equally vulnerable. The DBMS_SQL package is an older method for dynamic SQL and is being replaced by the ***execute immediate*** statement. Some applications use a combination of DBMS_SQL and ***execute immediate*** statements.

(i) Embedded SQL

Embedded SQL always executes compile-time-fixed SQL statement text. Dynamic SQL may execute compile-time-fixed SQL statement text or may execute run-time-created SQL statement text.

(ii) EXECUTE IMMEDIATE STATEMENT

The ***execute immediate*** statement is used to execute dynamic SQL in PL/SQL code. The statement fully supports bind variables, but also can be executed using a concatenated string.

The syntax for ***execute immediate*** is –

```
EXECUTE IMMEDIATE dynamic_string
[INTO {define_variable[, define_variable]... | record}]
[USING [IN | OUT | IN OUT] bind_argument
[, [IN | OUT | IN OUT] bind_argument]...]
[{RETURNING | RETURN} INTO bind_argument[, bind_argument]...];
```

An execute immediate statement subject to SQL injection attacks may be written like –

```
CREATE OR REPLACE PROCEDURE demo(name IN VARCHAR2) AS
sqlstr VARCHAR2(1000);
code VARCHAR2(100);
BEGIN
...
sqlstr := 'SELECT postal-code FROM states WHERE state-name = '" || name || "'';
EXECUTE IMMEDIATE sqlstr INTO code;
IF code = 'IL' THEN ...
...
END;
```

SELECT statement in the above code example would be meaningful in a SQL injection attack. It cannot be readily exploited by using set operations (e.g., UNION) or by concatenating another SQL statement as this is not permitted by ***execute immediate*** unless a PL/SQL block is used (i.e., BEGIN...END). Manipulating the outcome of the WHERE clause probably won't accomplish much. However, this statement can easily be exploited by inserting standard database functions (i.e., UTL_HTTP) or known functions that may cause buffer overflows.
To prevent SQL injection and to improve application performance, bind variables should always be used.

```
CREATE OR REPLACE PROCEDURE demo(name IN VARCHAR2) AS
sqlstr VARCHAR2(1000);
code VARCHAR2(100);
BEGIN
...
sqlstr := 'SELECT postal-code FROM states WHERE state-name = :name';
EXECUTE IMMEDIATE sqlstr USING name INTO code;
IF code = 'IL' THEN ...
...
END;
```

Execute immediate can be also used for anonymous PL/SQL blocks. Anonymous PL/SQL blocks are more vulnerable to SQL injection attacks since an attacker can insert multiple PL/SQL commands and SQL statements.

```
CREATE OR REPLACE PROCEDURE demo(value IN VARCHAR2) AS
BEGIN
...
— vulnerable
```

```
EXECUTE IMMEDIATE 'BEGIN updatepass('" || value || '"); END;';
— not vulnerable
cmd := 'BEGIN updatepass(:1); END;';
EXECUTE IMMEDIATE cmd USING value;
...
END;
```

(iii) DBMS_SQL PACKAGE

The DBMS_SQL package allows execution of dynamic SQL statements. DBMS_SQL is more complicated than ***execute immediate***, but basically performs the same function. Just as with ***execute immediate,*** bind variables should always be used instead of concatenating the SQL string together.

This procedure uses DBMS_SQL and is vulnerable to injection attacks –

```
CREATE OR REPLACE PROCEDURE demo(name IN VARCHAR2) AS
cursor_name INTEGER;
rows_processed INTEGER;
sqlstr VARCHAR2(150);
code VARCHAR2(2);
BEGIN
...
sqlstr := 'SELECT postal-code FROM states WHERE state-name = '" || name || '"';
cursor_name := dbms_sql.open_cursor;
DBMS_SQL.PARSE(cursor_name, sqlstr, DBMS_SQL.NATIVE);
DBMS_SQL.DEFINE_COLUMN(cursor_name, 1, code, 10);
rows_processed := DBMS_SQL.EXECUTE(cursor_name);
DBMS_SQL.CLOSE_CURSOR(cursor_name);
...
END;
```

The same procedure that uses bind variables is not open to attack –

```
CREATE OR REPLACE PROCEDURE demo(name IN VARCHAR2) AS
cursor_name INTEGER;
rows_processed INTEGER;
sqlstr VARCHAR2;
code VARCHAR2;
BEGIN
...
sqlstr := 'SELECT postal-code FROM states WHERE state-name = :name';
cursor_name := dbms_sql.open_cursor;
DBMS_SQL.PARSE(cursor_name, sqlstr, DBMS_SQL.NATIVE);
DBMS_SQL.DEFINE_COLUMN(cursor_name, 1, code, 10);
DBMS_SQL.BIND_VARIABLE(cursor_name, ':name', name);
```

```
rows_processed := DBMS_SQL.EXECUTE(cursor_name);
DBMS_SQL.CLOSE_CURSOR(cursor_name);
...
END;
```

(iv) DYNAMIC CURSORS

PL/SQL allows static and dynamic cursors. Cursor SQL statements can be dynamically generated just as ***execute immediate*** or DBMS_SQL statements can. Dynamic cursors are not regularly used, therefore, they may be overlooked in code reviews.

```
CREATE OR REPLACE PROCEDURE demo(name IN VARCHAR2) AS
sqlstr VARCHAR2;
...
BEGIN
...
sqlstr := 'SELECT * FROM states WHERE state-name = '" || name || "'';
OPEN cursor_states FOR sqlstr;
LOOP
FETCH cursor_states INTO rec_state
EXIT WHEN cursor_states%NOTFOUND;
...
END LOOP;
CLOSE cursor_status;
...
END;
```

Just as with ***execute immediate*** and DBMS_SQL, a bind variable would eliminate any possibility of SQL injection.

SQL Injection with JDBC

JDBC (Java Database Connectivity) is a standard Java interface for connecting from Java to relational databases. JDBC is used by most Java development architectures to connect to Oracle databases. Java Server Pages (JSP), Java Servlets, and Enterprise Java Beans (EJB) all use JDBC for database connectivity, as well as many other Java application architectures. By definition, all SQL statements in a JDBC application are dynamic. Dynamic SQL is executed with the Statement interface, specifically the ***CallableStatement*** and ***PreparedStatement*** subinterfaces. From a SQL injection perspective, both the ***CallableStatement*** and ***PreparedStatement*** interfaces can be vulnerable to SQL injection. In Oracle, only a single SQL statement will be executed by a ***PreparedStatement*** call. Other databases (e.g., SQL Server) may support multiple SQL statements in a single call.

PREPAREDSTATEMENT

The ***PreparedStatement*** interface is used to execute dynamic SQL statements. The standard JDBC ***PreparedStatement*** interface may be used or ***OraclePreparedStatement*** may be used if Oracle specific data types or other Oracle extensions are required. A ***PreparedStatement*** that is vulnerable to SQL injection may look something like this –

```
String name = request.getParameter("name");
PreparedStatement pstmt =
conn.prepareStatement("insert into EMP (ENAME) values ('" + name + "')");
pstmt.execute();
pstmt.close();
```

To prevent SQL injection, a bind variable must be used –

```
PreparedStatement pstmt =
conn.prepareStatement ("insert into EMP (ENAME) values (?)");
String name = request.getParameter("name");
pstmt.setString (1, name);
pstmt.execute();
pstmt.close();
```

CALLABLESTATEMENT

The ***CallableStatement*** interface is used to execute PL/SQL stored procedures and anonymous PL/SQL blocks. The standard JDBC ***CallableStatement*** interface may be used or the ***OracleCallableStatement*** may be used if Oracle specific data types or other Oracle extensions are required.

CallableStatement has two basic forms –Stored Procedure and Function Calls

```
prepareCall( "{call proc (?,?)}" );
```

Anonymous PL/SQL Block Calls

```
prepareCall("begin proc1(?,?); ? := func1(?); ...; end;");
```

The anonymous PL/SQL block call is much more vulnerable to SQL injection attacks since multiple SQL statements and PL/SQL commands can be inserted. A vulnerable anonymous PL/SQL block is –

```
String name = request.getParameter("name");
String sql = "begin ? := GetPostalCode('" + name + "'); end;";
CallableStatement cs = conn.prepareCall(sql);
cs.registerOutParameter(1, Types.CHAR);
cs.executeUpdate();
String result = cs.getString(1);
cs.close();
```

An attacker could alter the SQL statement from what the developer anticipated –

begin ? := GetPostalCode('*Illinois*'); end;
to either of the following statements or many other possibilities –
begin ? := GetPostalCode('*'); delete from users; commit; dummy(*''); end;
begin ? := GetPostalCode('*'||UTL_HTTP.REQUEST('http://192.168.1.1/')||* ''); end;
The simple fix is to use a bind variable –

```
String name = request.getParameter("name");
CallableStatement cs = conn.prepareCall ("begin ? := GetStatePostalCode(?); end;");
cs.registerOutParameter(1,Types.CHAR);
cs.setString(2, name);
cs.executeUpdate();
String result = cs.getString(1);
cs.close();
```

Protection Against SQL Injection Attack

SQL Injection attacks can be easily defeated with simple programming changes, however, developers must be disciplined enough to apply the following methods to every web accessible procedure and function. Every dynamic SQL statement must be protected. A single unprotected SQL statement can result in comprising of the application, data, or database server.

BIND VARIABLES

The most powerful protection against SQL injection attacks is the use of bind variables. Using bind variables will also improve application performance. Application coding standards should require the use of bind variables in all SQL statements. No SQL statement should be created by concatenating together strings and passed parameters. Bind variables should be used for every SQL statement regardless of when or where the SQL statement is executed. This is Oracle's internal coding standard and should be your organization's standard also. A very complex SQL injection attack could possibly exploit an application by storing an attack string in the database, which would be later executed by a dynamic SQL statement (referred to as a second-order attack). The use of bind variables is simple, but does require at least one more line of code per variable. Since a typical SQL statement may be using 10-20 values, the additional coding effort may be substantial. There are a few rare occasions when a developer must dynamically create a SQL statement.

INPUT VALIDATION

Every passed string parameter should be validated. Many web applications use hidden fields and other techniques, which also must be validated. If a bind variable is not being used, special database characters must be removed or escaped. For

Oracle databases, the only character at issue is a single quote. The simplest method is to escape all single quotes – Oracle interprets consecutive single quotes as a literal single quote. The use of bind variables and escaping of single quotes should not be done for the same string. A bind variable will store the exact input string in the database and escaping any single quotes will result in double quotes being stored in the database.

FUNCTION SECURITY

Standard and custom database functions can be exploited in SQL injection attacks. Many of these functions can be used effectively in an attack. Oracle is delivered with hundreds of standard functions and by default may have grants to PUBLIC. The application may have additional functions which perform operations like changing passwords or creating users that could be exploited. All functions that are not absolutely necessary to the application should be restricted.

ERROR MESSAGES

If an attacker cannot obtain the source code for an application, error messages become critically important for a successful attack. Many Java applications do not return detailed error messages, but testing and analysis should be performed to determine if the application returns detailed error messages. Rather than returning detailed database error messages to the user, this information should be written to a log file.

PL/SQL Gateway (modplsql)

The PL/SQL Gateway can be configured to display varying levels of error messages. The more information returned in an error message, the more useful the message is to an attacker. All PL/SQL Gateway applications should be designed to return an application generated error page when an Oracle error is encountered rather than allowing the gateway to return an error message. However, some errors like procedure not found must be returned by the gateway. The ERROR_STYLE setting in the "wdbsvr.app" configuration file determines the level of information returned to the user. Since these types of errors are most likely caused by an attacker rather than errors in normal application processing, only minimal or no information should be returned. The ERROR_STYLE parameter should be set to "WebServer" instead of "Gateway" or "Gateway Debug". ERROR_STYLE can be set at either the global or DAD level, so both sections of the configuration file must be checked.

COMMON EXCEPTIONS

Bind variables should be used for all dynamic SQL statements in PL/SQL and Java. Although, on rare occasions bind variables cannot be used, such as dynamically including table or column names.

DYNAMIC TABLE NAMES AND WHERE CLAUSES

When generating a dynamic SQL statement, bind variables cannot be used for table names or column names. For most applications, valid database object names (i.e., table and column names) can contain only alphanumeric characters and the underscore (_), dollar sign ($), and pound sign (#). Single quotes and other special characters are not valid. Any dynamic table or column name should be validated and all invalid characters should be stripped from the string, especially single quotes.

In PL/SQL, the TRANSLATE function can be used to easily removed invalid characters from an object name –

```
translate(upper(<input string>),
'ABCDEFGHIJKLMNOPQRSTUVWXYZ1234567890_#$@.
'~!%^*()-=+{}[];":"?/><,|\',
'ABCDEFGHIJKLMNOPQRSTUVWXYZ1234567890_#$@.');
```

LIKE CLAUSES

Bind variables are valid in a LIKE clause and should be used. % and _ characters should be directly appended to the string rather than concatenating the SQL statement.

The following concatenation should not be used –

```
String name = request.getParameter("name");
conn.prepareStatement("SELECT id FROM users WHERE name LIKE '%" + name + "%'");
```

Rather multiple statements and a bind variable are required to properly create the SQL statement –

```
String name = request.getParameter("name");
name = query.append("%").append(name).append("%");
pstmt = conn.prepareStatement("SELECT id FROM users WHERE name LIKE ?");
pstmt.setString (1, name);
```

DYNAMIC PROCEDURE AND FUNCTION CALLS

When generating a procedure or function call dynamically, a bind variable cannot be used for the procedure or function name. For most applications, valid database object names (procedure and function names) can contain only alphanumeric characters and the underscore (_), dollar sign ($), and pound sign (#). Period (.) and at sign (@) are used to specify package names and database links. Single quotes and other special characters are not valid. Any dynamically called procedure or function should be validated and all invalid characters should be stripped from the string.

In PL/SQL, the TRANSLATE function can be used to easily removed invalid characters from an object name –

```
translate(upper(<input string>),
```

‘ABCDEFGHIJKLMNOPQRSTUVWXYZ1234567890_#$@.`~!%^*()-=+{}[];”:”?/
><,|\’,
‘ABCDEFGHIJKLMNOPQRSTUVWXYZ1234567890_#$@.’);

ORACLE FUNCTIONS

By default, Oracle supplies over 1,000 functions in about 175 standard database packages that potentially can be exploited in a SQL injection attack. Many of these functions have PUBLIC grants.

DETERMINE FUNCTION PRIVILEGES

All the available functions for PUBLIC can be found with the following query –

```
select * from dba_tab_privs p, all_arguments a
where grantee = ‘PUBLIC’
and privilege = ‘EXECUTE’
and p.table_name = a.package_name
and p.owner = a.owner
and a.position = 0
and a.in_out = ‘OUT’
order by p.owner, p.table_name, p.grantee
```

RESTRICTING ACCESS TO FUNCTIONS

Access to specific functions within a package can not be restricted – only access to the entire package. To revoke PUBLIC access to a package use the following SQL command as a privileged database user

–

REVOKE EXECUTE ON <package_name> FROM public

As an example, to revoke access to the UTL_HTTP package the command is –

REVOKE EXECUTE ON sys.utl_http FROM public

STANDARD FUNCTIONS

Buffer overflows have been discovered in three standard Oracle database functions: BFILENAME, TZ_OFFSET, TO_TIMESTAMP_TZ, FROM_TZ, UMTOYMINTERVAL, and NUMTODSINTERVAL. These functions reside in the STANDARD database package and there is no way to restrict access to these functions. To fix known buffer overflows in standard Oracle database functions, you must apply a recent Oracle Critical Patch Update.

ORACLE SUPPLIED FUNCTIONS

Oracle supplies hundreds of functions in standard database packages. Most of these packages are prefixed with DBMS_ and UTL_. The following packages should be reviewed. If the package is not used by the application, access should be restricted.

DBMS_JAVA_TEST
DBMS_LOCK
DBMS_PIPE
DBMS_RANDOM
UTL_FILE
UTL_HTTP
UTL_SMTP
UTL_TCP

CUSTOM APPLICATION FUNCTIONS

Functions and functions within packages written for the application can also be exploited by a SQL
injection attack.

Access to all custom functions should be reviewed to determine –

1. Does the web application need access to this function?
2. If the function is exploited, what is the impact to the application?
3. Is the function marked as "PRAGMA TRANSACTION"? These functions can be executed
and write to the database from a SELECT statement

References

- Using Database Functions in SQL Injection Attacks
- http://www.integrigy.com/security-resources
- OWASP Guide to Building Secure Web Applications
- http://www.owasp.org/index.php/Category:OWASP_Guide_Project
- Additional Information on SQL Injection Attacks –
- http://www.securityfocus.com/infocus/1644
- http://www.nextgenss.com/papers/advanced_sql_injection.pdf
- http://www.spidynamics.com/whitepapers/WhitepaperSQLInjection.pdf
- Oracle Database Security Checklist –
- http://otn.oracle.com/deploy/security/
- SQL Injection: Are your Web Applications Vulnerable- SPI Dynamics http://www.spidynamics.com/support/whitepapers/WhitepaperSQLInjection.pdf
- Blind SQL Injection: Are your Web Applications Vulnerable - SPI Dynamics
- http://www.spidynamics.com/support/whitepapers/Blind_SQLInjection.pdf
- Advanced SQL Injection in SQL Server Applications, Chris Anley - NGSSoftware
- http://www.nextgenss.com/papers/advanced_sql_injection.pdf
- More advanced SQL Injection, Chris Anley - NGSSoftware
- http://www.nextgenss.com/papers/more_advanced_sql_injection.pdf
- Web Application Disassembly with ODBC Error Messages, David Litchfield - @stake
- http://www.nextgenss.com/papers/webappdis.doc

- SQL Injection Walkthrough
- http://www.securiteam.com/securityreviews/5DP0N1P76E.html
- Blind SQL Injection" - Imperva
- http://www.imperva.com/application_defense_center/white_papers/blind_sql_server_injection.html
- SQL Injection Signatures Evasion - Imperva
- http://www.imperva.com/application_defense_center/white_papers/sql_injection_signatures_evasion.html
- Introduction to SQL Injection Attacks for Oracle Developers - Integrigy
- http://www.net-security.org/dl/articles/IntegrigyIntrotoSQLInjectionAttacks.pdf

Grid and Cluster Computing

Vishal Virmani
Technical Architect,4 People Technologies, Delhi

Abstract
We are experiencing what can only be called the Perfect Storm of innovation, in not just one but many of the fundamental technologies of our day. Computing systems, storage systems, and networking systems are seeing exponential growth in capacity and capabilities, while their costs are declining at an equally astonishing rate. The emergence of this new innovation-driven economics is sending shock waves through the information technology marketplace. Technologists and business managers are reassessing how much and what kinds of systems and services they should purchase and where and how these systems should be deployed. Grid deployments in research and academic institutions are serving as useful test beds as Grid Computing transitions to commercial enterprises. Grid deployments are using unique combinations of commercial and public domain open source software to build extremely powerful grids, which are solving problems in a wide array of disciplines. Early indications from industry grid deployments are clearly pointing to tremendous enterprise productivity and infrastructure performance gains.

Keywords: *Grid Computing, Cluster Computing, Bioinformatics, High Performance Computing*

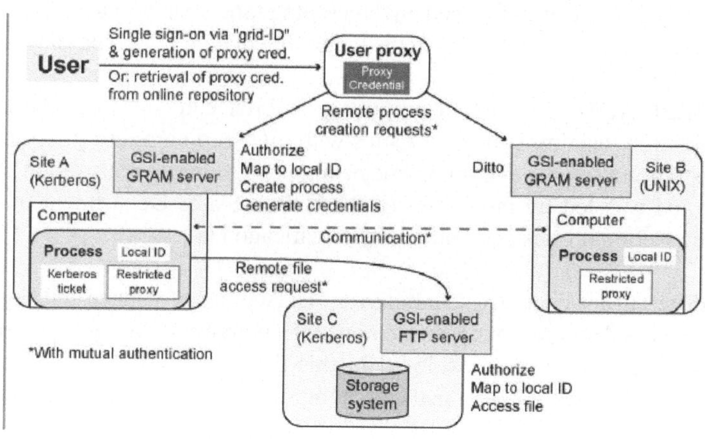

Figure 1: Grid Computing Technology—An Overview

Advances in microprocessor, networking, and storage technologies have been nothing short of astounding. This core technology ensemble has contributed to creating an extremely powerful infrastructure for consumer and business applications. The timing is right for new technologies, such as grid computing, to leverage the ever-increasing power and declining costs of these core technologies. The power of the desktop has become too significant to ignore. The exponential increase in microprocessor and storage capacity has made desktop computers extremely powerful resources. The near ubiquitous deployment of these computers provides companies with latent resources that can be utilized by grid technologies to make a substantial impact on business processes and increase productivity.

The global telecommunication infrastructure built over the past few years is mostly unused today. The price of telecommunication services have also dramatically come down, thus making it easier to build and acquire high-speed networks for Grid Computing applications.

We have developed an appreciation for standards. Many of the companies that were adherent to proprietary, closed end systems were forced to take a close look at open systems and, by the end of the 1990s, most had converted. This is already benefiting the Grid Computing technology evolution. Vendors, large and small, have committed from the beginning to open standards for Grid Computing and are active participants in their definition.

In the early-to-mid 1990s, there were numerous research projects underway in the academic and research community that were focused on distributed computing. One key area of research focused on developing tools that would allow distributed high performance computing systems to act like one large computer.

At the IEEE/ACM 1995 Super Computing conference in San Diego, 11 high speed networks were used to connect 17 sites with high-end computing resources for a demonstration to create one super "metacomputer." This demonstration was called **I-Way** and was led by Ian Foster of the United States Department of Energy's Argonne National Labs and University of Chicago.[1]

Sixty different applications, spanning various faculties of science and engineering, were developed and run over this demonstration network. Many of the early Grid Computing concepts were explored in this demonstration as the team created various software programs to make all computing resources work together.

The success of the **I-Way** demonstration led the United States government's DARPA agency, in October 1996, to fund a project to create foundation tools for distributed computing. The research project was led by Ian Foster of ANL and Carl

Kesselman of University of Southern California. The project was named **Globus** and the team created a suite of tools that laid the foundation for Grid Computing activities in the academic and research communities. At the 1997 Super Computing Conference, 80 sites worldwide running software based on the Globus Toolkit were connected together.

This effort started to be referred to as Grid Computing—coined to play on the analogy to the electrical power grid. Grid computing would make tremendous computing power available to anybody, at anytime, and in a truly transparent manner, just as, today, the electric power grid makes power available to billions of electrical outlets.

Grid Computing in the academic and research communities remained focused on creating an efficient framework to leverage distributed high-performance computing systems. But with the explosion of the Internet and the increasing power of the desktop computer during the same period, many efforts were launched to create powerful distributed computing systems by connecting together PCs on the network.

In 1997, **Entropia** was launched to harness the idle computers worldwide to solve problems of scientific interest. The **Entropia** network grew to 30,000 computers with aggregate speed of over one teraflop per second. A whole new field of philanthropic computing came about in which ordinary users volunteered their PCs to analyze research topics such as patient's response to chemotherapy, discovering drugs for AIDS, and potential cures for anthrax.

Although none of the above projects could be successfully monetized by companies, they did, however, attract a lot more media attention than any of the earlier projects in the academic and research world. Starting in late 2000, articles on Grid Computing moved from the trade press to the popular press. In rapid fire succession articles appeared in, for example, New York Times, Economist, Business 2.0, Red Herring, Washington Post, Financial Times, Yomiuri Shimbum,

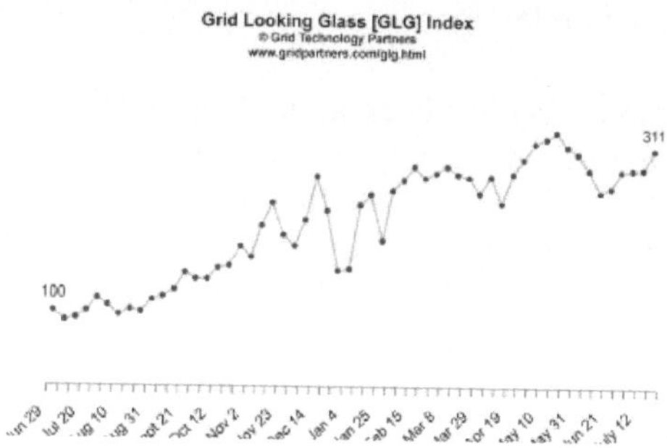

Figure 2 : GLG Index

In fact, the trend has only accelerated recently. An analysis of **Lexus-Nexis** data shows that Grid Computing references in popular U.S. media is up dramatically to 500 citations from 100 in Q4 of 2001. Grid Technology Partners' Grid Looking Glass Index (see Figure above) which tracks Grid Computing related searches on the Google search engine tripled in the first year of its inception.

Cluster Computing

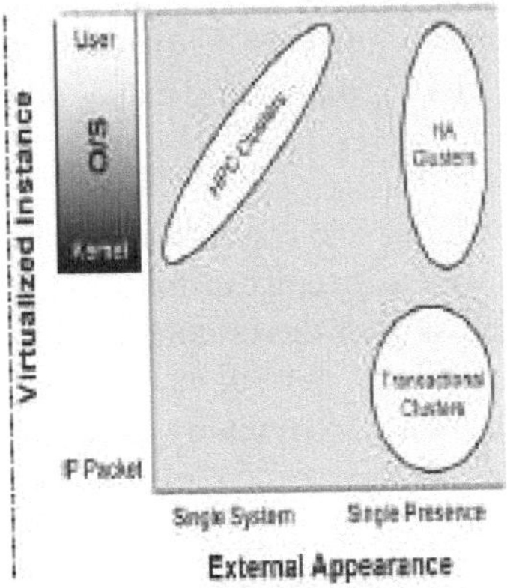

Figure 3: Cluster Computing Arrangements

Cluster computing came about as a response to the high prices of supercomputers, which made those systems out of reach for many research projects. Clusters are high-performance, massively parallel computers built primarily out of commodity hardware components, running a free-software operating system such as Linux or FreeBSD, and interconnected by a private high-speed network. It consists of a cluster of PCs, or workstations, dedicated to running high-performance computing tasks. The nodes in the cluster do not sit on users' desks, but are dedicated to running cluster jobs. A cluster is usually connected to the outside world through only a single node.

Cluster computing has been around since 1994 when the first Beowulf clusters were developed and deployed. Since then, numerous tools have been developed to run and manage clusters. Platform Computing, a firm that is now a leader in Grid Computing, developed many of the early load-balancing tools for clusters. Additionally, tools have also been developed to adapt applications run in the parallel cluster environment. One such tool, Forge Explorer, can check if particular applications are suitable for parallelization and determine if they would be suitable to run on a cluster.

The exponential growth in microprocessor speeds over the last decade has now made it possible to create truly impressive clusters. This year an AMD® Athlon™based cluster at University of Heidelberg in Germany was tested at 825 Gflops, making it the 35th fastest high performance computer in the world. Clusters are widely deployed in industries such as life sciences, digital entertainment, finance, etc.

IEEE Computer Society Task Force on Cluster Computing conducts a yearly conference that is designed to bring together international cluster and Grid Computing researchers, developers, and users to present and exchange the latest innovations and findings that drive future research and products. It is expected that the Grid Computing community will benefit from the years of experience that the cluster community has in building tools that allow applications to share distributed computing resources.

Beowulf clusters were developed by Thomas Sterling and Don Becker while working at the Center of Excellence in Space and Data and Information Sciences, a division of University Space Research Association located at NASA Goddard Space Flight Center.

Case Study: Bioinformatics

Grid Computing is becoming more prevalent in both basic research and drug development—the industry that takes biotech from research to commercial applications. Computer technology is used at nearly every stage of the drug development process. In the early stages of pre-clinical testing, research, and development, bioinformatics technology allows researchers to analyze terabytes of data being produced by the Human Genome Project.

Bioinformatics is the discipline of obtaining information about genomic or protein sequence data. This may involve similarity searches of databases, comparing an unidentified sequence to the sequences in a database, or making predictions about the sequence based on current knowledge of similar sequences. Gene sequence databases, gene expression databases (which track how genes react to various stimuli), protein sequence databases, and related analysis tools all help scientists determine whether and how a particular molecule is directly involved in a disease process. That, in turn, aids in the discovery of new and better drug targets.

Bioinformatics may be the only way drug companies can deal with the gigabytes of data they produce and receive every day. The sequenced human genome has already increased the number of biological drug targets that can be explored from about 500 to more than 30,000—and that number will only get larger. The completion of a working draft of the human genome—an important milestone in the Human Genome Project—was announced in June 2000 and published in February 2001. Databases available via the Internet put this wealth of information at the disposal of the world's scientific community. At the same time, computational chemistry allows companies to synthesize more than 100 compounds per chemist per year, and advances in computing technology continue to raise that number even higher.

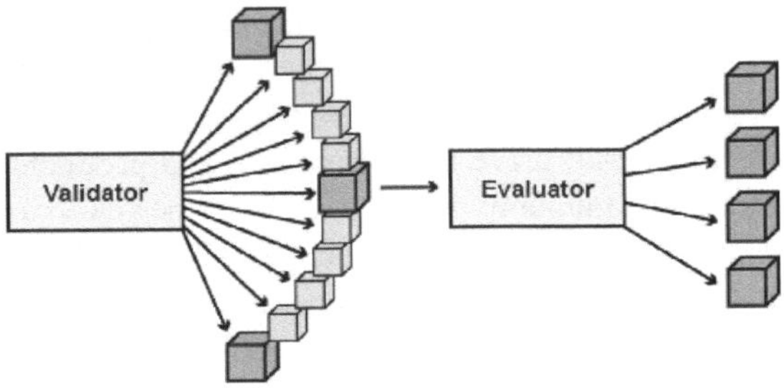

Figure 4: Sample Life Sciences Grid Application

Bioinformatics and High-Performance Computing

Bioinformatics in the life sciences industry is focused on the compilation of genomic information into databases and identifying and analyzing patterns within genetic data for viability as pharmaceutical products. Drug discovery and biotech research companies need powerful, high-performance solutions to search through and analyze huge amounts of data. High-speed, high-performance computing power and industrial-strength databases perform a wide range of data-intensive computing functions: mapping genetic and proteomic information, data mining to identify patterns and similarities, and text mining using huge libraries of information. These activities require high-performance computer infrastructures with access to huge databases of information.

Grid Computing and Bioinformatics

Database searching and comparison or sequencing is embarrassingly parallel with the application able to be split up and run independently—there is no need for communication between the processors doing the comparison, simply the sharing of results when complete. Grid Computing is emerging as one way to make this search happen fast, using untapped computing resources in the company or, in some cases, around the world via the Internet to run these sequences.

Most major pharmaceutical companies have grid-computing projects underway to explore the possibilities in this fast-growing area When PCs are not otherwise being used, Grid Computing harnesses spare computing power to run data comparison in parallel. This approach works well for bioinformatics applications, but does not fit when interaction between the processors is required, such as in molecular modeling.

The considerable "algorithmic complexity" of biological systems requires a large amount of detailed information for their complete description. There has been a vast quantity of information gathered for all kinds of biological systems at the molecular and cellular level that now require computational tools to be adequately interpreted.

Bioinformatics—An Excellent Grid Application

The ultimate goal of the field is to enable the discovery of new biological insights as well as to create a global perspective from which unifying principles in biology can be discerned. At the beginning of the genomic revolution, a bioinformatics concern was the creation and maintenance of a database to store biological information such as nucleotide and amino acid sequences. Development of this type of database involved not only design issues, but the development of complex interfaces whereby researchers could access existing data as well as submit new or revised data.

Because of their tremendous computational requirement, it is not a surprise that life sciences companies are early adopters of Grid Computing technology. Cluster and distributed computing have been a core component of the IT infrastructure of many of the large- and medium-sized life sciences companies. Penetration rates are 85 percent in large pharmaceutical companies and 65 percent in small- to medium-sized life science organizations.

Life sciences applications such as HMMER, CHARMm, LigandFit, GOLD, Delphi, and Archimedes also exhibit good parallel efficiency and are being deployed on grids today.

Example Grid Computing: Smallpox Research

The Smallpox Research Grid Project, being driven by the United States Department of Defense, shows the potential to harness spare computing power across the country for research. The project will be powered by a massive computing grid that will enable millions of computer owners worldwide to contribute idle computing resources to the task of developing a wide collection of potential anti-smallpox drugs.

The project is based on commercially available technologies and services used by many pharmaceutical and biotechnology companies to improve and accelerate drug discovery and development. The project will employ computational chemistry to analyze chemical interactions between a library of 35 million potential drug molecules and several protein targets on the smallpox virus in the search for an effective antiviral drug to treat smallpox post-infection. Past projects, such as one for anthrax, have been able to complete the billions of computer simulations in as little as a month.

Conclusion

Grid Computing is making an impact across numerous industries. The list of applications that are taking advantage of Grid Computing is also expanding at a feverish pace. The availability of tools to grid-enable applications and easier integration with grid middleware has been extremely successful in bringing new applications to the grid.

References

- *Fayyad U, Piatesetsky-Shapioro G, Smyth P and Uthurusamy , R .1996.* Advances in Knowledge Discovery and Data Mining. AAAI Press/The MIT Press.
- *Dyreson,C.* and Cook, James. 19196. Informational Retreival from an Incomplete Data Cube. In proceedings of te 22nd VLDB Conference 1996.
- *Srivastav,D.*Dar,S,Jagdish, H. V., and Levy A. 1996. Answering Queries with Aggregation Using Views. In Proceedings of the 22nd VLDB Conference 1996.
- *Zargham, M.*R. 1996. Computer Architecture Single and Parallel Systems. Prentice Hall.
- *Browning, Tim.* 1995.Capacity Planning for Computer Systems.AP Professional.
- *Corey,M.*J., Abbey,M., and Decheicho D. Jr. Storage Estimations for Multidimensional Aggregates in the presence of Hierarchies.
- *Tuecke, Czajkowski, Foster, Frey, Graham, and Kessleman*, "Grid Service Specification" 6/13/2002.
- Pfister, G. F., In Search of Clusters, Second Edition, Prentice Hall, 1998.
- *Savarese, D. F. & T. Sterling, Beowulf, in R. Buyya (ed.),* High Performance Cluster Computing, Volume 1, 625-645, 1999.
- *FLUENT on Hewlett-Packard Linux, HP-UX, and Windows NT Clusters*, Technical white paper, December 1999.

Key Management Using VoIP Signaling

Kapila Arora
Software Engineer, NDCC
A.K.Mohapatra
Sr. Lecturer, USIT, GGSIPU, Delhi

Abstract

Voice over Internet Protocol (VoIP) is an emerging technology and has been being penetrating into every segment to replace the traditional circuit switched infrastructure for telephony service.

Session Initiation Protocol (SIP), an application layer signaling protocol for initiating, managing and terminating voice sessions is widely being used for VoIP communication. RTP is the standard speech transmission protocol used with VoIP networks.

The use of SIP in public network infrastructure over unreliable Internet Protocol for exchange of private information has raised many security issues. One of the key areas in VoIP security is key exchange mechanism. Security of the media transport layer—the layer in which the actual voice datagrams are transmitted—depends on the secrecy of session keys and authentication of session participants.

A number of key exchange mechanisms have been proposed in literature: SDES, MIKEY and ZRTP. Each of these has some advantages and disadvantages. SDES is the most widely deployed mechanism. A new key exchange mechanism similar to SDES is proposed in this paper in order to counter some of the drawbacks of this mechanism.

Keywords— *VoIP, SIP, RTP, Security, Key Management, SDES, MIKEY, ZRTP*

Introduction

VoIP stands for Voice over Internet Protocol and is a technology for transmitting ordinary telephone calls over the Internet using packet linked routes. VoIP involves sending voice transmissions as data packets using the Internet Protocol (IP), whereby the user's voice is converted into a digital signal, compressed, and broken down into a series of packets. The packets are then transported over private or public IP networks and reassembled and decoded on the receiving side. A major advantage of VOIP is that it avoids the tolls charged by ordinary telephone service. In a VoIP network, a signaling protocol like SIP is used to set up individual sessions for voice connection between users and speech transmission protocol like RTP is used for exchange of data packets. During the set up process communication details are negotiated between users using the Session Description Protocol.

Session Initiation Protocol (SIP) is an application-layer control (signaling) protocol for creating, modifying, and terminating sessions with one or more participants. These sessions include Internet telephone calls, multimedia distribution, and multimedia conferences.

The two components that make up a SIP system include user agents and network servers.

User agent: A user agent (UA) is a logical function in the SIP network that initiates or responds to SIP transactions. A UA can act as either the client or the server in a SIP transaction. A UA might or might not directly interact with a human user. A UA is stateful that is, it maintains session or dialog state.

Proxy: A proxy is an intermediate entity in the SIP network that is responsible for forwarding SIP requests to the target UAS or another proxy on behalf of the UAC. A proxy primarily provides the routing function in the SIP network.

Redirect server: Redirection servers do not process calls and only respond with information containing the appropriate address of the next server.

Registrar server: A registrar is a UAS that accepts SIP REGISTER requests and updates the information from the request message into a location database.

Back-to-back user agent: A back-to-back user agent (B2BUA) is an intermediate entity that processes incoming SIP requests as a UAS. To answer the incoming SIP request, the B2BUA acts as a UAC, regenerates a SIP request, and sends it on the network. A B2BUA must maintain dialog state and participates in all transactions within the dialog.

The use of SIP in public network infrastructure over unreliable Internet Protocol for exchange of private information has raised many security issues. The Secure Real-time Transport Protocol (or SRTP) defines a profile of RTP (Real-time Transport Protocol), intended to provide encryption, message authentication and integrity, and replay protection to the RTP data and control data of RTP. A key derivation function is used to derive the different keys used in a crypto context (SRTP and SRTCP encryption keys and salts, SRTP and SRTCP authentication keys) from one single master key in a cryptographically secure way. Thus, the key management protocol needs to exchange only one master key, all the necessary session keys are generated by applying the key derivation function. This raises one important issue – how to securely exchange keys in an untrusted environment.

A number of key exchange mechanisms are proposed in literature each with some pros and cons. The key exchange mechanism can broadly be divided into two categories: one which relies on signaling for key exchange (e.g. SDES) and the other which uses media packets for the exchange of keys(e.g. ZRTP).

In this paper, we will present a new scheme for secure exchange of keys in SIP. It is similar to SDES but overcomes a serious drawback of this algorithm.

Earlier Work

Security of the media transport layer—the layer in which the actual voice datagrams are transmitted—depends on the secrecy of session keys and authentication of session participants. Key exchange protocols for VoIP sessions include SDP's Security DEscriptions for Media Streams (SDES) [1], Multimedia Internet KEYing (MIKEY) [2] and ZRTP [3].

SDES [1] is a way to negotiate the key for Secure Real-time Transport Protocol. It has been standardized by IETF in July 2006 as RFC 4568. The big advantage of this method is that it is extremely simple. The keys are transported in the SDP attachment of a SIP message. That means the SIP transport layer must make sure that no-one else can see the attachment. This can be done by using TLS transport layer, or other methods like S/MIME. Using TLS assumes that the next hop in the SIP proxy chain can be trusted and it will take care about the security requirements of the request. The use of TLS is however deprecated because TLS does not provide end-to-end protection over a chain of proxies. One of the biggest disadvantage of SDES is it's vulnerability to replay attacks as S/MIME does not provide any replay protection.

MIKEY [2] is another key exchange protocol for SRTP. MIKEY is defined in RFC 3830. It can operate in three different modes: pre-shared key with key transport, public key with key transport, public key with authenticated Diffie-Hellman (DH) key exchange. In pre-shared key (PSK) mode only symmetric encryption is used and only a small amount of data has to be exchanged. However, an individual key has to be shared with every single peer, which leads to scalability problems for larger user groups. In public-key mode the initial key is exchanged with the help of public key encryption. In larger systems, this requires a PKI to handle the secure distribution of public keys. In Diffie-Hellman mode, a Diffie-Hellman key exchange is used to set up the initial key. This method has a higher resource consumption (both computation time and bandwidth) than the previous ones, and needs a PKI like in the public-key case. However, it has the advantage of providing perfect forward secrecy. A disadvantage of MIKEY is that it requires either prior shared secrets, or a separate PKI, with all attendant problems such as certificate dispersal, revocation, and so on.

ZRTP [3] is a key agreement protocol which performs Diffie-Hellman key exchange during call setup in-band in the Real-time Transport Protocol (RTP) media stream which has been established using some other signaling protocol such as Session Initiation Protocol (SIP). This generates a shared secret which is then used to generate keys and salt for a Secure RTP (SRTP) session. One of ZRTP's features is that it does not rely on SIP signaling for the key management. ZRTP is potentially vulnerable to Denial of Service Attack.

A New Key Management Mechanism

Requirements of the key management protocol:

- *End-to-end security*. Only the participants involved in the communication have access to the generated key(s).
- *Simplicity*.
- *Efficiency*. Designed to have:
  - low bandwidth consumption,
  - low computational workload,
  - small code size, and
  - minimal number of roundtrips.
- Independence from any specific security functionality of the underlying transport.

The proposed scheme is similar to SDES. One of the biggest disadvantage of SDES is it's vulnerability to replay attacks as S/MIME does not provide any replay protection. Thus, during a session an attacker can monitor all the messages of that session and after the session is terminated, attacker can replay the original INVITE message generated by subscriber **A** and establish a new session with **B**. In order to counter the replay attacks, we use the following procedure.

The main problem with SDES is that the session key that is used to protect the media session does not include any randomness from the responder side. If that is done than we would be able to counter replay attacks also.

One of the random fields generated by the responder on the receipt of INVITE message is the To tag. We can utilize this tag and generate a final key that will be used for the media session encryption and authentication. The To tag is received by **A** in an INVITE response message which can be either of provisional or final messages. Provisional messages include 180 Ringing and 183 Session Progresses message and final response message on the successful establishment of a session is 200 OK. On the receipt of the Tag value **A** computes it's final session key by concatenating its original key with the To tag value.

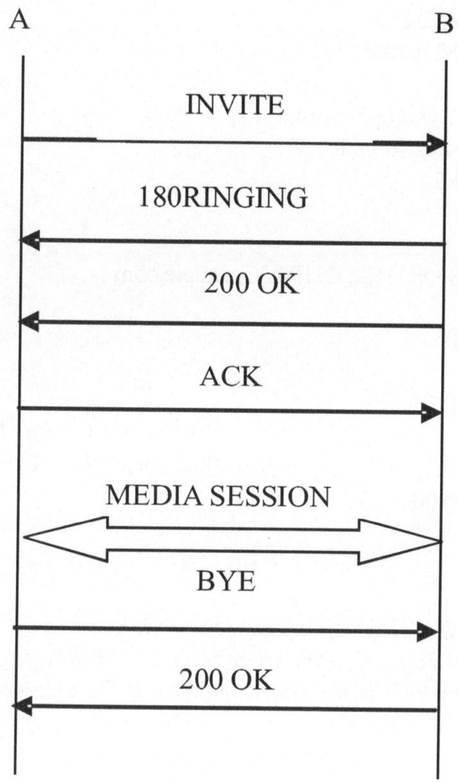

Figure 1: Example Call Flow

Figure 1 shows the call flow for establishment of a secure media session using this new key exchange mechanism. Various messages(M1 to M6) exchanged during this call are shown below:

M1: A '! B

When a subscriber A wants to establish a secures session with B, it sends a new INVITE message to B with a crypto attribute containing the crypto session parameters

INVITE sip:B@example.com SIP/2.0

Via: SIP/2.0/TCP A.example.com:5060; branch=z9hG4bK7
Max-Forwards: 70
From: A <sip:A@example.com>;tag=9fxced76sl
To: B <sip:B@example.com>
Call-ID: 3848276298220188511@A.example.com
CSeq: 1 INVITE
Contact: <sip:A@A.example.com;transport=tcp>
Content-Type: application/sdp
Content-Length: 151

v=0
o=A 2890844526 2890844526 IN IP4 A.example.com
s=-
c=IN IP4 192.0.2.101
t=0 0
m=audio 49172 RTP/SAVP 0
a=crypto:1 AES_CM_128_HMAC_SHA1_32
inline:WbTBosdVUZqEb6Htqhn+m3z7wUh4RJVR8nE15GbN
a=rtpmap:0 PCMU/8000

M2: B '! A

On the receipt of INVITE request subscriber B sends a 180 Ringing response with a tag value in To field. A on receiving this 180 Ringing response computes a new session key which is the concatenation of the original key value with the To tag value

SIP/2.0 180 Ringing
Via: SIP/2.0/TCP A.example.com:5060;branch=z9hG4bK7
;received=192.0.2.101
From: A <sip:A@example.com>;tag=9fxced76sl
To: B <sip:B@example.com>;tag=8321234356
Call-ID: 3848276298220188511@A.example.com
CSeq: 1 INVITE
Contact: <sip:B@B.example.com;transport=tcp>
Content-Length: 0

M3: B '! A

When subscriber B picks up the phone, it sends a 200 OK response with a crypto attribute containing the crypto session parameters

SIP/2.0 200 OK
Via: SIP/2.0/TCP A.example.com:5060;branch=z9hG4bK7
;received=192.0.2.101
From: A <sip:A@example.com>;tag=9fxced76sl
To: B <sip:B@example.com>;tag=8321234356
Call-ID: 3848276298220188511@A.example.com
CSeq: 1 INVITE
Contact: <sip:B@B.example.com;transport=tcp>
Content-Type: application/sdp
Content-Length: 147

v=0
o=B 2890844527 2890844527 IN IP4 B.example.com
s=-
c=IN IP4 192.0.2.201
t=0 0
m=audio 3456 RTP/AVP 0
a=crypto:1 AES_CM_128_HMAC_SHA1_32
inline:bmt4MzIzMmYxdnFyaWM3d282dGR5Z3g0c2k5M3Yx
a=rtpmap:0 PCMU/8000

M4: A '! B

For a three way handshake A sends an ACK request on the receipt of 200 OK response.

ACK sip:B@B.example.com SIP/2.0
Via: SIP/2.0/TCP A.example.com:5060;branch=z9hG4bK7
Max-Forwards: 70
From: A <sip:A@example.com>;tag=9fxced76sl
To: B <sip:B@example.com>;tag=8321234356
Call-ID: 3848276298220188511@A.example.com
CSeq: 1 ACK
Content-Length: 0

M9: A '! B

For terminating a session A sends a BYE request to B.

BYE sip:B@B.example.com SIP/2.0
Via: SIP/2.0/TCP A.example.com:5060;branch=z9hG4bKn
Max-Forwards: 70

From: A <sip:A@example.com>;tag=8321234356
To: B <sip:B@example.com>;tag=9fxced76sl
Call-ID: 3848276298220188511@A.example.com
CSeq: 2 BYE
Content-Length: 0

M10: B '! A

On the receipt of a BYE request A sends a 200 OK response

SIP/2.0 200 OK
Via: SIP/2.0/TCP A.example.com:5060;branch=z9hG4bKn
;received=192.0.2.201
From: A <sip:A@example.com>;tag=8321234356
To: B <sip:B@example.com>;tag=9fxced76sl
Call-ID: 3848276298220188511@A.example.com
CSeq: 2 BYE
Content-Length: 0

Conclusion and Future Work

The new key exchange mechanism that I suggested in this paper is purely dependent on the security of SIP body of the INVITE and 200 OK response messages. It works only for unicast communication streams. Unlike SDES it is able to counter the replay attacks in SIP.

In future, this work may further be enhanced by the development of a softphone using this new key exchange mechanism and by comparing it's performance with the other key exchange mechanisms.

References

- F. Andreasen, M. Baugher, and D. Wing. Session Description Protocol (SDP) Security Descriptions for Media Streams. IETF RFC 4568, July 2006.
- J. Arkko, E. Carrara, F. Lindholm, M. Naslund, and K. Norrman. MIKEY: Multimedia Internet KEYing. IETF RFC 3830, August 2004.
- P. Zimmermann. ZRTP: Extensions to RTP for Diffie-Hellman Key Agreement for SRTP. http://www1.tools.ietf.org/html/ draft-zimmermann-avt-zrtp-01,March 2006.
- Prateek Gupta, Vitaly Shmatikov, "Analysis of VoIP Protocols", IEEE Computer Society Foundation Symposium , 2007

- Marcus Goncalves "Voice Over IP Networks", McGraw Hill 1999.
- J. Rosenberg, H.Schulzrinne, "RFC3261", June 2002
- A. Johnston, S.Donovan, "SIP Basic Call Flow Examples" RFC 3665, December 2003
- A. B. Roach," Session Initiation Protocol (SIP)-Specific Event Notification" RFC 3265,June 2002
- R. Mahy," A Message Summary and Message Waiting Indication Event Package for the Session Initiation Protocol (SIP)" RFC 3842, August 2004
- A.Johnston, R.Sparks, "SIP Service Examples draft-ietf-sipping-service-examples-10", March 5 2006
- NIST SP 800-58, "Security Considerations for Voice Over IP Systems", 2005

Neural Virtual Physician

Shivani Joshi
Asstt. Professor, GNIM, Delhi

Abstract

This paper focuses on the neural networks which is somewhat able to think like human brain from the patterns and help in various fields. This paper elaborates the neural network capabilities in biological system and tells how it helps diagnosing the chronic diseases of the patients at early stage and helps the doctors, experts & practitioners to get the solution of the disease by the case history of the patient

Introduction

A neural network or neural computing, computer architecture modeled upon the human brain's interconnected system of neurons. Neural networks imitate the brain's ability to sort out patterns and learn from trial and error, discerning and extracting the relationships that underlie the data with which it is presented. Most neural networks are software simulations run on conventional computers. In neural computers, transistor circuits serve as the neurons and variable resistors act as the interconnection between axons and dendrites. As human brain consists of ten billion nerves so is the neural network consisting of integrated circuits, with 1,024 silicon "neurons," has also been developed. Each neuron in the network has one or more inputs and produces an output; each input has a weighting factor, which modifies the value entering the neuron. The neuron mathematically manipulates the inputs, and outputs the result. The neural network is simply neurons joined together, with the output from one neuron becoming input to others until the final output is reached.

Neural networks are good at providing very fast, very close approximations of the correct answer. Neural networks recognize shapes or patterns, learns from experience, or sorting relevant data from irrelevant. Their applications can be categorized into classification, recognition and identification, assessment, monitoring and control, and forecasting and prediction. They are also well suited for handwriting recognition, foreign language translation, process control, financial forecasting, medical data interpretation, artificial intelligence research, and parallel processing implementations of conventional processing tasks. In an ironic reversal, neural networks are being used to model disorders of the brain in an effort to discover better therapeutic strategies.

Discovery

A computer program operates in a manner analogous to the natural neural network in the brain. The neural networks was developed in 1943 by the neurophysiologist Warren McCulloch and the mathematician Walter Pitts. In 1954 Belmont Farley and Wesley Clark succeeded in running the first simple neural network. The primary goal of neural networks is their ability to emulate the brain's pattern-recognition skills. In business sector neural networks have been used to make investment decisions, recognize handwriting, and even detect bombs.

Medical Diagnosis

The major problem in medical field is to diagnose disease. Human being always make mistake and because of their limitation, diagnosis would give the major issue of human expertise. One of the most important problems of medical diagnosis, in general, is the subjectivity of the specialist. It can be noted, in particular in pattern recognition activities, that the experience of the professional is closely related to the final diagnosis. This is due to the fact that the result does not depend on a systematized solution but on the interpretation of the patient's signal (Lanzarini and Giusti, 1999).

Brause (2001) highlighted that almost all the physicians are confronted during their formation by the task of learning to diagnose. Here, they have to solve the problem of deducing certain diseases or formulating a treatment based on more or less specified observations and knowledge. For this task, certain basic difficulties have to be taken into account:-

- The basis for a valid diagnosis, a sufficient number of experienced cases, is reached only in the middle of a physician's career and is therefore not yet present at the end of the academic formation.
- This is especially true for rare or new diseases where also experienced physicians are in the same situation as newcomers.
- Principally, humans do not resemble statistic computers but pattern recognition systems. Humans can recognize patterns or objects very easily but fail when probabilities have to be assigned to observations.

Bra use(2001) also give an example of a study in the year 1971 showed these basic facts in the medical area. This study had shown that human have many limitations in diagnosis. The results of this experiment were as follows:-

- Best human diagnosis (most experienced physician): 79.7%
- Computer with expert data base: 82.2%
- Computer with 600 patient data: 91.1%

From this result we can see that humans can not ad hoc analyze complex data without errors.

Neural Network Capabilities

Here it is discussed how Neural Network approach can diagnose disease using patient medical data such as breast cancer, heart failure, medical images, acidosis diseases, and lung cancer.

- **Diagnose Breast Cancer**

Breast cancer is the second largest cause of cancer deaths among women. The automatic diagnosis of breast cancer is an important, real-world medical problem. A major class of problems in medical science involves the diagnosis of disease, based upon various tests performed upon the patient. When several tests are involved, the ultimate diagnosis may be difficult to obtain, even for a medical expert. This has given rise, over the past few decades, to computerized diagnostic tools, intended to aid the physician in making sense out of the confusion of data (Kiyan and Yildirim, 2003).

Neural network have been applied to breast cancer diagnosis.(Kiyan and Yildirim, 2003) employed Radial Basis Function, General Regression Neural Network and Probabilistic Neural Network in order to get the suitable result. From overall results, it is seen that the most suitable neural network model for classifying Wisconsin Breast Cancer data is General Regression Neural Network. This work also indicates that statistical neural networks can be effectively used for breast cancer diagnosis to help oncologists.

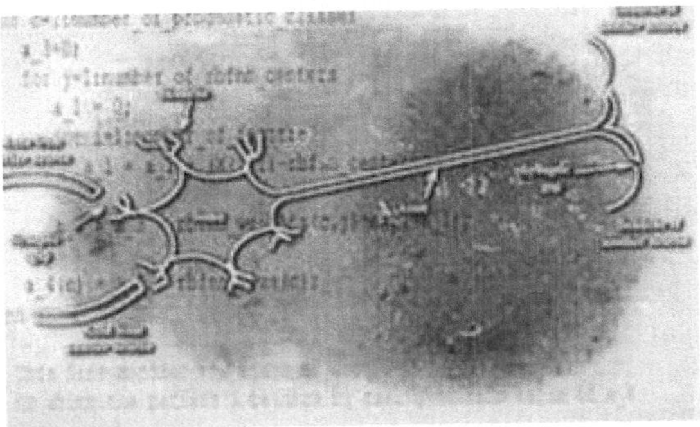

Figure 1: Development of cancer

- **Diagnose heart failure**

Making prognosis for patients with congestive heart failure is difficult due to the complex nature of this multisystem disease. No single criterion helps to identify patients at risk, and a combination of several prognostic parameters is recommended (Cowburn *et al.,* 1998). Neural networks are associative self learning techniques with the ability to identify multidimensional relationships and perform pattern recognition in non-linear domains. Atieza *et al.,* (2003) identified that classification is the best result for this cases.

- **Diagnose Acidosis Diseases**

Ultsch *et al.* (1995) used the capability of neural network to diagnose acidosis diseases by using knowledge based system in their hybrid system. The data set consists of 11 attributes originating from the blood analysis. Several classification methods according to (Deichsel and Trampisch, 1985) were used to explain these data. The Neural Network together with the UMatrix method was able to classify the data into the subcategories healthy, lacacidemia, metabolical acidosis, respiratory acidosis and one patient with cerebral deficiency. They used rule generation module to extracted rules out of the Neural Network, which were described by 4 or 5 attributes resembling more closely the decisions made by medical experts (Ultsch and Li, 1993).

- **Diagnose Lung Cancer**

Lung cancer is another diseases that commonly known as a deadly disease in the world. Many patients suffer from this disease. Early detection of this disease is very important to prevent this disease. Expertise have to measures for early stage lung cancer diagnosis mainly includes those utilizing X-ray chest films, CT, MRI, isotope, bronchoscopy, and needle biopsies. According to Zhou *et al.* (2001) at present, the specimens of needle biopsies are usually analyzed by experienced pathologists. Since senior pathologists are rare, reliable pathological diagnosis is not always available.

Zhou *et al.* (2001) named his an automatic pathological diagnosis procedure named Neural Ensemble based Detection (NED). It is proposed and realized in an early stage Lung Cancer Diagnosis System (LCDS). NED utilizes an artificial neural network ensemble to identify cancer cells in the images of the specimens of needle biopsies obtained from the bodies of the subjects to be diagnosed. A fast adaptive neural network classifier has been used to identify the lung cancer cell. Zhou *et al.* (2001) stated that a fast adaptive neural classifier that performs one-pass incremental learning with fast speed and high accuracy and does not require the user manually set up the number of hidden units.

Diagnose by Medical Images

Neural networks are extremely useful, since not only are they capable of recognizing patterns with the aid of the expert, but also of generalizing the information contained in the input data, thus showing relations which are a prior complex. (Laura and Armando, 1999) combined the processing of digital image and neural network to carry out the required recognition and classification. As a result, the solution to the problem can be divided in two parts: the segmentation of different elements, and their subsequent classification. In this case good results good results have been obtained thanks to the definition of a new clustering algorithm based on e re-definition of the input image. As for the classification stage, different solutions using neural networks have been compared, the results obtained being correct, with an error smaller than 10%.

Neural Networks are used in pattern recognition because of their ability to learn and to store knowledge. Because of their 'parallel' nature can achieve, Neural network can achieve very high computation rates which is vital in application like telemedicine (Siganos, 1995).

Applications of Neural Network in Medicine

The applications of neural network are divided into following domains:

- **Applications in Basic sciences**

In basic sciences, NN helps clinician to investigate the impact of parameter after certain conditions or treatments. It supplies clinicians with information about the risk or incoming circumstances regarding the domain. Learning the time course of blood glucose for example can help clinician to control the diabetes mellitus. By using feed forward NN for predicting the time course of blood glucose levels from the complex interaction of glucose counter regulatory hormones and insulin. Multi-Layer Perceptron (MLP) with sigmoidal Feed-Forward and standard Back-Propagation (BP) learning algorithm was employed as a forecaster for bacteria-antibiotic interactions of infectious diseases The conclusion is that one-month forecaster produces output correct to within occurrences of sensitivity. However, predictions for the two-month and three-month are less accurate

- **Applications in Clinical Medicine**

Patient who hospitalize for having high-risk diseases required special monitoring as the disease might spread in no time. NN has been used as a tool for patient diagnosis and prognosis to determine patients' survival. Bottaci and Drew (1997) investigate fully connected feed forward MLP and BP learning rule, were able to predict patients with colorectal cancer more accurately than clinic pathological methods. They indicate that NN predict the patients' survival and death very well compared to the surgeons.

Pofahl *et al.* (1998) compare the performance of NN, Ranson criteria and Acute Physiology and Chronic Health Evaluation (APACHE II) scoring system for predicting length of stay (LOS) more than seven days for acute pancreatitis patients'. Their study indicates that NN achieve the highest sensitivity (75%) for predicting LOS more than seven. Ohlsson *et al.* (1999) presents their study for the diagnosis of Acute Myocardial Infarction. In their study NN with 10 hidden nodes and one output neuron have been used as the classifier to classified whether the patient suffered from Acute Myocardial Infarction (1) or not (0). The results show that NN performance is 0.84 and 0.85 under *receiver-operating characteristics* (ROC).

- **Applications in Signal Processing and Interpretation**

Signal processing and interpretation in medicine involve a complex analysis of signals, graphic representations, and pattern classification. Consequently, even experienced surgeon could misinterpret or overlooked the data (Janet, 1997; Dybowski, 2000). In *electrocardiographic* (ECG) analysis for example, the complexity of the ECG readings of *acute myocardial infarction* could be misjudged even by experienced cardiologist (Janet, 1997). Accordingly the difficulty faced in ECG patient monitoring is the variability in morphology and timing across patients and within patients, of normal and ventricular beats (Waltrous and Towell, 1995). (Lager Holm *et al.,* 2000) employed Self-Organizing Neural Networks (Self-Organizing Maps or SOMs) in conjunction with Hermite Basis function for the purpose of beat clustering to identify and classify ECG complexes in *arrhythmia*. SOMs topological structure is a benefit in interpreting the data. The experimental results were claimed to outperform other supervised learning method that uses the same data.

Analysis of NN as ECG analyzer also proves that NN is capable to deal with ambiguous nature of ECG signal (Silipo and Marchesi, 1998). Silipo and Marchesi use static and recurrent neural network (RNN) architectures for the classification tasks in ECG analysis for *arrhythmia*, *myocardial ischemia* and chronic alterations. Feedforward network with 8-24-14-1 architecture was employed as a classifier for ECG patient monitoring (Waltrous and Towell, 1995). The analysis indicated that the performance of the patient-adapted network was improved due to the ability of the modulated classifier to adjust the boundaries between classes, even though the distributions of beats were different for different patients.

Multi layer RNN performance with 15-3-2 architecture had been studied and the performance of NN is compared with conventional algorithms for recognizing fetal heart rate abnormality (Lee *et al.*, 1999). The study reveals that the performance of NN is exceptional compared to conventional systems even with adjusted thresholds.

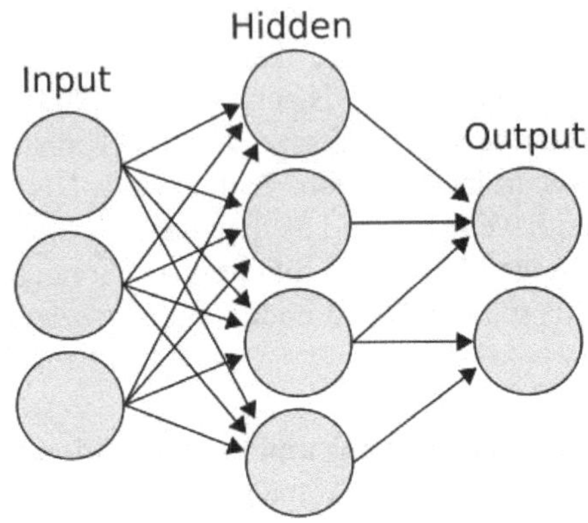

Figure 2: Signal processing

- **Applications in Medical Image Processing**

Image processing is one of the important applications in medicine as most of decision-making is made by looking at the images. In general the segmentation of medical images is to find regions, which represent single anatomical structures (Poli and Valli, 1995). Poli and Valli employed Hopfield neural network for optimum segmentation of 2-D and 3-D medical images. The networks have been tested on synthetic images and on real tomographic and X-ray images.

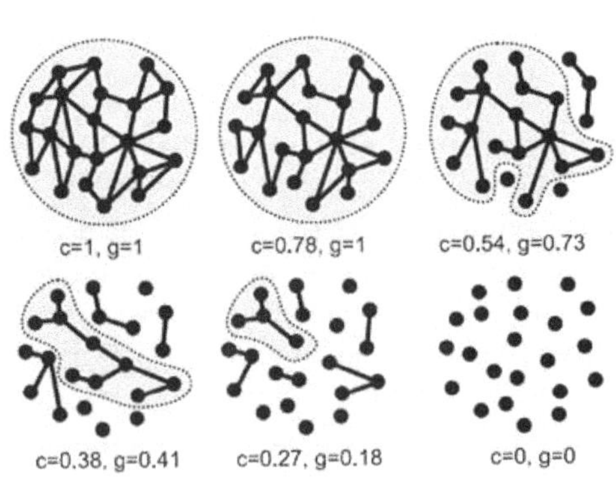

Figure 3: Image Processing

Ahmed and Farag (1998) uses two self-organizing maps (SOM) in two stages, self-organizing principal components analysis (SOPCA) and self-organizing feature map (SOFM) for automatic volume segmentation of medical images. They performed a statistical comparison of the performance of the SOFM with Hopfield network and ISODATA algorithm. The results indicate that the accuracy of SOFM is superior compare to both networks. In addition, SOFM was claimed to have advantage of ease implementation and guaranteed convergence.

- **Applications in Haematology**

There is an attempt to create an expert system to diagnose classes of anaemia and report presumptive diagnoses directly on the haematology form (Birndort et al., 1996). The purpose is to simulate the processes of human experts that can reliably achieve diagnostic separability by pattern analysis. In doing this, they constructed a hybrid expert system combining rule-based and artificial neural network (ANN) models to evaluate microcytic anaemia in a 3-layered program using haematocrit (HCT), mean corpuscular volume (MCV), and coefficient of variation of cell distribution width (RDWcv) as inputs. These measurements are available as standard output on most haematology analyzers. Three categories of microcytic anaemia were considered, iron deficiency (IDA), haemo globinopathy (HEM), and anaemia of chronic disease (ACD). The performance of the model was evaluated with actual case data. The results show that the model was successful in correctly classifying 96.5% of 473 documented cases of microcytic anaemia and anaemia of chronic disease. This result exhibits sufficient accuracy to be considered for use in reporting microcytic anaemia diagnoses on haematology forms.

The leukocyte-vessel wall interactions are studied in post capillary vessels by intravital video microscopy during in vivo animal experiments (Egmont-Petersen et al., 2000). Sequences of video images are obtained and digitized with a frame grabber. A method for automatic detection and characterization of leukocytes in the video images is developed. Individual leukocytes are detected using a neural network that is trained with synthetic leukocyte images generated using a novel stochastic model. This model makes it feasible to generate images of leukocytes with different shapes and sizes under various lighting conditions. Experiments indicate that neural networks trained with the synthetic leukocyte images perform better than networks trained with images of manually detected leukocytes. The best performing neural network trained with synthetic leukocyte images resulted in an 18% larger area under the ROC curve than the best performing neural network trained with manually detected leukocytes.

Conclusion

Neural network has been proven of their capabilities in many domains such as medical application. Neural network become powerful tool in medical diagnosis. Neural network show that experience from expertise is not enough in diagnosis. Nowadays, physicians combined this opportunity that give by neural network and their expertise to detect early stage of patients disease.

NN have been successfully implemented in many applications including medicine. NN, which simulates the function of human biological neuron, has potential of ease implementation in many applications domain. The main consideration of NN implementation is the input data. Once the network is train, the knowledge could be applied to all cases including the new cases in the domain. Studies have shown that NN predictive capability is a useful capability in medical application. Such capability could be used to predict patient condition based on the history cases. The prediction could help doctor to plan for a better medication and provide the patient with early diagnosis.

References

- Abidi S. S. R., and Goh, A. (1998). Neural Network Based Forecasting of Bacteria-Antibiotic Interactions for Infectious Disease Control. In 9th World Congress on Medical Informatics (MedInfo'98), Seoul August 18-22.
- Ahmed, M. N., and Farag, A. A. (1998). Two-stage Neural Network for Medical Volume Segmentation. Accepted for Publication in the Journal of Pattern Recognition Letters, 1998.
- Bottaci, L., and Drew, P. J. (1997). Artificial Neural Networks Applied to Outcome Prediction for Colorectal Cancer Patients in Separate Institutions. Lancet, Vol. 350, Issue 9076, pp. 469-473.
- Dybowski, R. (2000). Neural Computation in Medicine: Perspective and Prospects. In Malmgren, H., Borga, M., Niklasson, L. (eds.) Proceedings of the ANNIMAB-1 Conference (Artificial Neural Networks in Medicine and Biology), Goteborg, 13-16 May 2000. Springer, pp. 26-36.
- Fausett, L. (1994). Fundamentals of Neural Network: Architectures, Algorithms and Applications. Prentice Hall; Englewood Cliffs.
- Janet, F. (1997). Artificial Neural Networks Improve Diagnosis of Acute Myocardial Infarction. Lancet, Vol. 350, Issue 9082, pp. 935.
- Kemsley, D. H., and Martinez, T. R. (1992). A Survey of Neural Network Research and Fielded Applications. In International Journal of Neural Networks: Research and Applications, Vol. 2, No. 2/3/4, pp. 123-133.

- Lagerholm, M., Peterson, C., Braccini, G, Edenbrandt, L., and Sörnmo, L. (2000). Clustering ECG Complexes Using Hermite Functions and Self-Organizing Maps. *IEEE Transactions on Biomedical Engineering* 47, 838-848
- Ohno-Machado, L. (1996). Medical Applications of Artificial Neural Networks: Connectionist Model of Survival. *Ph.D Dissertation.* Stanford University.
- Partridge, D., Abidi, S. S. R., and Goh, A. (1996). Neural Network Applications in Medicine. *Proceedings of National Conference on Research and Development in Computer Science and Its Applications (REDECS'96)*, University Pertanian Malaysia: Kuala Lumpur, pp. 20 - 23.

Dynamic Implementation of K-Means Clustering Algorithm

Poonam Goyal
Asstt. Manager (Systems), SBI, Mumbai
R. L. Ujjwal
Sr. Lecturer, USIT, GGSIPU, Delhi

Abstract:
Developing an effective and an efficient data mining algorithms for a large dataset play an important role in helping users to effectively navigate summarize and organize the information. Clustering plays a crucial role in organizing large document collections. Clustering text data online as it comes in is a difficult problem. It is both hard to capture a meaningful notion of text data similarity and to cluster large amounts of data in a single pass. Recent studies have shown that partitioning based clustering algorithms are more suitable for clustering large datasets. The K-means algorithm is the most commonly used partitioning clustering algorithm because it can be easily implemented and is the most efficient one in terms of the execution time. The major problem is that it is sensitive to the selection of the initial partition and may converge to local optima. In this paper, we present a dynamic method for K-means clustering algorithm that performs fast document clustering. We are using cosine distance similarity to cluster the documents in a single pass, which gives certain running time guarantees & increase cluster weights when new document are added.

Keywords: *K-Means Clustering, Cosine Distance, Vector Representation.*

Introduction:

The data stream model has recently attracted attention for its applicability to numerous types of data, including telephone records, Web documents, and large data streams. For analysis of such data, the ability to process the data in a single pass, or a small number of passes, while using little memory, is crucial. We describe such a streaming algorithm that effectively clusters large data streams. We also provide empirical evidence of the algorithm's performance on synthetic and real data streams. Data mining, *the extraction of hidden descriptive or predictive information from large databases*, is a powerful new technology with great potential to help companies and data analysts focus on the most important information in their data repositories. Developing data mining algorithms for streaming and text data have emerged as an important problem. For streaming data, the assumption is that the data records can be examined only once. One of the main applications is to cluster large amounts of distributed network monitoring data. Simply integrating the distributed data in real time is expensive and for this reason low cost clustering algorithms for streaming data are of more interest. In many real data mining applications, data comes in as a continuous stream and presents several challenges to traditional static data mining algorithms. Application examples include topic detection from a news stream, intrusion detection from continuous network traffic, object recognition from video sequences, etc. Challenges lie in several aspects: high algorithm efficiency is required in real time; huge data volume that cannot be kept in memory all at once; multiple scans from secondary storage is not desirable since it causes intolerable delays; and mining algorithms need to be adaptive since data patterns change over time.

Data Clustering

Data mining, *the extraction of hidden descriptive or predictive information from large databases*, is a powerful new technology with great potential to help companies and data analysts focus on the most important information in their data repositories. Class identification, i.e. the grouping of the objects of a database into meaningful subclasses such that similarity of objects in the same group is maximized and similarity of objects in different groups is minimized, is called clustering. Representing data by fewer clusters necessarily loses certain fine details but achieves simplification. Thus the objects are clustered or grouped based on the principle of "maximizing the intraclass similarity and minimizing the interclass similarity". Clustering has its roots in many areas, including data mining, statistics, biology, and machine learning.

There exist many clustering algorithm from partition based, model based, non parametric density estimation based methods, graph theoretical based, to empirical and hybrid approaches. They all are underlying some concept about data organization and cluster characteristics to find interesting patterns or clusters in the given dataset. The partition-based algorithms are more suitable for clustering large datasets as they can be easily implemented and are most efficient one in terms of the execution time.

The most commonly used algorithm is K-Means clustering which is partitioning based algorithm. As this is the simplest algorithm but there are some limitations with this algorithm like the number of clusters (K) needs to be determined beforehand, means the algorithm is sensitive to an initial seed selection, it cannot be used for clustering problems whose results cannot fit in main memory, which is the case when data set has very high dimensionality or desired number of clusters is too big. So it is proposed to develop an efficient algorithm which tries to remove some or all the above given limitations.

Cluster Analysis

Cluster analysis is a collection of statistical methods, which identifies groups of samples that behave similarly or show similar characteristics. The key idea is to identify classifications of the objects that would be useful for the aims of the analysis. Cluster analysis is an important human activity. Early in childhood, one learns how to distinguish between cats and dogs, or between animals and plants, by continuously improving subconscious clustering schemes. The data stream model has recently attracted attention for its applicability to numerous types of data, including telephone records, Web documents, and large dataset.
Clustering is an unsupervised classification as it has no predefined classes and few of its typical application include:

- As a stand-alone tool to get insight into data distribution.
- As a pre-processing step for other algorithms.

A good clustering method will produce high quality clusters with high intra-class similarity and low inter-class similarity. The quality of a clustering result depends on both the similarity measure used by the method and its implementation. The quality of a clustering method can be measured by its ability to discover some or all of the hidden patterns. For analysis of such data, the ability to process the data in a single pass, or a small Number of passes, while using little memory, is crucial. In this paper, K-Means Clustering algorithm is dynamically implemented with the cosine distance similarity which also helps in achieving global optimality.

Related Work

Similarity Measurement

Similarity: The word "similarity" in k-means clustering means that data objects are closely related in terms of distance.
The usual axioms for a Similarity/Distance measure D are:

- D(x,y)=0
- D(x,y)=D(y,x)
- D(x,y)d" D(x,z)+D(z,y) the triangle inequality

Assume x=[x1, x2.....xn] and y=[y1, y2...yn]
There are following methods to measure distance between two objects of n dimensions-

1. Euclidean distance in n-dimensional feature space:
   $d_2(x_i, x_j) = (\sum_{k=1}^{n} (x_{ik} - x_{jk})^2)^{½}$

2. L_1 metric or city block distance:
   $d_1(xi, xj) = \sum_{k=1}^{m} |x_{ik} - x_{jk}|$
3. Minkowski metric (includes the Euclidean distance and city block distance as special cases):
   $d_p(x_i, x_j) = (\sum_{k=1}^{m} (x_{ik} - x_{jk})^p)^{1/p}$

K-Means Clustering

K-Means algorithm is one of the partitioning based clustering algorithm. The general objective is to obtain the fixed number of partitions/clusters that minimize the sum of squared Euclidean distances between objects and cluster centroid.

Let $X=\{x_i \mid i=1, 2, \ldots\ldots n\}$ be a data set with n objects, k is the number of clusters, m_j is the centroid of cluster cj where j=1, 2,…k. Then the algorithm finds the distance between a data object and a centroid by using the following Euclidean distance formula

Euclidean distance formula= $\mathrm{sqrt}(|x_i - m_j|^{2)}$
Starting from an initial distribution of cluster centers in data space, each object is assigned to the cluster with closest center, after which each center itself is updated as the center of mass of all objects belonging to that particular cluster. The procedure is repeated until convergence.

Algorithm

Input: //Set of *n* items to cluster
$D=\{d_1, d_2, d_2, \ldots\ldots\ldots d_n\}$
//No. of clusters randomly chosen i.e. *k*
//C is set of centroid of those clusters
$K=\{k_1, k_2, k_2 \ldots k_k\}$
$C=\{c_1, c_2, c_2, \ldots c_k\}$
Where $k_1=\{d_1\}$, $k_2=\{d_2\}, \ldots\ldots k_k=\{d_k\}$ and $c_1=d_1, c_2=d_2, c_2=d_2 \ldots\ldots\ldots c_k=d_k$
//Here *k*<=*n*

Output: //K is set of subsets of D as final clusters and C is set of centroid of these clusters
$K=\{k_1, k_2, k_2 \ldots k_k\}$
$C=\{c_1, c_2, c_2, \ldots c_k\}$

Algorithm:

1. *K-Means (D, K, C)*
2. Repeat until (No change in centroid)

3. for i= 1 to *n* do
4. Determine distance (m) between di and each centroid cj of any kj in K such that m is minimum. (1<=j<=k)
5. Assign di to cluster kj
6. Calculate new mean (centroid) for each cluster kj. (1<=j<=k).
7. End

In the above given K-Means clustering algorithms, the number of clusters (K) needs to be determined beforehand and this method is sensitive to an initial seed selection (Starting cluster centroid) due to which it is susceptible to a local optimum and may miss the global optimum. It may converge to suboptimal solutions.

Present Work: Dynamic Implementation of K-Means clustering algorithm

Approach

The dynamic implementation requires addressing the concept of vector space model and cosine distance similarity. In this algorithm, each document as well as each cluster is represented as a vector. There is a tremendous proliferation in the amount of information available on the largest shared information source, the world wide web. The specific instance of large dataset we want to focus on any web document containing information for cricket match. As data keeps on increasing day by day so it require to change the clusters over the time as new data comes. Due to the huge size of new dataset, it is not feasible to store all of the data. So if we partition the data within the fixed number of clusters then it can't be work life long as data keeps on increasing. So we need a dynamic method which can be used effectively. In this algorithm we are using vector in high dimensional vector space for representing documents as well as clusters and then we are using cosine distance between vectors. As the volume of dataset increases, management and analysis of data becomes very important.

The document is represented as a vector of terms <t1,t2,….,tn>.Each term ti represents a word or a phrase.

A set of documents is represented as a set of vectors that can be written as a matrix, where each row represent a document, each column indicates a term and each element xij represents the frequency of the ith term in the jth document.

$$\begin{pmatrix} x_{11} & \cdots & x_{1l} & \cdots & x_{1m} \\ \vdots & & \vdots & & \vdots \\ x_{j1} & \cdots & x_{jl} & \cdots & x_{jm} \\ \vdots & & \vdots & & \vdots \\ x_{n1} & \cdots & x_{nl} & \cdots & x_{nm} \end{pmatrix}$$

Cosine Distance

$$d(\vec{x}, \vec{y}) = 1 - \frac{\vec{x} \cdot \vec{y}}{|\vec{x}| \cdot |\vec{y}|}$$

Term frequency – inverted document frequency (tfidf)

Tfidf weighs the frequency of a term in a document with a factor that discounts its importance when it appears in almost all documents. Therefore terms that appear too rarely or too frequently are ranked lower than terms that balance between the two extremes.

Tfidf(t_k,d_j)=#(t_k,d_j)*log(|Tr|/#Tr(t_k)), where
#(t_k,d_j) denotes the number of times term t_k occurs in document d_j
#Tr(t_k) denotes the number of documents in Tr in which t_k occurs.
|Tr| denotes the number of documents.

Pre Processing involves the following tasks

- Word Filtering
- Vector construction

TFIDF approach is used to remove most frequent words from the document and after that it needs to convert to some vector form for the purpose to calculate distance with other document. Each possible word represents a dimension in this vector space, if an article contains a word it would have 1 added to that dimension. After that vector would be normalized.

Word filtering is done to save time for clustering and vector construction is done to represent the document in proper format after that cosine distance is measured which is compared with the word in other documents, with the help of which we don't need to define the number of clusters beforehand. And this algorithm is implemented in a single pass and as new data comes it keeps on adding in the clusters according to the cosine distance.

Framework

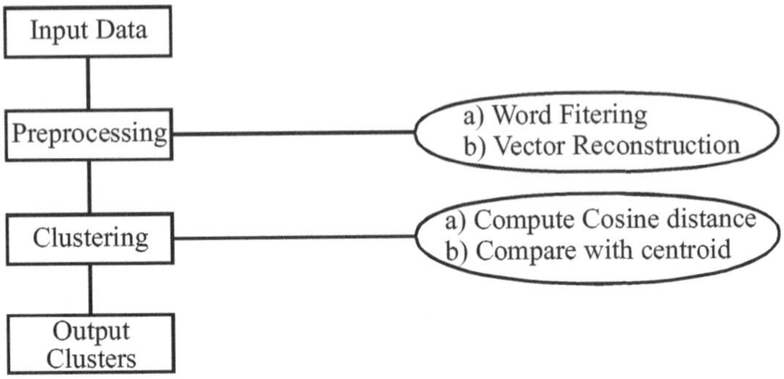

Figure 1: Framework for Dynamic Method

Algorithm:

Input: //Set of *n* Documents to cluster

$D = \{ d_1, d_2, d_2, \ldots\ldots.. d_n \}$

Output: //C is set of subsets of D as final clusters

$C = \{k_1, k_2, k_2, \ldots k_k\}$

Algorithm:

1. FOR EACH DOCUMENT
2. Begin
3. Perform Word Filtering to remove unwanted words
4. Count number of occurrence of each word using TFIDF and store in a text file.
5. Tfidf $(t\_k, d\_j) = \#(t\_k, d\_j) * \log(|T_r| / \#T_r(t\_k))$, Where
6. Create vector representation of each file using VSM <*t1, t2, ..., ti, ..., tn*>, Where each term *ti* represents a word or a phrase of the document.
   Repeat
7. Read vector for each file and compute the cosine distance between vectors by using cosine distance formula

$$d(\vec{x}, \vec{y}) = 1 - \frac{\vec{x} \cdot \vec{y}}{|\vec{x}| \cdot |\vec{y}|}$$ Where x, y are vector representation of documents

8. If (cosine distance is within threshold) Add to the cluster.
9. Else Begin a new cluster.
10. End

In this algorithm we don't need to define the number of clusters beforehand.

Results:

This algorithm is implemented using PERL Language and different results are compared using varying number of documents with different threshold values. Results are given below:

Comparison graph is given below:

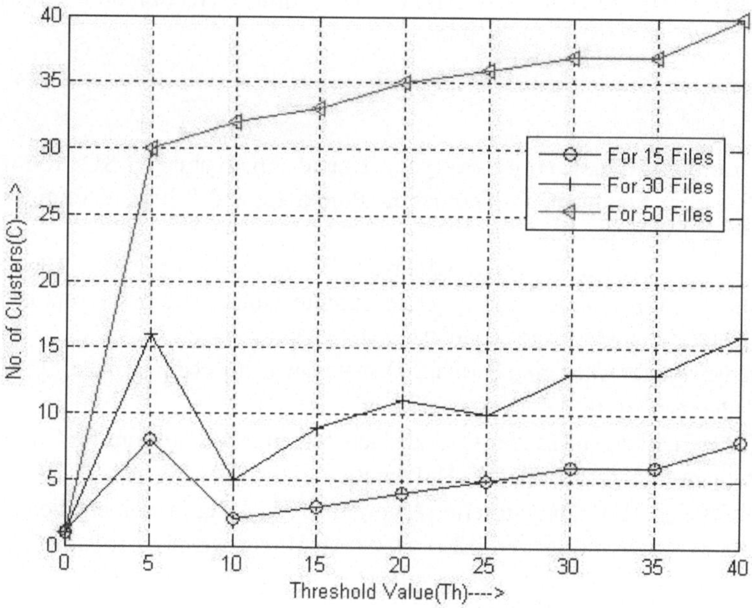

Figure 2: Comparison Graph

The above graph indicates generation of different numbers of clusters by considering various combinations of thresholds values and numbers of documents files. Here Red, Black and Blue plots show the 15,30 and 50 document files respectively. The above graph shows the plot by taking different threshold value and keeping number of documents 25. As we increase the threshold value the number of clusters also increased. Here value of threshold signifies the minimum permissible threshold to qualify in the existing clusters. For example if the cosine distance of a coming document D_c is greater than to the existing document D_e then we can say that, the current document D_c is more near to the document $D_{e.}$ Then if cosine distance is less then to given threshold value, so we have to create new cluster it means document D_c is not similar to any exists ting documents, second if it is greater then, so now D_c will be added in more similar document cluster.

Conclusion & Future work:

The proposed work assumes first data object as first cluster and then automatically generates all the clusters. It also considers the threshold limit which impacts final number of clusters to be formed. More the value of threshold limit lesser is the number of clusters or vice versa. The work shows how to generate clusters automatically but there is a grate impact of threshold limit on the number of clusters to be formed. In future one can consider this idea of generating clusters automatically independent of threshold limit. Outlier detection and removal is another area where work can be done.

References:

- Document Clustering Analysis Based on Hybrid PSO+K-means Algorithm,Xiaohui Cui, Thomas E. Potok,Applied Software Engineering Research Group.
- Charu C. Aggarwal, Jiawei Han, Jianyong Wang, and Phillip S. Yu. A Clustering Data Streams: Theory and Practice Sudipto Guha , Adam Meyerson Nina Mishra, Rajeev Motwani ,Liadan O'Callaghan.
- Framework for Clustering Evolving Data Streams. Proceedings of the 29th VLDB Conference, Berlin, Germany, 2003.
- Moses Charikar and Liadan O'Callaghan. Streaming Algorithms for Clustering Problems. Lecture, Princeton University.
- An Efficient K-Means Clustering Algorithm: Analysis & Implementation, Tapas Kanungo, Senior Member, IEEE, David M. Mount, Member, IEEE, Nathan S. Netanyahu, Member, IEEE, Christine D. Piatko, Ruth Silverman, and Angela Y. Wu, Senior Member, IEEE

Robotics Technology

'Robots are the future'

Deepti Sachdeva
Server Administrator, Computech System, Delhi

Abstract

In the near future human beings will be living in a ubiquitous world where all objects such as electronic appliances are networked to each other and robots will provide us with services of every variety by any device through any network, at any place anytime.

When it comes to robots, reality still lags science fiction. But, just because robots have not lived up to their promise in past decades does not mean that they will not arrive sooner or later. Indeed, the confluence of several advanced technologies is bringing the age of robotics ever nearer - smaller, cheaper, more practical and cost-effective.
There are 3 aspects of any robot: Brawn – strength relating to physical payload that a robot can move, Bone – the physical structure of a robot relative to the work it does; this determines the size and weight of the robot in relation to its physical payload, and Brain – robotic intelligence; what it can think and do independently; how much manual interaction is required.

Because of the way robots have been pictured in science fiction, many people expect robots to be human-like in appearance. But in fact what a robot looks like is more related to the tasks or functions it performs. A lot of machines that look nothing like humans can clearly be classified as robots. And similarly, some human-looking robots are not much beyond mechanical mechanisms, or toys.

Many early robots were big machines, with significant brawn and little else. Old hydraulically powered robots were relegated to tasks in the 3-D category – dull, dirty and dangerous. The technological advances since the first industry implementation have completely revised the capability, performance and strategic benefits of robots. For example, by the 1980s robots transitioned from being hydraulically powered to become electrically driven units. Accuracy and performance improved.

Introduction

Since 1950, inventions have revolutionized the way we live. Radio, Telephones, Television, Computers, Washing Machines. What's the next big thing? **Robots.** Of Course

Robot, the American Heritage dictionary says," is a mechanical device that sometimes resembles a human being and is capable of performing complex tasks on command or by programming in an advance"

When it comes to robots, reality still lags science fiction. But, just because robots have not led up to their promise in past decades does not mean that they will not arrive sooner or later. Indeed, the confluence of several advanced technologies is bringing the age of robotics ever nearer - smaller, cheaper, more practical and cost-effective.

However, current robots have a number of constraints to become wholly ubiquitous. The research attempts to eliminate the spatial limitations by introducing virtual robots into the physical world. Ubiquitous robot, Ubibot, is introduced to integrate three forms of robots: software robot (Sobot), embeded robot (Embot) and mobile robot (Mobot).

Sobot is a virtual robot, which has the ability to move to any place or connect to any device through a network, in order to overcome the spatial limitation. It has the capability to interpret the context and thus interact with the user.

Embot is embedded within the environment or in the Mobot. An Embot can recognize the locations of and authenticate the user or robot, and synthesize sensing information.

Mobot provides integrated mobile services. The services that will be provided by Ubibot will be seamless, calm and context-aware.

Brief History about Robots

The basic ability of man to imitate parts of the human body perhaps led to the first robot. A brief history of how robots evolved from being a mere figment of imagination to the working models of today.

Now robots has specialized in a wide range of fields. They have automated lawn mower robots, vacuum cleaner robots, robots which play with children, decorative butterflies which keep flapping the wings, robots that learn to live as a colony, wrestle with one another We even have frontier prowlers for surveillance near borders of countries and many other machines that save human lives during wars.

TYPES OF ROBOTS

Robots can be found in the manufacturing industry, the military, space exploration, transportation, and medical applications.
This section briefly examines some of the uses of Robots:

- **Robots on Earth**

Typical industrial robots do jobs that are difficult, dangerous or dull. They lift heavy objects, paint, handle chemicals, and perform assembly work. They perform the same job hour after hour, day after day with precision. They don't get tired and they don't make errors associated with fatigue and so are ideally suited to performing repetitive tasks. The major categories of industrial robots by mechanical structure are as below:

- **Robots in the Military**

In fact Military is a dangerous place for humans but it makes a logical application for robotics. For e.g. at left there is a Smart Crane Ammunition (Figure 1) Transfer System being developed by the Robotics Research Corporation. The goal is for one soldier to be able to unload the entire truck without ever leaving the cab. The system includes various cameras, video screens, force sensors and special grippers.

Figure 1

- **Entertainment Robots**

Entertainment Robots like Disney(as shown in the above Figure 2). With dancing bears and singing pirates Disney's imaginers have created thousands of robots. It is a robot dinosaur named Lucky. He walks on his two back legs and pulls a very large cart of "silk flowers". Really the cart is full of batteries. This was the only way they could get enough battery life for the robot to spend a meaningful amount of time wandering the amusement part.

Figure 2

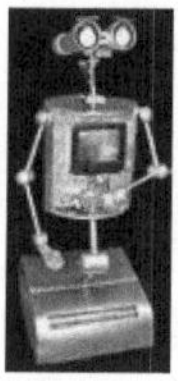

Figure 3

Some entertainment robots are not much more than rolling, remote-controlled speaker phones with video camera "eyes." They can wander around at parties and play pre-recorded jingles or display scrolling messages to promote a company's products or distribute promotional literature. Florida Robotics makes robots like as shown in the Figure 3. They also make more complex robots that have the capability to talk with on-lookers and include fiber optic hair, remote controlled water guns, on-board video camera and transmitter (robot can send video of what he sees to remote monitor or video wall), sound effects and smoke.

- **Industrial Robots**

Industrial Robots are true marvels of Engineering. Robots can do work 24 hours a day for years on end with no failures whatsoever. Though they are reprogrammable, in many applications (particularly those in the auto industry) they are programmed once and then repeat that exact same task for years .

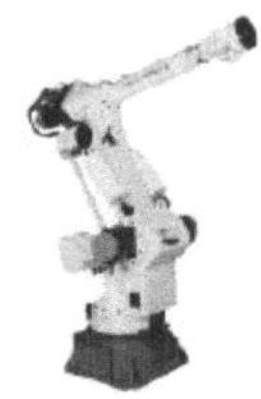

Figure 4

Fanuc makes this particular robot. Fanuc is the largest maker of these type of robots in the world and they are almost always yellow. This robot in Figure 4 has six independent joints, also called six degrees of freedom. Robots are also very useful in welding, painting and handling materials in auto industry sector.

- **Researched Robots**

The Robotics Research Corporation of America produced this robot in 1988 for NASA to study the possibility of using robots to perform maintenance on the International Space Station. Each of the robot's arms has 7 joints and they are mounted on a torso with 3 joints, giving the robot a total of 17 degrees of freedom. See the Figure 5. A number of researchers have embraced the idea of miniature robots working together in swarms. Powered by three watch batteries, it rides on track wheels and consists of an 8K ROM processor, temperature sensor, and two motors that drive the wheels. Enhancements being considered include a miniature camera, microphone, communication device, and a chemical micro-sensor

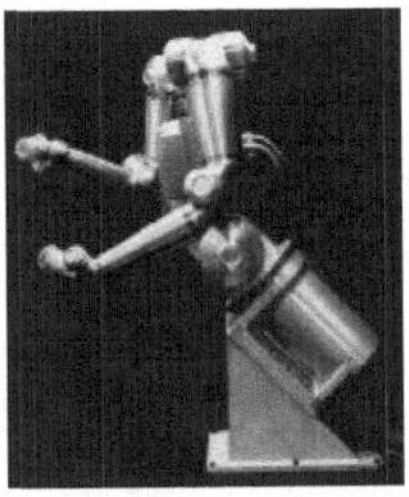

Figure 5

- **Undersea Robots**

Undersea operations are a great application for robotics to replace humans. Working underwater is both dangerous and difficult for humans. The Australian Centre for Field Robotics at the University of Sydney developed the robot shown in Figure 6 at left as a prototype for autonomous underwater robots that may one day explore and monitor the Great Barrier Reef. At present this robot (called Oberon) must remain

Figure 6

tethered to a ship on the surface, but its inventors predict that within a decade it would be possible for robots to be lowered to the ocean floor and left to get on with mapping the terrain on their own.

- **Robots in Radioactive Environment**

The folks working on the first atomic bombs pretty much defined telerobotics in this country. They had no other way of working with the radioactive materials The operator would stand on one side of a thick, leaded glass window while the robot manipulated the material on the other side. Cables, bands and tubes provided the coupling.

- **Robots in Space**

It is dangerous for humans to get to space, to be in space and to return from space. Keeping robots operating reliably in space presents some unique challenges for engineers. The conceptual robot at left has 21 independent joints. On earth it would be impossible for this robot to support its own weight, but in space, the design presents some unique capabilities. The robot can reach around obstacles and through port holes. It can continue to operate with excellent dexterity even after several joints fail.

Figure 7

Today, two important devices exist which are proven space robots. One is the Remotely Operated Vehicle (ROV) and the other is the Remote Manipulator System (RMS). An ROV can be an unmanned spacecraft that remains in flight, a lander that makes contact with an extraterrestrial body and operates from a stationary position, or a rover that can move over terrain once it has landed. Even the earliest and simplest spacecraft operated with some preprogrammed functions monitored closely from Earth. One of the best known ROV's is the Sojourner rover that was deployed by the Mars Pathfinder spacecraft. Several NASA centers are involved in developing planetary explorers and space-based robots. Robot arms are of two types. One is computer-operated and programmed for a specific function. The other requires a human to actually control the strength and movement of the arm to perform the task. To date, the NASA Remote Manipulator System (RMS) robot arm has performed a number of tasks on many space missions-serving as a grappler, a remote assembly device, and also as a positioning device.

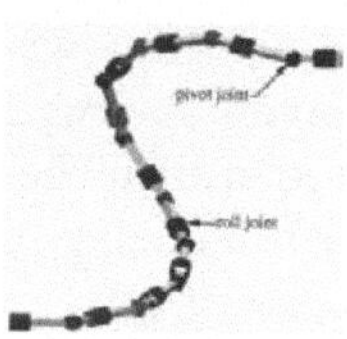

Figure 8

Applications

The Robotic Systems Section is infusing its technology into a number of applications for space mission and related terrestrial endeavors. An Aerobot is a robotic aerial vehicle that uses buoyancy to provide the lift needed to fly. Robotics Technology is helpful in following areas like:

- Driving
- Flying
- Landing
- Subsurface access
- Sampling
- Construction
- Simulation
- User Interface
- Military & Terrestrial
- Small body Orbiting

Future Robotics Technology

The future of robotics has certainly been addressed several times over. From books to movies, virtually everyone has at least some idea of how they believe the future of robotics technology will play out.

The future of robotics technology looks bright. It has been pondered however just how robotics technology will affect future generations. Robotics devices that can lead the blind, aid the elderly and even clean house when needed are all being considered although the timeline for these developments is far from being seen right now. Looking into the past you can see that changes come greatly with innovation.

The cotton gin, airplane and internet are all examples of how creative developments have made life much easier so it is very safe to assume that with research and new developments in the area of robotics technology, there may just be true robotics that will aid in disease curing and other important industries.

It is assumed that robotics will play a large role in law enforcement and security fields. As of today, robots are already being used for dangerous and hazardous tasks such as bomb disposal, hostage recovery and search and rescue operations. The effects of robotics technology in the future may well play a vital role in manufacturing computers, vehicles and better consumer and health products overall

Conclusion

The day when there are more of programmable tooling kinds of robots than all of the traditional robots that exist in the world today. There is an enormous sea change coming; the potential is significant because soon robots will offer not only improved cost-effectiveness, but also advantages and operations that have never been possible before.

One day Robots will definitely coming to school crossing near you and it will become a part of daily life.

Once relegated to science-fiction movies and automobile assembly lines, robots are expected to handle more complex tasks in health care and agriculture, among other areas.

Technology's interdisciplinary nature will help foster robotics advancements. The consumer space will create the need for cell phones and PDAs (personal digital assistants) with better batteries and these innovations will eventually be adapted to fit the robotics industry.

From this I conclude that a robot has to be safe and reliable. An unreliable robot may become the cause of unsafe conditions, high maintenance costs, inconvenience, etc

References

- Virtual Reality Technology - by Grigore C Burdea, Philippe Coiffe
- Telerobotics Automation and Human Supervisory –by Thomas B Sheridan
- The Robots in the Garden-by Ken Goldberg

A New Approach for Application and Implementation of Object Oriented Metrics

Anisha Chopra
Consultant,Headstrong Services Pvt. Ltd., Noida
Ashish Payal
Sr. Lecturer, USIT, GGSIPU, Delhi

Abstract:
Developing , Implementing an effective and an efficient Object Oriented Metrics Suite for Software Projects play an important role in helping users and managers to effectively measure various characteristics of Object Oriented Software and analysis of results after applying these metrics. Metrics plays a crucial role in assessing the quality and complexity of software systems, getting basic understanding of sensitive parts of Software. A key element of any engineering process is measurement. Measures are used to better understand the attributes of model that we create. Recent studies have shown that since object, oriented technology uses objects and not algorithms as its fundamental building blocks, the approach to software metrics for object oriented metrics must be different from the standard metrics set. Question here is "Which Object Oriented Metrics should a project use, and can any of traditional metrics be adapted to the object oriented environment?" The metrics are first defined, studied and then using simple object oriented example, the metrics are implemented. Object oriented analysis approaches the problem by looking for the system entities that combine them. Metrics plays an important role in some disciplines of software engineering and has been implemented by various authors over Basic Object Oriented Programs. The major problems are it is very difficult for project managers and practitioners to select measures for object-oriented systems and those measures could not be evaluated over a large data set and industrial object oriented software system . In this paper, we present a Object Oriented Metrics Suite which provide sufficient information over object oriented constructs like class, coupling, cohesion , inheritance and polymorphism .We will put emphasis on polymorphism concept over which less studies have been done till now. We are using object oriented metrics suite consisting of five metrics and then we will describe an empirical investigation into industrial object-oriented software comprising large lines of code. The System is a Financial System and in use by large number of users worldwide.

Keywords: *Object Oriented Software System, Coupling, Cohesion, Inheritance and Polymorphism.*

Introduction:

Object oriented design and development are popular concepts in today's software development environment. Software metrics are a valuable tool in helping software engineers to develop large, complex software systems. However, it is vital that transparency and precision are maintained at all stages. Object oriented software development requires a different approach from more traditional functional decomposition and data flow development methods. While the functional and data flow approaches commence by considering the system behavior or data separately, object oriented analysis approaches the problem by looking for system entities that combine them. Object oriented software engineers need a better understanding of the desirable and non-desirable properties of Object oriented systems design and their effect onto the quality factor .The desirable properties must represent those characteristics that ultimately lead to more efficient, reusable, maintainable and extensible software products. A mechanism is provided for comparing measures and their potential use, integrating existing measures, which examine the same concept in different ways, and facilitating more rigorous decision making regarding the definition of new measures. What entities do we measure in object-oriented design? In most object-oriented languages we find and can measure classes, operations (including methods and functions), variables (including the whole range from attributes to local variables) etc.

The objectives of our investigation — based upon a significant piece of industrial OO software — are twofold, first to contribute to our understanding Object oriented technology and second to explore the possibility of building prediction systems that are useful to practicing software engineers. Despite the need for empirical research into large-scale OO systems, the majority of object-oriented metrics research has concentrated upon defining sets of structural metrics, e.g. although this can be a useful Precursor to empirical work, on its own this type of approach has limited practical utility. Without empirical evidence, it is not possible to say how effective these measures are.

OO Metrics and Hypotheses

Our analysis focus on the set of Object Oriented metrics suite which consists of five metrics. Here, we will do comparative study of these metrics:

1) Size Metrics

WMC, Weighted methods per class .This metric measures the complexity of a class. Its value is computed as the sum of the complexity of each individual method of the class. For the sake of simplicity, we consider all methods of a class to be equally complex. Thus, the value of WMC represents the number of methods of the class.

Consider a class Order, with methods Sub1, ..., Sub n that are defined in the class. Let

C1...,.Cn be the complexity of the methods

$$WMC=\sum_{i=1}^{n} C_i$$

2) Coupling Metrics:

RFC, response for a class. This metric measures the number of methods that can be potentially executed in response to a message received by an object of a class. As in this paper e.g. for FSX2.0 and FSx2.1 there are methods which can be executed as data is passed by an object of class. Whenever a Sales Person places an order for New Subscription and Additional Subscription or Redemptions .Financial Data is passed to various queues for further processing. (Principal, Amount, Upfront Fee)

3) Cohesion Metrics:

Lack of Cohesion on Methods (LCOM) – This is the number of pairs of member functions without shared instance variables, minus the number of pairs of member functions with shared instance variables. However, the metric is set to 0 whenever the above subtraction is negative .A class with low cohesion among its methods suggests an inappropriate design, (i.e., the encapsulation of unrelated program objects and member functions that should not be together), this is likely to be fault-prone.

4) Inheritance Metrics:

4) DIT-The metrics for the hierarchical structure, Number of Children (NOC) and Depth in Tree(DIT) can also be graphically depicted as shown in Figure 10. A class with DIT = 0 is the "root" Of a hierarchy. If it is also a "leaf", NOC = 0, then it is standalone code that does not benefit from inheritance or reuse. Almost 66% of this project's classes are below other classes in the tree, which indicates a moderate level of reuse. Higher percentages for DIT's of 2 and 3 would show a higher degree of reuse, but increased complexity. There is one root in our application Funds and Clients as roots for which DIT is 0 .With the help of Clients and these funds Orders are being placed for further approval.

5) Polymorphic Metric:

For two methods to be polymorphic, they need to have the same name and signature (parameter types and return type) and the same effects (changing the state of the receiver in the same way and raising the same messages to other objects in the system).

Classes	Public Instance Methods
Order	
Subscription	
New Subscription	New Sub , Add Sub
Add Subscription	
Redemption	
Full Redemption	Full Redeem , Partial Share Redeem , Partial Amount Redeem
Partial Redemption By Share	
Partial Redemption By Amount	

Table 1: Part of Hierarchy in Sample Object Oriented Software

Let m be a method name. Let C1 and C2 be two classes existing in the model M. The methods named m are polymorphic in C1 and C2 in the model U if the following formula holds:

U |= Polymorphic (m, C1, C2)
Where the predicate Polymorphic is defined as follows:

Def a:
$\forall$□m: Name $\forall$C1, C2: Class ·
Polymorphic (m, C1, C2) $\leftrightarrow$ $\exists$m1, m2 · (m1 $\in$C1.operations $\wedge$ m2$\in$C2.operations $\wedge$ m1.name=m $\wedge$ m2.name=m $\wedge$ m1.Visibility=m2. Visibility
$\wedge$ hasSameSignature (m1, m2)
$\wedge$ hasSameBehavior (m, C1, C2))
The predicate hasSameSignature applied on two methods is true if both methods have the same signature.

Related Work

There are only 12.5 % of the total classes that have high coupling metric values. There are 4.1% classes with deep hierarchy. Since earlier empirical studies suggests that classes with more coupling and deep hierarchy are fault prone, the identified classes (12.5%) must be thoroughly checked during testing. Theoretical analysis of these metrics suggest that out of 14 class level metrics, six metrics (NOA, NOM, MPC, DAC, LCOM and LCC) provide sufficient information for usage and other metrics are either subset of these metrics or are providing same information in different format. The number of dimensions captured in PC analysis is only 5 which are much lower than the number of measures. This simply supports the conclusions drawn from theoretical analysis i.e. many of the metrics proposed are based on comparable ideas and therefore provide somewhat redundant information. The correlation analysis between different metrics and size shows that hardly any of the metric is strongly correlated to size. The measures could not be evaluated over a large data set but this is a problem that has plagued much of empirical software engineering research. More similar type of studies must be carried out with different data sets to give generalized results across different organizations. We plan to replicate our study on large data set and industrial Object-oriented software system.

Metric	Project2			
	Min	Max	Mean	Median
WMC	1	30	10	5
RFC	1	54	14	10
LCOM	0	1	0.5	0.5
DIT	0	1	0.5	0.5

Metric	Project1			
	Min	Max	Mean	Median
WMC	1	12	6	5
RFC	1	31	20	25
LCOM	0	1	0.5	0.5
DIT	0	1	0.5	0.5

Table 2: Correlation Analysis

Present Work:

The empirical study will be conducted on an industrial financial application. For confidentiality reasons, we cannot disclose neither functional details nor the producer of this application. In what follows, we refer to this application as Financial Systems.

Target Data

We collected data from three different Releases of Financial Systems, referred to as FSx2.0, FSx2.1 and FSx2.2, respectively. Such versions represent the evolution of the same software over time. At the time of this writing, all three releases operate in the field and all of them are maintained by the company as upcoming releases. All three releases are significantly different from each other in terms of offered functionality. Each release of Financial Systems consists of more than 2 million lines of Java code. The set of source files common to the three versions (common core files) accounts for 91.03% of the files in FSx2.0, 90.09% in FSx2.1 and 89.5% in FSx2.2. This suggests that the evolution of Financial Systems largely favored modification and adaptation of available code over implementation of new functionality in separate modules.

Application

WMC:

For some of the metrics, a simple histogram demonstrates prevailing and extreme values for two projects. For these projects (FSX2.0, FSX2.1) in Figure, a histogram of Weighted Methods per Class (WMC) reveals that, while most classes have a WMC of value around 50, there are a few classes with WMC greater than 100. Those few classes with the highest WMC are candidates for inspection and/or revision.This histogram is also useful for monitoring complexity over time.

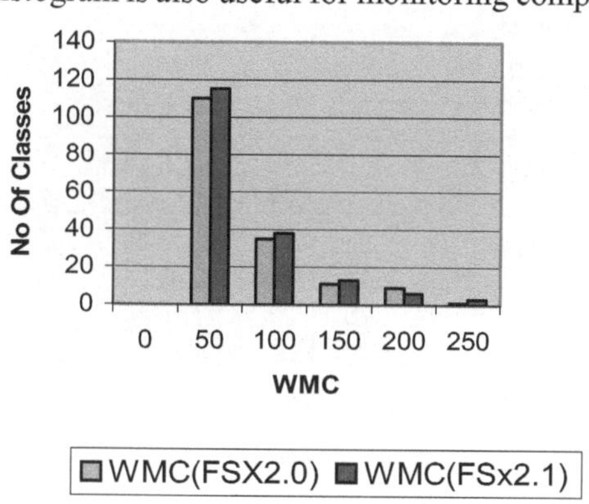

Figure 1: WMC

RFC:

A few classes in the projects shown in Figure are capable of invoking more than 150 methods. Classes with large RFC have a greater complexity and decreased understandability. Testing and debugging are more complicated. This information is useful when monitored over time also.

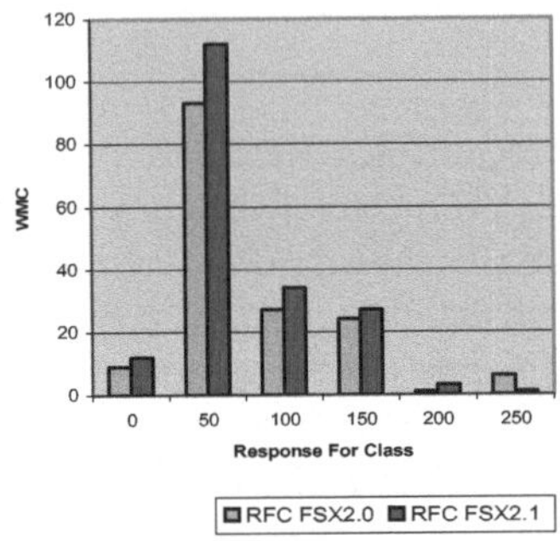

Figure 2: RFC

DIT::

The metrics for the hierarchical structure, Depth in Tree (DIT) can also be graphically depicted as shown in Figure 10. A class with DIT = zero, is the "root" of a hierarchy. If it is also a "leaf", NOC = zero, then it is standalone code that does not benefit from inheritance or reuse. Almost 58% of this project's classes are below other classes in the tree, which indicates a moderate level of reuse. Higher percentages for DIT's of 2 and 3 would show a higher degree of reuse, but increased complexity.

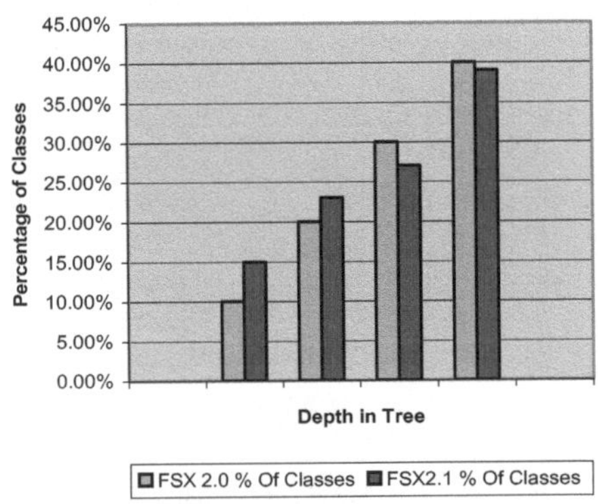

Figure 3: DIT

LCOM:

The value of Lack of Cohesion of Methods (LCOM) depends on the number of methods, so there is a maximum value possible. Figure is a plot of measured LCOM compared to possible maximums. While there is little experience with the LCOM metric, intuition says that the smaller actual LCOM is compared to its possible maximum, the better. In Figure we look at LCOM to identify the values closest to the line. Trend line shown in the graph to make comparisons between projects and between languages.

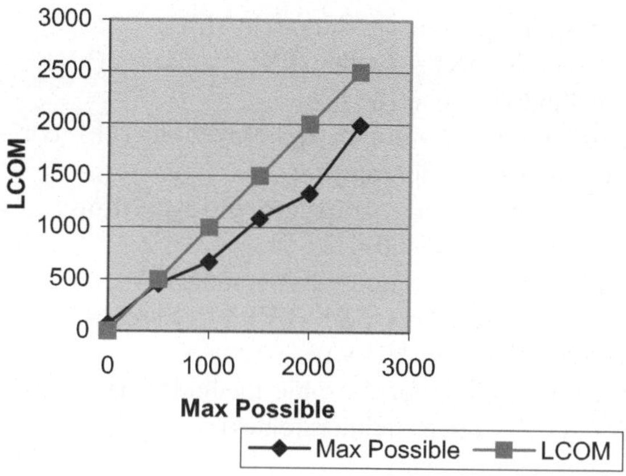

Figure 4: LCOM

Polymorphic Metric

The polymorphism metric is applied to the Projects we have considered in our paper. Polymorphic methods have been previously detected (using the definitions in OO Metrics and Hypotheses Section) and moved up in the hierarchy (i.e. the root class of the hierarchy is also the largest core class in the hierarchy). Methods appearing twice (or more times) as New Sub and Add Sub has same behavior (Both are used for placing the order of subscription) in the hierarchy , for example, the method Partial Redeem and Full Redeem : is non-polymorphic for Order.

Measuring Polymorphism to the Collection hierarchy:

polymorphism_measure (hC) = polymorphic_methods(hC) / #methods(hC) = polymorphic_methods(hC) / 178 (because #methods(hC) =178)= (width(hC) * #classes(hC)+ åhiÎchildren(hC) polymorphic-methods(hi – core(hC))) / 106 (from definition of polymorphic_methods(hC))

= (8 * 11 + åhiÎchildren(hC) polymorphic-methods(hi – core(hC))) /178 (because width(hC)=8, #(classes(hC)=11)= (66 + polymorphic-methods(sub-hierarchy-NotIndexedCollection) +

polymorphic-methods (sub-hierarchy-IndexedCollection)) / 178
= (88 + 7 + 51) / 178 = 0.82 (or 82 %)

Value to the NotIndexedCollection sub-hierarchy (hN):
polymorphic_methods(hN) = (width(hN) * #classes(hN) + åhiÎchildren(hN) polymorphic-methods(hi – core(hN)))
= (1 * 7 + åhiÎchildren (hN) polymorphic-methods (hi – core (hN))) = (1 * 7 + 0) = 7 (because children of hN are trivial hierarchies)

Value to the IndexedCollection sub-hierarchy (hX):
polymorphic_methods (hX) = (width (hX) * #classes (hX) + åhiÎchildren (hX) polymorphic-methods(hi – core(hX)))
= (4 * 9 + åhiÎchildren (hX) polymorphic-methods (hi – core (hX))) = (36 + polymorphic-methods(sub-hierarchy-FixedSizeCollection) + polymorphic-methods (sub-hierarchy-VariableSizeCollection)) = (48 + 0 + 3) = 51
Value to the VariableSizeCollection sub-hierarchy (hV):
polymorphic_methods (hV) = (width (hV) * #classes (hV) + åhiÎchildren (hV) polymorphic-methods (hi – core (hV)))
= (1 * 7 + åhiÎchildren (hV) polymorphic-methods (hi – core (hV))) = (7 + 0) = 7 (because children of hV are trivialhierarchies)
It can be observed in the outcome, the high degree of polymorphism of the Collection hierarchy (reaching the value of 82 %), which contributes potentially to the readability, extensibility, and ultimately to their Maintainability. However, some studies, that should further be confirmed, indicate that polymorphism may Increase the probability of faults in O-O software

Results

Metric Suite is defined and implemented on projects with large data

Metric	Project1				
	Min	Max	Mean	Median	Degree of Polymorphism
WMC	1	78	13	11	
RFC	1	113	41	38	
LCOM	0	1	0.7	0.7	
DIT	0	1	0.7	0.7	
Polymorphic					82%

Metric	Project2				
	Min	Max	Mean	Median	Degree of Polymorphism
WMC	1	69	17	14	
RFC	1	106	34	27	
LCOM	0	1	0.7	0.7	
DIT	0	1	0.7	0.7	
Polymorphic					78%approx

Table 3: Results of Correlation Analysis

Conclusion & Future Work

Although quality is not easy to evaluate since it is a complex concept compound by different aspects, several properties that make a good O-O design have been recognized and widely accepted by the software engineering community. We agree that both the traditional and the new O-O properties or attributes should be analyzed in assessing the quality of O-O design. But we believe that it is necessary to pay special attention to the concepts and metrics for polymorphism, since it should be considered one of the key concerns in determining the quality of an O-O software system.

The proposed work assumes has been done with metric suite comprises of five metrics and implemented on two projects. It also does stastical analysis of metrics which is of managerial use .In future one can define more metrics and then these metrics can be applied on other live projects with large data and stastical analysis can be performed which is helpful for managers and users.

References:

- Beyond Language Independent Object Oriented Metrics: Model Independent Metrics Michele Lanza lanza@iam.unibe.ch Software Composition Group Universit ´a di Berna, Svizzera St´ephane Ducasse ducasse@iam.unibe.ch Software Composition Group Universit ´e de Berne, Suisse
- An Empirical Evaluation of Object Oriented Metrics in Industrial Setting Giovanni Denaro Universit 'a di Milano Bicocca Dip. di Informatica,Sistemistica e Comunicazione I20126, Milano, Italy denaro@disco.unimib.it.

- Managerial Use of Metrics for Object- Oriented Software: An Exploratory Analysis Shyam R. Chidamber, David P. Darcy, and Chris F. Kemerer
- A Validation Of Object-Oriented Design Metrics as Quality Indicators*Victor R. Basili, Lionel Briand and Walcélio L.Melo *Technical Report, Univ. of Maryland, Dep. of Computer Science, College Park, MD, 20742 USA. April 1995*
- An Empirical Investigation of an Object-Oriented Software System Michelle Cartwright and Martin Shepperd Department of Computing Bournemouth University Talbot Campus Poole, BH12 5BB England {mcartwri, mshepper}@bmth.ac.uk

Cyber Crime and Suggestive Preventive Measures

Mukta Sharma
Asstt. Professor, RDIAS, Delhi

Abstract

Since the beginning of civilization, man has always been motivated by the need, to make progress by improving the existing technologies. This has led to tremendous development and progress which has been a launching pad for further developments. The great discovery in the field of Telecommunications is "Internet". But as every discovery comes with a share of its disadvantages, so does Internet Unlike conventional communities though, there are no policemen patrolling the information superhighway, leaving it open to everything from Trojan horses and viruses to cyber stalking, trademark counterfeiting and cyber terrorism. . The phenomenal growth of computers and Internet services has engendered the problem of cyber crime proliferation on the account of investigation difficulties and lack of strong evidences. This paper presents the issues faced by law enforcement agencies and attempt to look ahead in order to discern the research directions for cyber crime investigation and computer forensics. This paper is structured as follows. First, the types of cyber crime are presented. Next, there is a discussion on common tools and techniques used by cyber crime criminals along with classification of cyber crimes. Then we highlight reasons for cyber crime growth. This is followed by some preventive measures to counteract cyber crime.

Introduction to Cyber Crime

Cyber crime is the latest and perhaps the most complicated problem in the cyber world. Defining cyber crimes, as an "acts that are punishable by the Information Technology Act". A simple yet sturdy definition of cyber crime would be ***"unlawful acts wherein the computer is either a tool or a target or both".***

Cyber crime is hard to detect, thus giving the perpetrators plenty of time to flee the area in which the crime was committed, because of this fact the criminals can be in another country far away from the scene of the crime by the time it is detected. Cyber crime is an evil having its origin in the growing dependence on computers in modern life. In a day and age when everything from microwave ovens and refrigerators to nuclear power plants is being run on computers, cyber crime has assumed rather sinister implications. The first recorded cyber crime took place in the year 1820. Major Cyber crimes in the recent past include Cyber Terrorism in Mumbai Attacks on 26th Nov.' 2008 and the Citibank rip off. US $ 10 million were fraudulently transferred out of the bank and into a bank account in Switzerland.

Reasons for Cyber Crime

The reasons for the vulnerability of computers may be said to be:

1. *Capacity to store data in comparatively small space*- The computer has unique characteristic of storing data in a very small space. This affords to remove or derive information either through physical or virtual medium makes it much easier. Lakhs of pages of written matter can be stored in a CD ROM. Walking out of a godown with one lakh pages would be exceedingly difficult, but walking out of a secure location with a CD ROM containing a lakh of pages would be much simpler.
2. *Easy to access*- The problem encountered in guarding a computer system from unauthorised access is that there is every possibility of breach not due to human error but due to the complex technology. By secretly implanted logic bomb, key loggers that can steal access codes, advanced voice recorders; retina imagers etc. that can fool biometric systems and bypass firewalls can be utilized to get past many a security system.
3. *Complex*-The computers work on operating systems and these operating systems in turn are composed of millions of codes. Human mind is fallible and it is not possible that there might not be a lapse at any stage.
4. *Negligence*- Negligence is very closely connected with human conduct. It is therefore very probable that while protecting the computer system there might be any negligence, which in turn provides a cyber criminal to gain access and control over the computer system.
5. *Loss of evidence*- Loss of evidence is a very common & obvious problem as all the data are routinely destroyed. Further collection of data outside the territorial extent also paralyses this system of crime investigation.

Cyber Criminals

The cyber criminals constitute of various groups/ category. This division may be justified on the basis of the object that they have in their mind. The following are the category of cyber criminals-

1. *Children and adolescents between the age group of 6 – 18 years* –The simple reason for this type of delinquent behaviour pattern in children are seen mostly due to the inquisitiveness to know and explore the things. Other cognate reason may be to prove them to be outstanding amongst other children in their group. Further the reasons may be psychological even. E.g. the *Bal Bharati* (Delhi) case was the outcome of harassment of the delinquent by his friends.
2. *Organized or Political Hacktivists* These kinds of hackers are mostly organised together to fulfil certain objective. The reason may be to fulfil their political bias, fundamentalism, etc. The Pakistanis are said to be one of the

best quality hackers in the world. They mainly target the Indian government sites with the purpose to fulfil their political objectives. Further the *NASA* as well as the *Microsoft* sites is always under attack by the hackers.

3. Professional hackers / crackers – Their work is motivated by the colour of money. These kinds of hackers are mostly employed to hack the site of the rivals and get credible, reliable and valuable information. Further they are employed to crack the system of the employer basically as a measure to make it safer by detecting the loopholes.

4. *Discontented or Disgruntled employees*-This group include those people who have been either sacked by their employer or are dissatisfied with their employer. To avenge they normally hack the system of their employee.
5. Ex-Boy Friend or Divorced Spouse-These kinds of people try to defame their spouse.

Who can be the victim?

- Gullible
- Desperados and greedy people
- Unskilled & Inexperienced
- Unlucky People

Classification of Cyber Crime

The subject of cyber crime may be broadly classified under the following three groups. They are-

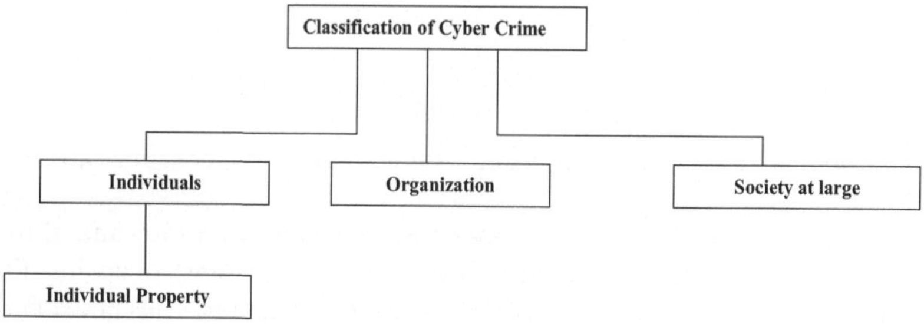

Figure 1: Classification of Cyber Crime

Against Individuals: –

i. Harassment via e-mails.
ii. Cyber-stalking.
iii. Dissemination of obscene material.
iv. Defamation.

v. Unauthorized control/access over computer system.
vi. Indecent exposure
vii. Email spoofing
viii. Cheating & Fraud

Against Individual Property: -
i. Computer vandalism.
ii. Transmitting virus.
iii. Unauthorized control/access over computer system.
iv. Intellectual Property crimes
v. Internet time thefts

Against Organization: -
i. Unauthorized control/access over computer system
ii. Possession of unauthorized information.
iii. Cyber terrorism against the government organization.
iv. Distribution of pirated software etc.

Against Society at large: -
i. Pornography (basically child pornography).
ii. Polluting the youth through indecent exposure.
iii. Trafficking
iv. Financial crimes
v. Sale of illegal articles
vi. Online gambling
vii. Forgery

Types of Crimes

Though criminals use many cyber crimes, some frequent cyber crimes are:-

(1) *Phishing:* Marketing the product through fake web site and through responses obtaining the credit card numbers and later misusing them. Criminals use e-commerce (design websites) for fraudulent sales like soliciting fund for charitable institution or for bogus investment as they enjoy direct access to millions of prospective victims.

(2) *Pedophilies:* Spread of Child pornography and sexually implicit material. This would include pornographic websites; pornographic magazines produced using computers (to publish and print the material) and the Internet (to download and transmit pornographic pictures, photos, writings etc). Recent Indian incidents revolving around cyber pornography include the Air Force Bal Bharati School case. A student of the Air Force Bal Bharati

School, Delhi, was teased by all his classmates for having a pockmarked face. Tired of the cruel jokes, he decided to get back at his tormentors. He scanned photographs of his classmates and teachers, morphed them with nude photographs and put them up on a website that he uploaded on to a free web hosting service. It was only after the father of one of the class girls featured on the website objected and lodged a complaint with the police that any action was taken. In another incident, in Mumbai a Swiss couple would gather slum children and then would force them to appear for obscene photographs. They would then upload these photographs to websites specially designed for pedophiles. The Mumbai police arrested the couple for pornography.

(3) *Marketing Strategy for Illegal Articles /* Trafficking*:* Selling narcotics, weapons etc. through bogus web sites. Trafficking may assume different forms. It may be trafficking in drugs, human beings, arms weapons etc. These forms of trafficking are going unchecked because they are carried on under pseudonyms. A racket was busted in Chennai where drugs were being sold under the pseudonym of honey.

(4) *Intellectual Property Crimes:* This includes software piracy, copyright, infringement, trademarks violations, theft of computer code. New product plans, and product description, research, marketing plans, prospective customer lists etc. The complainant (software company based in Bangalore) alleged that some of the company's former employees had accessed the company's IT system and tampered with the source code of the software under development.

(5) *Email Spoofing:* A copying/ hacking email and password, criminal sent unwanted emails to one's acquaintances and spoils the image of original person. Recently spoofed mails were sent on the name of Mr. Na.Vijayashankar (naavi.org), which contained virus. Rajesh Manyar, a graduate student at Purdue University in Indiana, was arrested for threatening to detonate a nuclear device in the college campus. The alleged e- mail was sent from the account of another student to the vice president for student services. However the mail was traced to be sent from the account of Rajesh Manyar. ing/ hacking e-mail and password, criminal send unwanted e-mails to one's acquaintances and spoils the image of the original person.

(6) *E-murder:* By manipulating medical prescription in a hospital.

(7) *Political Crime*: Abusive Management of public funds by altering computer data. Bribery and corruption by manipulating data, Manipulation in election by adding more votes or denial of voting rights.

(8) *Theft of Telecommunication Services*: The criminals gain access to dial in/ out circuits of an organization and then make their own calls like framing duplicate calling cards.

(9) *Information Piracy* and *Forgery:* Digital technology permits perfect reproduction of the original documents, examples are birth certificates, passport, false identity, counterfeiting of currency, negotiable instruments etc. Counterfeit currency notes, postage and revenue stamps, mark sheets etc can be forged using sophisticated computers, printers and scanners. Outside many colleges across India, one finds touts soliciting the sale of fake mark sheets or even certificates. These are made using computers, and high quality scanners and printers. In fact, this has becoming a booming business involving thousands of rupees being given to student gangs in exchange for these bogus but authentic looking certificates

(10) *Money Laundering and Evasion*: Emerging technologies greatly assist in online gambling and concealing the origin of ill-gotten money. Legal money can also be concealed from taxation authorities. Due to the volume of electronic fund transfers the criminals bypass the banking system.

(11) *Electronic Terrorism*: Criminals use electronic intruding in government websites causing inconvenience by bringing them down within no time. There is a subtle difference between the cyber terrorism and cyber crime though both are criminal acts. A cyber crime is generally a domestic issue, which may have international consequences, however cyber terrorism is a global concern, which has domestic as well as international consequences. Technology savvy terrorists are using 512-bit encryption, which is next to impossible to decrypt. The recent example may be cited of – *Osama Bin Laden*, the *LTTE*, attack on *America's army deployment system* during Iraq war. Cyber terrorism may be defined as "*the premeditated use of disruptive activities, or the threat thereof, in cyber space, with the intention to further social, ideological, religious, political or similar objectives, or to intimidate any person in furtherance of such objectives*"

(12) *Electronic Funds Transfer Fraud*: Financial institutions are using electronic fund transfer systems. Valid credit card numbers are intercepted electronically and the digital information stored on a card can be counterfeited. Stolen credit card numbers have been used by a Mumbai-Bangalore gang to book online tickets on Kingfisher, Jet Airways and Air Deccan. These have been sold at discounted rates to other customers. The fraud came to light when ICICI Bank monitored online credit of purchases of Kingfisher Airlines and noticed an unusual pattern in one credit card user.

(13) *Hacking:* To define hacking in short, we can say that an artistic criminal offense of breaking into another remote system without the owner's consent for the purpose of stealing information is known as hacking. Data theft, data destroy, stealing and altering information. Citibank rip off. US $ 10 million were fraudulently transferred out of the bank and into a bank account in Switzerland. A Russian hacker group led by Vladimir Kevin, a renowned hacker, perpetrated the attack. The group compromised the bank's security

systems. Vladimir was allegedly using his office computer at AO Saturn, a computer firm in St. Petersburg, Russia, to break into Citibank computers. He was finally arrested on Heathrow airport on his way to Switzerland. Hackers who are out to steal personal information, change a corporation's financial data, break security codes to gain unauthorized network access, or conduct other destructive activities are sometimes called "crackers."

(14) Email/ Logic Bombs: These are event/date dependent programs and are created to do something, only when a certain event occurs. Some viruses also act as logic bombs because they lie dormant throughout the year and become active on a particular date. Criminals send large number of e-mails to the victim till their server crashes. Example of threatening emails- The complainant was receiving threatening and obscene e-mails from unknown people. The e-mails contained the complainant's obscene morphed photographs. The accused threatened to post these on pornographic Websites and alleged that one such photograph was posted on a popular Website. Some of the major email related crimes are:

1. Email spoofing
2. Sending malicious codes through email
3. Email bombing
4. Sending threatening emails
5. Defamatory emails
6. Email frauds

(15) Internet Time thefts: By stealing user name and password, criminals use for themselves and steal the internet time allotted to the purchaser.

(16) Hate/Communal Crimes: As building a web page is not expensive and reaches to billions of people, criminals spread hate or communal information or rumors, by building a website and also recruits people for their operation through e-advertisement.

(17) Altering Websites: The hackers delete some pages of a website, upload new pages with the similar name and controls the messages conveyed by the web site.

(18) Spreading Computer Virus: Criminals uses malicious software for spreading computer virus. A virus program then attaches to a computer or to file and then circulates to other file or to other computers on a network. E.g. *love bug virus*, which affected at least 5 % of the computers of the globe. The losses were accounted to be $ 10 million. The world's most famous worm was the Internet worm let loose on the Internet by *Robert Morris* sometime in 1988. Almost brought development of Internet to a complete halt.

(19) *Cyber Defamation: This* occurs when defamation takes place with the help of computers and / or the Internet. E.g. someone publishes defamatory matter about someone on a website or sends e-mails containing defamatory information to all of that person's friends. In a recent occurrence, Surekha

(names of people have been changed), a young girl was about to be married to Suraj. She was really pleased. Then, one day when she met Suraj, he looked worried and even a little upset. When asked he told her that, members of his family had been receiving e-mails that contained malicious things about Surekha's character. He told her that, his parents were justifiably very upset and were also considering breaking off the engagement. Fortunately, Suraj was able to prevail upon his parents and the other elders of his house to approach the police instead of blindly believing what was contained in the mails. During investigation, it was revealed that the person sending those e-mails was none other than Surekha's stepfather. He had sent these e-mails so as to break up the marriage. The girl's marriage would have caused him to lose control of her property of which he was the guardian till she got married. Another famous case of cyber defamation occurred in America. All friends and relatives of a lady were beset with obscene e-mail messages appearing to originate from her account. These mails were giving the lady in question a bad name among her friends. The lady was an activist against pornography. In reality, a group of people displeased with her views and angry with her for opposing they had decided to get back at her by using such underhanded methods. In addition to sending spoofed obscene e-mails they also put up websites about her, that basically maligned her character and sent e-mails to her family and friends containing matter defaming her.

(20) Cyber Stalking: The Oxford dictionary defines stalking as "pursuing stealthily". Cyber stalking involves following a person's movements across the Internet by posting messages (sometimes threatening) on the bulletin boards frequented by the victim, entering the chat-rooms frequented by the victim, constantly bombarding the victim with emails etc A lady (the complainant) lodged a complaint that she was being harassed by a flood of telephone calls from unknown men with sexual intention at all odd hours and from various places around the world. Some men also visited the house, seeking her by name. It is the first registered cyber crime case in West Bengal.

(21) Denial of Service attack: This involves flooding a computer resource with more requests than it can handle. This causes the resource (e.g. a web server) to crash thereby denying authorized users the service offered by the resource. Another variation to a typical denial of service attack is known as a Distributed Denial of Service (DDoS) attack wherein the perpetrators are many and are geographically widespread. It is very difficult to control such attacks. The attack is initiated by sending excessive demands to the victim's computer(s), exceeding the limit that the victim's servers can support and making the servers crash.

(22) *Salami attacks-* This kind of crime is normally prevalent in the financial institutions or for the purpose of committing financial crimes. An important feature of this type of offence is that the alteration is so small that it would

normally go unnoticed. E.g. the *Ziegler case* wherein a logic bomb was introduced in the bank's system, which deducted 10 cents from every account and deposited it in a particular account.

How Can We Prevent Computer Crime?

Prevention is always better than cure. It is always better to take certain precaution while browsing the net. The following things we should keep in mind while surfing internet –

1. To prevent cyber stalking avoid disclosing any information pertaining to oneself. This is as good as disclosing your identity to strangers in public place.
2. Always avoid sending any photograph online particularly to strangers and chat friends as there have been incidents of misuse of the photographs.
3. Always use latest and up date anti virus software to guard against virus attacks.
4. Always keep back up volumes so that one may not suffer data loss in case of virus contamination.
5. Never send your credit card number to any site that is not secured, to guard against frauds.
6. Always keep a watch on the sites that your children are accessing to prevent any kind of harassment or depravation in children.
7. It is better to use a security programme that gives control over the cookies and send information back to the site as leaving the cookies unguarded might prove fatal.
8. Web site owners should watch traffic and check any irregularity on the site. Putting host-based intrusion detection devices on servers may do this.
9. Use of firewalls may be beneficial.
10. Web servers running public sites must be physically separate protected from internal corporate network.

Following are some general security tips for users as displayed in the Mumbai Police cyber crime Website:

1. ***Take a test before opening an e-mail attachment***

- Is the e-mail from someone that you know?
- Have you received e-mails with an attachment from this sender before?
- Were you expecting an e-mail with an attachment from this sender?
- Does the e-mail from the sender with the contents as described in the subject line and the name of the attachment(s) make sense?
- Does this e-mail contains a virus? To determine this, you need to install and use an anti-virus programme.

2. ***Use strong password***

- For each computer and service you use (for example, e-mail, chatting, online purchasing), you should have a password.
- You shouldn't write them down nor should you share them with anyone, even your best friends.
- Computer intruders use trial-and-error, or brute-force techniques, to discover passwords.
- Use alphanumeric characters and special characters in your password.
- The length of password should be as long as possible (more than eight characters).
- Do not write it on some place where it is visible to someone else.

3. ***Protect your Website***

- Stay informed and be in touch with security related news.
- Watch traffic to your side. Put host-based intrusion detection devices on your Web servers and monitor activity looking for any irregularities.
- Put in firewall.
- Configure your firewall correctly.
- Develop your Web content off-line.
- Make sure that the Web servers running your public Website are physically separate and individually protected from your internal corporate network.
- Protect your databases. If your Website serves up dynamic content from database, consider putting that database behind a second interface on your firewall, with tighter access rules than the interface to your Web server.
- Back up your Website after every update.

4. ***Tips for children***

- Do not give out identifying information such as name, home address and school name or telephone number in a chat room.
- Do not send your photograph to any one on the net without initially checking with the parent or guardian.
- Do not respond to messages or bulletin board items that are obscene, belligerent or threatening.
- Never arrange a face to face meeting without informing your parent or guardian.
- Remember that people online may not be who they seem to be.

Sailesh kumar Zarkar, technical advisor and network security consultant to the Mumbai Police Cyber crime Cell advocates the 5P mantra for online security:

1. Precaution,
2. Prevention,
3. Protection,
4. Preservation and
5. Perseverance.

Conclusion

With the outgrowth of computers and internet, cyber crimes are also growing proportionately, and to prevent it steps must be taken faster than criminals to control the cyber crimes. Criminals have outflanked the technology adopted by corporate houses and Law Enforcement agencies as they apparently seem to be better equipped in terms of availability of funds and possession of computer technology. Preventive measures have been suggested in this paper so that security systems are up-to-date. Concrete measures must be found in order to track electronics evidence, classify the material that needs to be search, and their preservation, so that systems are better protected from cyber intrusions.

References

- Ecommerce by Elias M. Awad
- www.symantec.com/avcenter/cybercrime
- www.cybercrimelaw.org
- www.crime-research.org/analytics
- www.cybercellmumbai.com
- www.pcmag.com/article2/0,2817,2331225,00.asp
- www.crimes-of-persuasion.com/Crimes/Delivered/internet.htm

Artificial Intelligence and Law: Stepping Stones to a Model of Legal Reasoning

Lalit Sharma
Sr. Lecturer (IT), Jaipuria Institute of Management, Noida (U.P.)

Abstract

Principles are abstract rules intended to guide decision-makers in making normative judgments in domains like the law, politics, and ethics. It is difficult, however, if not impossible to define principles in an intentional manner so that they may be applied deductively. The problem is the gap between the abstract, open-textured principles and concrete facts. On the other hand, when expert decision-makers rationalize their conclusions in specific cases, they often link principles to the specific facts of the cases. In effect, these expert-defined associations between principles and facts provide extensional definitions of the principles. The experts operationalize the abstract principles by linking them to the facts. AI and Law is much more than an applications area. Its concerns touch upon issues at the very heart of AI: reasoning, representation, and learning. This paper discusses the contribution of AI in law and ethics translation with extensionally defining principles, as well as citing past cases, to predict the principles and cases that might be relevant in the analysis of new cases. To investigate this phenomenon computationally, a large set of professional ethics cases was analyzed with reference to a computational model called SIROCCO, a system for retrieving principles and past cases.

A Brief History of AI and Law

The field of AI and Law is at least thirty years old. It has had a vibrant history.[1] Its concerns have often mirrored—and sometimes anticipated—streams of research in AI at large: from logic to expert systems and logic programming, from frames and scripts to cases and CBR and to hybrid systems, from theorem-proving to defeasible and nonmonotonic reasoning and to agents for e-commerce.

In their 1970, Buchanan and Headrick discussed the possibilities of modeling legal research and reasoning, particularly for advice-giving, legal analysis and argument construction, and even though they envisioned using goal-directed rule-based approaches, they presciently pointed out the importance of analogical reasoning. In 1977, the *Harvard Law Review* published a landmark paper by L. Thorne McCarty on his TAXMAN system, which pursued a theorem-proving approach to reasoning with issues in corporate tax law.

In the 1980s, work in AI and Law intensified tremendously. Anne Gardner's 1984 doctoral dissertation at Stanford focused on the problem of what happens "when the rules run out"—when the antecedent of a rule uses a predicate that is not defined by further rules—particularly due to the inherent open-textured nature of legal concepts and problems involving the relationship between technical and common-sense meaning of words. It drew attention to the fact well-known in the law that one cannot reason by rules alone, and that in response to failure, indeterminacy, or simply the desire for a sanity check, one examines examples.

While progress continued on rule-based reasoning (RBR) systems in the 1980s, there began to emerge a community of AI researchers who focused on reasoning with cases and analogies—that is, case-based reasoning. In 1984, Ashley first reported on the legal argument program HYPO and the mechanism of "dimensions". This line of research had grown out of Rissland's earlier work on example-based reasoning and "constrained example generation" in mathematics.[2] Initially concerned with the problem of generating hypothetical (hence its name), HYPO reached full maturity as a case-based argumentation program. It was the first true CBR system in AI and Law, and one of the pioneering systems in CBR in general. Thus by the mid 1980s, RBR and CBR approaches were making themselves felt in AI and Law.

The 1990s saw a renewal of interest in legal information retrieval, in part because of improved retrieval engines, new learning-based information extraction techniques, and the dramatic rise of the World Wide Web. For instance, in 1995, Hafner edited a special issue of *Artificial Intelligence and Law* devoted to intelligent legal text-based systems.

Introducing this Issue

In domains such as ethics and the law, principles, norms, or laws govern human behavior and inform reasoning and decision-making. While the consequences of violating abstract rules such as these can be far-reaching and severe, the rules themselves are often quite difficult to apply. Typically, abstract rules contain open-textured terms [6, 12] that cover a wide range of specific fact situations. The rules are subject to interpretation and may have different meanings in different contexts. There is a gap between the abstract rules and the concrete facts to which they apply. Often, there are no authoritative or readily available intermediate rules with which to "bridge the gap", that is, no rules of finer granularity that elaborate the abstract rules' meaning or explain how they apply in concrete circumstances.

Consider, for example, the following engineering ethics principles, taken from the National Society of Professional Engineers reference guide [11]:

NSPE Code I.1: "Engineers, in the fulfillment of their professional duties, shall hold paramount the safety, health, and welfare of the public in the performance of their professional duties."

NSPE Code III.2.b: "Engineers shall not complete, sign or seal plans and/or specifications that are not of a design safe to the public health and welfare and in conformity with accepted engineering standards."

NSPE Code II.1.c: "Engineers shall not reveal facts, data, or information obtained in a professional capacity without the prior consent of the client or employer except as authorized or required by law or this Code."

While most people would agree that abstract principles such as these are reasonable and appropriate, it is difficult to apply them in real-world situations [7]. Since the principles contain open-textured terms and phrases (e.g., how does one precisely define "fulfillment of professional duties", "design safe to the public health", or "prior consent"?), it is not possible for experts to define intermediate-level rules to cover all possible conditions to which the principles apply. Often even the principles' recommended actions are abstract (e.g., what exactly does it mean to "hold paramount" the safety, health, and welfare of the public?). Moreover, one can easily imagine fact situations pitting an engineer's obligation to public safety against his obligation to maintain his client's confidences.

For all of the reasons above—open texture, lack of authoritative intermediate rules, and conflicts among abstract rules—problem solving in ethics and law can be characterized as ill-defined.

In order to overcome these problems, a computational model called SIROCCO (**S**ystem for **I**ntelligent **R**etrieval of **O**perationalized **C**ases and **CO**des) was constructed. SIROCCO is a program that represents some of the extensional connections between abstract rules and scenarios made by decision-makers as they apply operationalization techniques. The program uses these connections to retrieve principles and past cases that are relevant to new fact situations.

Operationalization in the Ethics Domain

This paper involved a systematic study of the published opinions of the NSPE and its code of ethics [10]. The NSPE Board of Ethical Review, has written extensive explanations of how and why codes apply or do not apply to more than 400 fact situations, provides engineers with guidance on a wide range of ethical issues such as protecting public safety, employment duties, fairness in advertising, conflicts of interest, and confidentiality.

The analysis confirmed that the operationalization techniques were identifiable and repeated across a large segment of the NSPE cases, and that the techniques in Figure 1

---

1. Principle Instantiation: Instantiating a principle by linking it to clusters of questioned and critical facts.
2. Fact Hypotheses: Hypothesizing facts that affect how a principle applies.
3. Principle Revision: Revising a principle over time in light of new cases or changes in culture.
4. Conflicting Principles Resolution: Resolving conflicting principles in a specific case.
5. Principle Grouping : Grouping principles in a specific case to bolster an argument.
6. Case Instantiation : Instantiating a case as a precedent by linking it to clusters of questioned and critical facts, and by analogizing or distinguishing it.
7. Principle Elaboration: Applying, defining or elaborating issues and principles from past cases.
8. Case Grouping : Grouping cases to bolster an argument.
9. Operationalization Reuse: Reusing a specific application of any of the above techniques from previous analyses.

Figure 1: Operationalization technique used by NSPE BER

Principle Instantiation is used to cite a principle and then connect that principle to selected facts of a case with the purpose of either bolstering or rhetorically challenging a conclusion. The *Case Instantiation* technique is used to cite a past case and draw an analogy to that case (through selected facts of the current case) for the purpose of supporting or contradicting a conclusion. *Principle* and *Case Grouping* are techniques in which the board cites *multiple* principles or cases in support of a conclusion. Finally, *Operationalization Reuse* is applied when the board reaches back to a previous analysis and reuses some of its reasoning (specifically, the reasoning associated with one of the eight other techniques) in the analysis of a new case.

An Overview of SIROCCO

SIROCCO is an interpretive case-based reasoning (CBR) program [8]. Interpretive CBR is a sub-field of case-based reasoning in which complex, ill-structured, and highly linguistic fact situations are evaluated in the context of previous experience.

SIROCCO operates by (1) accepting a target case expressed in the Ethics Transcription Language (ETL), (2) searching for relevant information in a case base of source cases expressed in the Extended Ethics Transcription Language (EETL), and (3) producing suggested code provisions and past cases, as well as other suggestions. ETL is the constrained, narrative language used to represent target or input cases. EETL is an extension of ETL that supports representation of the argument made by the board for a case and is the language of the source cases. EETL is also the language used to represent the operationalization techniques.

Representing target cases: The ethics transcription language

The facts of a sample target case are shown in Figure 2. In this case, Engineer A is confronted with conflicting obligations. He has an obligation to protect the public, but he also has an obligation of confidentiality to his client. The facts are as follows. Engineer A is hired to analyze the structural integrity of an inhabited apartment building. Engineer A's client, the owner of the building, instructs the engineer that his findings are to be held in confidence. The engineer does not find anything structurally wrong with the building, but the client confides that there are problems with the electrical and mechanical systems of the building. Although Engineer A knows these problems could be safety hazards, he does not contact the authorities. Rather, he just mentions these problems in the final report he provides only to the owner. The question raised by this case is whether it was ethical for Engineer A not to report the safety violations to the proper authorities. The ETL representation for the same is shown in Figure 3.

As enforced by the grammar shown in Figure 4, ETL represents the actions and events of an engineering scenario as a *Fact Chronology*, which is an ordered list of *Facts* (i.e., individual sentences). Each Fact consists of: (1) *Actors and Objects*, instances of general actors and objects that appear in the scenario; (2) a *Fact Primitive,* the action or event in which the actors and objects participated; and (3) *Time Qualifiers*, temporal relations that specify how the Fact relates to other Facts in time. For instance, in the case representation (Figure 3), the fourth Fact of the Fact Chronology contains the Actor "Engineer A", the Object "Apartment House P", the Fact Primitive "inspects", and the Time Qualifiers "Occurs during 1, 2; After the conclusion of 3". [9].

At least one Fact in every chronology is the *Questioned Fact*; this is the action or event corresponding to an ethical question raised in the scenario. In Figure 3, Fact 10 is the Questioned Fact: it describes Engineer A's failure to alert the authorities about his findings. If more than one question is raised in the context of the same Fact Chronology, a typical situation, the Questioned Facts are enumerated (e.g.,

"Questioned Fact 1", "Questioned Fact 2", etc.) and a separate *Case* is created for each question.

To input a target case, a case enterer must transcribe the textual facts of a case (Figure 2) into a Fact Chronology (Figure 3). To support this process a web-based case acquisition tool was developed (www.pitt.edu/~bmclaren/ethics). The web site helps the case enterer by providing a transcription template and transcription instructions.

Facts: Engineer A is retained to investigate the structural integrity of a 60-year old occupied apartment building that his client is planning to sell. Under the terms of the agreement with the client, the structural report written by Engineer A is to remain confidential. In addition, the client makes clear to Engineer A that the building is being sold "as is" and he not planning to take any remedial action to repair or renovate any system action to repair or renovate any system within the building prior to its sale.

Engineer a performs several structural tests on the building and determines that the building is structurally sound. However, during the course of providing services, the client confides in Engineer A and informs him that the building contains deficiencies in the electrical and mechanical systems that violate applicable codes and standards. While Engineer A is not an electrical nor mechanical engineer, he does realize those deficiencies could cause injury to the occupants of the building and so informs the client.

In his report, Engineer A makes a brief mention of his conversation with the client concerning the deficiencies; however, in view of the terms of the agreement, Engineer A does not report the safety violations to any third party.

Question: Was it ethical for Engineer A not to report the safety violations to the appropriate public authorities ?

Figure 2: Sample Target Case

1.	Client X <hires the services of> Engineer A.	Pre-existing fact
2.	Apartment House P <may be hazardous to safety>	Pre-existing fact
3.	Client X <instructs> Engineer A <to> (Engineer A<withholds Information from> Any Third Parties <regarding> Structural Report R)	Occurs during 1, 2

	Fact	Time qualifier
4.	Engineer A <inspects> Apartment House P. After the conclusion of 3	Occurs during 1, 2
5.	Engineer A <discovers that> (Apartment House P <fails standards and may be hazardous to safety>)	Occurs during 4
6.	Engineer A <know> (Government Authority <should be informed about the Hazard or potential hazard>)	Immediately after the conclusion of 5
7.	Engineer A <informs> Client X <that> (Apartment House P <fails standards and may be hazardous to safety>	Immediately after the conclusion of 5
8.	Engineer A <writes paper/article> Structural Report R <about> Apartment House P.	After the conclusion of 7
9.	Engineer A <provides limited information to> Client X <regarding> (Engineer A <discovers that> (Apartment House P <fails standards and may be hazardous to safety>))	Occurs as part of 8
10.	Engineer A <does not inform> Any Third Parties <that> (Apartment House P <fails standards and may be hazardous to safety> [Questioned fact]	

Figure 3: ETL representation of the Case

<Fact-Chronology>	:=	<Fact> [<Fact> ....]
<Fact>	:=	<Fact-#> <Fact-Phrase> [(Questioned Fact <X>) } <Time-Qualifier> [<Time-Qualifier>,.......]
<Fact-Phrase>	:=	<Fact-Primitive> [<Fact-Modifier>] <Actor-Or-Object> [<Actor-Or-Object> (<Fact-Phrase>)] [<Actor-Or-Object> (<Fact-Phrase>)]
<Fact-#>	:=	<Positive-Integer>
<Fact-Primitive>	:=	An instance of a Fact-Primitive
<Actor-Or-Object>	:=	An instance of an Actor or an object
<Fact-Modifier>	:=	partially substantially limited extensive
<Time-Qualifier>	:=	Pre-existing fact

After the start of <Fact-#> [, <Fact-#>, ...]
Starts at the same time as <Fact-#> [, <Fact-#>, ...]
<Time-Period> after the start of <Fact-#>[, <Fact-#>, ...]
After the conclusion of <Fact-#> [, <Fact-#>, ...]
Immediately after the conclusion of <Fact-#> [, <Fact-#>, ...]
<Time-Period> after the conclusion of <Fact-#> [, <Fact-#>, ...]
Ends <Fact-#> [, <Fact-#>, ...]
Occurs during <Fact-#> [, <Fact-#>, ...]
Occurs as part of <Fact-#> [, <Fact-#>,......]
Occurs concurrently with <Fact-#> [, <Fact-#>, ...]

<Time-Period> := <Y> Days <Y> Weeks |<Y> Months <Y> Years
<Y> := Empty <Positive-Integer>
<Y> := Many Several <Positive-Integer>
<Positive-Integer> := 1.........N

Key: = Alternative ; [ ] = Optional; < > = Grammer element
Regular font indicates literal placement (e. g., "Pre-existing fact"]
Italicized font indicates a general description of a terminal item not shown in this figure

Figure 4: The grammar for the ethics Translation Language (ETL)

Abstraction in SIROCCO

Although Fact Primitives are specified at the most detailed level in the Fact Chronologies, SIROCCO is able to reason with the primitives at a more abstract level using an *Action/Event Hierarchy*. The Action/Event Hierarchy is a characterization and abstraction of the most-important actions and events that occur in engineering ethics scenarios. Cases may potentially be retrieved and matched based on similarity at higher levels of the hierarchy. A portion of SIROCCO's Action/Event Hierarchy is shown in Figure 5.

Fact Primitives are displayed in italics as the leaves of the hierarchy. Abstract categories are the inner nodes of the hierarchy. The depth of the hierarchy ranges from 2 to 5 levels and there are a total of 33 first level abstraction categories (i.e., those categories directly beneath the Fact-Primitive-Root). Note that the Action/ Event Hierarchy is not a strict tree; for instance, the Fact primitive "reviews-and-analyzes" has two parents.

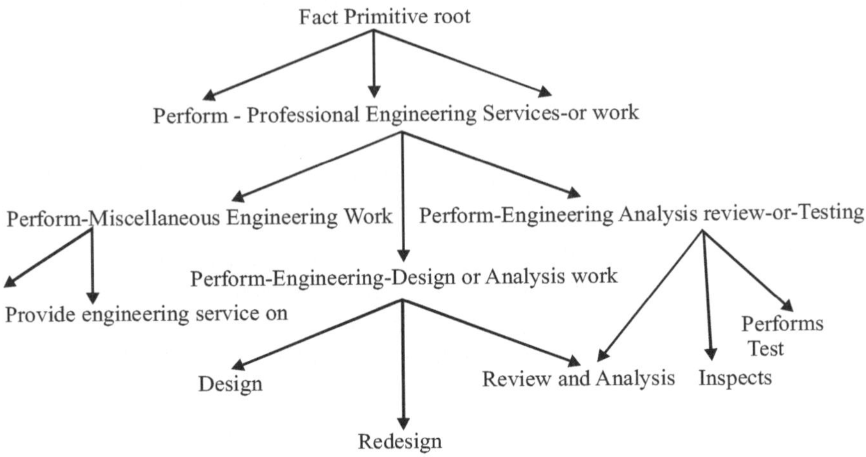

Figure 5: A portion of SIROCCO's action/event hierarchy

Representing operationalizations in source cases: The Extended Ethics Transcription Language

After entering a source case in the case base the board's analysis of the case i.e. represented using the Extended Ethics Transcription Language (EETL). EETL represents the protagonist whose action is questioned, a conclusion about that action (e.g., ethical, unethical, or unknown), and justifications for that conclusion. EETL models arguments as a set of operationalizations, some of which support the conclusion reached in the scenario, some of which conflict with the conclusion, and some of which provide relevant background information. Excerpts from the EETL representation of the board's analysis of case are depicted in Figure 6.

The three tables of Figure 6 include codes and past cases that support the board's conclusion (Table 1), that conflict with the board's conclusion (Table 2), and that the board deemed otherwise relevant to the present case (Table 3). At the top of Table 1, the heading "Code" indicates a code cited by the board, here NSPE Code I.1, the public safety code discussed earlier. "Code Status" indicates whether the cited code was violated or not in this instance. Here, the board said that Code I.1 was violated. "How Cited" indicates whether the code or case was cited explicitly or implicitly? "Grouped With" indicates other codes and cases that were discussed together with the cited code or case. "Overrides" shows whether the cited code overrides another cited code in this instance. Here, Code I.1 was found to override Code II.1.c. "Why Relevant?" provides a rationale for the citation and links the cited code to specific steps of the Fact Chronology.

Questioned Fact (s):	Fact 10
Questioned Actor or Actors :	Engineer A
The Board's conclusion:	Unethical

Table 1: The board cited the following evidence in support of their conclusion:

Code	Code Status	How Cited	Grouped With	Over rides	Why Relevant?	Why Violated, Not Violated Changed, or Not Applicable?
I. 1	Violated	Explicitly discussed	None	II. 1. c.	Engineer is involved in a professional situation in which a safety, health or welfare issue is at stake [1,2,4,5]	Engineer's action does not hold paramount the safety, health, and welfare of the public [10]
...	...	...	...	...	...	...
Code	**Citation Type**	**How Cited**	**Grouped With**	**Q#**	**Why Relevant ?**	**Why Distinguished or Analogous ?**
84-5	Analogous Precedent	Explicitly Discussed	None	1	A client overrules Engineer's judgment [1,3] Engineer complies with the client's judgment [10]	Engineer's complicity could result in a potentially dangerous situation [2,5]

Table 2: The board cited the following evidence that conflicts with their conclusion:

Code	Code Status	How Cited	Grouped With	Over rides	Why Relevant?	Why Violated, Not Violated Changed, or Not Applicable?
II. 1.c	Non violated	Explicitly discussed	None	None	Engineer has a client [1] Engineer obtains confidential facts, data, or information through work for the client [4,5]	Engineer does not reveal confidential facts, data, or information to unauthorized parties [10]
...	...	...	...	...	...	...

Table 3: The board cited the following information that neither directly supports nor confects with the conclusion:

Code	Citation Type	How Cited	Grouped With	Q#	Why Relevant ?	Why Distinguished or Analogous ?
87-2	Relevant, but Not Controlling	Explicitly discussed	85-4, 82-2	1	Engineer has a client [1] Engineer obtains confidential facts, data, or information through work for the client [4,5]	NA
...	...	...	...	...	...	...

Figure 6: EETL tables representing BER analysis of the Case

Conclusion

The computational model described in this paper represents information about how abstract principles have been applied in analyzing past problems and uses it to retrieve information relevant for analyzing new cases. Although abstract principles are rules, they cannot be applied without some way to "bridge the gap" between the rules' abstractions and concrete fact situations. Ill-defined domains like ethics and the law often lack authoritative or readily-available intermediate rules that can be used to bridge this gap.

The work that is reported in this paper is significant in at least two respects. First, it demonstrates the importance of operationalization as a method for dealing with abstract principles using past case explanations. In particular, the work shows the value of operationalization in an ill-defined domain, engineering ethics, by identifying, cataloguing, implementing, applying, and testing operationalization techniques. The work's second major contribution is to demonstrate how AI techniques make possible an empirical investigation of a phenomenon in an ill-defined domain. Indeed, without AI, theorists in the domain probably could not study the phenomenon experimentally. Ethicists would agree that operationalization is important. They speak of a dialectical interaction in which principles inform the decisions of cases and decided cases modify and refine the meanings of principles.

References

- Cook et al.'s, The application of artificial intelligence to law: A survey of six projects, in proceedings of AFIPS National Computer Conference, 1981
- Edwina L. Rissland, Kevin D. Ashley, Constrained Example Generation (CEG) model to generate counter-examples in mathematics, Third Biennial Conference of Canadian Society for computational studies of intelligence, 1980
- Edwina L. Rissland, Kevin D. Ashley, R.P. Loui "AI and Law: A fruitful synergy" AAAI, 2003
- K.D. Ashley, Modeling Legal Argument: Reasoning with Cases and Hypotheticals, MIT Press, Cambridge, MA, 1990.
- L.K. Branting, Reasoning with Rules and Precedents, Kluwer, Dordrecht, 2000.
- A. Gardner, An Artificial Intelligence Approach to Legal Reasoning, MIT Press, Cambridge, MA, 1987.
- A.R. Jonsen, S. Toulmin, The Abuse of Casuistry: A History of Moral Reasoning, California Univ. Press, Berkeley, CA, 1988. *B.M. McLaren / Artificial Intelligence(2003)*
- J. Kolodner, Case-Based Reasoning, Morgan Kaufmann, San Mateo, CA, 1993.
- B.M. McLaren, Assessing the relevance of cases and principles using operationalization techniques, 1999.
- National Society of Professional Engineers (NSPE), Opinions of the Board of Ethical Review, Vols. I–VIII, National Society of Professional Engineers, Alexandria, VA, 1958–1998.
- National Society of Professional Engineers (NSPE), The NSPE Ethics Reference Guide, National Society of Professional Engineers, Alexandria, VA, 1996.
- W. Twining, D. Miers, How to Do Things With Rules, Cox and Wyman, London, 1976.
- WWW. ElsevierComputerScience.com

Scope of Compression in Programming for Embedded Systems

Manpreet Kaur
Lecturer, GTBIT, Delhi
A.P. Singh
Sr. Lecturer, USIT, GGSIPU, Delhi

Abstract

Today, the focus of the world is towards miniaturization means maximum utilization of available resources. No field is left, whether it is hardware or software. The resources like power and memory are increasing the need of optimum utilization with their limited availability. In the field of coding, programming for embedded systems has focused towards the compression of the code in order to save the memory. As a consequence of it there is saving of power and size. In last two decades a lot of researches have been done and experiments are carried out in order to find a optimized method to compress the code. This paper discusses the various reasons that lead to need of code compression. The paper is organized as Part I details Introduction and the need of code compression. Part II summarizes the various techniques available for code compression, Part III conclude and discusses the most efficient technique.

Keywords : *Compression, Compression Ratio, Microcontroller, Memory, Processors, Decompression Engine, and Dictionary based Compression, Bit masks.*

Introduction

Data Compression or Source Coding is a process in which data is encoded using fewer bits. Data Compression is classified as lossless compression and lossy compression techniques. In lossless compression the statistical redundancy is removed, in such a way that there is no error in the transmitted data. e.g. Run Length Encoding, Dictionary Coders: LZ77, LZ78,LZW etc. Lossy Compression techniques are applicable to the area where some fidelity loss is acceptable. e.g. wavelet compression, vector quantization.

For the code compression we cannot trade off the accuracy of compression technique with size that is why usually **for embedded systems lossless compression** is used.

Figure below shows the traditional code compression and decompression flow where the compression is done off-line (prior to execution) and the compressed program is loaded into the memory. The decompression is done during the program execution (online).

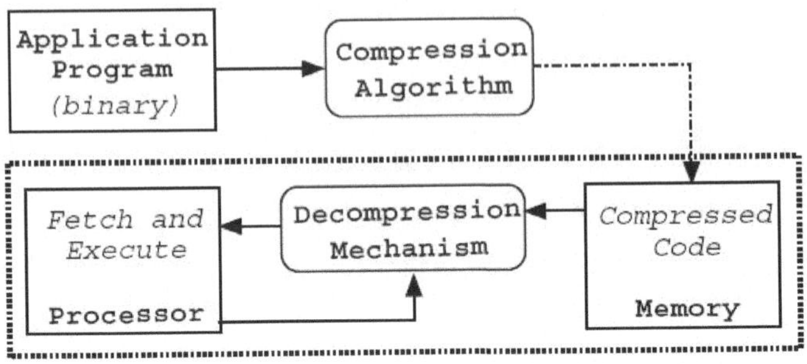

Figure 1: Code Compression and Decompression Flow

Compression ratio, widely accepted as a primary metric for measuring the efficiency of code compression, is defined as:

$$\text{Compression Ratio} = \frac{\text{Compressed Program Size}}{\text{Original Program Size}}$$

The paper has been organized as Part I comprises of dictionary based compression techniques that are best suitable for code compression. Part II discusses the challenges of implementing this technique to variable length instruction set. Part III conclude the paper and suggested future prospects in this field.

Overview of Existing Proposed Techniques

The proposed techniques have considered two ways one fixed codeword processors and second variable length codeword.

The main problems with variable length instruction set are

1. Instruction boundaries are not distinguishable at the decompression end.
2. Instructions which are frequently used are small in length and providing it a long codeword will not lead to compression.
3. While decompressing, a specified number of instructions cannot be fetched.

To overcome this problem various solutions have been proposed some of them are discussed below.

Dipankar et. all. have developed an algorithm that compresses the code of variable length. The experiment carried by them has tested the performance in terms of cycle count and memory access of the RISC processor.

The scope of the compression is done by finding out the ratio of average length of the code to the entropy of the code. This experiment is done for ARM7TDMI and CR16C.

Ultimately the scope forCR16C variable length instruction set is very less as compared to the fixed length instruction set processor.

A concept of trap instruction has been introduced where trap instruction is a frequently occurring bunches of instructions. These are used to indicate that the current instruction is a codeword and not a normal instruction. Trap Instruction consists of codeword and usable portion (4-6bits) that indicates dictionary offset.

Another approach is to extract the pipeline decoder logic for an embedded processor in software at system development time. This can be done by the designing of IFetch (Instruction Fetch) mechanisms for these compression schemes and discusses their performance and cost. In particular, the degree of compression for the ROM doesn't necessarily translate into an improvement in instructions delivered per cycle. Experiments found that when the misprediction penalty of the added Huffman decoder stage was taken into account, a Tailored ISA approach produced higher performance.

Lekatsas et.all. proposed running prototype of a one-cycle code decompression unit that decompresses compressed instructions on-the-fly
The problems that must be accounted for design are

1. Decompressing in one cycle
2. Meeting the clock cycle delay budget
3. Decompression engine should be transparent to the existing setup.
4. Decompression engine should be smaller than CPU.

A tree algorithm is formed that do the decompression while overcoming above mentioned problems.
This implementation has one limitation that it can only be applied to the systems that do not change their code during execution. This is the case for most of the embedded systems.

Seong & Mishra has worked on bit masked dictionary based code compression algorithm that provides cost benefits in the form of increased number of matching patterns. Also, it doesn't provide any decompression penalty.
The experiments have been carried out using applications from various domains and compiled them for different architectures. Experiment results show a 55% to 65% compression ratio.

The above mentioned techniques have targeted the different problems and with experiment results have suggested optimum methods to counteract them.

It can be concluded that among the above methods, for microcontroller based embedded systems bit masked dictionary based code compression shows a promising compression and its corresponding decoding hardware is the efficient one.

Dictionary Based Compression Technique

The above discussion shows that dictionary based compression method is best for code compression of the embedded systems. Below the variants of dictionary based algorithms are explained.

Dictionary Based Approaches

The basic idea is to take the advantage of commonly occurring instruction sequences by using a dictionary. The repeating occurrences are replaced by a codeword that points to the index of the dictionary that contains the pattern. The compressed program consists of both code words and uncompressed instructions. The binary consists of ten 8-bit patterns i.e., total 80 bits. The dictionary has two 8-bit entries. The compressed program requires 62 bits and the dictionary requires 16 bits. In this case, the compression ratio is 97.5%

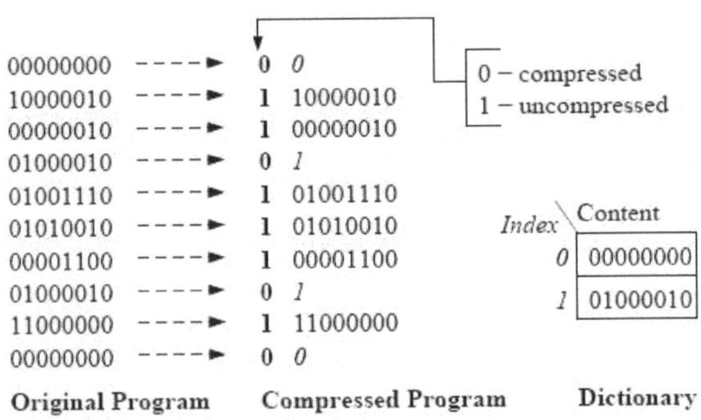

Figure 2: Dictionary Based Approach

Improved Dictionary-based Approach

The basic idea is to determine the instruction sequences that are different in few bit positions (hamming distance) and store that information in the compressed program and update the dictionary.

This example considers only 1-bit change. An extra field is necessary to indicate whether mismatches are considered or not. In case a mismatch is considered, another field is necessary to indicate the bit position that is different from an entry in the dictionary. For example, the third pattern (from top) in the original program is different from the first dictionary entry (index 0) on the sixth bit position (from left). The compression ratio for this example is 95%.

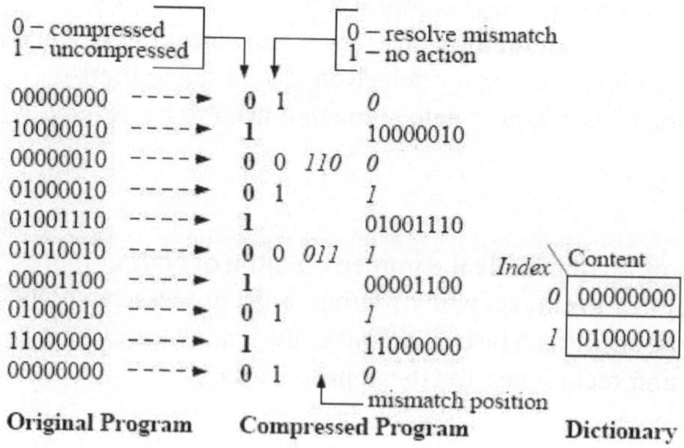

Figure 3: Improved Dictionary Based Approach

Bit Mask Approach

The basic idea is to determine mask type for the given application and then saving the mask type, its location and mask pattern as the compressed program. Following is the same example explaining the bit mask approach.

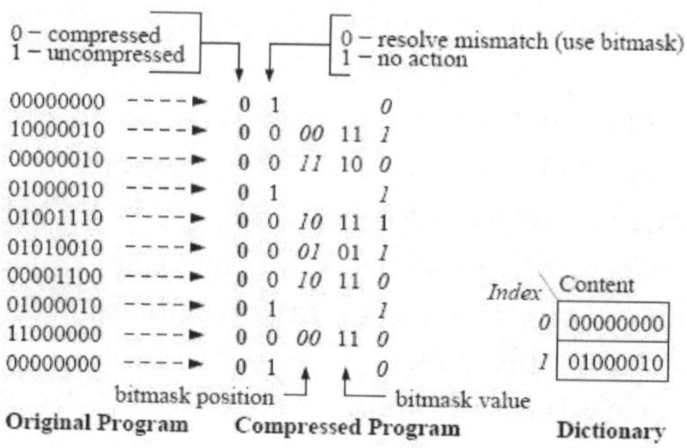

Figure 4: Bit Mask Based Approach

Conclusion

Embedded systems have a main constraint of memory size.
Code compression can reduce this problem by compressing the code of application.
While implementing the code compression
By providing bit masks the first challenge is to select the size and contents of the mask. Then optimal dictionary selection is a nondeterministic polynomial time hard problem. Thus a appropriate algorithm need to be devised.

Future Scope

Our future work will include the implementation of code compression in different domains (application areas) with different target processors i.e. 89C51, IC51 etc A series of experiments can be carried out to determine the efficiency and utilization of compression techniques for these processors.

References

- Wolfe and A. Chanin. " Executing compressed programs on an embeded risc architecture". In Proceedings of International Symposium on Microarchitecture (MICRO), pages 81–91, 1992.
- H. Lekatsas, Jorg Henkel, and Venkata Jakkula. "Design of an one-cycle decompression hardware for performance increase in embedded systems". In Proceedings of Design Automation Conference (DAC), pages 34–39, 2002.
- Dipankar Das, Rajeev Kumar, and P.P. Chakrabarti. "Dictionary based code compression for variable length instruction encodings". In Proceedings of VLSI Design (VLSID), pages 545–550, 2005
- Seok. W.Seong,Prabhat Mishra "A Bitmasked based code compression technique for embedded systems". IEEE Transactions on computer-Aided Design of Integrated Circuits and Systems,VOL. 27, NO. 4, APRIL 2008.
- J. Prakash, C. Sandeep, P. Shankar, and Y. Srikant. A simple and fast scheme for code compression for vliw processors. In Proceedings of Data Compression Conference (DCC), page 444, 2003.
- A Simple Dictionary-Based Compression Algorithm By Robert Jasku_la (robak_1983@o2.pl), September 2007.

Vital Information Resources Under Siege: Problem in Today's Scenario

Neetu Goel
Sr. Lecturer , RDIAS, Delhi

Abstract

Computer viruses generally refer to programs that unintentionally get into computers, disrupt the normal operation, and cause damage to data and programs. A virus is best identified not by what it does, but by how it spreads and infects other programs. This paper presents the general information of viruses i.e. the categorization of viruses, what they infect & how, basic symptoms, how to deal with them.

Introduction

VIRUS stands for "Vital Information Resources Under Siege".

It is a computer program designed to copy itself into other programs, with the intention of causing mischief or damage. A virus will usually execute when it is loaded into a computer's memory. On execution, it instructs its host program to copy the viral code into any number of other programs and files stored in the computer. A virus may also execute several different sequences of execution one or more times to attempt replication. Virus replication consists of a sequence of execution of any combination of the following general operations like - open, read, write, search and close. The corrupted programs may continue to perform their intended functions while also executing the virus's instructions, thus further propagating it. The infection may transfer itself to other computers through storage devices, computer networks, and on-line systems.

Categorization of Malicious Program

In order to replicate itself, a virus must be permitted to execute code and write to memory. For this reason, many viruses attach themselves to executable files that may be part of legitimate programs. If a user tries to start an infected program, the virus' code may be executed first.
On the basis of their behavior when they are executed:
1. Nonresident
2. Resident

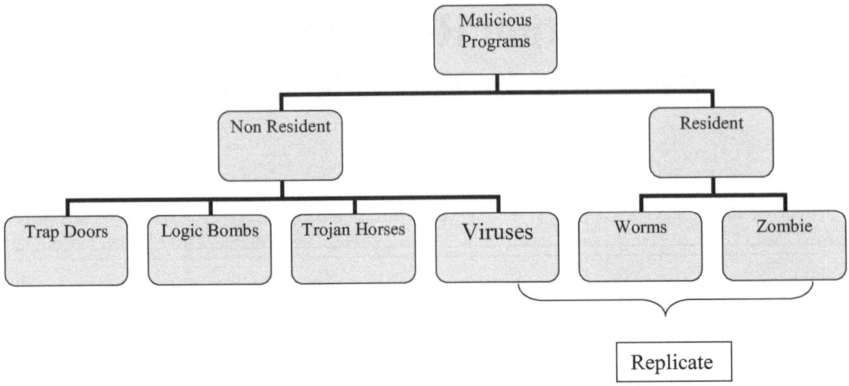

Figure 1: Classification of Malicious Program

Non resident

Non resident viruses which requires host programs for its functioning & can be thought of as consisting of a finder module and a replication module. The finder module is responsible for finding new files to infect. For each new executable file the finder module encounters, it calls the replication module to infect that file.

Trap Doors – Trap Door is a secret entry point into a program that allows some one that is aware of the trap door to gain access without going through the usual security access procedures. In other words Trap Door is a code that recognizes some special sequence of inputs or is triggered by being run from a certain user id or by an unlikely sequence of events

Logic Bombs – One of the oldest type of program threat. The Logic Bomb is code embedded in some legitimate programs that is set to "explode" when certain conditions are met. Once triggered a bomb may alter or delete data or entire file cause a machine halt or do some other damage.

Trojan Horses - A Trojan Horse is useful program containing hidden code that, when invoked, performs some unwanted or harmful functions. The Trojan Horses are usually masked so that they look interesting, for example a saxophone wav file that interests a person collecting sound samples of instruments. A Trojan horse differs from a destructive virus in that it doesn't reproduce.

Viruses - A computer virus is a program, a block of executable code, which attaches itself to, overwrite or otherwise replace another program in order to reproduce itself without knowledge of a PC user.

There are a couple of different types of computer viruses: Boot Sector viruses, Parasitic viruses, Multi-partite viruses, Companion viruses, Link viruses and Macro viruses. These classifications take into account the different ways in which the virus can infect different parts of a system.

Resident

Resident viruses also known as Independent program which doesn't require any host program for its functioning, it contain a replication module that is similar to the one that is employed by nonresident viruses. However, this module is not called by a finder module. Instead, the virus loads the replication module into memory when it is executed and ensures that this module is executed each time the operating system is called to perform a certain operation. For example, the replication module can be called each time the operating system executes a file. In this case, the virus infects every suitable program that is executed on the computer.

Worms - A worm is a program which spreads usually over network connections. Unlike a virus which attaches itself to a host program, worms always need a host program to spread. In practice, worms are not normally associated with one person computer systems. They are mostly found in multi-user systems such as UNIX environments.

Zombie - A Zombie is a program that secretly takes over another internet attached computer and then uses that computer to launch attacks that a difficult to trace. Zombies are used in denial-of-service attacks.

Stages in the Life of a virus

During its lifetime, a typical virus goes through the following four stages:

Dormant phase - In this phase, the virus is idle and will eventually be activated by some event such as the occurrence of a certain date or the presence of another program or file. For instance, according to the system date, the virus gets activated.
Propagation phase -. In this phase, the virus places an identical copy of itself into other programs or into certain system areas on the disk. Each infected program will now contain a clone of the virus, which will itself enter a propagation phase.
Triggering phase- At this point, the virus is activated to perform its intended function. As with the dormant phase, the triggering phase can be caused by a variety of system events, including a count of the number of times that this copy of the virus has made copies of itself.
Execution phase- The actual function of the virus is performed in the execution phase. The function may be harmless, such as displaying some messages on screen, or damaging, such as destroying programs and data files.

Virus Generations

When the first viruses were written, they could be classified into five generations of viruses. Each new generation of viruses has incorporated new features that make the viruses more difficult to detect and remove.

First generation (simple). The first generation of viruses consisted of simple viruses. These viruses did nothing very significant other than replicate. First-generation viruses do nothing to hide their presence on a system, so they can usually be found simply by noting an increase in the size of files or the presence of a distinctive pattern in an infected file.

Second generation (self-recognition). First generation viruses repeatedly infect the host, which leads to depleted memory and then early detection. To prevent this unnecessary growth of infected files, second-generation viruses usually implant a unique signature that signals that the file or system is infected. The virus will check for this signature before attempting infection. If the signature is not present, it will place the signature soon after the infection has taken place; however, if the signature is present, the virus will not re-infect the host.

Third generation (stealth). Most viruses may be identified on a contaminated system by scanning the secondary storage and searching for a pattern of data unique to each virus. To counteract such scans, some resident viruses employ stealth techniques. These viruses subvert selected system service call interrupts when they are active. Requests to perform these operations are intercepted by the virus code. If the operation exposes the presence of the virus, the operation is redirected to return false information.

Fourth generation (armored). As anti-virus researchers have developed tools to analyze new viruses, authors have turned to methods to obfuscate the code of their viruses. This "armoring" includes adding confusing and unnecessary code to make it more difficult to analyze the virus code. These viruses may also perform directed attacks against anti-virus software, if present on the affected system.

Fifth generation (polymorphic). These most recent class of viruses to appear on the scene is also called self mutating viruses. These viruses infect their targets with a modified or encrypted version of themselves. By varying the code sequences written to the file, or by generating a different, random encryption key, the virus in the altered file will not be identifiable through the use of simple byte matching. To detect the presence of these viruses requires that a more complex algorithm be employed that, in effect, reverses the masking (decryption) to determine the presence of the virus.

How Viruses Activate?

We are always afraid that viruses do something harmful to files when they get active, but not all the viruses activate. Some viruses just spread out, but when viruses activate they do very different things. Might play a part of melody or play music in the background, show a picture or animated picture, show text, format hard disk or do changes to files.

Viruses can not do any harm to hardware but they can do harm to programs and for example to BIOS so that computer does not start after that. Usually you can start the computer from a boot diskette if the computer does not start otherwise.

Symptoms of a Computer Virus

If you suspect or confirm that your computer is infected with a computer virus, obtain the current antivirus software. The following are some primary indicators that a computer may be infected:

- The computer runs slower than usual.
- The computer stops responding.
- The computer crashes, and then it restarts every few minutes.
- The computer restarts on its own. Additionally, the computer does not run as usual.
- Applications on the computer do not work correctly.
- Disks or disk drives are inaccessible.
- You cannot print items correctly.
- You see unusual error messages.
- You see distorted menus and dialog boxes.
- There is a double extension on an attachment that you recently opened, such as a .jpg, .vbs, .gif, or .exe.
- An antivirus program is disabled for no reason. Additionally, the antivirus program cannot be restarted.
- An antivirus program cannot be installed on the computer, or the antivirus program will not run.
- New icons appear on the desktop that you did not put there, or the icons are not associated with any recently installed programs.
- Strange sounds or music plays from the speakers unexpectedly.
- A program disappears from the computer even though you did not intentionally remove the program.

How to Protect Computer from Viruses

You can protect yourself against viruses with a few simple steps:

- If you are using an unsecured operating system, then buying virus protection software is a nice safeguard.
- Never open an e-mail attachment from someone you don't know.
- Avoid opening an e-mail attachment from someone you know, unless you know exactly what the attachment is. The sender may be unaware that it contains a virus.
- It is good to take a backup of the file that was infected. Virus program could do some damage to the file and that is why it is good to have a backup.
- One possibility on Windows Me, Windows XP and Windows Vista is a tool known as System Restore, which restores the registry and critical system files to a previous checkpoint.
- Reinstalling the operating system is another approach to virus removal.
- Use an Internet firewall

Conclusion

Computer viruses have been around for over fifteen years. The total number of viruses and Trojan horses have passed the 1 million mark by the end of 2008 (Source: computerworld.com). In recent years, the number viruses have increased dramatically. The damages they cause are estimated to be several billions of U.S. dollars per year. Most often, the origin of the virus is difficult to trace.

The proliferation of the Internet and Web, have enabled viruses to spread quickly on a massive scale, by taking advantage of several security loopholes. The continual challenge is to have quick and effective responses to these virus attacks.

Various kinds of anti-virus software have been developed which detect viruses and take corrective actions. But its not enough, user awareness is the key factor to tackle with the current situation. For this Preventive Measures should be taken like the anti-virus software needs to be continually updated to cope with newer types of viruses.

References:

- http://www.computerworld.com/action/ article.do?command = viewArticleBasic&articleId=9075118
- http://www.research.ibm.com/antivirus/SciPapers/Chess/Future.html
- http://support.microsoft.com/kb/129972
- http://www.tml.tkk.fi/Opinnot/Tik-110.501/1997/viruses.html
- http://www.virus-scan-software.com/virus-scan-help/answers/the-history-of-computer-viruses.shtml
- Virus Attack IT Magazine, September edition 2006
- "Virus Symptoms" McAfee Company, Virus Bulletin editorial 2006.

CMS Framework for Value Addition in Education System

Vinay Kumar Saini
Lecturer, Maharaja Agrasen Institute of Technology, Delhi

Abstract

This paper is intended to propose a basic architecture that on implementation shall add value to the existing education system prevailing in the affiliated institutes to GGS Indraprastha University. The existing system doesn't have an information system that can help various institutions to collaborate and synchronize there academic activities. Furthermore there is no usual procedure to conduct subjects under NUES. So there are a number of serious tribulations coupled with this pattern. The projected architecture is based on the concept of Content Management System (CMS) and targets to provide an easily accessible online system which shall provide a solution to stated problems and hence facilitate a smooth interaction between the faculty and the student mass all across the university and other sister concerns as well.

Keywords: *Content Management System (CMS), Non University Examination Scheme (NUES)*

Introduction

Education system plays a vital role in the social and economic development of our nation. The economic progress of a country is strongly linked with the quality of education. Guru Gobind Singh Indraprastha University established by Government of NCT of Delhi is an affiliating and teaching University that aims to facilitate and promote studies, research and extension work in emerging areas of higher education with focus on professional education in the disciplines of engineering, technology, architecture, management, medicine, pharmacy, physiotherapy, nursing, education, law, journalism and mass communication, etc. The existing education system of GGSIPU includes two six month semester in a year. Every semester include subject wise teaching based on the university prescribed syllabus that includes theory classes along with tutorials and practical exercises. The evaluation of the students is done on the basis of two terminal examinations and one end term examination. The examination papers for terminal exams are framed by subject coordinator and same question paper is used in all the engineering colleges for that subject. There is a concept of Non University Examination Scheme NUES for management courses for multidimensional development of the students. But there are some serious problems associated with the system:-

- Acute shortage of well qualified faculty forces the management to appoint fresh engineering graduates as faculty who are required to engage classes immediately after joining the institutions without being given any training and preparation time [1].
- Synchronization among the subject coverage in various institutions is missing.
- Variance in the content delivery to the students in various institutions.
- Difference in the standard of quality teaching imparted to the students.
- No eccentric or innovative methodology / content is available in concrete.
- Lack of uniform evaluation for subjects under Non University Examination Scheme (NUES).
- No centralized interface to facilitate student - student and student – faculty interaction.

All these problems causes decline in the quality of teaching in the institutions. Poor quality teachers and poor quality students results in indiscipline and bad work culture in the institution.

Proposed Solution

The above mentioned problems are seriously a matter of concern for the future of institutions and the career of the students passing out. The need is to provide a effective information system using the web technologies that provide a centralized platform for student –faculty interactions. There are many website development technologies that can be used for developing the required information system. Content Management System (CMS) concept is an alternative that can be used to develop the desired information system. Many organizations have already used this concept to add value to the Education Sector. Some of the success stories are as follows.

- Content management system (CMS)-based web site for the Joint Information Systems Committee (JISC) [2], a UK strategic advisory body.
- Campusuite CMS [3] for higher education empowers you and your staff to take control of web content with a set of friendly tools designed to make their jobs — and yours — easier and more professional. Use Campusuite's content management tools to keep your site "connected" quickly and simply with fresh content. Even your non-techie users can intuitively reach your tech-savvy users.
- Web Portal with Content Management System [4] is a complete educational institute information portal with the core objective to provide information on educational institutes.
- cyn.in [5] is an Internet based collaboration and content management platform. cyn.in helps educational institutes to solve big problems even on a very small budget all over the world. It has a zero Infrastructure setup which means, you

have: reduced management overheads, no worries of upgrading aging technology and complete protection from unforeseen expense spikes.

Referring to these success story CMS prove out to be the best solution for overcome the above stated problems in the Introduction Section. Content Management is now seen as a key strategic requirement that add values to the organizations [6]. So there is a need of a customized framework that can be referred for designing the desired information system. Following Sections covers the CMS concept in detail and the proposed CMS Framework.

Content Management System (CMS)

CMS is a computer application used to create, edit, manage, search and publish various kinds of digital media and electronic text. CMSs are frequently used for storing, controlling, versioning, and publishing industry-specific documentation such as news articles, operators' manuals, technical manuals, sales guides, and marketing brochures. The content managed may include computer files, image media, audio files, video files, electronic documents, and Web content [7].

A typical CMS can be divided into two sections namely admin section and public section. Admin section is provided for the Administrator to manage (add, edit, delete) content and members registered with the system. Public section on the other hand is the interface available for public access where users can register themselves and can make use of the facilities provided in the system. Figure 1 show the architectural view of a typical CMS, where in Administrator and content editors are having access to Admin section to manage the content of the system by working on different sections of the system. The published website is available for public access.

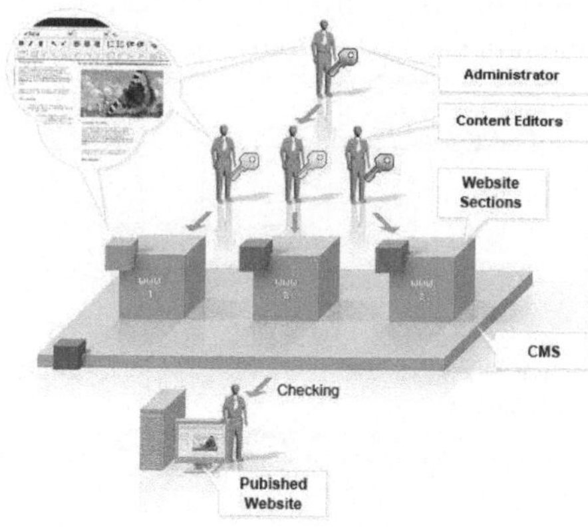

Figure 1: Architecture of CMS based System

Figure 2 shows the Flow Diagram of a typical CMS that shows how actually the above mentioned operations are actually realized. A web server (Apache here) executes the various transactions like member management, and content editing onto the database (MySQL here). The website is published by extracting the data from the database and then presenting it to the user as per the website design.

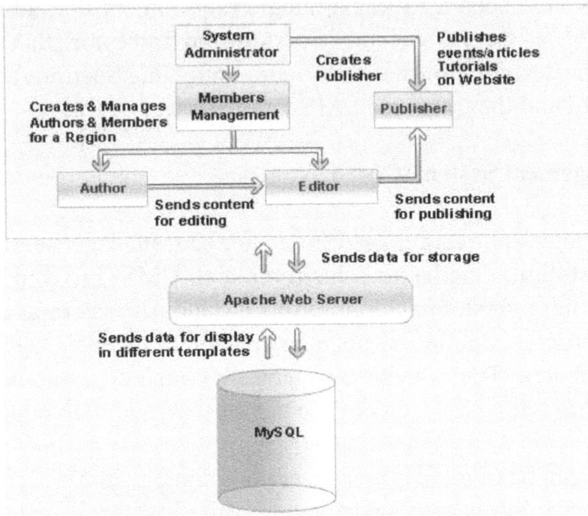

Figure 2: Flow Diagram of the CMS

CMS Framework for Education System

The proposed CMS framework for education system provides design guidelines for a dynamic system that shall facilitate open interaction among students and faculties across the University affiliated Engineering colleges. Figure 3 shows the components of the proposed CMS framework.

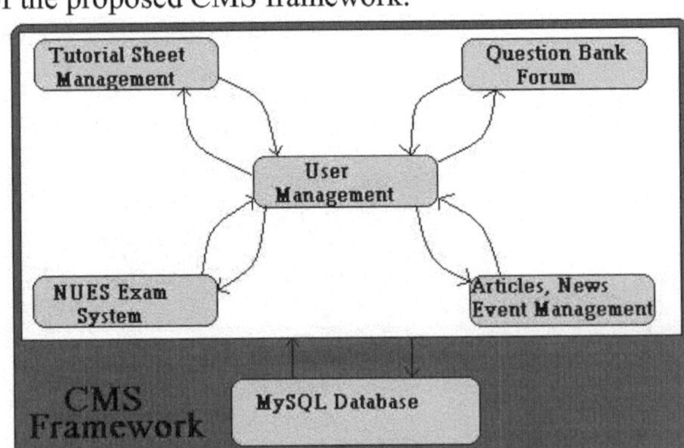

Figure 3- CMS Framework for Education System

- **User Management**

Managing User Groups to represent roles, and permissions can be granted to user groups. An example could be creating a User Group called "Tutorial Sheet Content Authors". Rather than granting access of tutorial sheet content management to individual users, access is granted to this group. When users leave or join, they are simply added to the User Group, and no changes are required to the permissions of the pages within the tutorial sheet management section of the website. Permissions can be Read, Write or Administrative. If a user has Read permission for a particular section, they are able to view the section of the website via their browser. If a user has Write permission for a particular section, they are able to view and update the content for that section. Finally if a user has Administration permission they are also able to change the status, edit site settings, permissions, and the workflow of the system.

- **Tutorial Sheet Management**

This section of the Framework provides facility to the registered teachers to upload tutorial sheets and they are allowed to make changes and update the tutorial sheets uploaded by them. This section can be accessed by student members of the website in a read only mode. They can download the tutorial sheets and can post questions related to the tutorial sheets. They can also post answers. If any student posts any undesirable content then that content can be deleted without intimation to the user and his/her account can be blocked by the administrator. An advance search facility is the highlight of this section that allows student to access specific tutorial sheets out of the whole archive available on the server pertaining to various subjects.

- **Question Bank Forum**

Question Bank forum section is a component that facilitates student – teacher interaction. Students can post any question pertaining to the academic area. If any students posts any undesirable content then administrator has every right to take appropriate action against the user, like deactivating his/her membership and deleting his/her content without intimation. This section also have a search facility where in students can search existing question bank to check if there doubt related questions are already exists in the bank and if not they can post fresh questions, that can be answered by others.

- **NUES Exam System**

NUES exam system includes multiple choice questions based online exam facility. The registered faculties are allowed to add questions to the database that are managed subject wise in the database. The registered users can appear for the test after registering for the test. This section is designed to provide a facility of maintaining standard interface for NUES based subject evaluation. This system can be used under the supervision of the concerned faculties of the affiliated institutions and out of the 100 marks approved by the University some percentage can be reserved for evaluation based on this system. This shall add standardization to the NUES evaluation.

- **Articles, News and Events**

This section is the most important part of the framework that allow registered users to post Articles, News, and Events on to the website, that gets published on the website only after the approval of the administrator. All the editing and managerial permissions on the content in this section are reserved with the author of the content and the administrator. This section provides a platform where students throughout the university can convey there ideas and can notify any events, or news that of the interest of all the students. This facilitates open communication that is lagging in the existing system. This section can further be extended to provide facility for event management, for example an institution is organizing a cultural fest, then its notification can be posted and registrations related to that can be invited through the same interface and updates regarding the event can be published there only.

- **Database**

Database is a structured collection of records or data that is stored in a computer system. The structure is achieved by organizing the data according to a database model. The model in most common use today is the relational model. The need of framework is to manage the storage of the along with the option of manipulation and concurrent access to the database. To achieve a Database management system is required. There are many Relational Database management Systems (RDBMS), available like SQL Server, Oracle, MySQL. Database plays the role of backend component in the CMS Framework. The database structure designed using normalization results in better performance. Proposed CMS Framework considers a normalized database that includes all the entities like tutorial, article, event, news, member, question_bank, and Reply. More entities can be added to extend the capability of the CMS.

Proposed CMS Framework's features are:

- Identification of all key users and their content management roles.
- Enable faculty – faculty interaction to allow young and fresh faculties to gain experience by getting consultations with the experience faculties.
- The ability to assign roles and responsibilities to different content categories or types.

- Definition of workflow tasks for collaborative creation, often coupled with event messaging so that content managers are alerted to changes in content.
- The ability to capture content the ability to publish the content to a repository to support access to the content.
- Easing of the process of student - student and student – faculty interaction through question bank, articles, and events sections.

Available Technologies for Implementation

A typical website can be divided into three components. These components need to be integrated properly to develop a successful website. These three components are Web Server, Server Side Scripting language and Back-end database. Following sections throws light on these three components and available technologies and products for these three components.

- **Web Server**

A Web Server is a computer that delivers (*serves up*) web pages to the clients who send request to the web server. Every Web server has an IP address and possibly a domain name. For example, if you enter the URL in your browser, this sends a request to the server whose domain name is mentioned in the URL. The server then fetches the page named *index.html* and sends it to your browser. Any computer can be turned into a Web server by installing server software and connecting the machine to the Internet. There are many Web server software applications, including public domain software from NCSA and Apache, and commercial packages from Microsoft, Netscape and others.

- **Server Side Scripting**

Server side scripting facilitates writing programs that are executed on the server, and can be used in many ways. Template based web sites and shopping carts are just two examples. The languages used for these tasks are normal programming languages with special libraries/packages for server side scripting. Following is summarized comparison of most common programming languages used for server side scripting.

ASP/ASP.net

ASP, or Active Server Pages, is a technology developed by Microsoft for making advanced web pages. The most common language for programming ASP is VBScript. It is available in most web hosting accounts on Microsoft servers. .NET framework provide many reusable components that can be used to create and developing commercial websites, corporate intranets and extranets, online publishing portals and custom vertical applications. .NET framework also contain Extensible architecture, fully-exposed API, Integration of ASP.NET controls and custom modules which are completely customizable through Visual Studio .NET. So ASP.net is the next generation ASP technology which allows you to use any .net-enabled language to program your site. The 2 most common languages for .net web programming is VB.net and C#. Both are good choices for both desktop and web applications.

JSP/Servlets

Java is perhaps the most popular language for enterprise level applications, so professional programmers can take their skills to the web. JSP means Java Server Pages and consists of JSP tags mixed in with html. It is best used as the presentation layer of a Java web application, although you can build JSP-only applications. The logic behind the application is normally hidden below a JSP and is a pure Java program called a servlet. JSP's are also compiled into servlets by the JSP engine the first time it is executed for faster execution time on later requests.

ColdFusion

A scripting language developed by Allaire, and then bought by Macromedia. Macromedia ColdFusion Server is not free, the Standard edition of ColdFusion MX 6.1 costs $1299/server. ColdFusion [8] is a programming language based on standard HTML (Hyper Text Markup Language) that is used to write dynamic web pages. A ColdFusion application is very simply a collection of pages, similar to a static Web site. But unlike the pages in a static Web site, the pages in a ColdFusion application include the server-side ColdFusion Markup Language (CFML) in addition to HTML.

Perl

Perl has been the most used scripting language for web applications. It is a very powerful language with many advanced features, and there are 1000's of perl scripts available for free in various scripting directories. Perl scripting is available in most cheap web hosting packages.

PHP

PHP Hypertext Preprocessor is an open source language and has gained enormous popularity the last years. It is easy to learn and there are many readymade scripts available. Almost every cheap web hosting package includes PHP. It is easy to learn for a programming language with many books and web sites dedicated to it.

Python

Although Python was created in 1989, it is not yet as widespread as PHP, ASP or Perl, and Python is not a language that is supported by most web hosting companies. It is easy to learn though, has a clean, elegant syntax and is perfectly suited to typical web applications. The drawback is that there really is no standard web application framework for Python. Besides its usefulness in web applications,

Python is also a good choice for many other types of programs, like GUI applications and utility scripts.

- **Back End Database**

There are many different vendors that currently produce relational database management systems (RDBMS). Relational databases vary significantly in their capabilities and in costs. Some products are proprietary while others are open source. The leading vendors [9] of RDBMS are listed below:

RDBMS Vendors	RDBMS
Oracle Corporation	Oracle
IBM	DB2
Microsoft Corporation	MS Access
Microsoft Corporation	SQL Server
MySQL AB	MySQL

Table 1: Leading Vendors of RDBMS

Out of the listed RDBMS in Table 1 products MySQL (RDBMS) runs as a server providing multi-user access to a number of databases. MySQL is owned and sponsored by a single for-profit firm, the Swedish company MySQL AB, now a subsidiary of Sun Microsystems, which holds the copyright to most of the code base. The project's source code is available under terms of the GNU General Public License, as well as under a variety of proprietary agreements. MySQL RDBMS provides many advantages like low cost, easy to configure and manage.

Proposed Technologies for Implementation

Software experts and researchers on open source software have identified several advantages of open source development [10]. The main advantage is low cost of development, marketing and logistical services. It also helps companies to keep abreast of all technology developments. Open Source communities are a big support group that helps in any development related issues if any. The Open Source development approach has helped produce reliable, high quality software quickly and inexpensively.

Open source PHP content management systems using Apache Web server along with MySQL as back end database offers wide range of features for developing content management system based on the proposed CMS Framework. Additional features can be integrated to such open source CMS frameworks or other management systems can be integrated with CMS through enterprise integration services. PHP CMS development reduces layout and content interdependence to zero and either of these can be updated without worrying about the other aspect of website. This facilitates you to manage website through different source points. Every person having best access to information can update the related section of the website.

Conclusion

Proposed system shall facilitate open interaction among students and faculties across the University affiliated Engineering colleges. Easy GUI based interactive interfaces will allow bridging the gap between the gurus and the students and will allow them to interact even after the formal teaching hours. For the proposed framework, System analysis approach has been followed to identify the problems, draft functional and nonfunctional requirements. Further Comparison has been done to evaluate commercial and open source systems. The understanding of advantages and pitfalls of each system helps in polishing strategy to efficiently manage digital content in a cost effective manner. The proposed system after successful implementation shall add value to the existing education system and will provide solution to the existing problems in the education system. The system development and implemented is proposed to follow CMS Framework designed to simplify the publication and management of Web content to Web sites, in particular allowing content creators to submit content without requiring technical knowledge of HTML or the uploading of files.

References

- Prasad. G, Bhar. C, Srivastav. V (2007) "A Critical Review of Examination Related Problems in Technical Education in India".
- The JISC web site http://www.jisc.ac.uk/
- Campusuite CMS http://www.campusuite.com/content-management-system-higher-education/
- Web Portal with Content Management System
- http://www.elegantmicroweb.com / web_portal_with_content_management_system.htm
- cyn.in http://www.cynapse.com/products/cynin
- Gregory Booth, Research Project (2005) "Developing an Event and Content Management System".
- Wikipedia free encyclopedia http://en.wikipedia.org/wiki/Content_management_system
- ColdFusion, http://www.fusionauthority.com/cfintro.cfm
- RDMS vendors list http://rdbms.ca/database/vendors.html
- Open source software http://en.wikipedia.org/wiki/Open_source_software

Web 3.0 : A Transformation from HTML to Semantic web

Shikha Singh
Lecturer, BCIIT, Delhi

Abstract

As the barriers of distances in networking are removed through Internet technology. It is the time to have new era in the field of database, AI and IR and web. This is coming up in the form of semantic Web.The word semantic define 'meaning'. As the semantic database is the latest trend in database technology and it is incorporating the new generation of knowledge representation and Information Retrieval for Semantic Web. This paper presents the in depth discussion on the transformation from HTML to OWL , Information Retrieval system and Semantic web.We will be discussing the different techniques used in IR systems for Semantic Web.

Introduction

Internet has provided new ways to float the information in every field. This is achieved mainly through WWW which provide the highway of information. As this is the Information age and thus need arises to manage that information in a better way to provide fast and relevant information to the users and thus arises **Semantic Web**.

Database provides a key role in storing information as facts. But the current database management system i.e RDBMS or ORDBMS provides access to information on keyword based not on the basis of meanings which results in wastage of time. So emergence of Semantic database plays a vital role in redefining scenario of database system.

Semantic database constitutes 'meaning' of information as 'facts' about the objects.

Semantic Database= Semantic (meaning) + Information

Semantic web is the vision of ***Tim Berners-Lee.*** The semantic web is introduced as an extension of the World Wide Web(Web 3.0), which define the semantics of information and services on the web, making it possible for the web to understand and satisfy the requests of people and machines to use the web content.

Traditional search engine is based on keywords –search. The only documents retrieved are those containing user-specified keywords. But many documents convey desired semantic information without containing these keywords. This limitation can be overcome by introducing query expansion mechanisms based on the statistical co-occurrence of terms. This problem can be solved by indexing documents according to context an meaning rather than keywords, but this is a lengthy process which requires a method of converting words to meanings and the creation of a meaning –based index structure. Requirement arises for the development of new category of search engine which will overcome these limitations. So 'Semantic search' crop up to provide search with meaning.

Semantic web is defines as web with meaning. To be meaningful (semantic), information must be logical. For an entire worldwide web of information to be semantic (meaningful) the entire web of information must be structured according to what is called **universal logic**. Semantic web will be used to make web pages machine readable so that they can perform more of the tedious work involved in finding, sharing and combining information on the web without interference of humans.

Objective of semantic web is to combine information from multiple sources. The vision of the "Semantic Web" is to have all public (www) 'data' encoded in a way that ANY application program can use it – even programs that have no encoding to anticipate the meaning of the data.

Information retrieval technology has been vital to the success of the Web. For semantic web documents or annotations to have an impact, they will have to be compatible with Web based indexing and retrieval technology These annotations will provide metadata about the documents as well as machine interpretable statements capturing some of the meaning of document content

Transformation from HTML to OWL

WWW Language—HTML

Now a day's information in computer can be loosely divided into documents and data. Documents like articles, messages, reports, and brochures are read by humans. Data, like calendars, address books, playlists, and spreadsheets are presented using an application program which lets them be viewed, searched and combined in many ways. Currently Web pages are stored in HTML HTML is full of tags that can be used to represent a visually-abstract content, but these were designed to markup pages, so they contain semantics about paragraphs, tables, images, but they cannot markup things like invoices, mathematics formulas, car spare parts, etc.

Example of HTML code:

```
<H1>Introduction to AI</H1>
<UL><LI>Teacher: Frank van Harmelen
<LI>Students: 1AI, 1I
<LI>Requirements: none
</UL>
```

Metadata

Metadata is data about data. HTML brought the **<meta>** tag to allow page authors to help indexing of the page by placing keywords that specified the page content. The best search engine make extensive use of these tags, when available, to categorize the information. Metadata will not be displayed on the page, but will be interpretable by machines. Metadata tags, for example

```
<meta name="keywords" content="semantic, Intelligent web, Web 3.0">
<meta name="description" content="New research in web">
<meta name="author" content="Shikha Singh">
```

Metadata provide a method by which computers can categories the content of web pages. But still that does not provide powerful approach to search engines. So the new language was introduced to provide advantage over HTML i.e. XML.

WHY XML?

(eXtensible Markup Language)

XML does not specify fixed tag set. In fact XML is really a meta-language for describing markup languages. In other words, XML provides a facility to define tags and the structural relationships between them. Since there's no predefined tag set, there can't be any preconceived semantics. All of the semantics of an XML document will either be defined by the applications that process them or by style sheets. XML is considered to be the basis for all semantic web languages - the "machine code" of the new generation web.

An XML document is parsed in two levels.

Ø **Well-formed**. A XML document is well formed if it is having start tag(<>) and its corresponding end tag(</>).

Ø **Valid.** A valid document additionally conforms to semantic rules, either user-defined or in an XML schema, especially DTD; e.g. if a document contains an undefined element, then it is not valid; a validating parser is disallowed from processing it.

Now lets take example of XML tags.

<course date=" ">
<title>...</title>
<teacher>
<name>...</name>
<subject>....</subject>
</teacher>
<student>..</student>
</course>

It can be shown in tree like structure, which will become the basis for search in web.

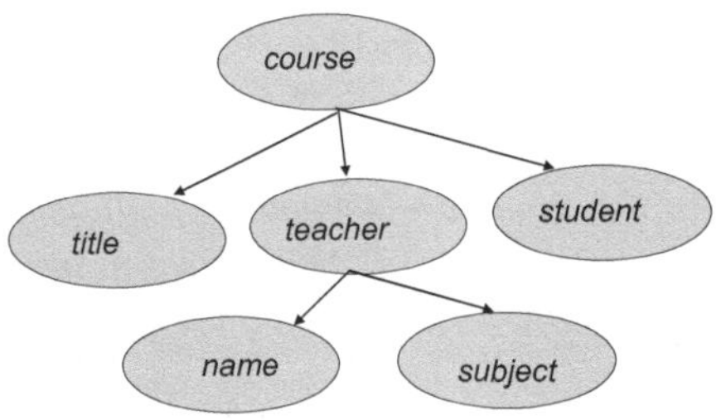

Figure 1: Tree Representation of XML

Any XML document whose nested tags form a balanced tree is a well-formed XML document. Furthermore it is possible to enforce constraints on which tags should be used, and which nesting of these tags is allowed. In XML 1.0 this is done in a Document Type Definition (DTD)

Limitations in XML

Let us suppose we want to express the following fact:
Shikha Singh is a lecturer of Computer Science

There are various ways of representing this sentences in XML .Three possibilities are

<course name="Computer Science">
<lecturer>Shikha Singh</lecturer>
</course>

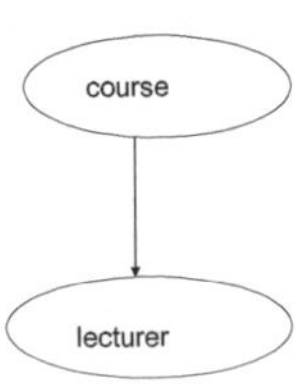

Figure 2: Graph for lecturer and course

```
<lecturer name="Shikha Singh">
   <teaches>Computer Science</teaches>
</lecturer>
```

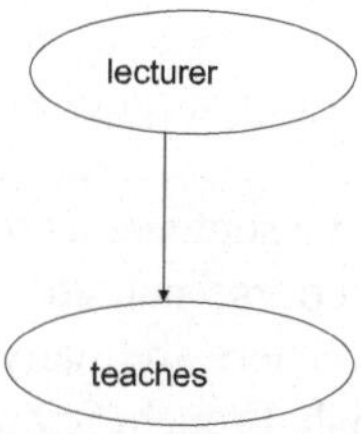

Figure 3: Graph showing link of lecturer and teaching

- Here in all the statements, same relationship is shown but there is no specification to show relationships, it is up to the application to understand itself. So, there is no standard way of assigning meaning to tag nesting.
- XML is aiming at the structure of documents and does not impose any common interpretation of the data contained in the document. This is the major limitation of XML: since XML just describes grammars there is no way of recognizing a semantic unit from a particular domain of interest.
- If the files are defined by a DTD or Schema, the files will not be extensible.

In a nutshell, this means that XML is very suitable for data interchange between applications that both know about what the data is, but not in situations where the addition of new communication partners occurs frequently.

XML Schema

An XML schema describes the structure of XML document, typically expressed in terms of constraints on the structure and content of documents of that type, above and beyond the basic syntactical constraints imposed by XML itself. An XML schema provides high level of abstraction to the view of the document. Different languages are developed to describe XML schema like DTD (Document Type Definition) etc. Two other very popular, more expressive XML schema languages are XML Schema (W3C) and RELAX NG.

RDF (Resource Description Framework)

The limitations of relationship associated with the XML are overcome by RDF. XML describes the *syntax* and RDF describes the *semantic*.

- Syntax: the structure of your data
- Semantics: the meaning of your data

Syntax being the science of how signs can be put together to create sentences. *Semantics* being how these signs relate to the world so that one can give the sentence a truth value.

Lets take the above sentence i.e

Shikha Singh teaches computer science.

The above sentence is referring to three things. One person named *Shikha Singh*, second course named *computer science* and the relationship between them i.e teaches. There are many ways to represent the same relationship i.e you can write in English, French, Spanish Java or in XML. But all of them will be describing the same thing but in different syntax.

As I referred above XML describes the syntax of the document and RDF describes the semantics. So RDF can be written in many ways like RDF/XML, N3, N-Triple or as Turtle.

RDF describes the framework for meta-data of web document. RDF is used to describe relationship between different Entities in the world.

RDF provides information like title, author, modification date, content, and copyright information of a Web page

The RDF data model can be said to have resemblance with entity-relationship diagram. The RDF data model, however, does not provide method for declaring the properties, nor does it provide any mechanisms for defining the relationships between the properties and other resources. That is the role of RDF Schema.

RDFS Schema

For describing any Resource there is requirement to say certain things about certain kinds of resources. For describing bibliographic resources, for example, descriptive attributes including "author", "title", and "subject" are common. For digital certification, attributes such as "checksum" and "authorization" are often required. The declaration of these properties (attributes) and their corresponding semantics are defined in the context of RDF as an *RDF schema.* A schema defines not only the properties of the resource (e.g., title, author, subject, size, color, etc.) but may also define the kinds of resources being described (books, Web pages, people, companies, etc.).

By definition
RDF schema is a semantic extension of RDF. The RDF schema language is used for declaring basic class and types when describing the terms used in RDF and are used to determine characteristics of other resources, such as the domains and ranges of properties.

The 'rdfs' namespace is used here to define core vocabulary, and is identified by the URI reference http://www.w3.org/2000/01/rdf-schema#.This specification also uses the prefix 'rdf' to refer to the core RDF namespace http://www.w3.org/1999/02/22-rdf-syntax-ns#.

RDF/XML

RDF is not designed for being displayed to people XML language used by RDF is called RDF/XML. RDF uses XML to describe metadata so that information can easily be exchanged between different types of computers using different types of operating systems and application languages.

RDF/RDFS allows anyone to write their own name-space document (a 'schema'). This defines properties and classes in some application domain.

These form vocabularies which can be used globally for sharing the meaning of tags

Along with its formal semantics, RDF data structure is effectively modeled using a directed graph. In RDF data model the metadata statements are represented as triples: nodes are used to represent two parts of the triple, and the third part is represented by a directed link that describes the relationship between the nodes. The triples are stored in a logical network.

Triple is defined as (subject, predicate, object) for instance (Shikha Singh, teaches, computer science)

RDF identifies everything as URI(Uniform Resource Identifier) which gives a uniformity in accessing anything on the web. This URI could link to a machine or human readable definition, or the URI could merely serve as a unique identifier with no real link to information content

RDF triple can be taken as (Resource, property, value).

- A Resource is anything that can have a URI, such as "http://www.abc.com/RDF"
- A Property is a Resource that has a name, such as "creator" or "homepage"
- A Property value is the value of a Property, such as "Shikha Singh" or "http://www.abc.com"

Property value can either be literal or another URI.Let's look at some example statements to get a better understanding:
Statement:

"The creator of http://www.abc.com/RDF is Shikha Singh".

· The subject of the statement above is: http://www.abc.com/RDF
· The predicate is: creator
· The object is: Shikha Singh

So here property value is literal(string).

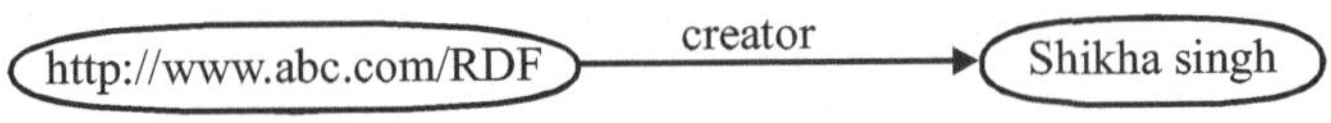

Figure 4 : RDF triple with object as literal value

Statement: "The homepage of http://www.abc.com/RDF is http://www.abc.com".

Ø The subject of the statement above is: http://www.abc.com/RDF
Ø The predicate is: homepage
Ø The object is: **http://www.abc.com**

In the above example the property value is URI.

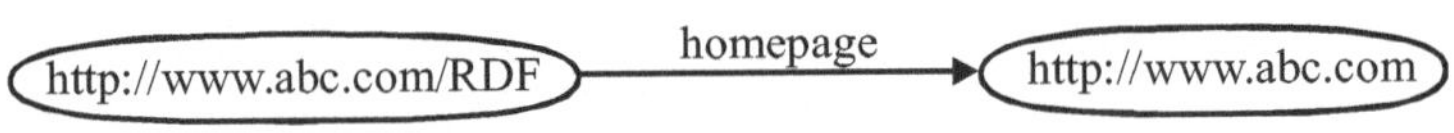

Figure 5: RDF triple with object as URI

Root Element

<rdf:RDF> is the root element of an RDF document. It defines the XML document to be an RDF document. It also contains a reference to the RDF namespace:

Description

rdf:Description is a container for information about a resource identified by the about attribute. In this case each resource is a book, its identification (URI) is its name. Each book has an author and the specified number of pages.

Source (RDF/XML document)

```
<rdf:RDF
   xmlns:rdf="http://www.w3.org/1999/02/22-rdf-
   syntax-ns#"
   xmlns:lib="http://www.zvon.org/library">
 <rdf:Description about="Matilda">
<lib:creator>Roald Dahl</lib:creator>
<lib:pages>240</lib:pages>
 </rdf:Description>
 <rdf:Description about="The BFG">
      <lib:creator>Roald Dahl</lib:creator>
      <lib:pages>208</lib:pages>
 </rdf:Description>

 <rdf:Description about="Heart of Darkness">
      <lib:creator>Joseph Conrad</lib:creator>
      <lib:pages>110</lib:pages>
 </rdf:Description>

 <rdf:Description about="Lord Jim">
      <lib:creator>Joseph Conrad</lib:creator>
      <lib:pages>314</lib:pages>
 </rdf:Description>
<rdf:Description about="The Secret Agent">
  <lib:creator>Joseph Conrad</lib:creator>
  <lib:pages>249</lib:pages>
  </rdf:Description>
 </rdf:RDF>
```

Author	Title	Pages
Roald Dahl	Matilda	240
Roald Dahl	The BFG	208
Joseph Conrad	Heart of Darkness	110
Joseph Conrad	Lord Jim	314
Joseph Conrad	The Secret Agent	249

Table 1 : Output of RDF/XML

Graphical representation of XML and RDF

Lets take the example of xml schema (ABC1)

```
d"Persone"
    d"namee"shikha singhd"/namee"
    d"mboxe"ss@yahoo.comd"/mboxe"
    d"knowse"
        d"Persone"
            d"namee"Deeptid"/namee"
            <mboxe" deepti@yahoo.com
            d"/mboxe"
        d"/Persone"

        d"Persone"
            d"namee"Jonathan Storyd"/namee"
            d"mboxe" Jonathan.Story@eg.edu
            d"/mboxe"
        d"/Persone"
    d"/knowse"
d"/Persone"
```

Next see ABC2 showing additional information

```
d"AddressBooke"
    d"Persone"
        d"namee"Jonathan Storyd"/namee"
        d"mboxe"Jonathan.Story@eg.edud"/mboxe"
        d"addresse"
        d"Countrye"Franced"/Countrye"

        d"/addresse"
    d"/Persone"
    d"Persone"
        d"namee"Tim Brayd"/namee"
        d"mboxe"Tim.Bray@eg.Comd"/mboxe"
        d"addresse"
        d"Countrye"Canadad"/Countrye"
        d"/addresse"
    d"/Persone"
d"/AddressBooke"
```

Now we can have transformed statements of XML into *N3 relations* of ABC1.

[a :Person;
:name "shikha singh";
:mbox d"mailto:ss@yahoo.come";
:knows [a :Person;
:name "Deepti";
:mbox d"mailto:deepti@yahoo.come"
];
:knows [a :Person;
:name "Jonathan Story";
:mbox d"mailto:Jonathan.Story@eg.edue"
];
].

The above relations can be shown as a graph as below.

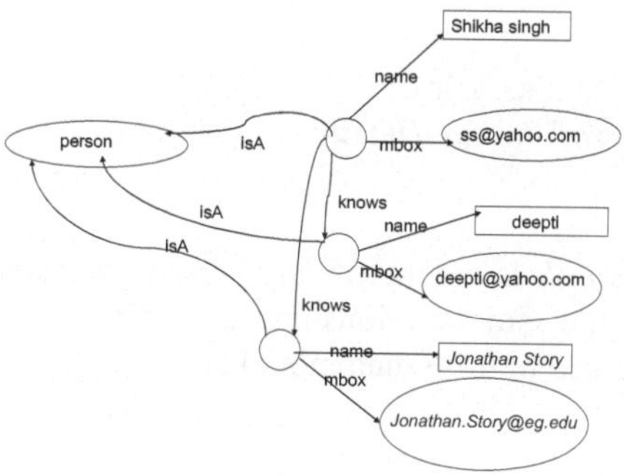

Figure 6: RDF statements of ABC1 schema

Now the ABC2 can be shown as *N3 relation* as below
[a :Person;
:name "Tim Bray";
:mbox d"mailto:Tim.Bray@eg.come"
:address [a :Address;
:country "Canada"@en
]]
[a :Person;
:name "Jonathan Story";
:mbox d"mailto:Jonathan.Story@eg.edue"
:address [a :Address;
:country "France"@en

]

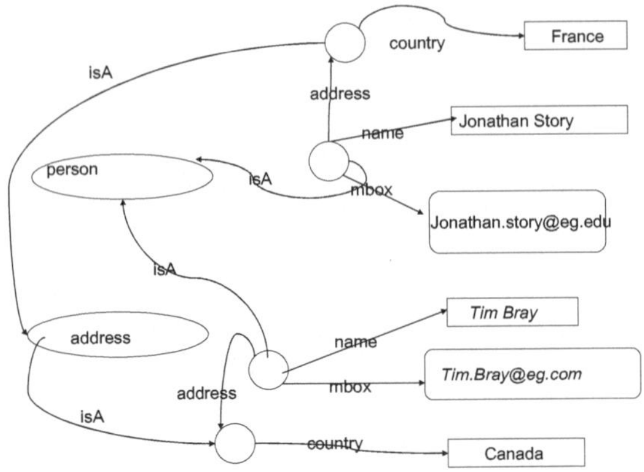

Figure 7:RDF triple graph of ABC2

RDF data Model

Now lets take the statement as below:
Shikha singh is teacherof Rahul Thakur.

RDF statement is
http://www.abc.com/s.singh is teacherof *http://www.abc.com/r.thakur.*
both statements shows the same relationship but in different manner. The above statement can be expressed in RDF data model as

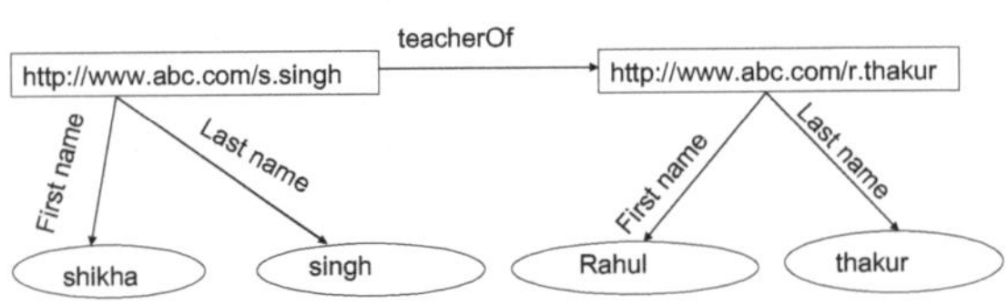

Figure 8: RDF data Model

Here in above example statement shows subject and predicate both are having properties as *first name* and *last name* with literal values .

Layered structure of RDFS

The RDF data model can be transformed in layered structure of RDFS and its namespace. As I have mentioned earlier that RDFS specifies the schema for RDF and it also specifies classes and properties to be used in RDF modeling. So using those classes and properties , the above example can be shown as a layered structure.

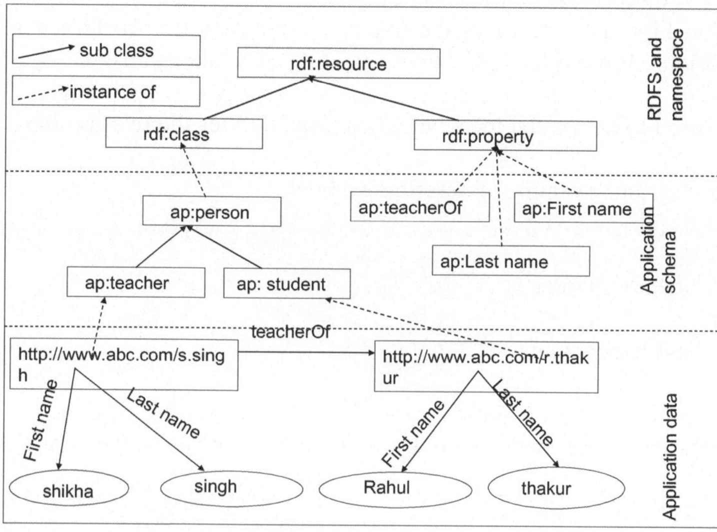

Figure 9: RDF model and RDFS structure

Again the RDF is having certain limitations in terms of vocabulary for specifying the metadata and their relationships, which is overcome by introduction of *Ontology.*

Ontology

The term ontology has different meaning in different terms.

In general ontology represents an idea or concept. It is a kind of model depicting a concept. Ontology is knowledge representation showing model consists of properties and relationship.

In philosophy , ontology is defined as metaphysics, which deals with the nature of reality-of what exists.

In computer science ontology is a conventional representation of a set of concepts within a domain and the relationships between those concepts. Ontology provides hierarchical structure of concepts.

An 'Ontology' is an agreed on, shared, common understanding of a domain written as an explicit, formal specification.

Ontology is defined as classification of things. It bequeath a better organisations of relationships. It categorises the object or things in the world according to specifications. It provides better understanding of relationships.

As RDF used to define the metadata , Ontology defines the relationships.

Lets take the same example of describing a book.

Book
    hasPart chapter
Chapter
    hasElement page
Page
    hasElement paragraph
So the information regarding a book can be represented as above or as below.
book
hasTitle text
hasDescription text
    hasSubject descriptor
    hasDatePublished date

These are the simplest way of writing the ontologies.
Basics components of Ontology in any field are:

- Ø *Classes*
- Ø *Attributes*
- Ø *Relationships*
- Ø *Rules*
- Ø *Restrictions*
- Ø *Axioms*

Classes *can be expressed as domain of the problem or we can say it specify the kind of thing, or collection of objects etc.*

Attribute *are used to represent set of properties which a thing poses or characteristics.*

Relationship *shows the link between classes or individuals or it describes how classes are related to each other.*

***Rules** define the logical inferences that can be taken from an assertion.*

***Restriction** specifies the conditions under which a statement can be true.*

***Axioms** defined the logical form of assertions.*
There are two "kinds" of ontology: representation ontology (axiomatization of basic operations used in many applications) and application ontology which are domain specific.

OWL (Web Ontology Language)

W3 has endorsed a language to define ontologies and is called as OWL.OWL is mainly based on two semantics: OWL DL and OWL Lite semantics are based on Description Logics, which have attractive and well-understood computational properties, while OWL Full uses a novel semantic model intended to provide compatibility with RDF Schema. OWL ontologies are most commonly serialized using RDF/XML syntax. OWL is considered one of the fundamental technologies underpinning the Semantic Web, and has attracted both academic and commercial interest.

Structure of Semantic Web

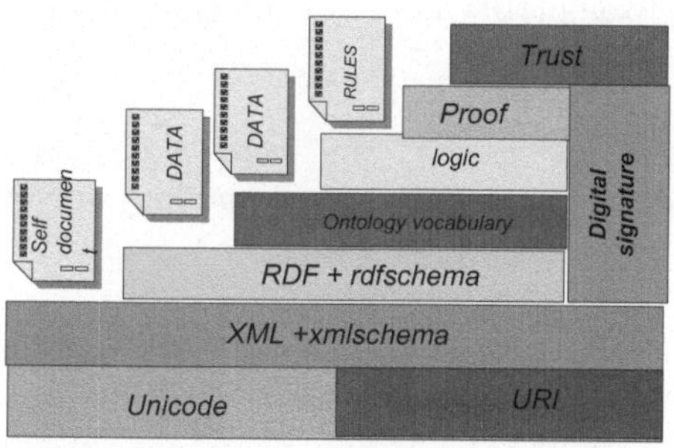

Figure 10: Semantic Architecture in Layer

The upper layers are:

Logic Layer: creates new pieces of knowledge information by applying assertions to existing web data.

Proof Layer: validates information so that it can be accredited. Ontologies will be retrieved from the Semantic Web and processed locally to create and provide proofs for other machine processes in the Semantic Web.

Trust Layer: Digital signatures will have to be applied to all layers from the RDF Layer up to the Proof Layer, validating the results of each component. This is the reason why the Semantic Web also has the Web of Trust moniker.

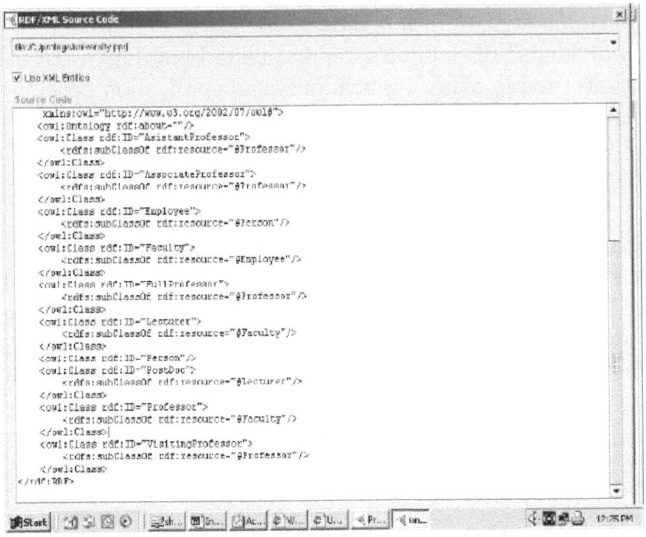

Figure 11: Example of Ontology written in OWL/RDF format

Related Work

All ready study conducted on comparison of ontology and other formalism and which describe as

1. *Ontologies vs. XML Schema*: In general, XML Schema is proposed as a mechanism to define the syntax for XML documents.

   Because data can be encoded in different ways using XML, this allow parties to agree on a defined structure and labeling for the exchange of data [12]. While XML Schemas define the structure of the document, they do not define any meaning. Ontologies on the other hand are formalized in a way that limits possible interpretations. In particular, on the basis of possible interpretations, an OWL-aware tool can tell that two classes or individuals are equivalent or different. While XML and XML-Schema have strength in exchanging data, ontologies are used to exchange information.

2) *Ontologies vs. Database Schema*: Database schemas can be distinguished into the conceptual and the physical Schema and logical schema. The physical

schema results from the mapping of the conceptual schema to physical storage objects—e.g. tables of a relational database. In particular, a conceptual database schema mostly reflects only a single or a limited viewpoint— namely that of its creators. When requirements change, the viewpoint and the schema respectively need to be modified.

Ontologies in general are required to be shared, that is, reflect multiple viewpoints (domain ontologies in particular).

A domain ontology does not need to be modified to meet changes in requirements but can be flexibly used to model any data requirements related to a particular domain. An important distinction between ontologies and database schemas is their behavior at runtime. After being translated to physical tables, the ontology is also available for retrieval and inferencing of new facts at runtime. The ontology can potentially increase semantic interoperability not only of the resources exchanged among systems but also of the data stored in physical databases. For instance, the formal descriptions of two differently labeled concepts may yield the same interpretations and so the corresponding tables can be inferred as containing semantically the same data despite the different table names. Therefore, when queries are formulated using ontology concepts, they can be processed also by external systems that may use different labels for the elements of the physical schema.

Information Retrieval in Semantic web

Different techniques are being used to extract data from semantic web. As data is stored in many forms like XML and RDF or in the form of RDBMS etc. in semantic web. Here I am discussing about two languages for IR i.e XQuery and SPARQL which have already developed.

A query language that uses the structure of XML intelligently can express queries across all these kinds of data, whether physically stored in XML or viewed as XML via middleware. This specification describes a query language called XQuery, which is designed to be broadly applicable across many types of XML data sources. The SPARQL Protocol and RDF Query Language (SPARQL) is a query language and protocol for RDF. XQuery is a language to query a document, SPARQL is a tool to query the world.

An XQuery can only query one document. RDF helps you to extract the content of many documents, as a set of facts, drop them in one big container, and query that container in one go, essentially allowing one to make relations between facts stated in different documents. This is the fundamental difference between these two technologies, and why they are both needed.

Relational OWL

Currently all databases are based on relational theory, so there is need arises to develop a relational OWL for the semantic web so as to relate current web databases with futuristic semantic database. So relational OWL have been developed.

Relational OWL is a Semantic Web-based representation format for relational data and schema components, which is particularly appropriate for exchanging items among remote database systems or to expose relational data on the Semantic Web. OWL, originally created for the Semantic Web enables us to represent not only the relational data itself, but also a part of its interpretation, i.e. knowledge about its format, its origin, its usage, or its original embedment in specific frameworks.So formulation of relational OWL from current RDBMs will be like this statement as given below.
Database has tables.
Tables has columns.
Tables are identified by primary key.
Foreigne key refer to primary key of another table.

So graphical representation of this kind of Ontology is relational OWL.Jena toolkit is being used for the development of such OWL.

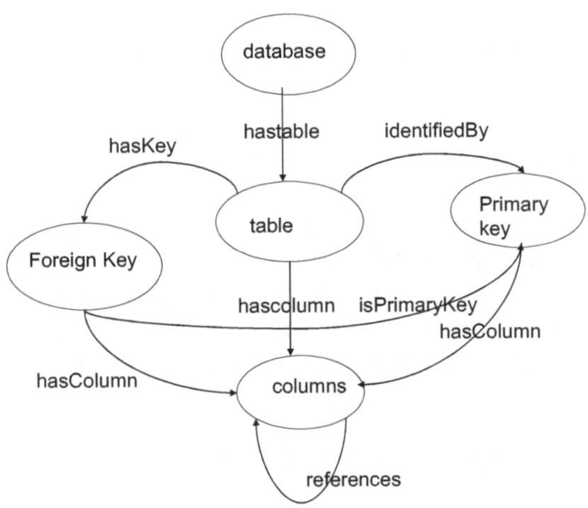

Figure 12: Relational OWL of RDBMS

Jena is based on java and uses JDBC for database connectivity. It converts the relational RDF/OWL into RDBMS and also convert data extracted from RDBMS into relational RDF/ OWL representation.

Discussion and Future Work

In this paper I have discussed about a new age of web and that is semantic web. So how transformation has been taking palce from HTML to OWL. Here I have discussed various KR of data in semantic web and how current database can be connected with the futuristic semantic web. As semantic web is the future web , which will provide meaningful information without wastage of time. I have discussed already developed query language for semantic search .My future work will be based on development of query language for joining of multiple ontologies and implementation of RDBMS concepts of constraints etc.

References

- T. Berners-Lee, J. Hendler, and O. Lassila, "The semantic web," Scientific American, vol. 284, no. 5, pp. 34–43, 2001.
- X. Lopez and S. Stephens, "Semantic Data Integration for the Enterprise," March 2006. [Online].Available: "http://www.oracle.com/technology/tech/ semantic technologies/pdf/semantic grid wp 0603.pdf"
- G. Schreiber, H. Akkermans, A. Anjewierden, R. de Hoog, N. Shadbolt,W. V. de Velde, and B. Wielinga, Knowledge Engineering and Management: The CommonKADS Methodology. MITpress, 2000.
- M. A. Musen, "Domain ontologies in software engineering: Use of prot´eg´e with the EON architecture," Methods of Information in Medicine, vol. 37, pp. 540–550, 1998.
- O´Corcho, A. Go´mez-Pe´rez, M. Ferna´ndez-Lo´pez, and M. Lama, "ODE-SWS: A semantic web service development environment," in Proceedings of SWDB'03, The first International Workshop on SemanticWeb and Database, I. F. Cruz, V. Kashyap, S. Decker, and R. Eckstein, Eds., 2003, pp. 203–216.
- A. Haller, E. Cimpian, A. Mocan, E. Oren, and C. Bussler, "WSMX - A semantic service-oriented architecture," in ICWS. IEEE Computer Society, 2005, pp. 321–328.
- H. Knublauch, "Ontology-Driven Software Development in the Context of the Semantic Web: An Example Scenario with Protege/OWL," 1st International Workshop on the Model-Driven Semantic Web (MDSW2004),2004.
- M. Brodie, C. Bussler, J. de Brujin, T. Fahringer, D. Fensel, M. Hepp,H. Lausen, D. Roman, T. Strang, H. Werthner, et al., "Semantically Enabled Service

Oriented Architectures: A Manifesto and a Paradigm Shift in Computer Science," DERI TR-2005-12-26, Tech. Rep., 2005.

- T. R. Gruber, "A translation approach to portable ontology specifications,"Knowledge Acquisition, vol. 5, no. 2, pp. 199–220, 1993.
- M. Uschold and M. Gr¨uninger, "Ontologies and semantics for seamless connectivity," SIGMOD Record, vol. 33, no. 4, pp. 58–64, 2004.
- M. Dean and G. Schreiber, "OWL Web Ontology Language Reference. W3C Recommendation," World Wide Web Consortium (2004) Latest version: http:/ /www. w3. org/TR/owl-ref, vol. 7.
- "XML schema part 1: Structures, W3C recommendation," W3Consortium, May 2001. [Online].Available: http://www.w3c.org/TR/xmlschema-1/
- N. Shadbolt, T. Berners-Lee, and W. Hall, "The semantic web revisited," IEEE Intelligent Systems, vol. 21, no. 3, pp. 96–101, 2006.
- K. Wolstencroft, P. Lord, L. Tabernero, A. Brass, and R. Stevens, "Protein classification using ontology classification," in ISMB (Supplement of Bioinformatics), 2006, pp. 530–538.
- I. Singh, B. Stearns, and M. Johnson, Designing Enterprise Applications with the J2EE Platform, Second Edition. Addison- Wesley Professional, June 2002. [Online]. Available: http://java.sun.com/blueprints/guidelines/designing enterprise applications 2e/titlepage.html
- D. Riehle, M. Tilman, and R. Johnson, "Dynamic Object Model,"Proceedings of PLoP2000. Technical Report# wucs-00-29, Dept. of Computer Science, Washington University Department of Computer Science, October, 2000.
- M. Volkel and Y. Sure, "RDFReactor-from ontologies to programmatic data access," Proceedings of the International Semantic Web Conference- Demo Session, Galway, Ireland, NOV, 2005.
- I. Horrocks, P. Patel-Schneider, H. Boley, S. Tabet, B. Grosof, and M. Dean, "SWRL: A Semantic Web Rule Language Combining OWL and RuleML," W3C Member Submission, vol. 21, 2004.
- B. Motik and U. Sattler, "A Comparison of Reasoning Techniques for Querying Large Description Logic ABoxes," Proc. of the 13th International Conference on Logic for Programming Artificial Intelligence and Reasoning (LPAR 2006), Phnom Penh, Cambodia, November, 2006.
- T. Tran, P. Cimiano, and A. Ankolekar, "Rules for an Ontologybased Approach to Adaptation," in Proceedings of the 1st International Workshop on Semantic Media Adaptation and Personalization, Athen,Greece, 2006.
- "The Semantic Web - on the respective Roles of XML and RDF" Stefan Decker, Frank van Harmelen , Jeen Broekstra Michael Erdmann, Dieter Fensel, Ian Horrocks, Michel Klein, Sergey Melnik

- ”SPARQL Protocol for RDF “ Kendall Grant Clark , Lee Feigenbaum W3C Recommendation 15January2008 http://www.w3.org/TR/2008/REC-rdf-sparql-protocol-20080115/
- RelationalOWL - A Data and Schema Representation Format Based on OWL; Cristian Pérez de Laborda and Stefan Conrad;Conceptual Modelling 2005, Second Asia-Pacific Conference on Conceptual Modelling (APCCM2005); pp 89-96
- Querying Relational Databases with RDQL; Cristian Pérez de Laborda and Stefan Conrad; Berliner XML Tage 2005; pp 161-172
- Semantic Web Activities at the Databases and Information Systems Group D?orf - http://www.dbs.cs.uni-duesseldorf.de/RDF/
- Jena ? A Semantic Web Framework for Java - http://jena.sourceforge.net/
- “Relational.OWL - v 0.1 beta” http://dbs.cs.uni-duesseldorf.de/RDF/docs/ROWLApp/

Grid Security Architecture

Kamlesh Rana
Lecturer, VIPS, Delhi

Abstract
State-of-the-art and emerging scientific applications requirement access to large quantities of data and commensurately fast computational resources. Both resources and data are often distributed in a wide-area network with components administered locally and independently. Computations may involve hundreds of processes that must be able to acquire re- sources dynamically and communicate efficiently. This paper analyzes the unique security requirements of large-scale distributed (grid) computing and develops a security policy and corresponding security architecture. An implementation of the architecture within the Globus metacomputing toolkit is discussed.

Keywords: Grid Security Problem, Security Requirements, Grid Security Architecture, Implementation

Introduction

Ready access to large amounts of computing power has been a persistent goal of computer scientists for decades. Since the 1960s visions of computing utilities as pervasive and as simple as the telephone have driven users and system designers. It was recognized in the 1970s that such power could be achieved inexpensively with collections of small devices rather than expensive single supercomputers. Interest in schemes for managing distributed processors became so popular that there was even once a minor controversy over the meaning of the word distributed." As this early work made it clear that distributed computing was feasible, researchers began to take notice that distributed computing would be difficult. When messages may be lost, corrupted, or delayed, robust algorithms must be used in order to build a coherent system. Such lessons were not lost on the system designers of the early 1980s. Production systems such as Locus and Grapevine wrestled with the fundamental tension between consistency, availability, and performance in distributed systems. In summary, this paper makes four contributions to our understanding of distributed system security:

1) It provides an in-depth analysis of the security problem in computational grid systems and applications.
2) It includes the first detailed formulation of a security policy for grid systems.
3) It proposes solutions to specific technical issues raised by this policy, including local heterogeneity and scalability.

4) It describes a security architecture that uses these solutions to implement the security policy, and it demonstrates via large-scale deployment that this architecture is workable.

Grid Security Problem

We introduce the grid security problem with an example illustrated in Figure 1. This example, although somewhat contrived, captures important elements of real applications. We imagine a scientist, a member of a multi-institutional scientific collaboration, who receives e-mail from a colleague regarding a new data set. He starts an analysis program, which dispatches code to the remote location where the data is stored (at site C).

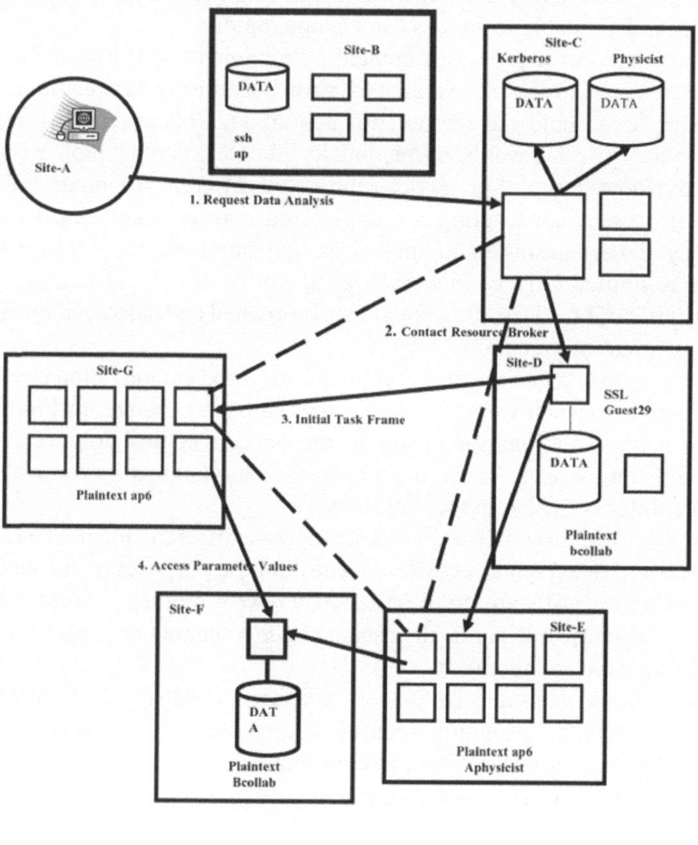

Figure 1: Example of a Large-scale distributed Computation

Once started, the analysis program determines that it needs to run a simulation in order to compare the experimental results with predictions. Hence, it contacts a resource broker service maintained by the collaboration (at site D), in order to locate idle resources that can be used for the simulation. The resource broker in turn initiates computation on computers at two sites (E and G). These computers access parameter values stored on a file system at yet another site (F) and also communicate among themselves (perhaps using specialized protocols, such as multicast) and with the broker, the original site, and the user. This example illustrates many of the distinctive characteristics of the grid computing environment:

1) The user population is large and dynamic. Participants in such virtual organizations as this scientific collaboration will include members of many institutions and will change frequently.
2) The resource pool is large and dynamic. Because individual institutions and users decide whether and when to contribute resources, the quantity and location of available resources can change rapidly.
3) A computation (or processes created by a computation) may acquire, start processes on, and release resources dynamically during its execution. Even in our simple example, the computation acquired (and later released) resources at five sites. In other words, throughout its lifetime, a computation is composed of a dynamic group of processes running on different resources and sites.
4) The processes constituting a computation may communicate by using a variety of mechanisms, including unicast and multicast. While these processes form a single, fully connected logical entity, low-level communication connections (e.g., TCP/IP sockets) may be created and destroyed dynamically during program execution.
5) Resources may require different authentication and authorization mechanisms and policies, which we will have limited ability to change. In Figure 1, we indicate this situation by showing the local access control policies that apply at the different sites. These include Kerberos, plaintext passwords, Secure Socket Library (SSL), and secure shell.
6) An individual user will be associated with different local name spaces, credentials, or accounts, at different sites, for the purposes of accounting and access control. At some sites, a user may have a regular account. At others, the user may use a dynamically assigned guest account or simply an account created for the collaboration.
7) Resources and users may be located in different countries. To summarize, the problem we face is providing security solutions that can allow computations, such as the one just described, to coordinate diverse access control policies and to operate securely in heterogeneous environments.

Security Requirements

Grid systems and applications may require any or all of the standard security functions, including authentication, access control, integrity, privacy, and no repudiation. In this paper, we focus primarily on issues of authentication and access control. Specifically, we seek to

1) Provide authentication solutions that allow a user, the processes that comprise a user's computation, and the resources used by those processes, to verify each other's identity; and
2) Allow local access control mechanisms to be applied without change, whenever possible. As will be discussed in Section 4, authentication forms the foundation of a security policy that enables diverse local security policies to be integrated into a global framework. In developing a security architecture that meets these requirements, we also choose to satisfy the following constraints derived from the characteristics of the grid environment and grid applications:

Single sign-on

A user should be able to authenticate once (e.g., when starting a computation) and initiate computations that acquire resources, use resources, release resources, and communicate internally, without further authentication of the user.

Protection of credentials

User credentials must be protected. Interoperability with local security solutions: While our security solutions may provide interdomain access mechanisms, access to local resources will typically be determined by a local security policy that is enforced by a local security mechanism. It is impractical to modify every local resource to accommodate interdomain access; instead, one or more entities in a domain must act as agents of remote clients/users for local resources.

Exportability

We require that the code be

1) Exportable and
2) Executable in multinational testbeds. In short, the exportability issues mean that our security policy cannot directly or indirectly require the use of bulk encryption.

Uniform credentials/certification infrastructure

Interdomain access requires, at a minimum, a common way of expressing the identity of a security principal such as an actual user or a resource. Hence, it is imperative to employ a standard (such as X.509v3) for encoding credentials for security principals.

Support for secure group communication.

A computation can comprise a number of processes that will need to coordinate their activities as a group. The composition of a process group can and will change during the lifetime of a computation. Hence, support is needed for secure (in this context, authenticated) communication for dynamic groups. No current security solution supports this feature; even GSS-API has no provisions for group security contexts.

Support for multiple implementations

The security policy should not dictate a specific implementation technology. Rather, it should be possible to implement the security policy with a range of security technologies, based on both public and shared key cryptography.

Grid Security Architecture

In the security policy we can construct specific security architecture. In doing so, we specify the set of subjects and objects that will be under the jurisdiction of the security policy and define the protocols that will govern interactions between these subjects and objects. The following components are depicted: entities, credentials, and protocols. The thick lines represent the protocols described later in the paper. The curved line separating the user from the rest of the figure signifies that the user may disconnect once the user proxy has been created; the dashed lines represent authenticated intercrosses communication. We are interested in computational environments. Consequently, the subjects and objects in our architecture must include those entities from which computation is formed. A computation consists of many processes, with each process acting on behalf of a user. Thus, the subjects are users and processes. The objects in the architecture must include the wide range of resources that are available in a grid environment: computers, data repositories, networks, display devices, and so forth.

Grid computations may grow and shrink dynamically, acquiring resources when required to solve a problem and releasing them when they are no longer needed. Each time a computation obtains a resource, it does so on behalf of a particular user. However, it is frequently impractical for that \user" to interact directly with each such resource for the purposes of authentication: the number of resources involved may be large, or, because some applications may run for extended period of time (i.e., days or weeks), the user may wish to allow a computation to operate without intervention. Hence, we introduce the concept of a *user proxy* that can act on a user's behalf without requiring user intervention

User Proxy Creation Protocol

A user proxy is a session manager process given permission to act on behalf of a user for a limited period of time. The user proxy acts as a stand-in for the user. It has its own credentials, eliminating the need to have the user on-line during a computation and eliminating the need to have the user's credentials available for every security operation. Furthermore, because the lifetime of the proxy is under control of the user and can be limited to the duration of a computation, the consequences of its credentials being compromised are less dire than exposure of the user's credentials. Within the architecture, we also define an entity that represents a resource, serving as the interface between the grid security architecture and the local security architecture.

Recall that a user proxy is an entity within our architecture that acts on behalf of a user. In practice, the user proxy is a special process started by the user which executes on some host local to that user. The main issue in the user proxy creation protocol is the nature of credentials given to the proxy and how the proxy can obtain these credentials. A user could enable a proxy to act on her behalf by giving the proxy the appropriate credentials. The proxy could then use those credentials directly. However, this approach has two significant Disadvantages: it introduces an increased risk of the credentials being compromised and does not allow us to restrict the time duration for which a proxy can act on the user's behalf. Instead, a temporary credential, C_{UP}, is generated for the user proxy; the user indicates her permission by signing this credential with a secret (e.g., private key). C_{UP} includes the validity interval as well as other restrictions imposed by the user, e.g., host names

Resource Allocation Protocol

In discussing resource allocation, we decompose the problem into two classes: allocation of resources by a user proxy and allocation of resources by a process. As process allocation is a generalization of user proxy allocation, we will start our discussion with allocation by a user proxy. Recall that operations on resources are controlled by an entity, called a *resource proxy*, which is responsible for scheduling access to a resource and for mapping a computation onto that resource. The resource proxy is used as follows. A user proxy requiring access to a resource first determines the identity of the resource proxy for that resource. It then issues a request to the appropriate resource proxy. If the request is successful, the resource is allocated and a process created on that resource. (The procedure would be similar if our goal was simply to allocate a resource, such as network or storage, with which no process was to be associated. However, for brevity, we assume here that process creation always follows resource allocation.)

Resource Allocation from a Process Protocol

While resource allocation from a user proxy is necessary to start a computation, the more common case is that resource allocation will be initiated dynamically from a process created via a previous resource allocation request. It defines the process by which this can be accomplished.

1) The process and its user proxy authenticate each other using C_P and C_{UP}.
2) The process issues a signed request to its user proxy, with the form S_{igP} {"allocate", *allocation request parameters}*
3) If the user proxy decides to honor the request, it initiates a resource allocation request to the specified resource proxy using Protocol
4) The resulting process handle is signed by the user proxy and returned to the requesting process.

Mapping Registration Protocol

A central component of the security policy and the resulting architecture is the existence of a \correct" mapping between a global subject and a corresponding local subject. We achieve this conversion from a global name into a local name (e.g., login name or user ID) by accessing a *mapping table* maintained by the resource proxy. While a mapping table can be created by the local system administrator, this approach imposes a certain administrative burden and introduces the possibility for error.1 hence; we have developed a technique that allows a mapping to be added by a user.

The basic idea behind this technique, presented as Protocol, is for a user to prove that he holds credentials for both a global and local subject. This is accomplished by authenticating both globally and directly to the resource using the local authentication method. The user then asserts a mapping between global and local credentials. The assertion is coordinated through the resource proxy, since it is in a position to accept both global and local credentials. In the first two steps, we show the different activities performed by user as it authenticates globally and to the resource

An Implementation of the Grid Security Architecture

In this section, we describe the Globus Security Infrastructure (GSI), an implementation of our proposed grid security architecture. GSI was developed as part of the Globus project, whose focus is to

1) Understand the basic infrastructure required to support the execution of wide range of computational grid applications,

2) Build prototype implementations of this infrastructure, and evaluate applications on large-scale testbeds. As specified by our security architecture, GSI provides support for user proxies, resource proxies (the Globus resource allocation manager (GRAM) , certification authorities, and implementations of the protocols described above. We describe here selected aspects of this implementation, focusing on our use of the Generic Security Services application programming interface (GSS-API), the Secure Socket Layer (SSL), and our experiences deploying the implementation in a large testbed.

Use of the Generic Security Services Application Programming Interface

The protocols defined above are expressed in terms of abstract security operations, such as signature and authentication, rather than in terms of specific security technologies, such as DES or RSA. Hence, these protocols can be implemented by using any of a number of modern security technologies and mechanisms, such as shared secrets and tickets, public key cryptography or smart-cards. This separation of protocol and mechanism is a desirable property in an implementation as well, since it enhances the overall portability and flexibility of the resulting system. To

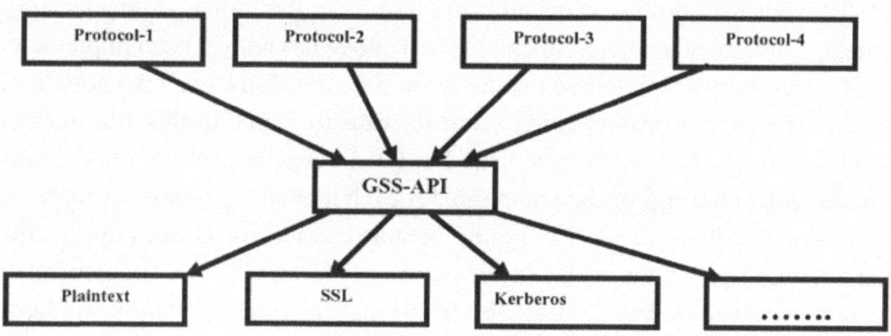

Figure 2: Use of GGS-API

Supports for Public Key Technology in GSI

The GSI implementation currently uses the authentication protocols defined by the Secure Socket Library (SSL) protocol [10]. At first glance, this may seem like an odd choice, since SSL defines a communication layer while GSS explicitly does not. However, in principle, it is possible to separate the authentication and communication components of SSL. To avoid confusion between the SSL authentication protocol and the SSL communication library, we use the term *SSL Authentication Protocol* or SAP to refer specifically to the authentication elements of SSL. We refer to our GSS implementation using SAP as GSS/SAP. The use of SAP was motivated by several factors.

First, there exists a high-quality, public-domain implementation of the SSL protocol (SSLeay), developed outside of the United States and hence avoiding export control issues. Second, SSLeay is structured in a way that allows a token stream to be extracted easily, thus making the GSS implementation straightforward. Third, SSL is widely adopted as the method of choice for authentication and secure communication for a broad range of distributed services, including HTTP servers, Web browsers, and directory services. By combining GSS/SAP with TCP sockets, we can, in fact, reconstitute the entire SSL protocol. Consequently, a computation can use GSI to access not only Globus services, but also generic Web services.

Deployment

GSI has been deployed in GUSTO, a grid testbed spanning some 20 sites in four countries. GUSTO includes NSF supercomputer centers, DOE laboratories, DoD resource centers, NASA laboratories, universities, and companies. The initial deployment in late 1997 was limited to the password implementation of GSI and involved installation of the GRAM resource proxy described previously and the establishment of a globus maps file that describes the global to-local mapping applicable at a particular site. Since Protocol above has not yet been implemented, this file is currently maintained manually by site administrators. (We note that, in practice, site administrators often seem to want to maintain this file manually, using it as a form of access control list.) The GRAM resource proxy runs as root so as to implement the appropriate mapping for each incoming request. As mentioned earlier, GSS/SAP is intended to be the default method for Globus applications. After obtaining export approval and license in early 1998, GSS/SAP implementation has been deployed on a wide-scale (both national and international) basis starting in spring 1998. The password implementation is no longer in production use. We are also operating a Globus certification authority to support certificate generation for users and resources. To date, resource proxies have been developed that provide

Gateways to local Kerberos and cleartext/rsh authentication mechanisms.
in this paper are workable. Particularly interesting in this regard is the experience of installing resource proxies at various sites. Because it runs as root, resource proxy code was subject to careful review by security administrators at different sites. The result to date has been unanimous approval

Conclusions

We have described security architecture for large-scale distributed computations. This architecture is immediately useful and, in addition, provides a firm foundation for investigations of more sophisticated mechanisms. We have also described an implementation of this architecture; this implementation has been deployed on a national-scale testbed. Our architecture and implementation address most of the requirements introduced in Section 3. The introduction of a user proxy addresses the single sign-on requirement and also avoids the need to communicate user credentials. The resource proxy enables interoperability with local security solutions, as the resource proxy can translate between interdomain and intradomain security solutions. Because encryption is not used within the associated protocols, export control issues and hence international use are simplified. Within the implementation, the use of GSS-API provides for portability. Group communication is one major requirement not addressed.

References

- E. Belani, A. Vahdat, T. Anderson, and M. Dahlin. The CRISIS wide area security architecture. In UsenixSecurity Symposium, January 1998.
- C. Catlett and L. Smarr. Metacomputing. Communi- cations of the ACM.
- I. Foster and C. Kesselman. The Globus project: A progress report. In Heterogeneous Computing Work- shop, March 1998.
- I. Foster, C. Kesselman, and S. Tuecke. The Nexus approach to integrating multithreading and communication. Journal of Parallel and Distributed Computing.

Security of MANET from Black Hole Attack in AODV Protocol

Ranjan Jakhar
Lecturer, DMIET, Sonipat

Abstract

A mobile ad hoc network (MANET) is a spontaneous network that can be established with no fixed infrastructure. This means that all its nodes behave as routers and take part in its discovery and maintenance of routes to other nodes in the network. A number of routing protocols like Ad Hoc On-Demand Distance Vector (AODV) routing, Dynamic Source Routing (DSR), Destination–Sequenced Distance Vector(DSDV) and temporarily Ordered Routing Algorithm (TORA) have been implemented. AODV is a prominent On Demand reactive routing protocol for mobile ad hoc networks .But in existing AODV there is no security provision against a well known "Black Hole" attack. In a black hole attack, a malicious node impersonates a destination node by sending a spoofed route reply packet to a source node that initiates a route discovery. By doing this, the malicious node can deprive the traffic from the source node. The encryption and authentication solutions, which are considered as the first line of defense, are no longer sufficient to protect MANETs. Therefore, Intrusion Detection Systems (IDSs) are needed to protect the network from such security problems. Many of the current IDSs for MANETS based on the Watchdog technique. This paper proposes a watchdog and Pathrater mechanism to detect the black hole attack and avoids routing packets through these nodes

Keywords : *Ad hoc Networks, Routing Protocols, AODV, Black Hole Attack.*

Introduction

This paper discusses a new approach to avoid ''Black-Hole" attack in a MANET, including information of MANET, Routing protocols in MANET, AODV, Security Attacks and new mechanism.

Mobile adhoc networks are being widely deployed currently since they provide some features, which are difficult or impossible to be achieved by conventional networks. The application area ranges from the battlefield (sensor nodes in hostile territory) to general transportation that provide useful infrastructure during disaster recovery. Due to the great importance of MANET, security in ad hoc networks is a hot research area and already significant research is done in this field. The use of wireless links in an ad hoc network generates the possibility of link attacks from passive eavesdropping to active impersonation, message replay and message distortion. Eavesdropping might give an attacker access to secret information thus violating confidentiality. Active attacks could be ranged from deleting data, injecting erroneous messages, impersonating a node etc. thus violating availability, integrity, authentication and non-repudiation.

Research carried out till present day provided us either general or their routing solutions are incomplete and inefficient. This inefficiency motivated us to take this as challenge to integrators a better security solution into the existing AODV routing protocol to satisfy the security needs of the ad hoc networks.

Problem Definition

There are basically four routing protocol AODV, DSR, DSDV, and TORA in mobile ad hoc network. However from the beginning of its design, almost none of the protocol specifies the security measures, but the nature of the wireless ad hoc network makes them vulnerable to malicious attacks as compared to traditional wired networks. An attack occurs when an intruder tries to exploit vulnerabilities of a system. This paper is focusing on special active-black hole attack. Black hole attack can occur when one of node on path directly attacks the data traffic intentionally by dropping the data traffic passing through it, so that network performance degraded tremendously against this type of attack.

What is MANET?

As the importance of computers in our daily life increases it also sets new demands for connectivity. Wired solutions have been around for a long time but there is increasing demand on working wireless solutions for connecting to the Internet, reading and sending E-mail messages, changing information in a meeting and so on. There are solutions to these needs, one being wireless local area network that is based on IEEE 802.11 standard. However, there is increasing need for connectivity in situations where there is no base station (i.e. backbone connection) available (for example two or more PDAs need to be connected). This is where ad hoc networks step in. In Latin, ad hoc means "for this," further meaning "for this purpose only." It is a good and emblematic description of the idea why ad hoc networks are needed. They can be set up anywhere without any need for external infrastructure (like wires or base stations). They are often mobile and that's why a term MANET is often used when talking about Mobile Ad hoc NETworks. MANETs are often defined as follows: A "mobile ad hoc network" (MANET) is an autonomous system of mobile routers (and associated hosts) connected by wireless links – the union of which forms an arbitrary graph. The routers are free to move randomly and organize themselves arbitrarily; thus, the network's wireless topology may change rapidly and unpredictably. Such a network may operate in a standalone fashion, or may be connected to the larger Internet.

The strength of the connection can change rapidly in time or even disappear completely. Nodes can appear, disappear and re-appear as the time goes on and all the time the network connections should work between the nodes that are part of it. As one can easily imagine, the situation in ad hoc networks with respect to ensuring connectivity and robustness is much more demanding than in the wired case.Ad hoc networks are networks are not (necessarily) connected to any static (i.e. wired) infrastructure. An ad-hoc network is a LAN or other small network, especially one with wireless connections, in which some of the network devices are part of the network only for the duration of a communications session or, in the case of mobile or portable devices, while in some close proximity to the rest of the network.

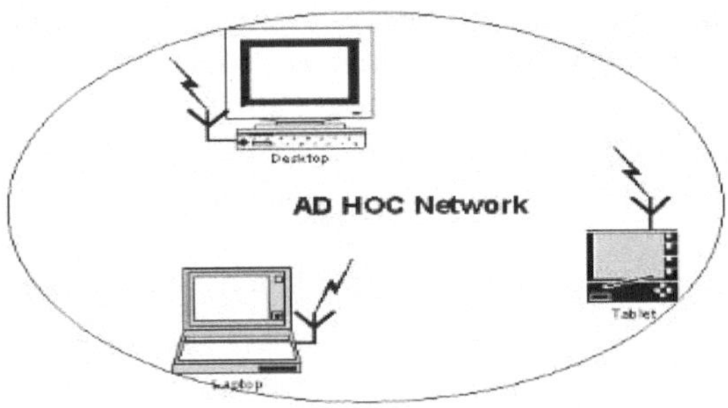

Figure 1: Ad Hoc Network

The ad hoc network (Figure-1) is a communication network without a pre-exist network infrastructure. In cellular networks, there is a network infrastructure represented by the base-stations, Radio network controllers, etc. In ad hoc networks every communication terminal (or radio terminal RT) communicates with its partner to perform peer to peer communication. If the required RT is not a neighbour to the initiated call RT (outside the coverage area of the RT), then the other intermediate RTs are used to perform the communication link. This is called multi-hope peer to peer communication. This collaboration between the RTs is very important in the ad hoc networks. In ad hoc networks all the communication network protocols should be distributed throughout the communication terminals (i.e. the communication terminals should be independent and highly cooperative).

Characteristics

Mobile Adhoc Network (MANET) is a collection of independent mobile nodes that can communicate to each other via radio waves. The mobile nodes that are in radio range of each other can directly communicate, whereas others needs the aid of intermediate nodes to route their packets. These networks are fully distributed, and can work at any place without the help of any infrastructure. This property makes these networks highly exible and robost.

The characteristics of these networks are summarized as follows:

- Communication via wireless means.
- Nodes can perform the roles of both hosts and routers.
- No centralized controller and infrastructure. Intrinsic mutual trust.
- Dynamic network topology. Frequent routing updates.
- Autonomous, no infrastructure needed.
- Can be set up anywhere.
- Energy constraints
- Limited security

Application Areas

Some of the applications of MANETs are

- Military or police exercises.
- Disaster relief operations.
- Mine site operations.
- Urgent Business meetings
- Robot data acquisition

Security Problems in Manets

MANETs are much more vulnerable to attack than wired network. This is because of the following reasons:

Open Medium - Eavesdropping is more easier than in wired network.

Dynamically Changing Network Topology - Mobile Nodes comes and goes from the network, thereby allowing any malicious node to join the network without being detected.

Cooperative Algorithms - The routing algorithm of MANETs requires mutual trust between nodes which violates the principles of Network Security.

Lack of Centralized Monitoring - Absence of any centralized infrastructure prohibits any monitoring agent in the system.

Lack of Clear Line of Defense - The only use of I line of defense - attack prevention may not su ce. Experience of security research in wired world has taught us that we need to deploy layered security mechanisms because security is a process that is as secure as its weakest link . In addition to pre-vention, we need II line of defense - detection and response.

Security Issues in Manets

Vulnerabilities of operating systems and upper layer applications that belong to user programs such as databases, browsers or client-server applications are not considered as a security issue for ad-hoc networks. General attack types are the threats against the routing layer of the ad-hoc networks; such as physical, MAC and network layer which is the most important function of wireless ad-hoc network for the routing mechanism, orienting the packets after a route discovery process. Other vulnerabilities are application security, network security, database security which are studied in different works which are not explained in detail here. Attacks to the wireless ad-hoc network in the networking layer usually have two purposes: not forwarding packets or adding and changing some parameters of routing messages; such as sequence number and IP addresses. These will be detailed in the subsequent sections. Using one of the key mechanisms such as cryptography or authentication, or both in a network, serves as a preventive approach and can be employed against '*attackers*'. However, these mechanisms protect the network against attacks that come from outside, malicious '*insiders*' which use one of the critical keys can also threaten the security. For instance, in a battle field where ad-hoc networks are used, even if keys

are protected by temper proof hardware that are used in the vehicles in the network, it is difficult to say that these vehicles exhibit the same behavior if the enemy captures them. On the other hand, a node may undeliberately misbehave as if it is damaged. A node with a failed battery which is unable to perform network operations may be perceived as an attack. Another malicious behavior of the nodes is selfishness. Selfish nodes refrain from consuming its resources; such as battery, by not participating in network operations. Therefore; failed and selfish nodes also affect the network performance as they do not correctly process network packets, such as in routing mechanism. We should, therefore ensure that everything is correctly working in the network to support overall security and know how an insider is able to attack the wireless ad-hoc network. Wireless ad-hoc networks should be protected with an intrusion detection system that can understand the possible actions of attackers and can produce a solution against these attacks.

Attack Types

Passive Eavesdropping

An attacker can listen to any wireless network to know what is going on in the network. It first listens to control messages to infer the network topology to understand how nodes are located or are communicating with another. Therefore, it can gather intelligent information about the network before attacking. It may also listen to the information that is transmitted using encryption although it should be confidential belonging to upper layer applications. Eavesdropping is also a threat to location privacy [1]. An unauthorized node can notice a wireless network that exists within a geographical area, just by detecting radio signals. To combat this, traffic engineering techniques have been developed.

Selective Existence (Selfish Nodes)

This malicious node which is also known as *selfish node* and which is not participating in the network operations, use the network for its advantage to enhance performance and save its own resources such as power. To achieve that, selfish node puts forth its existence whenever personal cost is involved. Therefore these selfish node behaviors are known as *selective existence attacks.* [2]. For instance, selfish nodes do not even send any HELLO messages and drop all packets even if they are sent to itself, as long as it does not start the transmission. When a selfish node wants to start a connection with another node, it performs a route discovery and then sends the necessary packets. When the node no longer needs to use the network, it returns to the "silent mode" After a while, neighboring nodes invalidate their own route entries to this node and selfish node becomes invisible on the network. Actually, dropping packets may be divided into two categories according to the aims of the attacking node. Attacker may want to drop the packets of only the other nodes that it will attack later. To do that it must look at the packet to see whether it comes from this node. If attacker looks at the content of all packets aggregating from the network, it spends CPU resource and naturally battery life. This is not desirable behavior for selfish nodes because it spends battery life. Therefore attackers are not interested in the content of the packets if its aim is not to consume its own resources. irst category of dropping packets cannot be evaluated as a selfish node behavior. Thus selectively dropping messages is not a selfish node behavior mentioned in [3]. Selective existence is kind of a passive attack, nodes just do not participate in the network operations and they do not change the content of packets.

Gray Hole Attack (Routing Misbehavior)

Gray hole attacks is an active attack type, which lead to dropping of messages. Attacking node first agrees to forward packets and then fails to do so. Initially the node behaves correctly and replays true RREP messages to nodes that initiate RREQ message. This way, it takes over the sending packets. Afterwards, the node just drops the packets to launch a (DoS) denial of service attack. If neighboring nodes that try to send packets over attacking nodes lose the connection to destination then they may want to discover a route again, broadcasting RREQ messages. Attacking node establishes a route, sending RREP messages. This process goes on until malicious node succeeds its aim (e.g. network resource consumption, battery consumption). This attack is known as routing misbehavior. [3] Dropping packets is also one of the behaviors of failed or overloading nodes

[1]. One should not evaluate every dropping packet action as a selective existence, gray or black hole attack. Actually most routing protocols have no mechanism to detect whether data packets have been forwarded, DSR being the only exception.

Black Hole Attack

The difference of Black Hole Attacks [4] compared to Gray Hole Attacks is that malicious nodes never send true control messages initially. To carry out a black hole attack, malicious node waits for neighboring nodes to send RREQ messages. When the malicious node receives an RREQ message, without checking its routing table, immediately sends a false RREP message giving a route to destination over itself, assigning a high sequence number to settle in the routing table of the victim node, before other nodes send a true one. Therefore requesting nodes assume that route discovery process is completed and ignore other RREP messages and begin to send packets over malicious node. Malicious node attacks all RREQ messages this way and takes over all routes. Therefore all packets are sent to a point when they are not forwarding anywhere. This is called a black hole akin to real meaning which swallows all objects and matter. To succeed a black hole attack, malicious node should be positioned at the center of the wireless network. If malicious node masquerades false RREP message as if it comes from another victim node instead of itself, all messages will be forwarded to the victim node. By doing this, victim node will have to process all incoming messages and is subjected to a sleep deprivation attack.

Gray hole attacks against one or two nodes in the network to isolate them, where as black hole attack affects the whole network. Moreover, the malicious node that attempts gray hole attacks cannot be perceived easily since it does not send false messages. Behavior of failed or overloaded nodes may seem like selfish nodes attacks or gray hole attacks due to dropping of messages. But, since failed nodes cannot fabricate a new control message, they cannot form a black hole attack although they will drop the message later.

Aodv Routing Protocol

Ad-hoc On-Demand Distance-Vector (AODV) routing protocol is specifically designed for mobile ad-hoc wireless network. It provides very quick and efficient route establishment between communicating nodes. In most of the protocols the overhead is incurred by the fact that each transmitted packet contains the source route to the destination information. AODV protocol eliminates this problem by maintaining only the next hop information to reach a particular destination. So routing message does not have an increasing size. A monotonically increasing sequence number is used to prevent replay attacks and to ensure loop free routing among the nodes.

Prevention Of Aodv From Black Hole Attack

For a better security solution into the existing AODV routing protocol to satisfy the security needs of the ad hoc networks from black hole aattacks, we propose a methodology i.e watchdog and Pathrater for identifying multiple black hole nodes and avoids routing packets through these nodes

Watchdog And Pathrater Technique

Watchdog is the base intrusion detection technique that many of the recent researches depended on. It was proposed by Sergio Marti et al. [Marti 2000], they proposed two techniques that improve throughput in MANETs in the presence of compromised nodes that agree to forward packets but fail to do so. A node may misbehave because it is overloaded, selfish, malicious, or broken. An overloaded node lacks the CPU cycles, buffer space, or available network bandwidth to forward packets. A selfish node is unwilling to spend battery life, CPU cycles, or available network bandwidth to forward packets not of direct interest to it, even though it expects others to forward packets on its behalf. A malicious node launches a DoS (Denial of Service) attack by dropping packets. A broken node might have a software fault that prevents it from forwarding packets.

They used two techniques to mitigate the decrease in the throughput due to the above node categories, the first one is the intrusion detection which is the Watchdogs that identify misbehaving nodes and the other is the response of the intrusion detection system which is a pathrater that helps routing protocols avoid these nodes. When a node forwards a packet, the node's Watchdog verifies that the next node in the path also forwards the packet. The Watchdog does this by listening promiscuously to the next node's transmissions. If the next node does not forward the packet, it is misbehaving. Every time a node fails to forward the packet, the Watchdog increments the failures counter. If the counter exceeds a certain threshold, it determines that the node is misbehaving; this node is then avoided using the pathrater. The pathrater, run by each node in the network, combines knowledge of misbehaving nodes with link reliability data to pick the route most likely to be reliable, it uses the reliability metric instead of shortest path. Each node maintains a rating for every other node it knows about in the network. It calculates a path metric by averaging the node ratings in the path. The Watchdog technique has its own advantages and weaknesses. Dynamic source routing (DSR) [Johnson 1996] with the Watchdog has the advantage that it can detect misbehavior at the forwarding level, not just at the link level. Watchdog's weaknesses are that it might not detect a misbehaving node in the presence of:

- Ambiguous collisions: These prevent node A from overhearing the transmission from node B, as shown in **Figure 2**.

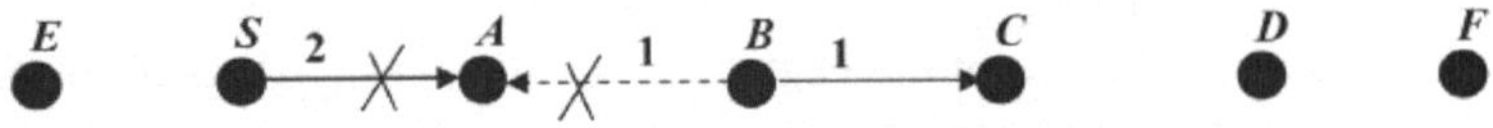

Figure 2: Node A does not hear node B forward packet 1 to C, because B's transmission collides at A with packet 2 from source S.

- Receiver collisions: Node A can only tell whether B has sent a packet, but not if node C received it or not, as shown in **Figure 3.**

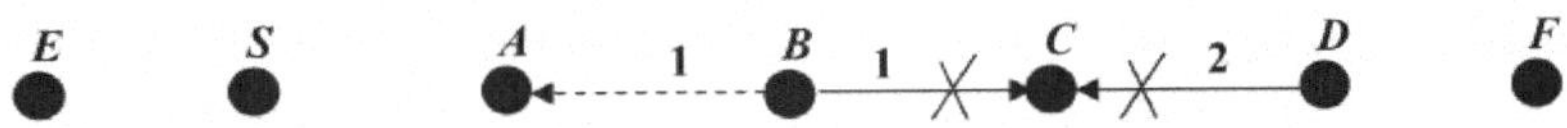

Figure 3: Node A believes that node B has forwarded packet 1 to C, although C never received the packet due to a collision with packet2.

- Limited transmission power: A misbehaving node could limit its transmission power such that the signal is strong enough to be overheard by the previous node but too weak to be received by the true recipient. As shown in **Figure 4**.

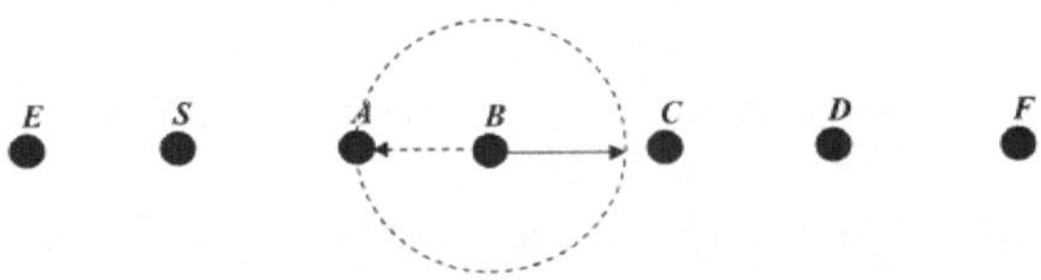

Figure 4: Node B limits its transmission power such that the signal is strong enough to be overheard by node A but too weak to be received by node C.

- False misbehavior: This occurs when a node falsely reports other nodes as misbehaving.

Partial dropping: A node can circumvent the Watchdog by dropping packets at a lower rate than the Watchdog's configured minimum misbehaving threshold.

Conclusion

The field of MANET is rapidly growing and changing. While there are still many challenges that need to be met, it is expected that such networks will see general use within the next few years. One of these challenges is security. Security of mobile ad hoc networks has recently gained momentum in the research community. Due to the open medium of ad hoc networks, and their inherent lack of infrastructure, Security exposures can be an obstacle to basis network operation. It is impossible to find a general idea that can work efficiently against all kinds of attack, since every attack has its own distinct characteristics.

In this paper we studied the routing security issues of MANETs, describing the cooperative black hole attack that can be mounted against a MANET and proposed a feasible solution for it in the AODV protocol. The proposed solution can be applied to 1.) Identify multiple black hole nodes cooperating with each other in a MANET; and 2.) Discover secure paths from source to destination by avoiding multiple black hole nodes acting in cooperation.

This paper show a new methodology based on watchdog mechanism against a well-known insider active attack' black hole attack"and the Pathrater avoids routing packets through these nodes.

Future Work

The solution in this paper covers a subset of all threats and is far from providing a comprehensive answer to many security problems in the MANET's field. Here we are discussing only the case whether a node behaves like a legitimate one or the malicious one. But this will be a hot area of research if we consider that one or more legitimate nodes behave legitimately at one time and maliciously at another time, i.e. behavior of a nodes change in the network with time.

References

- P. Yau and C. J. Mitchell, "Security Vulnerabilities in Adhoc Network".
- G. Vigna, S. Gwalani and K. Srinivasan, "An Intrusion Detection Tool for AODV- Based Ad hoc Wireless Networks", Proc. of the 20th Annual Computer Security Applications Conference (ACSAC'04).
- P. Ning and K. Sun, "How to Misuse AODV: A Case Study of Insider Attacks Against Mobile Ad-Hoc Routing Protocols", Proc.of the 2003 IEEE Workshop on Information Assurance United States Military Academy, West Point, NY., June 2003.

- D. Johnson, D. Maltz and J. Broch, "DSR the Dynamic Source Routing Protocol for Multihop Wireless Ad Hoc Networks". Ad Hoc networking, Chapter 5, page 139-172. Addison-Wesley, 2001.
- [Marti 2000] S. Marti, T. J. Giuli, K. Lai, and M. Baker, "Mitigating Routing Misbehavior in Mobile Ad-hoc Networks," *Proceedings of the 6th Annual International Conference on Mobile Computing and Networking (MobiCom'00)*, PP. 255-265, August 2000.
- **[Johnson 1996]** D. B. Johnson and D. A. Maltz, "Dynamic Source Routing in Ad-hoc Wireless Networks," *Mobile Computing, T. Imielinski and H. Korth, Eds., Kluwer,* 1996, pp. 153-81

AOP : A Cumulative Study

Ashwini Kumar "SushiNam"
Lecturer, DKES-SCS, Delhi

Abstract

AOP is a term used to describe a programming technique and a way of thinking about the construction of software applications that complements the forms of expression found in object-oriented programming. The goal of AOP is to improve the modularity of software applications, making them easier to develop, test, and maintain. In practical world there are many programming problems for which neither procedural nor object-oriented programming techniques are sufficient to clearly capture some of the important design decisions, the program must implement. This forces the implementation of those design decisions to be scattered throughout the code, resulting in "tangled" code that is excessively difficult to develop and maintain. The properties these decisions address will be called as aspects. The reason why they have been hard to capture is that they cross-cut the system's basic functionality Aspect-oriented programs comprise of a mixture of objects and aspects. Both encapsulate state and behavior, but whereas the behavior in an object is executed only when explicit calls are made to the object's methods, the behavior in an aspect can also execute at points in the runtime of the program determined by the aspect's specification.

Introduction

Aspect-Oriented Programming, is a new programming technique which makes it possible to clearly express programs involving aspects, including appropriate isolation, composition & reuse of the aspect-code.

Object-oriented programming (OOP) has been presented as a technology that can fundamentally aid software engineering, because the underlying object model provides a better fit with real domain problems. But we have found many programming problems where OOP techniques are not sufficient to clearly capture all the important design decisions the program must implement. Software design processes and programming languages exist in a mutually supporting relationship. Design processes break a system down into smaller and smaller units. Programming languages provide mechanisms that allow the programmer to define abstractions of system sub-units, and then compose those abstractions in different ways to produce the overall system.

A design process and a programming language work well together when the programming language provides abstraction and composition mechanisms that cleanly support the kinds of units the design process breaks the system into.

The exact nature of the decomposition differs between the language paradigms of course, but each unit is encapsulated in a procedure /function /object, and in each case, it feels comfortable to talk about what is encapsulated as a functional unit of the overall system. This last point may be so familiar that it feels somewhat redundant. But it is important that we give it explicit attention now, because in the course of this paper will be considering units of system decomposition that are not functional.

Separating software concerns

A concern is a particular goal, concept, or area of interest. In technology terms, a typical software system comprises several core and system-level concerns. For example, a credit card processing system's core concern would process payments, while its system-level concerns would handle logging, transaction integrity, authentication, security, performance, and so on. Many such concerns — known as crosscutting concerns — tend to affect multiple implementation modules. Using current programming methodologies, crosscutting concerns span over multiple modules, resulting in systems that are harder to design, understand, implement, and evolve.

Aspect-oriented programming (AOP) better separates concerns than previous methodologies, thereby providing modularization of crosscutting concerns.
In the early days of computer science, developers wrote programs by means of direct machine-level coding. Unfortunately, programmers spent more time thinking about a particular machine's instruction set than the problem at hand. Slowly, it migrated to higher-level languages that allowed some abstraction of the underlying machine. Then came structured languages; we could now decompose our problems in terms of the procedures necessary to perform our tasks. However, as complexity grew, we needed better techniques. Object-oriented programming (OOP) let us view a system as a set of collaborating objects. Classes allow us to hide implementation details beneath interfaces. Polymorphism provided a common behavior and interface for related concepts, and allowed more specialized components to change a particular behavior without needing access to the implementation of base concepts.

Programming methodologies and languages define the way we communicate with machines. Each new methodology presents new ways to decompose problems: machine code, machine-independent code, procedures, classes, and so on. Each new methodology allowed a more natural mapping of system requirements to programming constructs. Evolution of these programming methodologies let us create systems with ever increasing complexity. The converse of this fact may be equally true: we allowed the existence of ever more complex systems because these techniques permitted us to deal with that complexity.

Currently, OOP serves as the methodology of choice for most new software development projects. Indeed, OOP has shown its strength when it comes to modeling common behavior. However, as we will see shortly, and as you may have already experienced, OOP does not adequately address behaviors that span over many — often unrelated — modules. In contrast, AOP methodology fills this void. AOP quite possibly represents the next big step in the evolution of programming methodologies.

Crosscutting concerns

AOP is designed to handle cross-cutting concerns by providing a mechanism, the aspect, for expressing these concerns and automatically incorporating them into a system. AOP does not replace existing programming paradigms and languages; instead, it works with them to improve their expressiveness and utility. It enhances our ability to express the separation of concerns necessary for a well-designed, maintainable software system. Some concerns are appropriately expressed as encapsulated objects, or components. Others are best expressed as cross-cutting concerns.

A developer creates a system as a response to multiple requirements. We can broadly classify these requirements as core module-level requirements and system-level requirements. Many system-level requirements tend to be orthogonal (mutually independent) to each other and to the module-level requirements. System-level requirements also tend to crosscut many core modules. For example, a typical enterprise application comprises crosscutting concerns such as authentication, logging, resource pooling, administration, performance, and storage management. Each crosscuts several subsystems. For example, a storage-management concern affects every stateful business object.

The type of logging required in our example is a cross-cutting concern. It cannot be isolated or encapsulated in one or two specific classes; the logging involves changes in many places across the system. Our desire is to keep the system maintainable, and therefore we want our logging approach to keep the code as clean and simple as possible. We would also like to avoid significant structural changes to the system's architecture. So how do we implement a cross-cutting concern such as logging? We could refactor all of the code by creating a logging class and performing the appropriate insertions. However, in a large system, this would be a time-consuming, error-prone job.

Although crosscutting concerns span over many modules, current implementation techniques tend to implement these requirements using one-dimensional methodologies, forcing implementation mapping for the requirements along a single dimension. That single dimension tends to be the core module-level implementation. The remaining requirements are tagged along this dominant dimension. In other words, the requirement space is an n-dimensional space, whereas the implementation space is one-dimensional. Such a mismatch results in an awkward requirements-to-implementation map.

The fundamentals of AOP

AOP, at its core, lets you implement individual concerns in a loosely coupled fashion, and combine these implementations to form the final system. Indeed, AOP creates systems using loosely coupled, modularized implementations of crosscutting concerns. OOP, in contrast, creates systems using loosely coupled, modularized implementations of common concerns. The modularization unit in AOP is called an aspect, just as a common concern's implementation in OOP is called a class.

AOP involves three distinct development steps:

1. Aspectual decomposition: Decompose the requirements to identify crosscutting and common concerns. You separate module-level concerns from crosscutting system-level concerns. For example, in the aforementioned credit card module example, you would identify three concerns: core credit card processing, logging, and authentication.
2. Concern implementation: Implement each concern separately. For the credit card processing example, you'd implement the core credit card processing unit, logging unit, and authentication unit.
3. Aspectual recomposition: In this step, an aspect integrator specifies recomposition rules by creating modularization units — aspects. The recomposition process, also known as weaving or integrating, uses this information to compose the final system. For the credit card processing example, you'd specify, in a language provided by the AOP implementation, that each operation's start and completion be logged. You would also specify that each operation must clear authentication before it proceeds with the business logic.

AOP Benefits

AOP helps overcome the aforementioned problems caused by code tangling and code scattering. Here are other specific benefits AOP offers:

- Modularized implementation of crosscutting concerns: AOP addresses each concern separately with minimal coupling, resulting in modularized implementations even in the presence of crosscutting concerns. Such an implementation produces a system with less duplicated code. Since each concern's implementation is separate, it also helps reduce code clutter. Further, modularized implementation also results in a system that is easier to understand and maintain.

- Easier-to-evolve systems: Since the aspected modules can be unaware of crosscutting concerns, it's easy to add newer functionality by creating new aspects. Further, when you add new modules to a system, the existing aspects crosscut them, helping create a coherent evolution.
- Late binding of design decisions: Recall the architect's under/overdesign dilemma. With AOP, an architect can delay making design decisions for future requirements, since she can implement those as separate aspects.
- More code reuse: Because AOP implements each aspect as a separate module, each individual module is more loosely coupled. For example, you can use a module interacting with a database in a separate logger aspect with a different logging requirement.

An Aop Implementation for Java

AspectJ, a freely available AOP implementation for Java from Xerox PARC, is a general-purpose aspect-oriented Java extension. AspectJ uses Java as the language for implementing individual concerns, and it specifies extensions to Java for weaving rules. These rules are specified in terms of pointcuts, join points, advice, and aspects. Join points define specific points in a program's execution, a pointcut is the language construct that specifies join points, advice defines pieces of an aspect implementation to be executed at pointcuts, and an aspect combines these primitives.

In addition, AspectJ also allows the "aspecting" of other aspects and classes in several ways. Indeed, you can introduce new data members and new methods, as well as declare a class to implement additional base classes and interfaces. AspectJ's weaver — an aspect compiler — combines different aspects together. Because the final system created by the AspectJ compiler is pure Java byte code, it can run on any conforming JVM. AspectJ also features tools such as a debugger and selected IDE integration.

AspectJ is a language specification as well as an AOP language implementation. The language specification defines various constructs and their semantics to support aspect-oriented concepts. The language implementation offers tools for compiling, debugging, and documenting code.

AspectJ's language constructs extend the Java programming language, so every valid Java program is also a valid AspectJ program. The AspectJ compiler produces class files that comply with Java byte code specification, enabling any compliant JVM to interpret the produced class files. By choosing Java as the base language, AspectJ passes on all the benefits of Java and makes it easy for Java programmers to use it.

AspectJ, as one of its strong points, features helpful tools. It provides an aspect weaver in the form of a compiler, an aspect-aware debugger and documentation generator, and a standalone aspect browser to visualize how an advice crosscuts a system's parts. Moreover, AspectJ offers good integration with popular IDEs, including Sun Microsystems' Forte, Borland's JBuilder, and Emacs, making AspectJ a useful AOP implementation for Java developers.

To support AOP, AspectJ adds to the Java language concepts:

- Joinpoints: Points in a program's execution. For example, joinpoints could define calls to specific methods in a class
- Pointcuts: Program constructs to designate joinpoints and collect specific context at those points
- Advices: Code that runs upon meeting certain conditions. For example, an advice could log a message before executing a joinpoint

Pointcut and advice together specify weaving rules. Aspect, a class-like concept, puts pointcuts and advices together to form a crosscutting unit. The pointcuts specify execution points and the weaving rule's context, whereas the advices specify actions, operations, or decisions performed at those points. You can also look at joinpoints as a set of events in response to which you execute certain advices.

Joinpoints

Joinpoints, a central concept in AspectJ, are well-defined points in a program's execution. Candidate joinpoints include calls to a method, a conditional check, a loop's beginning, or an assignment. Joinpoints also have a context associated with them. For example, a method-call joinpoint could have the target object and its argument as part of the context.

Although any identifiable point in a program's execution is a joinpoint, AspectJ limits the available joinpoints to those usable in a systematic manner. AspectJ makes the following pointcuts available:

- Method call and execution
- Constructor call and execution
- Read/write access to a field
- Exception handler execution
- Object and class initialization execution

AspectJ does not expose finer execution structures such as if checks or for loops.

Pointcuts

Pointcuts, program constructs to designate joinpoints, let you specify a joinpoint collection. Pointcuts also let you expose context at the joinpoint to an advice implementation.

Advices

Advices specify the executable code when reaching certain pointcuts. AspectJ provides three ways to associate an advice with a joinpoint: before, after, and around a joinpoint's execution. A before advice runs just before the joinpoint, whereas an after advice runs just after. With an after advice, you can specify after normal return, after throwing an exception, or after returning either way from a joinpoint. An around advice surrounds a joinpoint and has control if the joinpoint's execution should proceed. It can also decide to proceed with a different argument set.

Aspects

Aspects act as AspectJ's unit of modularization, just as classes do in Java. An aspect puts together pointcuts and advices. Aspects resemble classes: an aspect can contain methods and fields, extend other classes or aspects, and implement interfaces. However, aspects differ from classes in that you cannot create an object for an aspect using new.

AspectJ allows classes to declare pointcuts. You must declare static pointcuts declared inside a class. However, AspectJ does not allow classes to contain advices; only aspects can contain advices.

An aspect can mark itself and any pointcut as abstract. Abstract pointcuts act similarly to a class's abstract methods: they let you defer the details to the derived aspects. A concrete aspect extending an abstract aspect can then provide concrete definitions of abstract pointcuts.

Conclusion

The study constructs an analysis of the problems that AOP is intended to solve, as well as an initial set of terms and concepts that support explicit AOP-based system design. Based on the analysis, the team of the authors of this paper has been able to develop aspect-oriented programming technology that supports clean abstraction & composition of both Components and Aspects. Components are properties of a system, for which the implementation can be cleanly encapsulated in a generalized procedure.

Aspects are properties of a system, for which the implementation cannot be cleanly encapsulated in a generalized procedure. Aspects and cross-cut components cross-cut each other in a system's implementation.

The key difference between AOP and other approaches is that AOP provides Component & Aspect Languages with different abstraction & composition mechanisms.

{i} The AOP conceptual framework is helpful to design the systems, and

{ii} the AOP-based implementations have proven to be easier to develop and maintain, while being comparably efficient to much more complex code written using traditional techniques.

A special language processor called an aspect weaver is used to coordinate the co-composition of the aspects and components.

References

- Aksit M., Wakita K., et al., Abstracting object interactions using composition filters, in proc. ECOOP'93 Workshop on Object-Based Distributed Programming, pp. 152-184, 1993.
- http://www.parc.xerox.com/spl/eca/oi/workshop- 94/foil/main.html
- Mendhekar A., Kiczales G., et al., RG: A Case-Study for Aspect-Oriented Programming, Xerox PARC, Palo Alto, CA. Technical report SPL97-009 P9710044, February, 1997.
- Rumbaugh J., Blaha M., et al., Object-Oriented Modeling and Design. Book published by Prentice Hall, 1991.
- AspectJ Project, The Eclipse Foundation, http:// www.eclipse.org/aspectj/.

Changing Face of IT Utilization Economics through Grid Computing

Ritika Wason
Lecturer (IT), IITM, Delhi

Abstract

This paper is an attempt to unveil how Grid Computing holds the potential to change the face of IT utilization across companies, organizations and universities. The use of grids across boundaries of organizations as a utility helps in not only increasing the underlying efficiency but can also enable organizations to share ideas and resources with each other as and when required. This idea of interconnection not only brings about economic benefits to organizations but can also help in realizing the dream of a virtual global organization over several physical organizations.

Introduction

Simply defined a grid is a flexible, secure, coordinated way of sharing resources among dynamic collections of individuals, institutions and organizations. Popularized only since the last decade, grid computing still remains an untapped technology in terms of potential and application. Despite much research and applications in this field, it still remains an unexplored mine of resources waiting to be tapped.

With the advent of high speed network technology, high performance, unconventional applications emerge by sharing geographically distributed resources in a well controlled, secure and mutually fair way. Such a coordinated worldwide resource sharing requires an infrastructure called Grid [8].Since first introduced the grid has expanded greatly in the last five years. From a few pioneering projects like Globus, Condor, Legion and Unicore. Today many countries have their own Grid projects [2].

Grid Computing is a collection of distributed computing resources (memory, processing and communication technology) available over a network that appears to an end user as one large virtual computing system. It dynamically links far flung computers and computing resources over the public Internet or a virtual private network on an as-needed basis. Thus this technology can be used to provide computing power on demand, much like a utility [7].

From practical point of view the goal of Grids is to support large-scale resource sharing. Conventional distributed environments differ from grids in that they are based on resources the user owns. Sharing and owing in this context is not necessarily related to ownership in a usual sense. Sharing here refers to temporarily utilizing resources where the user has no direct (login) access otherwise. Similarly, owing implies having permanent and unrestricted access to the resource. From semantical point of view a grid is nothing but an abstraction. The physical and virtual levels are completely split but there is a mapping in grid between resources and uses of the two layers [8].

Most companies, universities and organizations today use only a small fraction of the computing power available to them through the computing resources they already own. PC's, servers and mainframes all remain idle much of the time, while the people using them attend to other official and unofficial tasks. A recent IBM Corporation study points out, the above fact as a significant problem for three main reasons:

i) Companies and organizations continually want to do more with less by breaking out from the cycle of increasing infrastructure needs and costs.
ii) Much value remains hidden in the infrastructure that companies would like to release in the hope that it might change the way they do business.
iii) IT faces a continual pressure to deal with on-time delivery of projects to help deploy new business capabilities.

A solution to this underutilization of computing infrastructure: Although it is fairly easy to achieve 60-70 % utilization on a mainframe, but most companies are actually using only 15-20%.But the new emerging technology grid computing promises to attain 90% in the near future [7]. Owing to the tremendous potential grid computing holds it may even turn out to be a bigger phenomenon or paradigm shift from Internet or the World Wide Web.

Current IT Scenario

The history of commercial IT applications has been characterized by the astounding leaps, but nothing that has come before not even the introduction of PC or the introduction of the Internet-will match the upheaval that lies just over the horizon. IT today, like steam power and electricity before it, is what economists call a general-purpose technology. It is used by all sorts of organizations to do all sorts of tasks thus bringing widespread and fundamental changes to commerce and society. Due to its broad application as a general-purpose technology, IT offers the potential for considerable economies of scale if its supply can be consolidated. Today individual companies must purchase the various components required to use the technology, house those parts on site, weld them into a working system and hire a staff of specialists to maintain them. This fragmentation of supply forces large capital investments and heavy fixed costs in terms of technology and labor force for operating and maintaining it.

A perfect symbol of modern IT today is the PC dominating the desks of most office workers, it is a microcosm of the overall state of computing resources at the typical corporation fragmented, redundant and increasingly underutilized. The rise of robust, high-capacity networks has made the desktop PC less essential. The huge costs of maintaining and updating the huge fleet of PC's and their associated software. PC also represents the biggest security hole in today's companies, a gateway for hackers and a repository of ready evidence.

As a business resource or input, IT today looks a lot like electric power did at the start of the last century. The creation of tens of thousands of independent data centers, all using virtually the same hardware and for the most part running similar software, has imposed severe penalties on individual firms as well as on the broader economy. It has led to the overbuilding of IT assets, resulting in extraordinary low levels of capacity utilization.

A recent study of six corporate data centers revealed that most of their 1000 servers were using just 10-35% of their available processing power. Desktop computers fare even worse with IBM Corporation estimating an average capacity utilization rate of just 5% .Gartner Inc., the research consultancy based in Stanford, Connecticut, suggests that between 50-60% of a typical company's data storage capacity is wasted. Over capacity by no means is limited to hardware, software applications are also highly scalable i.e. able to serve additional uses at little or no incremental costs.

Replication of IT departments from company to company that share the same technical skills also represents an over investment in labor as well. According to a 2003 survey, about 60% of the average U.S. Company's IT staffing budget goes to routine support and maintenance functions. When overcapacity is combined with redundant functionality conditions are ripe for a shift to standardized supply [10]. To realize the statistics of the current situation let's consider the situation here with Oracle, a popular RDBMS product by Oracle Corp. From Oracle 10g onwards Oracle is empowered with the Grid Computing capabilities, but to use Oracle every organization has to bear a financial overhead in terms of tax to Oracle itself and hardware costs like procurement of a server and compatible client systems along with trained manpower to manage this utility effectively. Thus the whole Oracle package though desirable but is a costly affair both in terms of initial and maintenance costs.

Applications of Grid Computing

Grid Computing refers to a new technology infrastructure paradigm based on the web and the Internet (also other networks including the LAN, MAN and WAN). This technology enables one to exploit large scale sharing of resources within distributed and often loosely coordinated groups called virtual organizations [9]. Grid computing can be thought of as distributed and large-scale cluster computing and as a form of network-distributed parallel processing. Grids also provide a scalable, secure and reliable mechanism for discovering and negotiating access to remote resources.

Grid Computing has two main benefits: increased utilization of existing resources and computing power, hence enabling companies to share computing resources more effectively internally as well as with partners and even through public grids. This sharing of resources hence allows companies to boost their computational power by cutting costs. Grid computing thus redefines how companies pay for and manage IT.

Many approaches to Grid Computing are possible but according to IBM a utilities approach or pay for what you use-will be a significant component of computing within the next 5-10 years. Thus enabling companies to shift from making one large purchase of technology to making many smaller purchases. Business applications have been limited by lack of necessary software except for a few large companies. Grid Computing holds the potential of realizing the dream of transforming IT and its associated services to that of a true utility model. Today's piecemeal utility services exist as inputs into traditional data centers, individual companies still must connect them with their old hardware and software which is a difficult task. True utility computing can arrive only when an outside supplier takes responsibility for delivering all of a company's IT requirements from data processing to storage to applications. This utility model requires that ownership of the assets that have traditionally resided inside widely dispersed data centers be consolidated and transferred to utilities [6].

Grid Applications are no longer monolithic codes, rather they are being built from existing application components [1]. Many grid projects are being carried out worldwide in many developing and developed nations. A few main projects are:

- **CHINA Education and Research Grid (CERG)**

With the development of higher education in China, some universities still lack enough expensive research equipment resources due to insufficient budget. Many universities and research institutes are currently conducting researches on resource sharing technologies. However, the limitation by network bandwidth and server performance, user demands cannot be satisfied yet. These education resources dispersed on different nodes in CERNET (China Education and Research Network) have several disadvantages: the distributed resources are sufficient interconnected, and only connected by web links; it brings management problems, such as information redundancy and storage resources waste. The stored information is isolated in the so called information island, which makes it difficult to intercommunicate and share resources among universities. These resources are unable to filter, classify, and process the stored raw information to fit for different kinds of requirements of visitors, and all the visitors having different knowledge background now access information through the same channel.

In one of the largest implementations to date of grid computing IBM and China's Ministry of Education will use Grid technology to let universities across the country collaborate on research in science and education projects. The China Education and Research Grid was launched with six universities. Once complete, it is expected to link more than 200,000 students and faculty members at nearly 100 hundred universities across China. When the first phase of the project completed in 2006, the Grid performed more than 18 teraflops, or trillions of calculations per second, and eventually be capable of more than 300 trillion calculations per second by the end of second phase in 2010.

The China Grid aims to simplify how students and researchers access education and computing resources across China. Universities will be connected to a common virtual hub that will automatically find the appropriate application resources, from life sciences research to video courses and e-learning. China's university system hence saves on development costs, since each school can focus on its area of expertise e-learning or life sciences.

- **Grid Computing in India**

Oracle Open World, Oracle's global technology and business conference in 2006, started with a report on India results in Oracle Grid Index III. The report reveals that India leads the world in moving towards a grid IT environment with 60 percent of the organizations polled stating that a grid-based IT infrastructure was inevitable. Moreover, nearly half (48 percent) of organizations polled have embraced or are in the process of embracing grid technology. India is leading in the adoption of virtualization. Major grid computing based going on in India are:

GARUDA is a collaboration of science researchers and experimenters on a nationwide grid of computational nodes, mass storage and scientific instruments that aims to provide the technological advances required to enable data and compute intensive science for the 21st century. One of GARUDA's most important challenges is to strike the right balance between research and the daunting task of deploying that innovation into some of the most complex scientific and engineering endeavors being undertaken today.

The Department of Information Technology (DIT), Government of India has funded the Centre for Development of Advanced Computing (C-DAC) to deploy the nation-wide computational grid GARUDA. In Proof of Concept (PoC) phase, which ended on March 2008, 17 cities across the country were connected with an aim to bring "Grid" networked computing to research labs and industry. From April 2008 the Foundation phase is in progress with an aim to include more users' applications, providing Service Oriented architecture, improving network stability and upgrading grid resources. GARUDA will assist to accelerate India's drive to turn its substantial research investment into tangible economic benefits.

The principal goal of **EU-India Grid** is to support interconnection between the most relevant European Grid infrastructure (EGEE) and the Indian Grids to build a common infrastructure available to support data processing for e-Science application areas where strong collaborations already exist between Europe and India. Such common Grid infrastructure is intended to provide a concrete answer to specific requirements of several existing EU-India collaborative projects, characterized by very demanding computing needs. Coupled with this, the project is expected to trigger the use and development of Grids in India across a number of application areas and foster the creation of new Euro-Indian collaborations for the development of e-Science. The project began on 1st October 2006. The partners of this project are prominent actors on the European and Indian e-Infrastructures scene including: Italian National Institute of Nuclear Physics, INFN (project coordinator), Metaware SpA, Italian Academic and Research Network (GARR) and Cambridge University from Europe, Abdus Salam International Centre for Theoretical Physics (ICTP), Indian Education and Research Network (ERNET), University of Pune, SAHA Institute of Nuclear Physics, Kolkata, Centre for Development of Advanced Computing (CDAC), Bhabha Atomic Research Centre, Mumbai, TATA Institute for Fundamental Research (Mumbai) and National Centre for Biological Sciences (Bangalore) [12].

Realizing the Grid Computing Dream

The vision of grid computing is to create virtual dynamic organizations through secure, coordinated resource sharing among individuals and institutions [9]. Though the vision of grid computing is promising, the challenges of managing a grid infrastructure are daunting. Some difficulties are heterogeneity of devices on the grid, the need to operate in a geographically dispersed and complex envoirnment, the unpredictability of system performance and behavior over time, and the existence of multiple administrative domains. Usage-sensitive pricing, service-level agreements and network security issues introduce other serious concerns.

Future Suggestions & Summary

Every technologically sound nation today has some large-scale grid-based projects in the pipeline or already under implementation. The call of the hour however is to streamline these distributed efforts being made by various nations into a single consortium which works towards building a single virtual organization under which organizations from all corners of the world irrespective of their nationality can function by utilizing the required services of this virtual organization on a pay and utilize mode. The Internet turned into an phenomenon a few decades back as it was an umbrella which every individual and organization could use as and when required and for almost anything at a minimal cost and with minimal resources. Today when the slogan is more services for less, we can extend the same basis of Internet in Grid Computing to make an IT-services based utility we can coin as **"GridNet"** which can combine all organizations across physical boundaries by providing these organizations any required services as and when required.

To clarify this idea we try incorporating the same idea to the Oracle example we discussed before in the current IT Scenario. Today every organization wishful of using Oracle 10g or above has to bear heavy costs. If GridNet becomes a reality every organization irrespective of its size and nation will be able to build and maintain their databases using Oracle and all its features without having to bear costs of purchasing the required hardware's and employing trained man power. By just paying the cost of utilizing GridNet they will easily be able to use Oracle without having to worry about its maintenance.

Hence, we can now conclude that: Grid Computing promises to change the economics of IT utilization making existing and new types of applications and services more cost-effective. It shall also enable a variety of different technologies to be seamlessly inter-connected to create a vast network capable of gathering huge amounts of data. However, there are many challenges that must be overcome before the potential of this new architecture can be fully utilized [7].

The shift of IT from a fragmented capital asset to a resources centralized utility service will be momentous. It will overturn strategic and operating assumptions, alter industrial economies, upset markets and pose daunting challenges to every user and vendor [10].

Grids will be built to support different sets of user communities. Each of the systems, based on user requirements, will be built with different components [6].

The essence of Grid Computing lies in the efficient and optimal utilization of a wide range of heterogeneous, loosely coupled resources in an organization tied to sophisticated workload management capabilities or information virtualization [3]. Grid Computing aims at dynamic or runtime selection, allocation and control of computational resources such as processing power, disk storage or specialized software systems or even data, according to the demands of the end-users at any time and any location without any knowledge or reference to details such as the exact location or nature or quantity of the resource being drawn [9].

References

- Edelman Ewa, Blythe James, Pegasus: Mapping Scientific Workflows onto the Grid
- Graham P, EU Funded Grid Developments in Europe
- North Ken, Milestones in Grid Computing
- Open Grid Services Architecture, http://forge.gridforum.org/projects/ogsa-wg
- Zhao Henan, Sakellarion Rizos, A Low-Cost Rescheduling policy for Dependent Tasks on Grid Computing Systems
- Zsolt Nemeth, Grid Performance, Grid benchmarks, Grid Metrics,MTA Computer & Automation Research Institute
- Prabhu CSR, "Grid and Cluster Computing", PHI
- Wells April J., "Grid Database Design", Auerbach Publications
- Heather Smith and Benn Konsynski, Grid Computing, IT Sloan Management Review
- Nicholas G.Carr, The End of Corporate Computing, IT Sloan Review
- Wang Yuexuan, Wu Cheng,A Study on Education Resource Sharing Grid, International Journal of Information Technology,Vol 11 No.3
- www.euindiagrid.org
- http://www.thefreelibrary.com/

Fraud Detection using Data Mining

Rajan Gupta
Lecturer (IT), VIPS, Delhi.

Abstract

Fraud is a million dollar business and it's increasing every year. Everybody can recall some kind of fraud that has been all over the news. The numbers are shocking, all the more because over one third of all frauds are detected by 'chance' means. Fact is that fraud has become a serious part of our life and hence a serious cost to our economy. Forty-three percent of companies worldwide have fallen victim to economic crime in the years 2006 and 2007. The average financial damage to companies subjected to this survey was US$ 2.42 million per company over two years. There are several types of corporate fraud. The most prominent distinction one can make in fraud classification is internal versus external fraud. Management fraud is an example of internal fraud, where insurance fraud is a classic example of external fraud. The best detection method is internal control. So, it would be advisable to search for improvement of internal control systems. In this paper, we evaluate the use of data mining techniques for the purpose of fraud detection with theoretical background about fraud, internal control, data mining and supervised versus unsupervised learning.

Keywords: *Data Mining, Machine Learning, Fraud, Supervised learning, Unsupervised Learning, PGA*

Introduction

The emergence of fraud into our economic world did not go unnoticed. In 1985 the (US) National Commission on Fraudulent Financial Reporting (known as the Treadway Commission) was formed. To study the causes of fraudulent reporting and make recommendations to reduce its incidence, the Treadway Commission issued a final report in 1987 with recommendations for auditors, public companies, regulators, and educators. This report re-emphasized the importance of internal control in reducing the incidence of fraudulent financial reporting and included a recommendation for all public companies to maintain internal controls. The Committee of Sponsoring Organizations of the Treadway Commission (COSO) was formed to commission the Treadway Commission to perform its task. In response to this recommendation, COSO developed an internal control framework, issued in 1992 and entitled *Internal Control - Integrated Framework.*

More than half of offenders of serious incidents of economic crime in the industrial manufacturing sector came from within the company. Internal perpetrators were fairly likely to have come from the ranks of senior / top management in 2008. The average damage to the companies from tangible frauds (i.e. asset misappropriation, false pretences, and counterfeiting) was US$ 1.7 million according to the 'Global economic crime survey 2005' of PriceWaterhouseCoopers.

Fraud Detection / Prevention

Fraud *prevention* describes measures to stop fraud from occurring in the first place. These include elaborate designs, fluorescent fibers, multitone drawings, watermarks, laminated metal strips and holographs on banknotes, personal identification numbers for bankcards, Internet security systems for credit card transactions, Subscriber Identity Module (SIM) cards for mobile phones, and passwords on computer systems and telephone bank accounts. Of course, none of these methods is perfect and, in general, a compromise has to be struck between expense and inconvenience (e.g., to a customer) on the one hand, and effectiveness on the other.

In contrast, fraud *detection* involves identifying fraud as quickly as possible once it has been perpetrated. Fraud detection comes into play once fraud prevention has failed. In practice, of course fraud detection must be used continuously, as one will typically be unaware that fraud prevention has failed.

Fraud is detected in many ways, or at least one tries to detect it in many ways. Traditionally, a company relies most on its internal control activities and the internal auditor to prevent and detect fraud. If this isn't sufficient, external audit (as far as this isn't legally enforced yet), risk management systems, a whistle-blowing hotline, an investigations department, new technologies or other measures are installed, corresponding to the need the company experiences. The technological improvement that's partly responsible for the increasing trend in fraud is also part of the solution. Prevention and detection technologies are implemented, tested, customized and commercialized. Software companies sell 'The solution to all your business problems, including fraud'. The term 'data mining' is sold as an expensive, all-problems-solving word. ***If your business doesn't use data mining, you're not in the game.***

Fraud ???

The *Concise Oxford Dictionary* defines fraud as "criminal deception; the use of false representations to gain an unjust advantage." Fraud is as old as humanity itself and can take an unlimited variety of different forms.
According to *The American Heritage Dictionary, Second College Edition*, fraud is defined as *'a deception deliberately practiced in order to secure unfair of unlawful gain'*.

Classification of Fraud

Occupational fraud and abuse may be defined as: "*The use of one's occupation for personal enrichment through the deliberate misuse or misapplication of the employing organization's resources or assets.*" There are numerous ways of classifying occupational fraud. The classification most used is the one where two types of fraud are distinguished:

Financial statement balance fraud and asset-theft fraud. The main difference between the former and the latter is that there is no theft of assets involved in the former. Another classification classify fraud on many ways, amongst them fraud for versus against the company, internal versus external fraud, management versus non-management fraud and transaction versus statement fraud. Some of them overlap the above mentioned classification into financial statement balance fraud and asset-theft fraud. For example, asset-theft fraud will be fraud against the company and transaction fraud, without being classified as internal, external, management or non-management fraud. Various combinations can be made in this manner.

Data Mining and Machine Learning

A data analysis system has to be equipped with a substantial amount of background knowledge, and be able to perform reasoning tasks involving that knowledge and the data provided. In effort to meet this goal, researchers have turned to ideas from the **machine learning** field. This is a natural source of ideas, since the machine learning task can be described as turning background knowledge and examples (input) into knowledge (output). By doing so, the emergence of a new research area was set and frequently called data mining and knowledge discovery.

Data mining involves the use of sophisticated data analysis tools to discover previously unknown, valid patterns and relationships in large data sets. These tools can include statistical models, mathematical algorithms, and machine learning methods (algorithms that improve their performance automatically through experience, such as neural networks or decision trees). Consequently, data mining consists of more than collecting and managing data, it also includes analysis and prediction. If data mining results in discovering meaningful patterns, data turns into information. Information or -in this case- patterns that are novel, valid and potentially useful are not merely information, but knowledge. One speaks of discovering knowledge, before hidden in the huge amount of data, but now revealed. This brings us to the term 'Knowledge Discovery', which is usually called in the same breath as 'Data Mining'.

After clarifying the terms machine learning and data mining, it is worth looking at literature using these techniques for the purpose of fraud detection. The machine learning and artificial intelligence solutions that are explored may be classified into two categories: **'supervised'** and **'unsupervised'** learning. In supervised learning, samples of both fraudulent and non-fraudulent records are used. This means that all the records available are labeled as 'fraudulent' or 'non-fraudulent'. After building a model using these training data, new cases can be classified as fraudulent or legal. Of course, one needs to be confident about the true classes of the training data, as this is the foundation of the model. Another practical issue is the availability of such information. Furthermore, this method is only able to detect frauds of a type which has previously occurred.

In contrast, unsupervised methods don't make use of labeled records. These methods seek for accounts, customers, suppliers, etc. that behave 'unusual' in order to output suspicion scores, rules or visual anomalies, depending on the method.

Whether supervised or unsupervised methods are used, note that the output gives us only an indication of fraud likelihood. No stand alone statistical analysis can assure that a particular object is a fraudulent one. It can only indicate that this object is more likely to be fraudulent than other objects.

Fraud Detection

Fraud detection is a continuously evolving discipline. Whenever it becomes known that one detection method is in place, criminals will adapt their strategies and try others. Of course, new criminals are also constantly entering the field. Many of them will not be aware of the fraud detection methods which have been successful in the past and will adopt strategies which lead to identifiable frauds. This means that the earlier detection tools need to be applied as well as the latest developments. The development of new fraud detection methods is made more difficult by the fact that the exchange of ideas in fraud detection is severely limited. It does not make sense to describe fraud detection techniques in great detail in the public domain, as this gives criminals the information that they require to evade detection. Data sets are not made available and results are often censored, making them difficult to assess.

Many fraud detection problems involve huge data sets that are constantly evolving. Some of the fraud detection mechanisms are discussed here.

Internal Control as Fraud Detection:

Generally speaking, internal control implies a system of well designed processes and procedures for the purpose of fraud prevention and deterring. Are internal control systems sufficient as a fraud detection mechanism? Apparently not, since over one third of the fraud cases in the surveys are discovered by chance. Internal controls can be split into two groups: **active** and **passive** internal control systems. Active internal controls are signatures, passwords, segregation of duties etc. These can be compared with fences. They may appear insurmountable at first sight, but like all fences, they have their weakness to be defeated by clever fraud perpetrators. And like a fence, once evaded, there is little or no continuing value in preventing or deterring fraud. Passive internal controls operate at a different level. Instead of *preventing* fraud, like active controls attempt to, the emphasis here is on *deterring*. Passive internal control systems induce a state of mind in the would-be perpetrator that strongly motivates him "not to go there". Examples of passive control systems are surprise audits, customized controls and audit trails. Passive control systems, when turned active if a company feels the need to do so (they suspect fraud), mainly make use of reporting tools, like providing different numbers and statistics for manual analysis. Neither active nor passive control systems are best. They complement each other and should both be prevalent.

Supervised Methods of Fraud Detection

In supervised methods, samples of both fraudulent and non fraudulent records are used to construct models which allow one to assign new observations into one of the two classes. Of course, this requires one to be confident about the true classes of the original data used to build the models. It also requires that one has examples of both classes. Furthermore, it can only be used to detect frauds of a type which have previously occurred.

The use of supervised methods of data mining for fraud detection is investigated in several studies. An intensively explored method is **neural networks**. Neural Network technology can be used for detecting fraud in mobile phone networks and financial statement fraud. A fuzzy neural net, can also be used in the domain of fraudulent financial reporting. A Bayesian learning neural network can be implemented for credit card fraud detection. Artificial Neural Networks has been used for telecommunications fraud by researchers.

Spathis et al (2005) investigates the usefulness of Decision Trees, Neural Networks and Bayesian Belief Networks in the identification of fraudulent financial statements.

Unsupervised Method of Fraud Detection

Unsupervised methods do not need the prior knowledge of fraudulent and non-fraudulent transactions in historical database, but instead detect changes in behavior or unusual transactions. An advantage of using unsupervised methods over supervised methods is that previously undiscovered types of fraud may be detected. The use of unsupervised learning for fraud detection is not explored as intensively as the use of supervised learning. Outlier detection is a fundamental issue in data mining, specifically in fraud detection. Outliers have been informally defined as observations in a data set which appear to be inconsistent with the remainder of that set of data, or which deviate so much from other observations so as to arouse suspicions that they were generated by a different mechanism. The identification of outliers can lead to the discovery of useful knowledge and has a number of practical applications in areas such as credit card fraud detection, athlete performance analysis, voting irregularity analysis, severe weather prediction etc. **Peer Group Analysis (PGA)** is an unsupervised method for monitoring behavior over time in data mining

Bolton and Hand had monitored behavior over time by means of Peer Group Analysis. Peer Group Analysis detects individual objects that begin to behave in a way different from objects to which they had previously been similar. Another tool Bolton and Hand develop for behavioral fraud detection is Break Point Analysis. Unlike Peer Group Analysis, Break Point Analysis operates on the account level. A break point is an observation where anomalous behavior for a particular account is detected. Both the tools are applied on spending behavior in credit card accounts.

Conclusion

Prevention and detection technologies are implemented, tested, customized and commercialized. Software companies sell 'The solution to all your business problems, including fraud'. Also governments use one liners like 'the newest weapon to defeat fraud'. The term 'data mining' is sold as an expensive, all-problems solving word. If your business doesn't use data mining, you're not in the game. If this was really the case, then why is there still fraud? Because using data mining or machine learning technologies implies a lot of conditions. **First**, the term data mining is used many times in an improper manner. Most importantly, data mining is different from the traditional data analysis techniques. **Second**, the most promising results in fraud detection by means of data mining are attained with supervised learning. Having labeled data is however not a realistic view on most of company's problems.

Internal control systems seem to be an appropriate mean to combat internal fraud, since it is number two (after accidental detection) in detecting fraud. But, it still is number two. This has to be improved, and if we believe part of all the success stories of data mining and fraud detection, we have a candidate for the desired improvement: data mining techniques.

References:

- Association of Certified Fraud Examiners: 2006 ACFE Report to the nation on occupational fraud and abuse (2006)
- Bolton, R. J. and Hand. D.J. "Unsupervised Profiling Methods for Fraud Detection," *Credit Scoring and Credit Control VII, Edinburgh, UK, 5-7 Sept* (2001).
- PriceWaterhouse&Coopers: Economic crime: People, culture and controls. The 4th biennial Global Economic Crime Surve (2007)
- Spathis, C. (2002). Detecting false financial statements using published data: some evidence from Greece. Managerial Auditing Journal, 17(4), 179–191.

Enhanced Authentication Scheme in WiMax Network

Deepa Godara
Lecturer, GPMCE., GGSIPU, Delhi

Abstract

The importance of IEEE-Standard 802.16 WiMAX is growing and will compete with technologies such as UMTS. However, acceptance and adoption of technologies and services also depend on security. In the security mechanism of IEEE 802.16e, the network's base station (BS) authenticated the subscriber station (SS) through the X.509 certificate configured in the system of Worldwide Interoperability for Microwave Access (WiMax) that is mutual authentication was based on X.509 certificate and EAP. But RSA signature algorithm in the X.509 certificate had many hidden security trouble. RSA algorithm is based on generating large prime numbers but due to technology limitation generating large prime numbers is troublesome. This made encryption/decryption more difficult in some extent. In this paper, first of all security architecture of IEEE 802.16 will be given. It will summarize the most important elements of the WiMAX security architecture. Further, enhanced authentication scheme will be given by replacing RSA algorithm in X.509 certificate with ECC algorithm, doing this WiMax system's security performance can be enhanced accordingly. ECC is a subset of DLC where DLC is Discrete logarithm cryptography which is another area of cryptography where security is provided by difficulty in solving logarithmic equations over large finite groups. Then a comparison of two algorithms will be given based on operation speed and no of keys required. For example, the ECC key size equivalent of a 1024 bit RSA key is 160 bits.

Keywords: *WiMax, RSA, ECC*

Introduction

WiMAX system uses the radio channel, which is an open channel. Hence, security procedures must be included in order to protect the traffic confidentiality and integrity and to prevent different network security attacks such as theft of service. As WiMAX standards expand from considering a fixed LOS and PMP high frequency system (10—66 GHz) to including a lower frequency (2-11 GHz) NLOS mobile system, WiMAX is open to more security threats than other wireless systems. Since WiMAX uses air interface for the transmission medium, both the PHY and MAC layers are readily exposed to security threats. Privacy is accomplished by encrypting connections between the subscriber station and the base station. The base station protects against unauthorized access by enforcing encryption of service flows across the network. A privacy and key management (PKM) protocol is used by the base station to control the distribution of keying data to subscriber stations. In the security mechanism of IEEE 802.16d, the network's base station (BS) authenticated the subscriber station (SS) through the X.509 certificate configured in the system of Worldwide Interoperability for Microwave Access (WiMax). The X.509 certification carried its owner's related information, marked the BS status and contained the digital signature to BS; however this standard lacked mechanism of SS authenticating BS, which caused the camouflage aggressor to legitimate BS easily and carried on the spurious attack to SS. The IEEE802.16e had repaired this crack, increased digital authentication from SS to BS, and realized mutual authentication between the SS and BS. This kind of mutual authentication was based on X.509 certificate and EAP,it could ensure WiMax security effectively and could reduce the camouflage or invasion from illegal BS; whereas it could be seen that using the RSA signature algorithm in the X.509 certificate had many hidden security trouble, it was known, the RSA security was based on the mathematics problem that the large prime number was difficult to decompose, RSA algorithm was not to be discovered the obvious and serious existent security problem in practice; however, with the technology limitation of generating prime number, the RSA key's production was very troublesome, which also made the encryption/decryption more difficult in some extent[1]. The X.509 certificate was the important guarantee to WiMax's network security, which could be used in the existent cipher system to guarantee its security and efficiency. In this paper, an improved authentication scheme is given by replacing RSA algorithm of X.509 certificate with the ECC algorithm, by which WiMax system's security performance can be enhanced accordingly.

Security Architecture

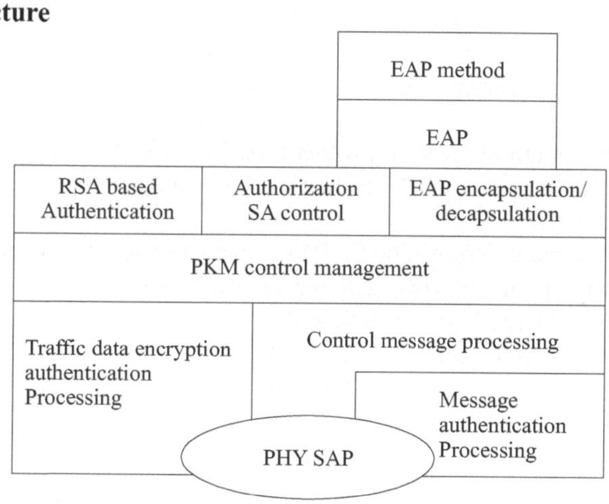

Figure1. Security Architecture

The Security sub layer has been redefined in the IEEE 802.16e amendment mainly due to the fact that 802.16-2004 had some security holes (e.g. no authentication of the BS) and that the security requirements for mobile services are not the same as for fixed services. The Security sub layer of WiMAX as it has been redefined in the IEEE 802.16e [2].

The security schemes involved in WiMAX network security architecture are authentication (including equipment authentication and user authentication), data encryption (including data confidentiality and integrity), access control and key management. By applying cryptographic transforms to MPDUs carried across connections between SS and BS, the security sublayer provides subscribers with privacy, authentication, or confidentiality across the broadband wireless network. Moreover, the BS can protect against unauthorized access to these data transport services by securing the associated service flows across the network. In addition, by adding digital certificate-based SS device-authentication to the key management protocol, the basic security mechanisms are strengthened. The Security sub layer has two main component protocols as follows [3].

1) A data encapsulation protocol for securing packet data across the fixed BWA network. This protocol defines a set of supported cryptographic suites, i.e. pairings of data encryption and authentication algorithms, and the rules for applying those algorithms to a MAC PDU payload.
2) A key management protocol (PKM) providing the secure distribution of keying data from the BS to the SS. Through this key management protocol, the SSs and BSs synchronize keying data. In addition, the BS uses the protocol to enforce conditional access to network services. The 802.16e amendment defined PKMv2 with enhanced features.

Wimax Authentication

Three distinct authentication protocol mechanisms are supported by WiMAX.

1. RSA authentication. (Rivest Shamir Adleman) This protocol is based on X.509 certificates.
2. EAP authentication. The EAP uses particular kinds of credential (subscriber identity module, password, token-based, X.509 certificate or other) depending on the EAP method implemented.
3. HMAC/CMAC authentication. The 802.16 standard securities include the use of a Hashed Message Authentication Code (HMAC) for some message authentication and integrity control. 802.16e added the possibility of using CMAC as an alternative to HMAC.

Authentication Procedure of IEEE 802.16

In WiMax network, the main entities include subscriber station (SS) and base station (BS), in IEEE802.16e, the authentication and key exchange process between SS and BS are as following.

1. SS sends an authentication information message to BS. The message includes X.509 digital certificate which contains the information of SS manufacturer, the legitimacy of the SS equipment can be verified by BS.
2. SS sends an authorization request message to BS for the sake of requesting BS to authenticate the legitimacy of the SS. The message includes manufacturers' X.509 certificates, the cipher algorithms supported by SS, SS basic ID number, 64-bit random number produced by SS and the RSA digital signature about the above information.
3. After BS verifies the identity of SS, BS will activate one of encryption algorithms and protocols which are shared with SS, then sends authorization key (AK) to SS and encrypts it using SS's public key by RSA algorithm, the reply message includes the BS's digital signature containing the entire authorized information encrypted by the RSA algorithm. If BS rejects the authorization request from SS, BS will not send messages to SS.
4. SS sends the confirmation message encrypted by RSA to BS. The information covers a random number produced by BS and authentication result code (Auth Result Code) which represents the success or failure of the certification. Only if the authorization request is rejected, the Error-code and display-string will appear with denoting request being refused and its reasons respectively.

In order to acquire re-authorization continuously, it is necessary for SS to send authorization request periodically to BS for updating the AK

RSA Authentication

RSA cryptography generates keys by taking two large prime numbers. The inherent security is in the difficultly of recovering this key via factorization of large integers. It is generally accepted that RSA keys should be a minimum of 1024 bits.

The PKM RSA authentication protocol uses X.509 digital certificates, the RSA public-key encryption algorithm that binds public RSA encryption keys to MAC addresses of SSs. X.509 certificates X.509 certificates are used to allow the base station to identify subscriber stations. The 802.16 standard states that 802.16-compliant SSs must use X.509 Version 3 certificate formats providing a public key infrastructure used for secure authentication.

Version
Serial Number
Signature Algorithm
Signature Value
Issuer
Validity
Subject
Subject Public Key Information
Issuer's Identifier (optional)
Subject's Identifier (optional)
Extensions

Figure2: X.509 Certificate Fields

Currently RSA-based authorization or RSA + EAP authorization/authentication is supported in 802.16 networks. The X.509 certificates have RSA encryption keys, between 1024 and 2048 bits.

ECC Based Authorization

Discrete logarithm cryptography (DLC) is another area of cryptography where security is provided by difficulty in solving logarithmic equations over large finite groups. ECC is a subset of DLC, where the discrete logarithm solution over an equation (plane curve). The elliptic curve equations can over finite groups on prime fields (F_p) or binary fields (F_2^m). For prime fields, where p is a large/odd prime > 3, curves are of the form $y^2 = x^3 + a*x + b$. For binary fields, the order of the field is a power of 2, the curves are of the form $y^2 + x*y = x^3 + a*x^2 + b$. The points on the curve and the point at infinity O form an abelian group together with the operation "addition". The operation in this group is given below [4]

1) Point Addition: If $P(X_1,Y_1)$ and $Q(X_2,Y_2)$ are points on the elliptic curve and if $-X_1$ □□ $\neq X_2$ (equally $P \neq -Q$), then, $R(X_3,Y_3)=P+Q$ can be defined geometrically In the case $P \neq Q$), Q, a line intersecting the curve at the points P and Q must also intersect the curve at a third point -R, and $R(X_3,Y_3)$ is the answer; if P=Q (point doubling),the tangent line is used;

If $P \neq Q$

$\lambda = (y_1+y_2) / (x_1+x_2);$

$x_3 = \lambda^2 + \lambda + x_1 + x_2 + a;$

$y = (x_1+x_3)\lambda + x_3 + y1;$

If $P=Q$

$\lambda = y1 / x_1 + x_1;$

$x_3 = \lambda^2 + \lambda + a;$

$y_3 = (x_1+x_3)\lambda + x_3 + y1;$

If $P=-Q$ then $P+Q=0$

2) Point Multiplication: Multiplication (also called Algorithm Signature Key exchange scalar multiplication) is defined by repeated addition.
   Q=kP=P+P+....+P.(k times addition)

The elliptic curve discrete logarithm problem (ECDLP), which is the ECC's security based on is described as follows. Given an elliptic and a point on it, To determine k from the Q=kP, where Q and P are points on the curve and kP means P added itself k times. It is easy to get Q from k and P- but is very hard to determine k from Q and P, especially for the big numbers [5].

ECC can be used for new cryptosystem. If A wants send message to B. First, A choose an elliptic curve and a point G on it, note that both and B should know G. Then A encodes message to the point Pm on the curve. B choose a random number a (B's private key), and compute aG (B's public key), and announce it. Then A choose another random number k, and compute Pm+k(aG) and kG, : and send C=(kG,Pm+kaG) to B. When B receives C, he can compute Pm=Pm-kaG-akQ and get Pm, then decode Pm to the message. Because of the ECDLP, attackers are very hard to get Pm.

Comparison of RSA/ECC Based Authentication

ECC keys can be smaller than RSA keys, because it is believed that the solution to a discrete logarithm is fundamentally more complex than the factorization of large integers. For example, the CC key size equivalent of a 1024 bit RSA key is 160 bits [3].

Following tables show comparison of ECC and RSA in terms of operation speedup and Energy cost of digital signatures and key exchange computations (mJ) [6]

	Operation Time [s]	Speedup
RSA 1024	10.99	1
ECC 160	0.81	13.6
RSA 2048	83.26	1
ECC 224	2.19	38

Table 1: Operation Speedup

Algorithm	Signature		Key Exchange	
RSA 1024	304	11.9	15.4	304
ECDSA 160	22.82	45.09	22.3	22.3
RSA 2048	2302.7	53.7	57.2	2302.7
ECDSA 224	61.54	121.98	60.4	60.4

Table 2: Energy cost of digital signatures and key exchange computations (mJ)

Authentication Process Based on ECC

Currently RSA-based authorization or RSA + EAP authorization/authentication is supported in 802.16 networks. The X.509 certificates have RSA encryption keys, between 1024 and 2048 bits. In this paper it is proposed to add elliptic curve cryptography (ECC)-based authorization to the suite of security protocols in IEEE 802.16m. This requires the use of ECC-based X.509 certificates that support key lengths of 160 - 224 bits. The structure of the certificates will have to be adjusted to match ECC requirements, and a new CA capable of supporting X.509-based ECC certificates will have to be created [6]. The ECC authorization should be added to the cryptographic suite of protocols and should be the preferred method, while maintaining use of RSA authorization for legacy MS [7].

Procedure of authentication is as follows:

1. SS sends authentication message to BS. The information contains the X.509 digital certificates issued by the SS manufacturers or other authority organizations (the manufacturers can download the relative information into the SS equipment). SS takes the manufacturers' X.509 digital certificate to BS through authentication messages; the certificate contains the SS manufacturer's information (MAC address, the manufacturer ID number, serial number, etc.), which can prove that the user station is legal equipment.

2. After BS verifies the SS manufacturer's X.509 digital certificate, BS will send the authentication information to SS. The information includes the X.509 digital certificates issued by the BS manufacturers or other authority organizations; then BS delivers the manufacturers' X.509 digital certificate to SS through authentication messages to prove the current BS's validity. If BS fails to validate the SS manufacturers' digital certificate, it will attach failure information on authentication message sent to SS.
3. Finishing checking up the identity of BS, SS will send authorization request message to BS. The information covers manufacturers' X.509 certificates, the cipher algorithm supported by SS, basic ID of SS, 64-bit random number produced by the SS and the ECC digital signature algorithm based on the above information, the information will be used to ask for BS to authenticate the certification legality of SS.
4. Completing verifying the identity of SS, BS will activate one of encryption algorithms and protocols, which are shared with SS. Authorization Key (AK)encrypted by SS public key through RSA algorithm will be sent to SS, the reply message usually includes BS's X.509 certificates, the Primary Authorization Key (PAK) encrypted by the ECC with the SS 1024-bit public key, a 4-bit PAK serial number, a survival cycle of the PAK privacy key, a single main security association logo, one or more static security association used for SS to acquire the accessing authorization from privacy key information, the 64-bit random number held by SS, a random number generated by BS and the signature of the entire authorized information. In addition, BS needs to determine whether the SS can acquire the authority of services.

   If BS rejects the SS authorization request, the refusal information will be sent to the SS, the information is based on the ECC encryption algorithm, including the following data: random number of SS, random number generated by BS, the error-code denoting the request rejected, the X.509 digital certificates held by BS, display-string expressing the reasons for the request refused and the digital signature based on the ECC signature algorithm for the information above.
5. The SS sends the confirm information encrypted by the ECC algorithm to BS. The information contains the random number produced by BS, the authentication result code (Auth Result Code) showing the successful or failing reasons in communication process, and the digital signature based on the ECC signature algorithm (only when the authorization request is rejected, error code indicating refused authorization request and display-string indicating refused request reason will appear in the confirmation message).

   The SS periodically sends the authorization request to BS in order to update the AK, re-authorization and authorization can perform the same process, however the SS will send the authentication messages no longer, in the process of re-authorization, in order to avoid the service being interrupted, the subsequent AK can overlap with the former during the key valid period.

Conclusion

In this paper, security architecture of IEEE802.16 is given. Further X.509 certificate is modified by using ECC algorithm and a comparison of RSA and ECC algorithms is given using certain data Compared with the RSA, public key system based on ECC has a lot of advantages not only in security strength but also in encryption efficiency. To provide the same security strength as RSA with 1024 bits key, ECC needs only a key of 160 bits, that is, the length of the X.509 certificate can be greatly reduced, and a higher level of security strength can be provided.

References

- Luo Wei, Guo Da, SONG Mei. The present status and development of WiMax security strategy [J]. Mobile Communications, 2006, 11-27.
- LANG Wei-min[1], ZHONG Jing-li[2], LI Jian-Jun[3] LANG "Research on authentication scheme of WiMax", IEEE Explore, 2008.
- Barker, Elaine, et al., "Recommendation for Key Management - Part 1: General (Revised)", NIST Special Publication 800-57, March 2007
- Leung, I.K.H. "A microcoded elliptic curve processor using FPGA technology" Leong, P.H.W.; Very Large-Scale Integration (VLSI) Systems, IEEE Transactions on Volume 10, Issue 5, Oct. 2002 Page(s):550 – 559
- Cano, M.-D., etc al., "A Certification Authority for Elliptic Curve X.509v3 Certificates", IEEE Third International Conference on Networking and Services, pg 49, June 2007.
- Ranga Reddy, US army, DJ Shyy Mitre, Sheng Sun Nortel,"Elliptic Curve Cryptography Based Authorization and Key aggrement for IEEE802.16m.
- Huixia Jin, Li Tu, Gelan Yang, Yatao Yang "An Improved Mutual Authentication Scheme in Multi-Hop WiMax Network 2008" International Conference on Computer and Electrical Engineering

Mining Software Repositories

Pooja Thakar
Lecturer , RDIAS, Delhi

Abstract

The term Mining Software Repositories has been coined to describe a broad class of investigations into the examination of software repositories. Here software repositories refer to artifacts that are produced and archived during software evolution. Software repositories contain a wealth of valuable information for empirical studies in software engineering. This paper presents an overview on Mining Software Repositories, discusses challenges associated with mining software repositories and current trends.

Introduction

As the size and complexity of software systems increases, software practitioners find themselves facing many challenges to deliver high quality software on time and within budget. Software managers are continuously estimating the quality of their software and predicting its reliability to ensure that no faulty software is released. Moreover, they endeavor with varying degrees of success to wisely allocate their limited testing and development resources to the parts of the most appropriate parts of the code.

Unfortunately, in many cases such attempts are based on ad-hoc techniques and rough approximations. Their success depends on their intuition, experience and chance.

Software developers spend a large amount of their time trying to comprehend source code as they modify it to implement the evolving requirements of the customers. They perform such complex tasks using simple text editors and tools. Such primitive tools are limited by the size of the software system and the amount of information a person can keep track of while jumping around the source tree.

The evolutionary history of a software project offers a great opportunity to assist these practitioners. Software repositories contain a wealth of valuable information about software projects. Using the information stored in these repositories, practitioners can depend less on their intuition and experience, and depend more on historical and field data.

Types of Software Repositories

The Mining Software Repositories field is maturing, thanks to the rich, extensive, and readily available software repositories. Various Types of Software repositories include:

1) **Historical repositories**

These include source control repositories, bug repositories, and archived communications, which record lots of information about the evolution and progress of a project.

Repository	Description
Source control repositories	These repositories record the development history of a project. They track all the changes to the source code along with meta-data about each change, e.g., the name of the developer who performed the change, the time the change was performed and a short message describing the change. Source control repositories are the most commonly available and used repository in software projects. CVS, subversion, Perforce, ClearCase are examples of source control repositories which are used in practice.
Bug repositories	These repositories track the resolution history of bug reports or feature requests that are reported by users and developers of large software projects. Bugzilla and Jira are examples of bug repositories.
Archived communications	These repositories track discussions about various aspects of a software project throughout its lifetime. Mailing lists, emails, IRC chats, and instant messages are examples of archived communications about a project.

Table 1: Hitorical Repositories

2) **Run-time repositories**

These include deployment logs contain information about the execution and the usage of an application at a single or multiple deployment sites. These repositories record information about the execution of a single deployment of a software application or different deployments of the same applications. For example, the deployment logs may record the error messages reported by an application at various deployment sites. The availability of deployment logs continues to increase at a rapid rate due to their use for remote issue resolution and due to legal acts.

3) **Code repositories**

These repositories archive the source code for a large number of projects. These include the source code of all the projects developed in the company. Many Open Source repositories such as Sourceforge.net and Google code contain the large open source code of various applications developed by several developers.

Use of Data Mining in Software Repositories

The data in these repositories is available for most large software projects and represents a detailed and rich record of the historical development of software systems.

Until recently these repositories were used primarily for their intended activities such as maintaining versions of the source code or tracking the status of a defect. Software practitioners and researchers are beginning to recognize the potential benefit of mining this information for other purposes. Various research has been done and now proceeding to uncover the ways in which mining these repositories can help support the maintenance of software systems, improve software design/ reuse, and empirically validate novel ideas and techniques. Figure 1 describes the process of "Mining Software Repositories". Lower layer represents all software repositories available, Middle layer represents the type of mining technique that can be applied on lowest layer for knowledge discovery and Top Layer represents the software engineering tasks on which this discovered knowledge can be utilized.

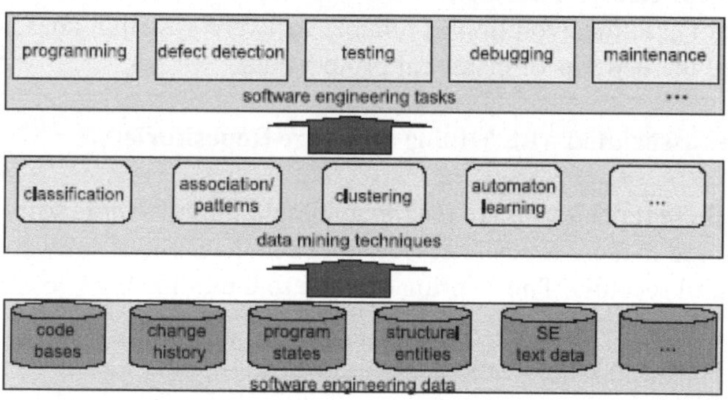

Figure1. Mining Software Engineering Data

Who will be benefited?

Approaches and techniques that use the evolutionary history of software projects can assist:

- Developers:
  - " in maintaining large software projects, to assist them in changing the software system and understanding it.
  - " in understanding legacy code and discovering the rationale behind the current software structure.
  - " in ensuring that changes are propagated to the appropriate parts of the code.
- Managers:
  - " in predicting the occurrence of faults in a software system.
  - " in improving the reliability of software systems
  - " in allocating their limited testing resources to the most appropriate parts of the software system.

Early Research

Software repositories have primarily been used for historical record keeping activities such as retrieving old versions of the source code or tracking the status of a defect. A few studies have emerged that use this data to study various aspects of software development such as software architecture, code reuse, development process and developer motivation.

Early Researchers have shown that software repositories can support developers in changing legacy systems by pointing out hidden code dependencies, historical information can assist developers in understanding large systems and demonstrated that historical change information can support management in predicting bugs and effort to ease the evolution of reliable software systems. These early studies highlighted the benefits of historical project data.

Challenges associated with Mining Software Repositories

Although these repositories are readily available for most large software projects, the data stored in these repositories has not been the focus of software engineering research until recently. This is primarily due to the following two reasons:

a) Limited Access to Repositories: Companies in many cases are not willing to give researchers access to such detailed information about their software systems. Another possible source for software repositories is academic projects and systems. Unfortunately, the repositories of such projects and systems are neither as rich nor as interesting as those of long-lived widely-deployed commercial software systems. In the past, Mining Software Repositories was almost subjected on industrial systems. Consequently, research efforts were limited to select a few software systems (and application domains) or hampered by lack of historical data that was publicly available.

b) Complexity of Data Extraction: Unfortunately, software repositories are not designed to facilitate empirical understanding of a software project. Software tools (such as version control and defect tracking systems) tend to have various anomalies and issues in their recorded information. Tools may be used differently in different projects, and different tools are often used in different organizations. More importantly, the quantities of interest such as development effort are usually not directly captured. A key challenge is to build useful theories and models of software development that can be empirically validated using the information in software repositories.

Most repositories are not designed with automated bulk data-extraction and mining in mind, so they provide limited support for automated extraction. The complexity of automated data extraction hindered the adoption and integration of software repositories in other software engineering research. In many cases, software engineering researchers do not have the expertise required nor do they have the interest to extract data from software repositories. Extracting such data requires a great deal of effort and time from researchers, instead they are more interested in gaining convenient access to the extracted data in an easy to process format.

There has been progress in overcoming some of these challenges by constructing tools and developing methods to extract, clean, and validate information from software repositories. But still many challenges require more research.

Current Trend in Mining Software Repositories

Recently, there has been a rapid paradigm shift with regards to the above situation, mostly attributed to the establishment and wide prevalence of open source software development. Arguably, the open source paradigm has been successful in producing numerous high-quality projects that continue to live and evolve. With the advent of open source systems, easy access to repositories of large software systems became a reality. Researchers now have access to rich repositories for large projects used by thousands of users and developed by hundreds of developers over extended periods of time.

Software repositories have traditionally been used for archival purposes. The mining software repositories field has shown that these repositories could be mined to uncover useful patterns and actionable information about software systems and projects. Mining Software Repositories researchers have proposed techniques which augment traditional software engineering data, techniques and tools, in order to solve important and challenging problems, such as identifying bugs, and reusing code, which practitioners must face and solve on a daily basis.

Many studies have emerged that use this data to support various aspects of software development within industrial and open source settings.

Conclusion

Software managers are routinely confronted with software projects that contain errors or inconsistencies and exceed budget and time limits. By mining software repositories with comprehensible data mining techniques, predictive models can be induced that offer software managers the insights they need to tackle these quality and budgeting problems in an efficient way.

References:

- Lehman M. On understanding laws, evolution and conservation in the large program life cycle. Journal of Systems and Software 1980.
- Lehman M, Ramil JF. An approach to a theory of software evolution. Proceedings International Workshop on Principles of Software Evolution (IWPSE'01). IEEE Computer Society Press: Los Alamitos CA, 2001.
- German DM, Cubranic D, Storey MAD. A framework for describing and understanding mining tools in software development. Proceedings 2nd International Workshop on Mining Software Repositories (MSR'05). ACM Press: New York NY, 2005.
- Buckley J, Mens T, Zenger M, Rashid A, Kniesel G. Towards a taxonomy of software change. Journal of Software Maintenance and Evolution: Research and Practice 2005.
- Robles G, Gonz´alez-Barahona JM, Ghosh RA. GlueTheos: Automating the retrieval and analysis of data from publicly available software repositories. Proceedings 1st International Workshop on Mining Software Repositories (MSR'04). University of Waterloo: Waterloo ON, 2004.

Grid Security

Mirtunjay Sinha
Lecturer, Hindu Institute of Management, Sonepat, Haryana

Abstract

Grid computing is known as next generation technology. It is simply stated as distributed computing taken to the next evolutionary level. It enables the sharing, selection and aggregation of geographically distributed heterogeneous resources for solving large scale problems in science, engineering and commerce. The resource in the grid are heterogeneous and geographically distributed, this created a lot of open space for intruders and make the grid vulnerable to third party attacks. It requires a lot of thinking and planning to secure such a heterogeneous and widely distributed grid.

A major requirement for Grid computing is security. At the base of any grid environment, there must be mechanisms to provide security, including authentication, authorization, data encryption, and so on. This paper describes how these challenges are being dealt within a given grid environment. It takes a look on challenges and the mechanism adopted to handle those challenges.

The organization of this paper includes the definition of Grid followed by basic terms involved in grid security terminology. Then it explains the mechanism of security by authentication, authorization and delegation followed by conclusion.

Introduction

Grid computing most simply stated as distributed computing taken to the next evolutionary level. The goal is to create a simple yet large powerful self managing virtual computer out of a large collection of connected heterogeneous system sharing various combinations of resources. This distributed and heterogeneous system has its own set of problem. This ranges from authentication to distribution. Grid security infrastructure found as the solution of this problem and discussed in detail in this paper.

The Grid

Grid is a type of parallel and distributed system that enables the sharing, selection, and aggregation of geographically distributed "autonomous" resources dynamically at runtime depending on their availability, capability, performance, cost, and users' quality-of-service requirements Grid infrastructure will provide us with the ability to dynamically link together resources as an ensemble to support the execution of large-scale, resource-intensive, and distributed applications.

Grid Security Requirements

The goal and purpose of Grid technologies is to support the sharing and coordinated use of diverse resources in dynamic, distributed virtual organizations (VOs). The basic security model must address the following security disciplines:

- *Authentication.* Provide plug points for multiple authentication mechanisms and the means for conveying the specific mechanism used in any given authentication operation. The authentication mechanism may be a custom authentication mechanism or an industry-standard technology
- *Delegation.* Provide facilities to allow for delegation of access rights from requestors to services, as well as to allow for delegation policies to be specified. When dealing with delegation of authority from an entity to another, care should be taken so that the authority transferred through delegation is scoped only to the task(s) intended to be performed and within a limited lifetime to minimize the misuse of delegated authority.
- *Single Logon.* Relieve an entity having successfully completed the act of authentication once from the need to participate in re-authentications upon subsequent accesses to managed resources for some reasonable period of time
- *Credential Lifespan and Renewal.* In many scenarios, a job initiated by a user may take longer than the life span of the user's initially delegated credential. In those cases, the user needs the ability to be notified prior to expiration of the credentials, or the ability to refresh those credentials such that the job can be completed.
- *Authorization.* Allow for controlling access to services based on authorization policies (i.e., who can access a service, under what conditions) attached to each service.
- *Privacy.* Allow both a service requester and a service provider to define and enforce privacy policies.
- *Confidentiality.* Protect the confidentiality of the underlying communication (transport) mechanism, and the confidentiality of the messages or documents that flow over the transport mechanism in grid infrastructure. The confidentiality requirement includes point–to–point transport as well as store-and-forward mechanisms.
- *Message integrity.* Ensure that unauthorized changes made to messages or documents may be detected by the recipient.
- *Secure logging.* Provide all services, including security services themselves, with facilities for time-stamping and securely logging any kind of operational information or event in the course of time - securely meaning here reliably and

accurately, i.e. so that such collection is neither interruptible nor alterable by adverse agents. Secure logging is the foundation for addressing requirements for notarization, non-repudiation, and auditing.

- *Firewall traversal.* A major barrier to dynamic, cross-domain Grid computing today is the existence of firewalls. Firewalls provide limited value within a dynamic Grid environment.

Grid Security terms

During the course of this paper, we go over many important security terms. The terms covered within this section provide the background as to how grid security works, below are some important security concepts that you should be aware of when reading this paper. These concepts are described in greater detail throughout the paper.

Symmetric encryption: Using the same secret key to provide encryption and decryption of data.

Asymmetric encryption: Using two different keys for encryption and decryption. The public key encryption technique is the primary example of this using a public key and a private key pair.

Secure Socket Layer/Transport Layer Security (SSL/TLS): These are essentially the same protocol. TLS has been renamed by the IETF, but they are based on the same RFC.

Public Key Infrastructure (PKI): The different components, technologies, and protocols that make up a popular asymmetric encryption solution.

Mutual Authentication: Two parties who want to communicate with one another use their public key stored in their digital certificate to authenticate with one another. These are all important concepts to remember and will give you a head start in understanding how grid security works.

The Certificate Authority

A Certificate Authority (CA) has many responsibilities.
The primary responsibilities are:

- Positively identifying entities requesting certificates
- Issuing, removing, and archiving certificates
- Protecting the Certificate Authority server
- Maintaining a namespace of unique names for certificate owners

- Serving signed certificates to those needing to authenticate entities
- Logging activity

One of the critical issues within a grid PKI environment is guaranteeing the system's trustworthiness. Before a CA can sign and issue certificates for others, it has to do the same thing to itself so that its identity can be represented by its own certificate. That means a CA has to do the following:

1. The CA randomly generates its *own key pair.*
2. The CA protects its *private key.*
3. The CA creates its *own certificate.*
4. The CA signs its certificate with its private key.

If a grid resource needs to securely communicate with another grid resource, it needs a certificate signed by a CA. The grid resource has to enroll with the CA by generating an unsigned digital certificate specifying his or her own information. The information submitted will be used by the CA to identify whether this grid resource is real and should be granted a certificate. The CA will then sign the digital certificate if the grid resource is eligible to receive the certificate. This certificate, after the CA signs the certificate, will be passed back to the requesting grid resource. So, one basic function of a CA is to create and issue certificates for a grid resource.

CA cross certification

Generally within a single grid environment, a CA will provide certificates to a fixed group of users. If two companies or virtual organizations (VOs) need to communicate with and trust one another, this may require that both CAs trust one another or participate in cross certification. Grid computers from different security domains or VOs will need to trust each others' certificates, so the roles and relationships between CAs have to be defined.

Digital certificates

Digital certificates are digital documents that associate a grid resource with its specific public key. A certificate is a data structure containing public key and pertinent details about the key owner. A certificate is considered to be a tamper-proof electronic ID when it signed by the Certification Authority for the grid environment A digital certificate is made up of a unique distinguished name (DN) and certificate extensions that contain the information about the individual or host that is being certified.

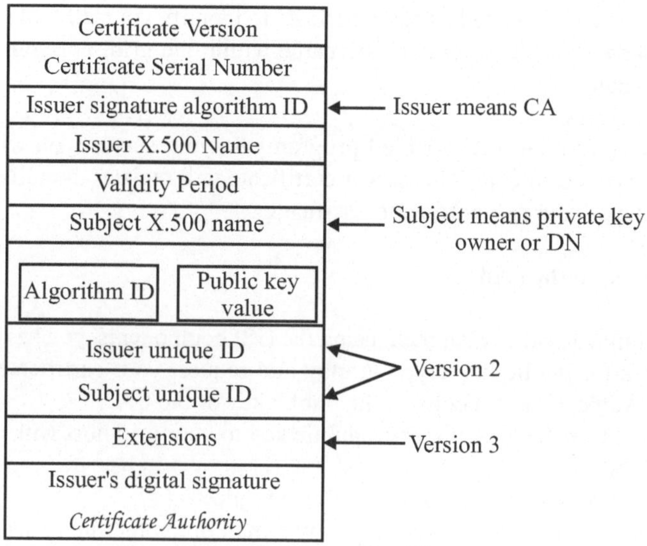

Figure 1: Digital Certificate

Obtaining a client or a server certificate from a CA involves the following steps:

1. The grid user requiring certification generates a key pair (private key and certificate request containing the public key).
2. The user signs its own public key and any other information required by the CA.
3. The signed information is communicated to the CA.
4. The CA verifies that the user does own the private key of the public key presented.
5. The CA needs to verify the user's identity. This can be done using e-mail, telephone, or face-to-face communication. A CA (or RA) can use its own record system or another organization's record system to verify the user's identity.
6. Upon a positive identity check, the CA creates a certificate by signing the public key of the user, thereby associating a user to a public key.

Verification of the user

The authentication described above is a one-time authentication for the purpose of certificate issuance.

Different types of certificates

There are two different types of certificates that are used within a grid environment.

User certificates

As a grid user, you will need a user certificate to identify yourself within the grid. This certificate will identify your user name within the grid, not your server or workstation name.

Server certificates

If you plan on running PKI-enabled programs on your server, you will need to register a server certificate. This server certificate will register the fully qualified domain name of your server to your certificate.

Getting access to the grid

In order to build a grid environment using the GSI components, you have to create a set of keys for public key cryptography and request your certificate from the Certificate Authority and a copy of the public key of the CA.

1. Copy the Certificate Authority's public key to your grid host with which you set up GSI.
2. Create your private key and a certificate request.
3. Send your certificate request to CA by e-mail or another more secure way if you are running a production system and need to positively identify the sender.
4. CA signs your request to make your certificate and sends it back to you.

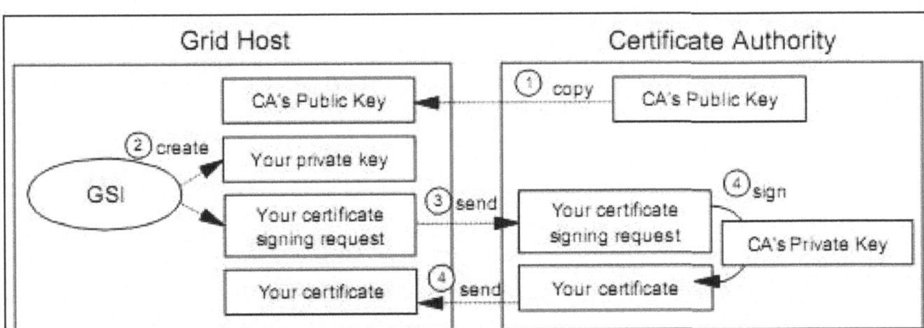

Figure 2: Preparation Procedure for GSI

When that procedure has been completed and you have received your signed digital certificate, you will have three important files on your grid host. They are:

The CA's public key

The grid host's private key

The grid host's digital certificate

Authentication and Authorization

Through the steps described below, grid host A is authenticated and authorized by grid host B. Almost all steps are for authentication, except the last authorization step:

1. A user or application on A sends its certificate to the host B.
2. Host B will get the public key for A and will use it to extract the subject from the certificate.
3. Host B creates a random number and sends it to host A.
4. Host A receives the number, encrypts it with its private key, and sends the encrypted number to host B.
5. Host B will decrypt the number and check that the decrypted number is really the one that it sent before. Then host B authenticates that the certificate is really that from the user on host A, because only that user on host A can encrypt the number with its private key.
6. The certificate is authenticated by host B, and the subject in the certificate is mapped to a local user name.

The subject is in the form of Distinguished Name (DN) like "O=Grid/O=Globus/OU=itso.grid.com/CN=your name", and it is the name that is used by LDAP to distinguish the entries in the directory service. The subject is used to specify the user identity in a grid environment. The user defined by the Distinguished Name is authorized by host B to act as a local user on host B.

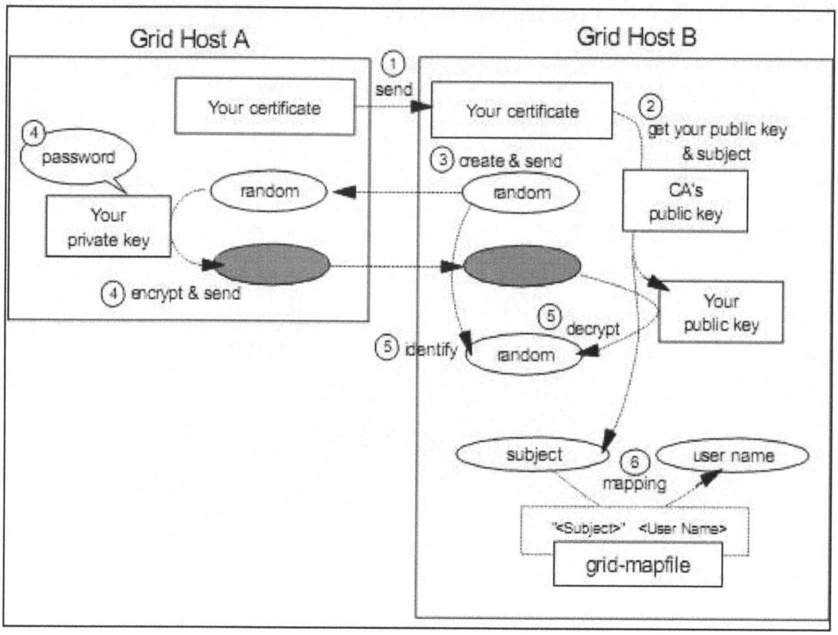

Figure 3: Authentication Procedure

Delegation

Imagine a situation where you distribute jobs to remote grid machines and let them distribute their child jobs to other machines under your security policy. In this situation, you can use the delegation function of GSI.

If you are on the side of host A, you can create your proxy at host B to delegate your authority. This proxy acts as yourself, and submits a request to host C on your behalf.

Proxy Creation

For proxy creation:

1. A trusted communication is created between host A and host B.
2. You request host B to create a proxy that delegates your authority.
3. Host B creates the request for your proxy certificate, and sends it back to host A.
4. Host A signs the request to create your proxy certificate using your private key and sends it back to host B.
5. Host A sends your certificate to host B.

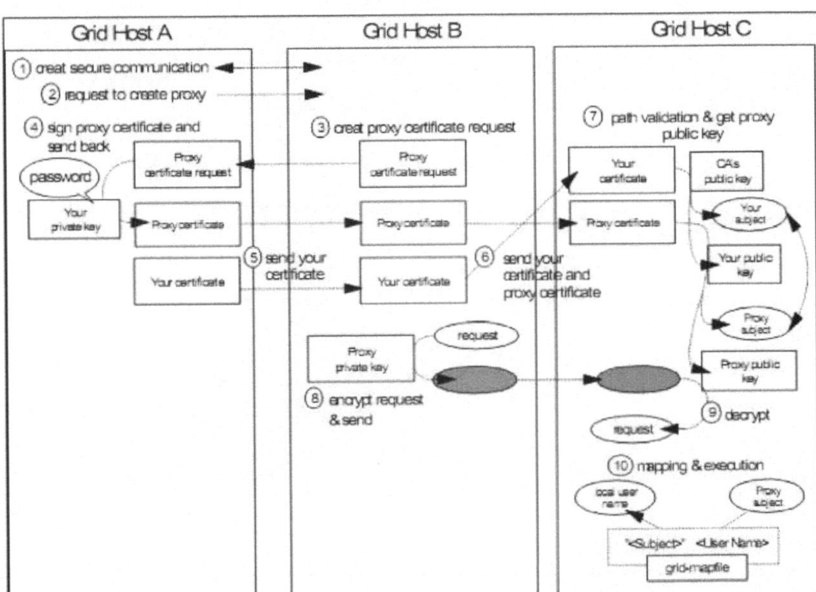

Figure 4: Delegation Procedure of User's Proxy

Proxy Action

For proxy action:

1. Your proxy sends your certificate and the certificate of your proxy to host C.
2. Host C gets your proxy's public key through the path validation procedure:
   a. Host C gets your subject and your public key from your certificate using CA's public key.
   b. Host C gets the proxy's subject and your proxy's public key from your proxy's certificate using your public key.
   c. The subject is a Distinguished Name. If it is validated, your proxy is authenticated by host C and able to act on your behalf.
3. The proxy encrypts a request message using its private key and sends it to host C.
4. Host C decrypts the encrypted message using the proxy's public key and gets the request.
5. Host C runs the request under the authority of a local user. The user is specified using a mapping file, which represents the mapping between the grid users and local users.

Grid Secure Communication

It is important to understand the communication mechanisms used within the Grid communication. By default, the underlying communication is based on the mutual authentication of digital certificates and SSL/TLS.

The digital certificates that have been installed on the grid computers provide the mutual authentication between the two parties. The SSL/TLS functions that OpenSSL provides will encrypt all data transferred between grid hosts. These two functions together provide the basic security services of authentication and confidentiality.

Mutual Authentication

The process of mutual authentication begins when two grid resources want to share resources. Instead of using a key repository, each grid resource authenticates with one another based on their digital certificate.

SSL Handshake

In order to establish the secure communication between the grid server and grid client, a handshake must be established. This handshake is responsible for determining the SSL settings, exchanging public keys and the basis for the mutual authentication process. The handshake process is as follows:

1. A grid client contacts a remote grid server to start a secure session by using a digital certificate.
2. The grid client automatically sends to the server the client's SSL version number, cipher settings, randomly generated data, and other information the server needs to communicate with the client using SSL.
3. The grid server responds, automatically sending the grid client the site's digital certificate, along with the server's SSL version number, cipher settings, and so on.
4. The customer's client examines the information contained in the server's certificate, and verifies that:
    a. The server certificate is valid and has a valid date.
    b. The CA that issued the server certificate has been signed by a trusted CA whose certificate is built into the client.
    c. The issuing CA's public key, built into the client, validates the issuer's digital signature.
    d. The domain name specified by the server certificate matches the server's actual domain name.
5. If the server can be successfully authenticated, the grid client generates a unique session key to encrypt all communications with the grid server using asymmetric encryption.
6. The user's client encrypts the session key itself with the server's public key so that only the site can read the session key, and sends it to the server.
7. The server decrypts the session key using its own private key.
8. The grid client sends a message to the server informing it that future messages from the grid client will be encrypted with the session key. The grid server then sends a message to the grid client informing it that future messages from the server will be encrypted with the session key.
9. An SSL-secured session is now established. SSL then uses symmetric encryption to encrypt and decrypt messages within the SSL-secured *pipeline*.
10. Now that the first grid resources have authenticated, the second grid resource will now authenticate using the same process.
11. Once the session is complete, the session key is eliminated. As long as both grid resources have a valid digital certificate, the process of mutual authentication will succeed.

Conclusion

To conclude that the expansion and invention of new technologies brings new methods of working this introduces new problems too. Grid computing is one of those breakthrough technologies which made everyone to think out of box. New features of grid introduced the need of improvement in security. This paper presented some of the techniques used in grid environment to provide secure communication. But still the world has to move a long way ahead.

References

- Behrouz A. Forouzan "Cryptography and Network Security", Tata McGraw-Hill Publishing Company Limited.
- Anirabn Chakrabarti "Grid Computing Security", Springer
- Bishop, M. Computer Security.Reading, MA: Addison-Wesley, 2005
- Rescorla, E. SSL and TLS. Redaing, MA: Addison-Wesley, 2001
- Soloman, D. Data Privacy and security. Berlin: Springer, 2003.
- Bart Jacob,Michel Brown, Kentaro Fukui,Nihar Trivedi, "Introduction to Grid Computing", IBM REDBOOKS.
- Nataraj Nagaratnam, Philippe Janson, John Dayka, Anthony Nadalin,Frank Siebenlist, Von Welch, Steve Tuecke,"The Security Architecture for Open Grid Services

Study of Location Based Services in GSM Technology

Jyotika Giri
Lecturer, DKES-SCS, Delhi

Abstract

A location-based service is able to provide targeted spatial information to mobile workers and consumers. These include utility location information, personal or asset tracking, concierge and route-guidance information, to name just a few of the possible LBS. The technologies and applications of LBS will play an ever increasingly important role in the modern, mobile, always-connected society.

This paper endeavors to provide some background to the technology underlying location-based services. These include whether wireless mobile technologies are ready to support LBS, which mobile positioning technologies can be used and what are their shortcomings.

Introduction

Mobile location-based commerce ("mobile e-commerce" or simply "l-commerce") refers to the provision of location-based information on mobile devices as a result of a user request. In other words, it "aims to provide specific, targeted information to users based on each specific user's location at any time" (Benson, 2001). In the case of emergency calls, it is obvious that if the call responders have information concerning the location of the people making the call, then the response time can be reduced. Hence security and safety are important considerations for a "mobile society". The second type of application is where location-specific information on something nearby (to the mobile device, or user's location) is sought. These are so-called "concierge services". The requested information may be related to points-of-interest such as hospitals, restaurants, cinemas, car parks, ATMs, and so on. Such a service may provide information about the point-of-interest, or route-guidance to find it.

In essence, LBS can only be provided through the integration of wireless communications and computing technologies, with 'spatial elements' such as positioning technologies and spatial data sets. These components form a network using wireless communication standards to transfer service requests and information between a mobile user and a service (or server) facility. The location-based service facility is able to perform spatial functions based on the user's location, generally with the aid of a Geographical Information System.

Mobile Wireless Communication Standard Lbs

In general, a wireless communication system consists of three main components: the Mobile Switching Centres (MSC) or central processing equipment, the base stations and the user handsets.

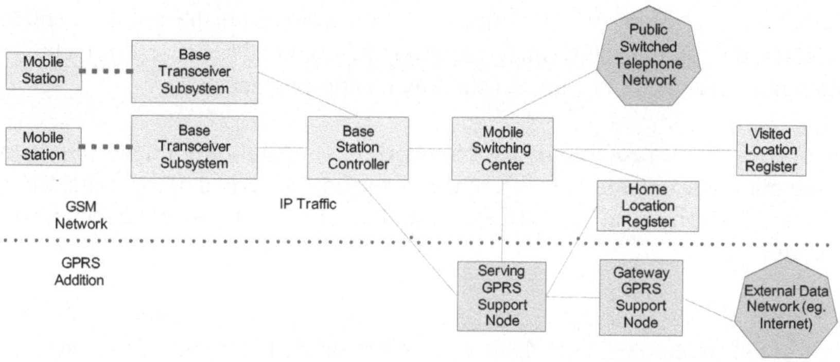

Figure 1. Mobile Wireless Components for GSM

The MSC is responsible for interacting with a large number of base stations, controlling call processing and billing. They make use of some very important databases, such as the home location register (HLR) and the visiting location register (VLR). The HLR contains subscriber registrations and service profile information. The VLR is used when a customer of a serving system area has 'roamed' into another area.

The base stations are the 'links' between the MSC and the handsets. A base station manages a cell within a wireless telephony network, containing many mobile handsets. The base station typically comprises a control unit, radio base station equipment and an antenna. The mobile handsets may be cell phones or small handheld computing devices known as Personal Digital Assistants (PDA). A mobile handset consists of a control/interface unit, a transceiver and an antenna system. When a user (calling party) makes a call from his/her cell phone, the calling base station receives the call and transfers it to the calling MSC. The calling MSC processes the call, retrieves the caller profile from the database and makes the relevant information available to the MSC. The called party receives the call via a called base station. Communication between MSCs is performed via the fixed telephone system.

Positioning And Lbs

Determining the location of mobile users is one of the most challenging tasks that must be undertaken in order to enable a location-based service. LBS providers currently use different methods to determine locations.

Non-gps Positioning Techniques

The most common non-GPS solutions for mobile positioning are:
Cell of Origin : Uses the cell identification information within the mobile telephony network to identify the approximate location of the caller. However, this technique is often not very useful because of the low positioning accuracy.

Time of Arrival: is a commonly used network-based solution for determining the position of mobile callers. The differences in the time of arrival of the signal from a user's mobile device to at least three base stations are used to calculate the location of that device.

Angle of Arrival : This technique seeks to determine the location of a mobile device based on the angle at which signals transmitted from the device arrive at the base station(s).

Enhanced Observed Time Difference: technique determines the location of a mobile device by using location receivers which are geographically dispersed across a wide area. These so-called Location Measurement Units (LMU) each have an accurate timing source. When it is possible for E-OTD (software-enabled) mobile devices and the LMUs to receive signals from at least three base stations, the time difference of arrival of the signal from each base station at the handset and at the LMU are calculated. The estimated location of the handset is calculated, based on the combination of the differences in time, through a hyperbolic positioning technique. The E-OTD technique offers an accuracy level from 50 to 125m.

Global Positioning System

GPS is a satellite-based navigation system developed and operated by the U.S. Department of Defense. GPS is a position, velocity and time determination system that is truly global, is able to operate 24 hours a day under all weather conditions, and charges no user fees. GPS offers comparatively high accuracy, when operational conditions are favorable. In cases of outdoor positioning, when signals from the constellation of GPS satellites are not obstructed, sub-decameter horizontal accuracy (<10m) is assured. GPS is a relatively mature technology, and current receiver hardware is smaller, lighter, cheaper and uses less power than earlier generation equipment. GPS does, however, have some serious limitations due to the strong attenuation of the satellite signals by buildings, foliage, etc. Therefore GPS does not operate well (or at all) in dense 'urban canyon' areas, or inside buildings. Yet these are often the very areas where demand for location-based services is the highest. Furthermore, in order to use GPS, the mobile handsets must be modified to integrate GPS receiver chips.

Assisted GPS : Assisted GPS (A-GPS) refers to the GPS positioning technique whereby there is assistance data provided from a special GPS server/base station by the mobile telephony network. A-GPS enables GPS positioning even in urban and indoor areas, where the signal is too weak to be acquired using standard signal tracking procedures within the receiver.

Geographical Information System

A Geographical Information System (GIS) refers to the computer-based capability to manipulate geographical data (i.e. all data that has a spatial attribute associated with it). A GIS includes functions to support the operations of acquisition, compilation, storage, update, management, retrieval, presentation and analysis of data. Spatial data in the form of maps or images can be stored in vector format or raster format. All GIS data are 'geo-referenced', so that all coordinate information is in a well-defined reference framework.

Data in GIS is of course spatial, and refers to a unique location on the earth's surface — its geographical location with respect to a datum. A spatial object must have following four characteristics defined:

Location: it exists at a known point on the earth's surface.

Form: it has a geometric representation, with any geographical feature being represented by one of three basic geometric types: point, line and polygon.

Attribute: properties that describe the nature of the object.

Spatial relationship with other objects — some basic relationships are boundary of an area, adjacent areas, distance between any two geometric objects, distance buffer of an object (consisting of all points within a given distance from that object), etc.

Lbs Issues

Diverse Mobile Mapping Standards : The issue of mobile mapping is important in the context of LBS as the ability to display mapping information on mobile devices such as cell phones and PDAs is limited. The spatial information may simply be text (street address of a point of interest, turn-by-turn directions, etc.), images (e.g. of current traffic conditions), map images (area of interest, shortest route from current location to a specific destination etc.), and so on. In general, attractive 'maps' are the best means of depicting spatial information, and are hence an essential element of LBS. Moreover, with the development of 3G telecommunications and the wireless Internet, users will be able to gain access to a wide variety of map information.

However, developing mapping applications for the mobile/wireless Internet is challenging, for several reasons. The major concern is the restricted display capability of mobile devices. Apart from the limited map features that can be displayed, the speed of data transmission to mobile devices is also slow in comparison to a wired network. Moreover, "Each device speaks a different wireless protocol and supports a variety of different Wireless Markup Languages (there are over 30 such languages) – these different standards preclude a web site developer from writing every application to individually support every single device available". For example, WAP-enabled cell phones support the WML. On the other hand, Palm Operating System devices support TTML (Tagged Text Markup Language), and voice-activated Internet applications support the VoiceXML and VoxML mark-up languages

Mobile mapping requires standards that allow data content to be easily transferred and displayed across the wireless Internet to any one of a large variety of mobile devices. For displaying spatial data on the standard Internet, Scalable Vector Graphics (SVG) and Geography Markup Language (GML) are two important standards. The data in these formats are delivered across the Internet via XML. In the case of the mobile/wireless Internet, there should be conversion of standard Internet markup languages (XML and HTML) to languages that mobile devices can understand (e.g. WML, Handheld Device Markup Language - HDML, VoiceXML and SMS).

Interoperability

Interoperability is a must for the widespread adoption of location-based services. "Achieving the full value for location services depends on consistent communication across different regions, technology platforms, networks, application domains, and classes of products". Moreover, interoperability ensures network security and privacy. It also helps to facilitate billing and revenue sharing. Therefore, "a truly interpretable Open Location Services Platform is essential for long-term success in this market". The issue of interoperability needs to be addressed across:

Wireless Systems/Networks (GSM, CDMA and TDMA).

Positioning Technologies (COO, AOA, TDOA, E-OTD and A-GPS).

Core Network (Multi-Vendor and Inter-Gateways).

Applications: Different network and contents interfaces (WAP, SMS and GPRS).

Different content formats (maps, routes and languages).

The Open GIS Consortium (OGC), which is the world's authoritative industrial organization for information processing matters related to spatial and location information, announced the Open Location Service (OpenLS) Initiative. The OpenLS Initiative focuses on developing interface standards "needed by industry to support implementation of the location services invoked by mobile or wireless Internet devices in end to end settings" (Hecht, 2000). "Similar to the way that HTTP protocols enabled the growth of activity in the World Wide Web, OpenLS standards, resulting from OGC's cooperative testbed process, have the potential to enable significant growth of Location Services markets in the Wireless Web" (Burnett, 2000).

The Location Interoperability Forum (LIF) is another organization dealing with specifications "pertaining to the query and response for the actual location or position of the mobile device". The following are the main objectives of the LIF:
"Reduce/limit multiplicity of positioning technologies to be deployed.
Promote common methods and interfaces for standards-based positioning technologies (Cell-ID, E-OTD, and A-GPS).

Define common interfaces and methods between applications and the wireless networks irrespective of their underlying air interfaces and positioning technologies.
Define/adopt common interfaces between applications and the different types of content engines and databases" (Location Interoperability Forum, 2001).

Market Capacity

Many computing and spatial information business analysts believe that LBS represent the ideal means by which spatial information can be provided to a wide range of public users. For mobile workers, all information needed to undertake the field work may be accessed from their mobile devices. For everyday activities LBS provide quick response to requests for location-related information. The capability of finding the nearest hotel or hospital location, and obtaining turn-by-turn directions to that destination, delivered via cell phones, is welcomed by everyone. Some even predict that LBS will, in the near future, be one of the most important sources of revenue for the wireless communications industry.

On the other hand, there are skeptical voices among analysts about the real attraction of location-based services. In addition, the LBS market seems to be speculative and "the real value and the future of mobile location-specific services lies in the developed relationships with customers and improved efficiencies of many business processes". The most important concern is whether consumers are really interested in LBS, and whether they are willing to pay for them.

In summary, the market for LBS is currently very speculative. There are some serious concerns, such as whether consumers are prepared to pay for LBS and how much revenue can be generated by LBS. However, the potential for LBS cannot be easily rejected.

User Privacy

Another important issue for LBS is wireless location privacy protection. The locations of customers, whose mobile devices have position-determination capability, may be known to accuracy better than 100m whenever they make a call. Hence their everyday 'tracks' can be recorded and analyzed unless safeguards are introduced. Such customers are worried about the privacy of information about their locations.

It is necessary for telecommunications carriers to understand how important customers' location privacy is. Currently, "vendors and carriers are being naive [about wireless privacy concerns from consumers] and haven't done the proper market research to detect that concern". The LBS vendors themselves have admitted that "privacy will be a concern" but "users must be assured that they have several ways to request receipt of location-based information (known as opt-in), as well as have opportunities to opt-out". Carriers should be able to distinguish between those customers that want location-based services (or location-based advertising), and those who do not.

Furthermore, carriers should protect their location information by not forwarding it to advertisers or other service providers unless the users authorize them to do so. In the U.S., The Location Privacy Protection Act has been introduced into the

Senate by Senator John Edwards. The bill requires companies that provide wireless location-based services to notify users when they collect information about their location. The bill also prohibits the use or sale of the information without permission of the user.

Protection Groups of consumers seem to be very concerned about such issues. The Center for Democracy and Technology (CDT), in the U.S., is calling upon location-based service developers to pay particular attention to mobile customer location privacy. CDT believes that a separate proceeding to craft strong, technology neutral privacy rules implementing the wireless location information provisions of section 222 of the Communications Act should commence immediately.

Conclusion

This paper concludes that out of different solutions discussed here, GPS is considered as first choice solutions for many mobile positioning applications even though it suffers from strong attenuation problems in urban areas. In urban areas this problem can be resolved with the help of Assisted-GPS (A-GPS).

References

- GSM Association Permanent Reference Document SE.23
- White Paper "Location Services in Wireless Ad Hoc and Hybrid Networks: A Survey" by Roy Friedman
- White Paper "Wireless Location Positioning based on Signal Propagation Data" by Jim McGeough
- White Paper "Cost-effective Wireless Location Solutions for Rural Carriers" from TruePosition
- http://www.mobilein.com/location_based_services.htm

HASKELL – The Next Programming Language

Varun Sapra
Deepak Sharma
Lecturer (IT), JIMS, Vasant Kunj, Delhi

Abstract:
Writing large software systems is really complex, difficult and expensive. Maintaining those systems is even more difficult and expensive. So it is more and more important to structure it well. Functional programming languages, such as Haskell, can make it easier and cheaper as compared to the conventional languages. Higher level programming languages can write the same program using less lines of code. Programmers can think/code the same number of lines of code in any language. As a result, if you use a higher level programming language, you'll save time. The number of bugs in a program is proportionate to the number of lines of code, so a shorter program has fewer bugs. Plus, some language features prevent certain types of bugs. Programs written in a higher level programming language have fewer bugs than if they were written in a lower level language. Haskell is the highest level programming language with shorter programs and less bugs. Even if we are not in a position to use Haskell in our programming projects, learning Haskell can make us a better programmer in any language. In this paper we show how Haskell originated and how Functional programming is better.

Keywords: *Functional Programming, Imperative Languages, Less Semantic Gap, Lazy Evaluation, No Core Dumps, Modularity.*

Introduction

This Paper is an attempt to elaborate the vitality of Functional Languages over convention languages. Haskell is one of the functional languages. Haskell is a purely functional programming language. It was designed in 1988. It is freely available and it is useful in teaching and research applications. For a beginner, it is an excellent language to step in to programming world, since it doesn't have any complex syntax. In Haskell, functions are expressions just like mathematical equations. In particular, it is a polymorphically statically typed, lazy, purely functional language, quite different from most other programming languages. The language is named for Haskell Brooks Curry, whose work in mathematical logic serves as a foundation for functional languages. Haskell is based on the lambda calculus, hence the lambda we use as a logo.

Haskell offers us:

- Substantially increased programmer productivity.
- Shorter, clearer, and more maintainable code.
- Fewer errors, higher reliability.
- A smaller "semantic gap" between the programmer and the language.

Now, the question arises what is functional language. The answer to this key question is that the programs are executed by evaluating expressions. This contrasts with imperative programming where programs are composed of statements, which change global state when executed. Functional programming, on the other hand, avoids using state and mutable data. Functional programming requires that functions are first-class, which means that they are treated like any other values and can be passed as arguments to other functions or be returned as a result of a function. Being first-class also means that it is possible to define and manipulate functions **nested** in code blocks.

Haskell is a purely functional language, all computations are done via the evaluation of expressions (syntactic terms) to yield values (abstract entities that we regard as answers). Every value has an associated type. (Intuitively, we can think of types as sets of values.) Examples of expressions include atomic values such as the integer 5, the character 'a', and the function \x -> x+1, as well as structured values such as the list [1,2,3] and the pair ('b',4). A function call can have no effect other than to compute its result. This eliminates a major source of bugs, and also makes the order of execution irrelevant - since no side-effect can change the value of an expression, it can be evaluated at any time.

Functions in Haskell are normally defined by a series of *equations*. For example, the function *inc* can be defined by the single equation:

inc n = *n+1*

Another kind of declaration is a *type signature declaration* with which we can declare an explicit typing for inc:

inc :: Integer -> Integer

Structured and Unstructured Programming

The most important difference between structured and unstructured programs is that structured programs are designed in a modular way. Modular design brings with it great productivity improvements. First of all, small modules can be coded quickly and easily. Secondly, general purpose modules can be re-used, leading to faster development of subsequent programs. When writing a modular program to solve a problem, one first divides the problem into subproblems then solves the sub-problems and combines the solutions. The ways in which one can divide up the original problem depend directly on the ways in which one can glue solutions together.

Glueing Functions

The modularization is the key feature of Functional Programming. It is easy for the functional programmers to write smaller, simpler and more general modules and glued them together with the new glues

listof X ::= nil | sams X (listof X)

which means that a list of Xs (whatever X is) is either nil, representing a list with no elements, or it is a sams of an X and another list of Xs. A sams represents a list whose first element is the X and whose second and subsequent elements are the elements of the other list of Xs.

For example, if X is "integer" then the definition says that a list of integers is either empty or a sams of an integer and another list of integers.

[] means nil

[1] means sams 1 nil

[1,2] means sams 1 (sams 2 (nil))

The other new kind of glue that functional languages provide enables whole programs to be glued together.

As we know a functional program is just a function form starting to end. For example if a and b are two programs then (a.b) is a program which computes a(b input). The program b computes its output which is used as an input for a.

Functional programming should be used as software becomes more and more complex, it is more and more important to structure it well. Well-structured software is easy to write, easy to debug, and provides a collection of modules that can be re-used to reduce future programming costs. Conventional languages place conceptual limits on the way problems can be modularised. Functional languages push those limits back.

How Functional programming is Better?

Brevity: Functional programs tend to be much more **concise** than their imperative counterparts.

Ease Of Understanding: Functional programs are often easier to understand. You should be able to understand the program without any previous knowledge of logic.

No Core Dumps: Most functional languages, and Haskell in particular, are strongly typed, eliminating a huge class of easy-to-make errors at compile time. In particular, strong typing means no core dumps! There is simply no possibility of treating an integer as a pointer, or following a null pointer.

Code Reuse: Strong typing is available in many imperative languages, such as Ada or Pascal. However, Haskell's type system is much less restrictive than, say, Pascal's, because it uses polymorphism.

Recursion: Recursion is heavily used in functional programming, as it is the canonical and often the only way to iterate. Loops are naturally expressed using tail recursion.

Lazy Evaluation: Pure computations are referentially transparent they can be performed at any time and still yield the same result. This makes it possible to defer the computation of values until they are needed, that is to compute them *lazily*.

Features Of HASKELL

Characteristic features of Haskell include pattern matching, currying, list comprehensions, guards, definable operators, and single assignment. The language also supports recursive functions and algebraic data types, as well as lazy evaluation. Unique concepts include monads, and type classes. The combination of such features can make functions, which would be difficult to write in a procedural programming language almost trivial to implement in Haskell.

HASKELL as Language

HASKELL 98 is one of the standardised version of Haskell language. HUGS is an interpreter used for Haskell. We select HUGS, because it is simple for people who were learning the basics of Haskell. It offers speedy compilation and more execution speed. One can download hugs98 from www.Haskell.org.

Make a directory named hask in your linux platform. Copy the packages like 'hugs98-Mar2005-patched.tar.bz2'to the newly created folder hask.

Unzip the package and then untar it; you will get the package like 'hugs98-Mar2005-patched'.

The next step is to compile and install the package. For that, the following procedures are needed:

```
cd hugs98-Mar2005.patched
./configure
make
make install
```

The interpreter may be started with a command line of the form hugs[option...][file...]

This is how we can write a program in Haskell. First open a file named try.hs and write the following

```
main = print"Hello, world"
To run the program
hugs  hello.hs
```

Other Tools Available for Haskell

The Glasgow Haskell Compiler
The Glasgow Haskell Compiler (GHC) is a state-of-the-art, open source, compiler and interactive environment for the functional language Haskell. In addition to the Haskell 98 native-code generation across much architecture, GHC implements many cutting-edge features including Software Transactional Memory providing much easy implementation of highly concurrent programs.x

Haskell Mode for Emacs
A basic Haskell mode for Emacs that provides syntax highlighting and automatic indentation. In addition, this elisp package comes with inferior Haskell interactive modes for both Hugs and GHCi.

LIBRARIES

Data.StringMap: A library providing maps from String keys to values. Use this library to build simple dictionary style databases in your Haskell programs.

HaXml: Haskell and XML: Need to deal with XML effectively? HaXml is a collection of utilities for parsing, filtering, transforming, and generating XML documents using Haskell. Its basic facilities include: a simple XML parser, a separate error-correcting parser for HTML, an XML validator, and pretty-printers for XML and HTML.

MissingPy: Call Python and C libraries or use the Python interpretter from your Haskell program. This library does not support calling Haskell code from Python.

Although Haskell has a comparatively small user community, its strengths have been well applied to a few projects. Audrey Tang's Pugs is an implementation for the long-term forthcoming Perl 6 language with an interpreter and compilers that proved useful already after just a few months of its writing; similarly, GHC is often a testbed for advanced functional programming features and optimizations. Darcs is a revision control system, with several innovative features.

Why People Are Not Using HASKELL?

The fact that Perl, Python and Ruby have become popular while Haskell has stayed a marginal language is a failure of the Haskell community. The Haskell community has failed to build a useful distribution Haskell, and it has failed to position the language as something that people can use to solve their problems. The community sells Haskell as a language instead of Haskell as a solution to our problems. There is no standard distribution containing a wealth of libraries for doing snazzy things. And there is an air of staleness: where new versions of these other languages appear frequently, the Haskell community is offering Hugs98.

References:

- http://www.jelovic.com
- http://www.haskell.org
- http://fsugtsr.org
- http://harold.hotelling.net/haskell.html
- Simon Thompson: *Haskell: The Craft of Functional Programming*, Addison-Wesley
- Richard Bird: *Introduction to Functional Programming using Haskell* Prentice Hall Press
- H. Abelson and G.J. Sussman. Structure and Interpretation of Computer.
- Watson, I. and Gurd, J. (1982). A practical data flow computer.
- Wadler, P., Taha, W., and MacQueen, D. (1988). How to add laziness to a strict language, without even being odd. In
- Workshop on Standard ML, Baltimore.
- Turner, D. A. (1982). Recursion equations as a programming language. In Darlington, J., Henderson, P., and Turner, D.,editors, Functional Programming and its Applications. CUP.
- The Implementation of Practical Functional Programming Languages. Ph.D. thesis, Imperial College, London.

A Study of Multi-Dimensional Databases

Sunil Kumar
Section Officer, GGSIPU, Delhi

Abstract

The information used in industry all around the world has witnessed a tremendous growth in depth, requiring new ways to implement the way database structures work. From flat-file databases to relational and distributed relational technologies, new technologies have always had to evolve to keep pace with the increasing demands of data overload on such database systems.

There is a tremendous amount of data generated by day-to-day operations in large organisations, in addition to valuable information obtained from external resources such as market research organisations, consultancy firms and test environments.

To meet this increase in demand, the latest step in database evolution is the multi-dimensional database system. This paper will give an overview of the concepts behind the multi-dimensional database structure broader discussion of the advantages for industry of this new technology. In contrast to previous technologies, these databases view data as multidimensional cubes that are particularly well suited for data analysis. Multidimensional models categorize data either as facts with associated numerical measures or as textual dimensions that characterize the facts. Queries aggregate measure values over a range of dimension values to provide results such as total sales per month of a given product. Multidimensional database technology is being applied to distributed data and to new types of data that current technology often cannot adequately analyze.

Introduction

E.F. Codd introduced relational data model in 1970. In 1993, E.F. Codd presented On line Analytical Processing (OLAP) due to advent of large data warehouses which requires high performance access and analysis of large amounts of related data across several applications, operating in different parts of the organization. The applications operate in a multi-tier environment, and often use different technologies operating on different platforms. The database management systems then matured into powerful transaction processing systems. The large systems needs capability of handling huge volumes of data in terabytes and ways to implement the database structures in new and sophisticated ways. The explosive growth in the size of data results in a need of organizing and manipulating the raw data into actionable information.

The latest step in database evolution is the multi-dimensional database model which address the need of increase in demand. The multi-dimensional database may also offer a better concept for visualizing the way we already think of data in the real world. For example, most business managers already think of data in a multi-dimensional way, such as when they think of specific products in specific markets over certain periods of time.

The multi-dimensional database attempts to present such data to the end user in a useful way. The multi-dimensional database model is used to *analyze* data rather than to perform online transactions as this technology views data as multidimensional *cubes,* which is well suited for data analysis. Such perspective defines data as *facts* with associated *measures or dimensions* that characterize the facts. Viewing data as cubes facilitates support hierarchies in dimensions and formulas without duplicating the data definitions. The dimensions are used for selecting and aggregating data at certain level of detail and the facts represent the subject or event in the enterprise that must be analyzed to understand.

Multidimensional data-base technology is a key factor in the interactive analysis of large amounts of data for decision-making purposes. In contrast to previous technologies, these databases view data as multidimensional cubes that are particularly well suited for data analysis. Multidimensional models categorize data either as facts with associated numerical measures or as textual dimensions that characterize the facts. Multidimensional database technology is being applied to distributed data and to new types of data that current technology often cannot adequately analyze. For example, classic techniques such as preaggregation cannot ensure fast query response times when data-such as that obtained from sensors or GPS-equipped moving objects-changes continuously [Pedersen]. Multidimensional database technology will increasingly be applied where analysis results are fed directly into other systems.

Spreadsheets and relational structures

A spreadsheet is a useful tool for analyzing sales data such as product sold, number of purchases, and city of sale. A pivot table is a two-dimensional spreadsheet with associated subtotals and totals that supports viewing more complex data by nesting several dimensions on the *x*- or *y*-axis and displaying data on multiple pages. Pivot tables generally support interactively selecting data subsets and changing the displayed level of detail. Spreadsheets are an inadequate tool for managing and storing multidimensional data because they tie data storage too tightly to the presentation—they do not separate the structural information from the desired views of the information. Thus, adding a third dimension such as time or grouping the data into higher-level product types requires a considerably more complex setup. The obvious solution is to use a separate spreadsheet for each dimension, but this will work only to a limited extent because analyzing the additional values of the extra dimension quickly becomes unwieldy.

Spreadsheets and relational databases provide adequate support for a small volume of data that has only a few nonhierarchical dimensions, but they do not fully support the requirements for advanced data analysis. The only robust solution is to use database technology that offers inherent support for the full range of multidimensional data modeling.

Dimensional Database

A *dimensional database* is one which, rather than storing data in multiple two dimensional tables (as a relational database does), represents key data entities as different dimensions. That is, multidimensional database systems offer an extension to the relational system to provide a multi-dimensional view of the data [Rand]. For example, in multi-dimensional analysis, data entities such as products, regions, customers, dates etc. may all represent different dimensions.

Some further advantages to this database model are:

- The ability to analyse large amounts of data with very fast response times.
- To "slice and dice" through data, and "drill down or roll up" through various dimensions of the defined data structure.
- To quickly identify trends or problem areas that would have been otherwise overlooked in an industry environment.

Relational Vs. Multi-dimensional Database Structure

The relational database model uses a two-dimensional structure of rows and columns to store data, in tables of records corresponding to real-world entities. Tables can be linked by common key values. E.F. Codd first designed this model in 1970, while working for IBM, and it's simplicity revolutionised database usage at the time. Codd's work was in many ways ahead of it's time, as computing power could not support the overheads of his database system (Hasan, 1999).

In the 1980s the power of computers had grown to the point where these overheads were no longer a problem, and today relational database management systems (DBMS) are available on local desktops, as well as large organisational database management servers.

The techniques of entity-relationship (ER) modelling and the structuring of data in normalised tables have become popular with trained database administrators and designers, who routinely use relational DBMS to store huge volumes of organisational data with very high transaction rates. Although it looks simple to design and operate, relational database simplicity for the end-user does fall down when it comes to running queries. Accessing data from relational databases may require complex joins of many tables and is not easy for untrained end-users, who may be forced to hire IT professionals to structure such queries in a query language, such as SQL. When queries of a writing nature are run, such as INSERT, DELETE and ALTER TABLE, the consequences of getting it wrong are greatly increased when they are employed on a live system environment.

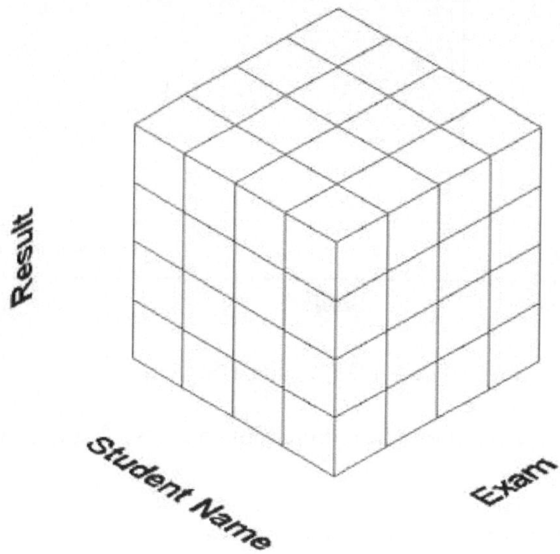

Figure 1: A typical 3D Hypercube

In a multi-dimension database system, the data is presented to the user in such a way as to represent a hypercube, or multi-dimensional array, where each individual data value is contained within a cell accessible by multiple indexes. A simple example is presented in the *Figure 1,* where a fictional student exam result database is given. This database contains three dimensions, namely *Result, Student Name* and *Exam*. In this database, an individual student (represented by Student Name) may have their exam results for several exams compared over a period of time, for example a four-year undergraduate course. This ability to present data in such a top level view is unique to multi-dimensional systems, and shows just how powerful these systems can be. Of course a multi-dimensional system is not limited to three dimensions as in the given example, but when we go beyond that amount, it becomes more difficult to present such structures in a pictorial view. If we stick with the example presented in *Figure 1,* we now add a fourth dimension called *Subject*. Assume our students study computer science, with subjects in *Databases, Programming* and *Software Engineering.* If we imagine this new dimension as being a box containing our previous three dimensions, then we would have three such boxes, namely one for each subject that our students were tested on, as shown in *Figure 2.*

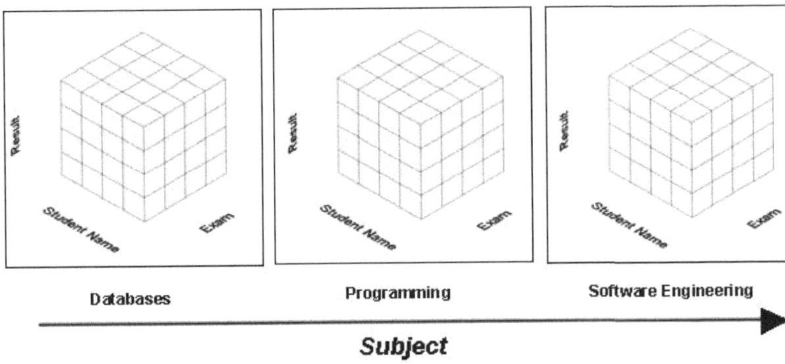

Figure 2: A 4 D Dataabase Structure.

This model can be extended to a fifth dimension, and a sixth and so on, until all requirements are met.

Features of Multi-dimensional Database Systems

- **Cubes**

Multidimensional databases view data as cubes that generalize spreadsheets to any number of dimensions. In addition, cubes support hierarchies in dimensions and formulas without duplicating their definitions. A collection of related cubes comprises a multidimensional database or data warehouse. Because dimensions in a cube are first-class, built in concepts with associated domains, cubes can easily manage the addition of new dimension values. Although the term implies three dimensions, a cube can theoretically have any number of dimensions; in fact, most real-world cubes have four to 12 dimensions [Thomsen]. Current tools often experience performance problems when a so-called hypercube contains more than 10 to 15 dimensions. Combinations of dimension values define a cube's cells. Depending on the specific application, the cells in a cube range from sparse to dense. Cubes tend to become sparser as dimensionality increases and as the dimension values' granularities become finer.

Product	Number of purchases by city			
	Aalborg	Copenhagen	Los Angeles	New York City
Milk	123	555	145	5,001
Bread	102	250	54	2,010
Jeans	20	89	32	345
Light bulbs	22	213	32	9,450

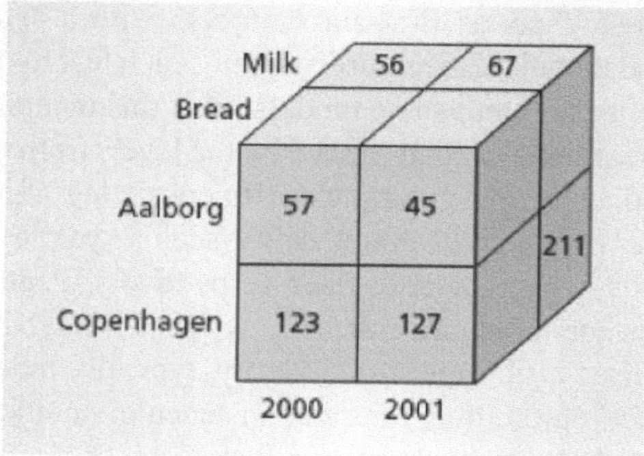

Figure 3: Sample Cube Capturing Sales Data. [*Source:* Pedersen, Jensen, Collins]

- **Dimensions**

Dimensions are an essential and distinguishing concept in multidimensional databases. An important goal of multidimensional modeling is to use dimensions to provide as much context as possible for facts. In contrast to relational databases, controlled redundancy is generally considered appropriate in multidimensional databases if it increases the data's information value. Because multidimensional cube data is often derived from other sources—for example, a transactional relational system—rather than being "born" in the multidimensional cube, the redundancy problems related to updates can be managed more readily [Kimball]. There is usually no redundancy in the facts, only in the dimensions. Dimensions are used for selecting and aggregating data at the desired level of detail. A dimension is organized into a containment-like hierarchy composed of numerous levels, each representing a level of detail required by the desired analyses. Each instance of the dimension, or dimension value, belongs to a particular level.

Unlike the linear spaces used in matrix algebra, multidimensional models typically do not include ordering or distance metrics for the dimension values. Rather, the only ordering is that higher-level values contain lower-level values. However, for some dimensions such as time, an ordering of the dimension values is used to calculate cumulative information such as total sales to date. Most models require dimension hierarchies to form balanced trees—the hierarchy must have uniform height everywhere, and each non-top value have precisely one parent.

- **Facts**

Facts represent the subject—the interesting pattern or event in the enterprise that must be analyzed to understand its behavior. In most multidimensional data models, facts are implicitly defined by their combination of dimension values; a fact exists only if there is a nonempty cell for a particular combination of values. However, some models treat facts as first-class objects with a separate identity. Most multidimensional models also require mapping each fact to one value at the lowest level in each dimension, but some models relax this mapping requirement. Each fact has a certain granularity determined by the levels from which its combination of dimension values is drawn. Granularities consisting of higher- or lower-level dimension values than a given granularity—such as year by type by city and day by product by city—are coarser or finer, respectively [Pedersen].
Data warehouses commonly include three types of facts [Kimball]:

- ***Events***, at least at the finest granularity, typically model real-world events, with one fact representing the same instance of an underlying phenomenon. Examples include sales, clicks on a Web page, or movement of goods in and out of a warehouse.
- ***Snapshots*** model an entity's state at a given point in time, such as store and warehouse inventory levels and the number of Web site users. The same instance of the underlying real-world phenomenon— such as a specific can of beans on a shelf—may occur in several facts at different points in time.
- ***Cumulative snapshots*** handle information about activity up to a certain moment. For example, the total sales up to and including the current month this year can be easily compared to the figure for the corresponding month last year.

- **Measures**

A measure consists of two components:

- a fact's numerical property, such as the sales price or profit; and
- a formula, usually a simple aggregation function such as *sum*, that can combine several measure values into one.

In a multidimensional database, measures generally represent the properties of the fact that the user wants to optimize. Measures then take on different values for various dimension combinations. The property and formula are chosen to provide a meaningful value for all combinations of aggregation levels. Because the metadata defines the formula, the data is not replicated as in a spreadsheet. Most multidimensional data models have measures, but some rely on using dimension values to make computations at the expense of user friendliness [Pedersen]. Three classes of measures behave quite differently in computations:

- ***Additive*** measures can be meaningfully combined along any dimension. For example, it makes sense to add total sales for the product, location, and time because this causes no overlap among the real-world phenomena that generated the individual values.
- ***Semiadditive*** measures cannot be combined along one or more dimensions. For example, summing inventory across products and warehouses is meaningful, but summing inventory levels across time does not make sense because the same physical phenomenon could be counted several times.
- ***Nonadditive*** measures cannot be combined along any dimension, usually because the chosen formula prevents combining lower-level averages into higher-level averages.

- **Querying**
- A multidimensional database naturally lends itself to certain types of queries:
- ***Slice-and-dice*** queries make selections to reduce a cube. For example, we can slice the cube in *Figure 3* by considering only those cells that concern bread, then further reduce this slice by considering only the cells for the year 2000. Selecting a single dimension value reduces the cube's dimensionality, but more general selections are also possible.
- ***Drill-down* and *roll-up*** queries are inverse operations that use dimension hierarchies and measures to perform aggregations. Rolling up to its top value corresponds with omitting the dimension.
- ***Drill-across*** queries combine cubes that share one or more dimensions. In relational algebraic terms, this operation performs a join.
- ***Ranking or top n/bottom n queries*** can return only those cells that appear at the top or bottom of the specified order—for example, the 10 bestselling products in Copenhagen in 2000.
- ***Rotating*** a cube allows users to see the data grouped by other dimensions. Drill-down and roll-up queries can be combined with slice-and-dice queries.

- **Rotation**

Due to the layout of data in a multi-dimensional database, certain views of the data can be generated at ease by a multi-dimensional system. In fact, viewing a multi-dimensional view (or *slice*) is similar to viewing data on a spreadsheet table.
If we imagine a slice of a database being a view of one of the faces of the hypercube, then for this example we have 6 available slices. In fact, the number of possible slices increases exponentially with the number of dimensions [Kenan], so a two-dimensional array has two views, a three-dimensional has six, a four-dimensional has 24 and a five has 120 views.

The six available views for our student database in following example are:

1. *Student Name* by *Exam*.
2. *Exam* by *Student Name*.
3. *Exam* by *Semester*.
4. *Semester* by *Exam*.
5. *Student Name* by *Semester*.
6. *Semester* by *Exam*.

The mechanism by which a view is selected is often referred to as data rotation. For example, if we can imagine that we are looking at the *Student Name* by *Exam* face (view) of the cube in *Figure 4*, now if we rotate that view 90 degrees clockwise around the *y*-axis (i.e. the *Student Name* dimension), then we are now looking at a different view of the database, namely *Student Name* by *Semester*. In a multi-dimensional database system, it is possible to view the data from any such rotation.

- **Ranging**

A well-designed multi-dimensional database allows users to range in on particular subsets of the database, to their specification. For example, an example of a range might be an array containing all results for semesters 1 and 2 for the subjects Databases and Programming. Ranging is comparable to complex queries in a rational system, and is often referred to as *data dicing* because it is scoped down to a subset of the overall array. The performance of ranging in a multi-dimensional system is once again greater than the relational equivalent, as few overheads are incurred in the multi-dimensional system to obtain the required view of the data.

- **Hierarchies, Roll-Up and Drill-Down**

As previously discussed, users may want to view data from several perspectives, although sometimes these views may be very similar. For example, a user might want to view exam results for a class, or the entire school for a particular year. There is a natural relationship between this entities, it is simply a matter of scale that separates them apart. Multi-dimensional databases are designed with these natural relationships in mind. Although it would be possible to create a separate dimension for *Class* and *School*, a more powerful solution is to create two related aggregates on the same dimension, which can then be used as part of the same dimension.

Therefore, as all examples of a Class are contained within a *School, School* is a higher-level aggregation within the overall dimension we can now call *College*. When we relate each position along the *Class* aggregation to a position along the *School* aggregation, we have defined a *hierarchy* within the overall *College* dimension.

The ability to move up and down along these newly created hierarchies is referred to as *roll-up* and *drill-down*. The chosen level along each dimension now defines each view, which can also be rotated or ranged.

ADVANTAGES

If we look again at our example of a student exam result dataset, there are many reasons why it is more efficient to represent our dataset with a multi-dimensional array rather than a relational table. For example, all similar information is lined up in a single dimension, like *Results*, so that they can be very quickly summed up to a total or quickly compared to get an immediate idea of how student results are fairing this semester.

The multi-dimensional array structure represents a higher level of organisation than the relational table. The structure itself represents a more intelligent view of the data it contains, because our perspectives of this data are embedded directly into the structure as dimensions, as opposed to being placed into fields. For example, if we were to design a fictional relational table for our student results, it might look something like the following table :

Student Name	Exam	Result
A	Databases	70
A	Programming	72
A	Operating Systems	60
B	Databases	80
B	Programming	99
B	Operating Systems	70
C	Databases	80
C	Programming	90
C	Operating Systems	99

Table 1: Fictional Relational Table for Student Results

The structure of this relationship table can tell us nothing of the nature of the contents of these fields, only that there are three fields *Student Name, Exam* and *Result*, and there are nine records. If we were to present a three-dimensional view of this data, while adding a third dimension called *Semester*, it might look something like the following:

As we can see from *Figure 4*, there is no need to have *Result* as a dimension, because the exam results are going to be contained within the cells of the database structure. Another obvious advantage is the removal of the duplication in the relational table, where each student name was repeated three times for each exam that they participated in. In the multi-dimensional view, the *Student Name* and the *Exam* become dimensions, or in effect indexes into that data, so having duplicates does not make any sense.

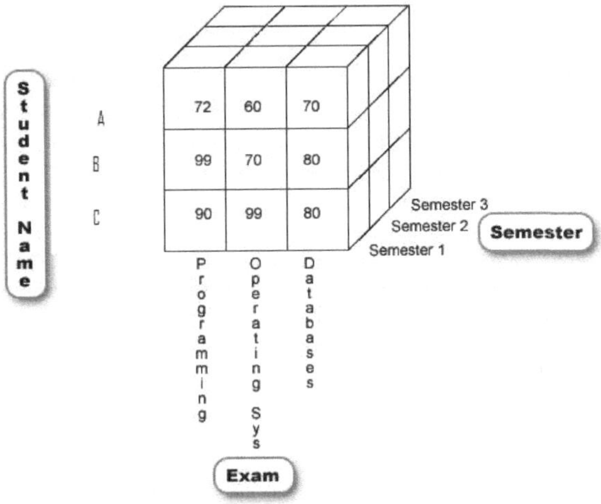

Figure 4: Student, Result & Exam [*Source:* Collins, Kenan]

Notice how all related information neatly lines up in the multi-dimensional view, for example all programming results for John Collins over all three semesters lines up along the *z* axis (i.e. from the diagram view perspective, the *Semester* dimension), while all exam results for John Collins in all subjects line up on the *x*-axis (the *Exam* dimension). Programming results for all students line up on the *y*-axis (the *Student Name* dimension). From this example, it is clear to see the inherit intelligence in this database structure; in the ER table such views of specific data would not be possible without writing complex SQL queries.

Apart from the inherit advantages of using a multi-dimensional array structure, multi-dimensional databases also contain the following advantages [Kenan]:

1. **Enhanced Data Presentation and Navigation**: Intuitive spreadsheet-like views of the data are the output of multi-dimensional databases. Such views are difficult to generate in relational systems without the use of complex SQL queries, while others cannot be performed by SQL at all, e.g. top ten exam results.

2. **Ease of Maintenance:** Multi-dimensional databases are very easy to maintain, because data is stored in the same way as it is viewed, that is according to its fundamental attributes, so no additional computational overhead is required for queries of the database. To compare this to relational systems, where complex indexing and joins may be used that require significant maintenance and overhead.
3. **Increased Performance:** Multi-dimensional database achieve performance levels that are well in excess of that of relational systems performing similar data storage requirements. These high performance levels encourage and enable OLAP applications. Performance can be improved in relational systems through database tuning, but the database cannot be tuned for every possible on-the-fly query. In relational systems, tuning is quite specific, therefore decreasing flexibility, and also requires expensive database specialists.

Conclusion

This paper has described some of the main characteristics of the multi-dimensional database structure, and provided an analysis of its effectiveness when compared to that of more traditional entity relationship database systems. The paper concludes that multi-dimensional database systems are a complementary technology to entity relational systems.

Where multi-dimensional systems excel over their relational system counterparts is in the area of data presentation and analysis, where the data in question lends itself to being suitable for multi-dimensional systems, such 2as where complex inter-relationships exist. The top-level views of data over many combinations of dimensions make multi-dimensional systems particularly useful for trend analysis over time by management staff of organisations, due to the ease of viewing the data in a more naturally intuitive way.

Multidimensional database technology is also being applied to new types of data that current technology often cannot adequately analyze. For example, classic techniques such as preaggregation cannot ensure fast query response times when data—such as from sensors or moving objects such as Global Positioning System equipped vehicles—is continuously changing.

Finally, multidimensional database technology will increasingly be applied where analysis results are fed directly into other systems, thereby eliminating human intervention. When coupled with the need for continuous updates, this context poses stringent performance requirements.

References

- E.F. Codd, S.B. Codd, and C.T. Salley, "Providing OLAP (On-Line Analytical Processing) to User-Analysts: An IT Mandate," Nov. 2001.
- Jacobson, R.: Microsoft SQL Server 2000 Analysis Services Step By Step, Microsoft Press, 2000.
- E. Thomsen, OLAP Solutions: Building Multidimensional Information Systems, John Wiley & Sons, New York, 1997.
- T.B. Pedersen, C.S. Jensen, and C.E. Dyreson, "A Foundation for Capturing and Querying Complex Multidimensional Data," Information Systems, vol. 26, no. 5, 2001, pp. 383 423.
- R. Kimball, The Data Warehouse Toolkit: Practical Techniques for Building Dimensional Data Warehouses, John Wiley & Sons, New York, 1996.
- A. Eisenberg and J. Melton, "SQL Standardization: The Next Steps," ACM SIGMOD Record, vol. 29, no. 1, 2000, pp. 63-67.
- J. Collins, "An assessment of multi-dimensional databases and their use", School of Computer Science, Ireland.
- H-J. Lenz and A. Shoshani, "Summarizability in OLAP and Statistical Data Bases," Proc. 9th Int'l Conf. Scientific and Statistical Database Management, IEEE CS Press, Los Alamitos, Calif., 1997, pp. 39-48.
- Baum D. (1996) Data Warehouses, Building Blocks for the Next Millennium, Oracle Magazine, March/April, 34-43.
- Rand Systems (2001), Data Warehousing - For Better Business Decisions.
- Hasan Helen (1999) Effective Information for Managers: Using Multi-Dimensional Data Structures to Support Research Management, 10th Australian Conference on Information Systems, 1999.
- J. Gray et al., "Data Cube: A Relational Aggregation Operator Generalizing Group-By, Cross-Tab and Sub-Totals," Data Mining and Knowledge Discovery, vol. 1, no. 1, 1997, pp. 29 54.

From Cluster-Grid to Cloud .....

Somendra Kumar
Lecturer (IT), RDIAS, Rohini, Delhi
Nitin Saraswat
Lecturer (IT), JIMS, Rohini, Delhi

Abstract

This paper emphasizes on the evolution of cloud computing and its pros and cons over Cluster and Grid computing. Grids are not clouds and clouds are not grids, although most clouds reside on some form of grid infrastructure. This is the standard explanation everyone hear from vendors trying to convince you of the merits of their latest offerings. But what, exactly, does that mean in the real world? If you're an enterprise manager with a specific problem to be solved, how do you know whether you need a cloud or a grid? As with any evolving technology, nailing down exactly what clouds and grids are and what they are supposed to do can be difficult. Often, by the time one mindset becomes common, vendors and the user communities are halfway to redefining the technology for entirely new purposes Initially, grids were an extension of cluster computing, with the main hurdle being to define "data residency" to allow servers to access data wherever it was on the network and, by extension, allow users to tap into computing resources the way we tap into electricity. The cloud, which came of age with Amazon's Simple Storage Service (S3), combines grid technology with the SaaS approach to offer computing services over the Web on a commercial basis.

Keywords : *Cluster Computing, Grid Computing, Cloud Computing, Cloud Architecture.*

Introduction

Cluster computing is the technique of linking two or more computers into a network (usually through a local area network) in order to take advantage of the parallel processing power of those computers.

An eternal struggle in any IT department is in finding a method to squeeze the maximum processing power out of a limited budget. Today more than ever, enterprises require enormous processing power in order to manage their desktop applications, databases and knowledge management. Many business processes are extremely heavy users of IT resources, and yet IT budgets struggle to keep pace with the ever growing demand for yet more power.

IT Limitations

Unfortunately, though some of the largest enterprises require the processing power of a supercomputer, few enterprises can rustle up supercomputer-sized IT budgets. While there have been significant advances in mainframe computing in recent years, investment in a single large source of processing power may be the most cost-effective or flexible solution.

Instead, many enterprises are now choosing to invest their IT budgets in computer clusters – networks of high-powered, low-cost desktop computers – that provide an attractive alternative to mainframe computers.

Types of Computer Clusters

There are several different varieties of computer clusters, each offering different advantages to the user. These are:

- **High Availability Clusters**

HA Clusters are designed to ensure constant access to service applications. The clusters are designed to maintain redundant nodes that can act as backup systems in the event of failure. The minimum number of nodes in a HA cluster is two – one active and one redundant – though most HA clusters will use considerably more nodes.

HA clusters aim to solve the problems that arise from mainframe failure in an enterprise. Rather than lose all access to IT systems, HA clusters ensure 24/7 access to computational power. This feature is especially important in business, where data processing is usually time-sensitive.

- **Load-balancing Clusters**

Load-balancing clusters operate by routing all work through one or more load-balancing front-end nodes, which then distribute the workload efficiently between the remaining active nodes. Load-balancing clusters are extremely useful for those working with limited IT budgets. Devoting a few nodes to managing the workflow of a cluster ensures that limited processing power can be optimized.

- **High-performance Clusters**

HPC clusters are designed to exploit the parallel processing power of multiple nodes. They are most commonly used to perform functions that require nodes to communicate as they perform their tasks – for instance, when calculation results from one node will affect future results from another.

Benefits of Computer Clusters

Computer clusters offer a number of benefits over mainframe computers, including:

Reduced Cost: The price of off-the-shelf consumer desktops has plummeted in recent years, and this drop in price has corresponded with a vast increase in their processing power and performance. The average desktop PC today is many times more powerful than the first mainframe computers.

Processing Power: The parallel processing power of a high-performance cluster can, in many cases, prove more cost effective than a mainframe with similar power. This reduced price per unit of power enables enterprises to get a greater ROI from their IT budget.

Improved Network Technology: Driving the development of computer clusters has been a vast improvement in the technology related to networking, along with a reduction in the price of such technology. Computer clusters are typically connected via a single virtual local area network (VLAN), and the network treats each computer as a separate node. Information can be passed throughout these networks with very little lag, ensuring that data doesn't bottleneck between nodes.

Scalability: Perhaps the greatest advantage of computer clusters is the scalability they offer. While mainframe computers have a fixed processing capacity, computer clusters can be easily expanded as requirements change by adding additional nodes to the network.

Availability: When a mainframe computer fails, the entire system fails. However, if a node in a computer cluster fails, its operations can be simply transferred to another node within the cluster, ensuring that there is no interruption in service.

A computer cluster can offer cost-effective service in specific applications, but may be limited to a single type of computing node that allows all nodes to run a common operating system. Alternatively, the canonical definition of grid is one that allows any type of processing engine to enter or leave the system dynamically. This is analogous to an electrical power grid on which any given generating plant might be active or inactive at any given time.

The key distinction between clusters and grids is mainly lie in the way resources are managed. In case of clusters, the resource allocation is performed by a centralized resource manager and all nodes cooperatively work together as a single unified resource. In case of Grids, each node has its own resource manager and don't aim for providing a single system view.

What is Grid Computing?

Because it is an emerging technology, grid computing can mean different things to different people. But here is a simple, serviceable definition for the concept of grid computing:

Grid computing allows you to unite pools of servers, storage systems, and networks into a single large system so you can deliver the power of multiple-systems resources to a single user point for a specific purpose. To a user, data file, or an application, the system appears to be a single enormous virtual computing system.

Grid computing is the next logical step in distributed networking. Just as the Internet allows users to share ideas and files as the seeds of projects, grid computing lets us share the resources of disparate computer systems so people can actually start working on those projects. Grid computing takes the ability for computers (and their users) to communicate a step further: With grid computing, you can reach out and use computational or storage resources on machines other than your own.

With grid computing, an organization can transform its distributed and difficult-to-manage systems into a large virtual computer that can be set loose on problems and processes too complex for a single computer to handle efficiently. The problems to be solved can involve data processing, network bandwidth, or data storage. The systems linked in a grid might be in the same room or distributed around the world. They might be running different operating systems on many hardware platforms. They might even be owned by different organizations. Regardless of the depth of a grid's resources, all the grid user experiences is the processing resources of a very large virtual computer.

Since the concept of putting grids into real-world practice is still relatively new, another good way to describe a grid is to describe what it isn't. The following are not grids:

- Clusters
- Network-attached storage devices
- Scientific instruments
- Networks

Each might be an important component of a grid, but by itself, doesn't constitute a grid. Being able to tie together several million computers — clusters, workstations, desktop PCs, supercomputers — with data storage, instruments, visualization devices is the dream grid computing strives to achieve and the reality of grid computing could be revolutionary to science and industry. So, what does it take to make the vision of the grid computing concept a reality? It requires standard and seamless, open general-purpose protocols and interfaces, all of which are being defined now and are similar to those that enable access to information from the Web.

The First Generation

The early Grid efforts started as projects to link supercomputing sites; at this time this approach was known as metacomputing. The origin of the term is believed to have been the CASA project, one of several US Gigabit testbeds around in 1989. Larry Smarr, the former NCSA Director, is generally accredited with popularizing the term thereafter.

The early to mid 1990s mark the emergence of the early metacomputing or grid environments. Typically, the objective of these early metacomputing projects was to provide computational resources to a range of high performance applications. Two representative projects in the vanguard of this type of technology were FAFNER and I-WAY .

The Second Generation

The emphasis of the early efforts in grid computing was in part driven by the need to link a number of US national supercomputing centres. The I-WAY project successfully achieved this goal. Today the grid infrastructure is capable of binding together more than just a few specialized supercomputing centers. A number of key enablers have helped make the Grid more ubiquitous, including the take up of high bandwidth network technologies and adoption of standards, allowing the Grid to be viewed as a viable distributed infrastructure on a global scale that can support diverse applications requiring large-scale computation and data. This vision of the Grid was presented in [Foster98] and we regard this as the second generation, typified by many of today's grid applications. There are three main issues that had to be confronted:

- Heterogeneity
- Scalability
- Adaptability

The Third Generation

The second generation provided the interoperability that was essential to achieve large-scale computation. As further grid solutions were explored, other aspects of the engineering of the Grid became apparent. In order to build new grid applications it was desirable to be able to reuse existing components and information resources, and to assemble these components in a flexible manner. The solutions involved increasing adoption of a service-oriented model and increasing attention to metadata – these are two key characteristics of third generation systems. In fact the service-oriented approach itself has implications for the information fabric: the flexible assembly of grid resources into a grid application requires information about the functionality, availability and interfaces of the various components, and this information must have an agreed interpretation which can be processed by machine. Whereas the Grid had traditionally been described in terms of large scale data and computation, the shift in focus in the third generation was apparent from new descriptions. The third generation is a more holistic view of grid computing and can be said to address the infrastructure for e-Science – a term which reminds us of the requirements (of doing new science, and of the e-Scientist) rather than the enabling technology. The anticipated use of massively parallel computing facilities is only part of the picture that has emerged: there are also a lot more users, hence loosely coupled distributed computing has not been dominated by deployment of massively parallel machines.

Cloud computing is often confused with grid computing ("a form of distributed computing whereby a 'super and virtual computer' is composed of a cluster of networked, loosely-coupled computers, acting in concert to perform very large tasks"), utility computing (the "packaging of computing resources, such as computation and storage, as a metered service similar to a traditional public utility such as electricity") and autonomic computing ("computer systems capable of self-management").Indeed many cloud computing deployments as of 2009[update] depend on grids, have autonomic characteristics and bill like utilities — but cloud computing can be seen as a *natural next step* from the *grid-utility model*

What is Cloud Computing?

Cloud Computing is an emerging computing paradigm where data and services reside in massively scalable data centers and can be ubiquitously accessed from any connected devices over the internet. It is

- Virtual – Physical location and underlying infrastructure details are transparent to users
- Scalable – Able to break complex workloads into pieces to be served across an incrementally expandable infrastructure
- Efficient – Services Oriented Architecture for dynamic provisioning of shared compute resources
- Flexible – Can serve a variety of workload types – both consumer and commercial

The term **Cloud Computing** derives from the common depiction in most technology architecture diagrams, of the Internet or IP availability, using an illustration of a cloud. The computing resources being accessed are typically owned and operated by a third-party provider on a consolidated basis in Data Center locations. Target consumers are not concerned with the underlying technologies used to achieve the increase in server capability, and is sold simply as a service available on demand. Grid computing is a technology approach to managing a cloud. In effect, all clouds are managed by a grid but not all grids manage a cloud. More specifically, a compute grid and a cloud are synonymous, while a data grid and a cloud can be different.

Cloud computing gained attention in 2007 as it became a popular solution to the problem of horizontal scalability.

Cloud Architecture

Cloud architecture, the systems architecture of the software systems involved in the delivery of cloud computing, comprises hardware and software designed by a cloud architect who typically works for a cloud integrator. It typically involves multiple cloud components communicating with each other over application programming interfaces, usually web services.

This closely resembles the Unix philosophy of having multiple programs doing one thing well and working together over universal interfaces. Complexity is controlled and the resulting systems are more manageable than their monolithic counterparts.

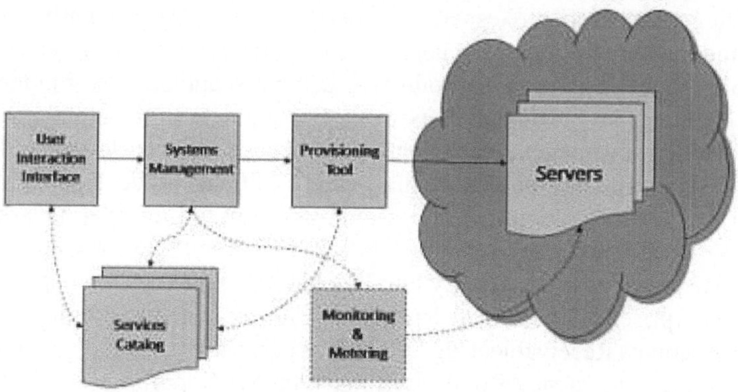

Figure 1 : Cloud Computing Architecture

Cloud architecture extends to the client, where web browsers and/or software applications access cloud applications.

Cloud storage architecture is loosely coupled, where metadata operations are centralized enabling the data nodes to scale into the hundreds, each independently delivering data to applications or users.

Cloud Storage

Cloud storage is a model of networked data storage where data is stored on multiple virtual servers, generally hosted by third parties, rather than being hosted on dedicated servers. Hosting companies operate large data centers; and people who require their data to be hosted buy or lease storage capacity from them and use it for their storage needs. The data center operators, in the background, virtualize the resources according to the requirements of the customer and expose them as virtual servers, which the customers can themselves manage. Physically, the resource may span across multiple servers. In some services, such as Nirvanix, the system may span multiple data centers or even continents.

Some Cloud Web Services

- EC2: Elastic Compute Cloud
- S3: Simple Storage Service
- SQS: Simple Queue Service
- SDB: Simple Database

Advantages of The Cloud

According to a Google spokesperson, Cloud computing is particularly valuable to small and medium businesses, where effective and affordable IT tools are critical to helping them become more productive without spending lots of money on in-house resources and technical equipment. Storing data in the cloud already has some distinct advantages over client-based access. We can leverage the sheer processing power of the cloud to do things that traditional productivity applications cannot do. Cloud computing offers almost unlimited computing power and collaboration at a massive scale for enterprises of all sizes. "The Force.com Platform-as-Service provides the necessary building blocks to make cloud computing real for the enterprise. Our customers have already developed applications in the cloud such as Accounts Receivable, Bug Enhancement Tracking, Employee Compliance and Training, Emergency Room Staffing, Expense Reporting, Food Ingredient Management, Recruiting, Time Management".

The cloud computing is all about the following parameters:

1. SaaS

These type of cloud computing delivers a single application through the browser to thousands of customers using a multitenant architecture. On the customer side, it means no upfront investment in servers or software licensing; on the provider side, with just one app to maintain, costs are low compared to conventional hosting. Salesforce.com is by far the best-known example among enterprise applications, but SaaS is also common for HR apps and has even worked its way up the food chain to ERP, with players such as Workday. And who could have predicted the sudden rise of SaaS "desktop" applications, such as Google Apps and Zoho Office?

2. Utility computing

The idea is not new, but this form of cloud computing is getting new life from Amazon.com, Sun, IBM, and others who now offer storage and virtual servers that IT can access on demand. Early enterprise adopters mainly use utility computing for supplemental, non-mission-critical needs, but one day, they may replace parts of the datacenter. Other providers offer solutions that help IT create virtual datacenters from commodity servers, such as 3Tera's AppLogic and Cohesive Flexible Technologies' Elastic Server on Demand. Liquid Computing's LiquidQ offers similar capabilities, enabling IT to stitch together memory, I/O, storage, and computational capacity as a virtualized resource pool available over the network.

3. Web services in the cloud

Closely related to SaaS, Web service providers offer APIs that enable developers to exploit functionality over the Internet, rather than delivering full-blown applications. They range from providers offering discrete business services — such as Strike Iron and Xignite — to the full range of APIs offered by Google Maps, ADP payroll processing, the U.S. Postal Service, Bloomberg, and even conventional credit card processing services

4. Platform as a service

Another SaaS variation, this form of cloud computing delivers development environments as a service. You build your own applications that run on the provider's infrastructure and are delivered to your users via the Internet from the provider's servers. Like Legos, these services are constrained by the vendor's design and capabilities, so you don't get complete freedom, but you do get predictability and pre-integration. Prime examples include Salesforce.com's Force.com, Coghead and the new Google App Engine. For extremely lightweight development, cloud-based mashup platforms abound, such as Yahoo Pipes or Dapper.net.

5. MSP (managed service providers)

One of the oldest forms of cloud computing, a managed service is basically an application exposed to IT rather than to end-users, such as a virus scanning service for e-mail or an application monitoring service (which Mercury, among others, provides). Managed security services delivered by SecureWorks, IBM, and Verizon fall into this category, as do such cloud-based anti-spam services as

Postini, recently acquired by Google. Other offerings include desktop management services, such as those offered by CenterBeam or Everdream.

6. Service commerce platforms

A hybrid of SaaS and MSP, this cloud computing service offers a service hub that users interact with. They're most common in trading environments, such as expense management systems that allow users to order travel or secretarial services from a common platform that then coordinates the service delivery and pricing within the specifications set by the user. Think of it as an automated service bureau. Well-known examples include Rearden Commerce and Ariba.

7. Internet integration

The integration of cloud-based services is in its early days. OpSource, which mainly concerns itself with serving SaaS providers, recently introduced the OpSource Services Bus, which employs in-the-cloud integration technology from a little startup called Boomi. SaaS provider Workday recently acquired another player in this space, CapeClear, an ESB (enterprise service bus) provider that was edging toward b-to-b integration. Way ahead of its time, Grand Central — which wanted to be a universal "bus in the cloud" to connect SaaS providers and provide integrated solutions to customers — flamed out in 2005.

Potential advantages of any cloud or grid computing approach include:

- Location of infrastructure in areas with lower costs of real estate and electricity.
- Sharing of peak-load capacity among a large pool of users, improving overall utilization.
- Separation of infrastructure maintenance duties from domain-specific application development.
- Separation of application code from physical resources.
- Ability to use external assets to handle peak loads (not have to engineer for highest possible load levels).
- Not have to purchase assets for one-time or infrequent intensive computing tasks.

Conclusion

Grid technology; reveals the early thoughts on interconnecting Clouds for dynamically creating an atmospheric computing environment along with pointers to future community research; and concludes with the need for convergence of competing IT paradigms for delivering our 21st century vision. Cloud computing is a new and promising paradigm delivering IT services as computing utilities. In this paper we have discussed the emergence of Cloud computing from cluster and grid. As the computing industry shifts toward providing Platform as a Service (PaaS) and Software as a Service (SaaS) for consumers and enterprises to access on demand regardless of time and location, there will be an increase in the number of Cloud platforms available. Recently, several academic and industrial organisations have started investigating and developing technologies and infrastructure for Cloud Computing. Several companies are already engaged in providing cloud services like Saas, Paas, DBas, Haas etc. The challenges include resource allocation, security and many more. The road ahead is tough though achievable. The primary goal is to provide low-risk, low-effort, "pay-as-you-go" access to services for small to midsize companies that are currently unable to move beyond technical computing on the desktop.

References

- M. Jelasity, R. Guerraoui, A.-M. Kermarrec, and M. van Steen. The peer sampling service: Experimental evaluation of unstructured gossip-based implementations. In H.-A. Jacobsen, editor, Middleware 2004, volume 3231 of Lecture Notes in Computer Science, pages 79–98. Springer-Verlag, 2004.
- M. Jelasity and A.-M. Kermarrec. Ordered slicing of very large-scale overlay networks. In Proceedings of the Sixth IEEE International Conference on Peer-to-Peer Computing (P2P 2006), 2006. to appear.
- M. Jelasity, A. Montresor, and O. Babaoglu.Gossip-based aggregation in large dynamic networks. ACM Transactions on Computer Systems, 23(3):219–252, August 2005.
- M. Jelasity, A. Montresor, and O. Babaoglu. The bootstrapping service. In Proceedins of the 26th International Conference on Distributed Computing Systems: Workshops (ICDCS WORKSHOPS), 2006. International Workshop on Dynamic Distributed Systems (IWDDS), to appear.
- Hand E., Head in the clouds, Nature, Vol. 449, 24 October 2007, p. 963
- Delic K., On Dependability of Corporate Grids, ACM Ubiquity, Volume 6, Issue 45 (December 7-13, 2005) Robison S., A Bright Future in the Cloud, Financial Times, March 4, 2008
- The Economist: When Clouds Collide, February 7, 2008.
- http://www.web2journal.com/read/612033.htm
- http://www.ebizq.net/blogs/saasweek/2008/03/distinguishing _cloud_computing/
- http://www.datacenterknowledge.com/archives/2008/Mar/25/ whats_in_a_name_utility_vs_cloud_vs_grid.html

Impact of Information & Communication Technology on Public Life

Aditi Chawla
MSc (IT), MCA

Abstract

Today in the World of Computers, everyone is amazed at how pervasive computers have become important in our lives. In just a time span of few decades they seem to be everywhere: from our laptops, to our desktops, to our cars, even our dish washers. In absence of computers, we would not be able to receive or send mails round the clock, anywhere on the globe or even from within the skies.

But, is this really amazing? Not when you think about the true nature of this device. Because it is different, very different in its basic nature than any tool ever manufactures before. Think about all our other implements for a while. Levers and pulleys, and all the things we can make from them, like cranes and earth-moving equipment, are extensions of our muscles.

Our transportation systems are extensions of our legs. They take us farther, higher and faster than we could go otherwise. Even our communications systems are extensions of our physical senses, be they telephones (voice) or video (vision). All of the tools which we have created throughout human history have been extensions of physical capabilities.

An attempt has been made to highlight the impact of use of various forms of information and communication technology on various walks of public lives including public governance, business and commerce, medicine and public health, travel, tourism and public transport, journalism and mass media, education and teaching-learning, etc.

Introduction

Information and communication technologies are definitely gaining ground, even in the remote corners of the world. ICT is about digital information passing between devices. The most prolific example is the Internet, a worldwide network of computers linked together by telephone lines. There are, however, other examples like mobile phones, interactive television and personal organisers. When ICT is applied in businesses it can lower costs, raise productivity and improve customer & supplier relationships. In learning, ICT widens participation and raises attainment. In public services, ICT engages people with services more effectively and in communities ICT links people to economic opportunity and brings together those with common agendas. We see the letters ICT everywhere - particularly in education. But what does it mean? A brief introduction to this important and fast-changing subject follows.

ICT is an acronym that stands for **Information Communications Technology.** However, apart from explaining an acronym, there is not a universally accepted definition of ICT. Why? Because the concepts, methods and applications involved in ICT are constantly evolving on an almost daily basis. Its difficult to keep up with the changes - they happen so fast. Let us focus on the three words behind ICT: **Informatio, Communicationsand Technology**

A good way to think about ICT is to consider all the uses of digital technology, which already exist to help individuals, businesses and organisations use information. **ICT covers any product that will store, retrieve, manipulate, transmit or receive information electronically in a digital form,** for example, personal computers, digital television, email, and robots.

So ICT is concerned with the **storage, retrieval, manipulation, transmission** or **receip**t of digital data. Importantly, it is also concerned with the way these different uses can work with each other. In business, ICT is often categorized into two broad types of product: 1) **the traditional computer-based technologies** (things you can typically do on a personal computer or using computers at home or at work); and 2) the more recent, and fast-growing range of **digital communication technologies** (which allow people and organizations to communicate and share information digitally).

Traditional Computer Based Technologies

ICT refers to the **communication** of data by electronic means, usually over some distance. This is often achieved via **networks** of sending and receiving equipment, wires and satellite links. The technologies involved in communication tend to be complex. You certainly don't need to understand them for your ICT course. However, there are aspects of digital communications that you need to be aware of. These relate primarily to the **types of network** and the ways of connecting to the Internet. Let's look at these two briefly (further revision notes provide much more detail to support your study).

Internal networks: Usually referred to as a **local area network (LAN),** this involves linking a number of hardware items (input and output devices plus computer processing) together within an office or building. The aim of a LAN is to be able to share **hardware** facilities such as printers or scanners, software applications and data. This type of network is invaluable in the office environment where colleagues need to have access to common data or programmes.

External networks: Often you need to communicate with someone outside your internal network, in this case you will need to be part of a **Wide Area Network (WAN)**. The Internet is the ultimate WAN - it is a vast network of networks.

Application Standard Office Application	**Use Main Examples**
Word processing	E.g. Microsoft Word: Write letters, reports etc
Spreadsheets	E.g. Microsoft Excel; Analyse financial information; calculations; create forecasting models etc
Database software	E.g. Oracle, Microsoft SQL Server, Access; Managing data in many forms, from basic lists (e.g. customer contacts through to complex material (e.g. catalogue)
Presentation software	E.g. Microsoft PowerPoint; make presentations, either directly using a computer screen or data projector. Publish in digital format via email or over the Internet
Desktop publishing	E.g. Adobe Indesign, Quark Express, Microsoft Publisher; produce newsletters, magazines and other complex documents.
Graphics software	E.g Adobe Photoshop and Illustrator; Macromedia Freehand and Fireworks; create and edit images such as logos, drawings or pictures for use in DTP, web sites or other publications
Specialist Applications	**Examples (list is not complete)**
Accounting package	E.g. Sage, Oracle; Manage an organisation's accounts including revenues/sales, purchases, bank accounts etc. A wide range of systems is available ranging from basic packages suitable for small businesses through to sophisticated ones aimed at multinational companies.
Computer Aided Design	Computer Aided Design (CAD) is the use of computers to assist the design process. Specialised CAD programs exist for many types of design: architectural, engineering, electronics, roadways
Customer Relations Management (CRM)	Software that allows businesses to better understand their customers by collecting and analysing data on them such as their product preferences, buying habits etc. Often linked to software applications that run call centres and loyalty cards for example.

Table 1: Traditional Computer Based Technologies

The Potential Uses Of Ict

ICT applications are useful in numerous instances to facilitate the developments of various aspects of the society. This section briefly examines some of these aspects:

***Public Administration**

Public administration is a key aspect of civil society and it includes a range of services to citizens and industry. It provides various functions that enhance the social, economic and political developments of the citizenry. Most importantly, it provides public information that is useful to the community at large. ICTs facilitate these public administration activities. For instance, e-Government, a concept that defines a situation where government activities and public information can be made available by using ICTs. In India, Union government and several provincial governments has expressed their intention of transforming itself into an e-government where information can be accessed at any time through the Internet/ WWW, with public Internet kiosks provided for universal access.

***Urban and Rural Development**

ICT applications are useful in facilitating development programmes in many countries. These technologies help in supporting economic and social developments. Mansell & Wehn (1998: 83) note that "*diverse current and historical data sets on health, education, water supplies, sanitation, and population growth and movement can be captured, collated, manipulated, and presented*" They also note that "*economic development can be fostered by tele-working and tele-services in some of the developing countries*" (ibid.). The establishment of information kiosks in rural communities can facilitate economic empowerment. Mobile telephony can also help rural entrepreneurs in keeping in touch with their market outside their communities.

***Transport Sector**

In transport sector, ICT applications can be used to improve road, air and rail transportation. ICT applications are noticeable in the air transport control, monitoring of freight and the day-to-day transport system. For example, the development of smart cards helps facilitate the smooth operations of the transport system. These operations include payment for parking metres, identification of authorised parking space occupants. In Africa the smart card system is not widely used, however, in South Africa the smart cards used to ease the hassles of boarding public transportation. For example, the SABTA (South Africa Black Taxi Association) trial application in Bloemfontein was to address the growing demand for prepayment services. Minibus taxis are the preferred mode of transport between the townships and places of work in South Africa. These taxis are licensed to carry up to 14 passengers. The Taxi proprietors were pleased with the tighter controls the system offers and more especially that it reduced the risk of loss cash in the system (Townsend, 1996). Currently, some Taxi operators are using the smart card system.

*** Health**

ICT applications are becoming valuable resources in the medical field. They support efficient exchange of information between health professionals, they enable transfer of patient records between sites and they can improve clinical effectiveness, continuity, and quality of care by health professionals (Mansell and Wehn 1998). ICT applications facilitate telemedicine - "*the use of ICTs to provide medical demand independent of person-to-person contact.*" Telemedicine provides medical service to people in geographically diverse settings: at home and in isolated places or in emergencies. An example of the impact of ICTs on medicine is the recent operation that was performed at the Chris Hani Baragwanath Hospital. Separated by 8917km, two surgeons made South African medical history when they jointly performed an operation on a two-year-old. Dr Bob at Chris Hani Baragwanath Hospital in Soweto and Professor Benno Ure at his offices in Hannover, Germany, made use of the latest advancement in surgery - the telemonitoring system, 'Socrates' - to perform a laparoscopic surgery (Green, 2003). 'Socrates' works by linking surgeons in the operating room with colleagues anywhere in the world. A voice-controlled robotic arm (Aesop) positions and holds an endoscope (a minute camera used to view internal organs) which is inserted into the patient via the navel.

*** Physically Challenged**

For many people with physical disabilities, ICTs can be extremely useful in providing access to communication, education and open up opportunities for them. The use of Braille keyboards and printers can help alleviate some common literacy and numeracy problems for visually impaired or blind people. Most telecommunications infrastructures are now being designed with the capabilities of meeting the special needs of the physically challenged. For instance, the Short Message Service (SMS) can be used to send and receive messaged by the hearing impaired, the voice activated dialling service can be used by visually impaired.

ICTs have changed the lives for disabled people for betterment. They are used by following categories of people:

- Severely disabled people to communicate;
- Dyslexic people;
- The blind and visually impaired;
- Those with learning difficulties.

The hardware may be standard hardware, or it may be modified to the specific needs of the disabled person. The device shown below in figure 1 is called **ahead**

mouse. The disabled person can move their head, and the mouse will behave on the screen just like a normal mouse that we move with our hand.

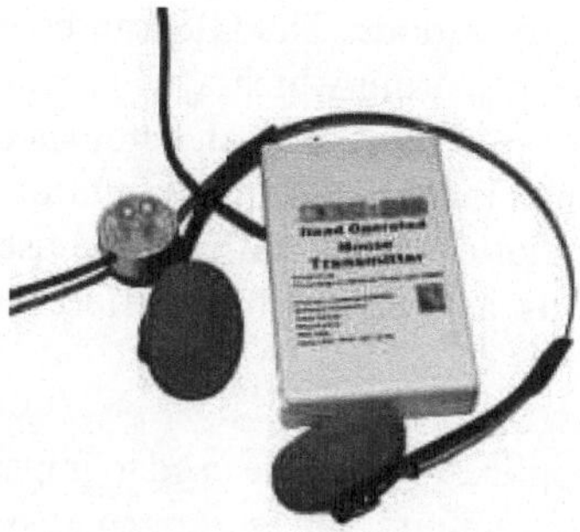

Figure 1: A head Mouse

ICT has given many career opportunities to disabled people. Self-employed disabled people have been able to take careers in:

- Web designers
- Photography
- Free lance writers
- Ceramics, trade crafts

Employment opportunities have been made available through ICT as:

- Teachers, at the Internet college
- ICT technicians
- Call centre operators
- Factory worker, storekeeper, shop assistant, trainee.

*** Education**

The education sector is arguably one major area that ICTs are playing remarkable a role. These technologies help in facilitating learning and exchange of educational materials. ICTs are helping library professionals store and manage academic information. Libraries have migrated from the traditional Dewey cataloguing system to an on-line system, which is a web-based cataloguing and search application. The online learning system is another web-based application that is revolutionising the learning platform of education. This system compliments the traditional face-to face teaching and learning format. In the on-line system, students can access class notes, submit assignment and also join a discussion group with other learners.

*** Environment**

ICT applications can help in collecting data about environmental issues. They allow access to information and provide support system to manage and monitor environmental issues. For example, the Geographical Information focuses on the collection, storage, analysis, display and application of geographic data (Mansell et. al., 1998). The Geographic Information System (GIS) is one of the Geographic Information Technology applications. The GIS can be regarded as an advanced equivalent of a traditional map from which a wide array of information can be extracted for specific purposes. The GIS is an automated system that enables the capture, storage, checking, integration, manipulation, analysis, display, and modelling of complex spatial data. The GIS can be useful in the integration of information on climate, soils, and terrains from different sources.

*** Agriculture**

At the micro level, ICTs applications can be used to impart information directly to farmers and the farming community. There are expert system designed to handle agricultural issues such as water utilisation and management, pest control, harvest management and so forth.

*** Manufacturing**

ICTs applications are linking the process chains in manufacturing as opposed to improving or facilitating single steps in the production lines. The old 'Fordist' or mass production of goods and services is gradually giving way to a network-based production and manufacturing system. There has been a shift from the old production system to a new mode which is facilitated by information and communication technology. While the old production and manufacturing system is energy-intensive, standardised and departmentalised the new manufacturing system facilitated by ICTs is information-intensive, customised, networked and integrated. Furthermore, the design stage of product manufacturing benefits enormously from the use of ICTs. For instance, the use of Computer-aided-design (CAD) has improved the design stages of machine tools.

*** Electronic Commerce**

Electronic commerce or e-commerce is the use of telecommunications or the Internet to carry out business of any type. Common examples of e-commerce are business-to-business e-commerce, online shopping, online banking, online stock trading etc. One of the advantages of e-commerce is the reduction of transaction costs. Electronic transaction of business activities has 'redefined' the concepts of 'market', 'seller' and 'buyers', as they all converge now on the electronic space. Billions of dollars worth of transactions are completed on the Internet. This development has warranted national government involvement in regulating e-commerce activities.

*** Travel and Tourism**

The travel and tourism industry has been heavily affected by ICT applications. The Internet, in particular, has been useful in many regards to the travel and tourism sector. It is used to provide multimedia information about destination to prospective travellers. It also affects auxiliary industries, such as the transport sector, which plays a major role in the tourism industry. With the aid of ICT applications, prospective travellers can view a destination, book accommodation, book the flight and other forms of transport and pay for all these without leaving their homes. The use of ICTs has permeated the travel and tourism industry. ICTs in this industry consist of various components that include computerised reservation systems, teleconferencing, video, video brochures, management information systems, airline electronic information systems, electronic funds transfer, digital telephone networks, smart cards, mobile communication, e-mail, and Internet (Mansell & When, 1998). These various communication technologies are being used in all sectors travel and tourism industry and related sectors (see Figure 2).

Figure 2: ICTs for Integrated Tourism and Local Economy

*** ICT in Banking**

Banks have been pioneer in making use of ICTs for providing better and faster services to their customers. As a matter of fact, banks have been making extensive use of following ICT applications for many years.

- Magnetic Ink Character Recognition (MICR)
- Bankers' Automated Clearing Services (BACS)
- Automated Teller Machines (ATM)
- Electronic Funds Transfer at Point of Sale (EFTPOS)
- Electronic Funds Transfer (EFT)
- Electronic data interchange (EDI)
- Smart Cards

We will look at each of these in turn:

- **MICR**

These are the strange looking numbers at the bottom of a cheque. They are written in a special magnetic ink, and have the advantage that they can be read by a reader connected to a computer, or by a person. One the cheque is written the bank sort code, the account number, the cheque number. When the cheque is being **cleared**, the cheque amount is also written.

- **BACS**

The **Bankers Automated Clearing Services** have used computers to carry out most financial transactions between banks. These include:

- clearing cheques
- paying in salaries
- payment of standing orders or direct debits

The BACS does its processing by batch processing, in which all transactions from the previous day are processed at one time. The processed data is passed between banks on magnetic tapes. Logs are kept of all the transactions. Banks were among the first organisations to use mainframe computers. Many of these are still at work today, as they are very good at this routine number crunching. It still takes up to a week for a cheque to clear.

- **ATM**

Automatic teller machines (Figure 3) are familiar to most bank customers. They insert a card in the wall, type in a PIN number and out comes the money.

Figure 3: A Bank ATM

They are connected to the bank via telephone lines and pass the details of each transaction to a transaction file. This is updated at the end of the day to debit the customers' bank accounts with the appropriate sums of money. The ATM allows the customer to:

- Get cash out
- Find out the balance in their account
- Change their Personal Identification Number (PIN)
- Request a statement.

Putting money into the account still requires handing it over to a cashier. Lloyds Bank have a system called *Credit point* where the customer deposits money in a special envelope. It is, in effect, a posting box; all the subsequent cash handling operations are manual. For the customer, the ATM:

- is more anonymous.
- provides a 24-hour a day service, seven days a week; ideal for customers who work irregular hours.
- causes fewer queues since the transactions are quicker.

For the bank the ATM:

- frees up staff from performing routine transactions so that more profitable sales-orientated work can be done.
- reduces the number of staff, since the computer does the work.
- provides a continuous service outside normal hours.
- prevents customers withdrawing money that is not in the account.

- **EFTPOS**

Electronic Funds Transfer at Point of Sale (Figure 4). One might have seen these devices at the checkouts of many shops:

Figure 4: Electronic Funds Transfer at Point of Sale

The cashier swipes the card through and the transaction is logged so that funds will be transferred from the customer's account to the retailer's account. Although in theory it would be possible for the transfer to be made on the spot, in fact the transaction is carried out when all the other transactions are updated later on in the day. Transactions made after about 16.00 are carried out the next day. Figure 5 shows the general scheme to ensure security: To prevent fraud, SMART cards are being more widely used, and soon customers will have to put in a PIN number into the machine.

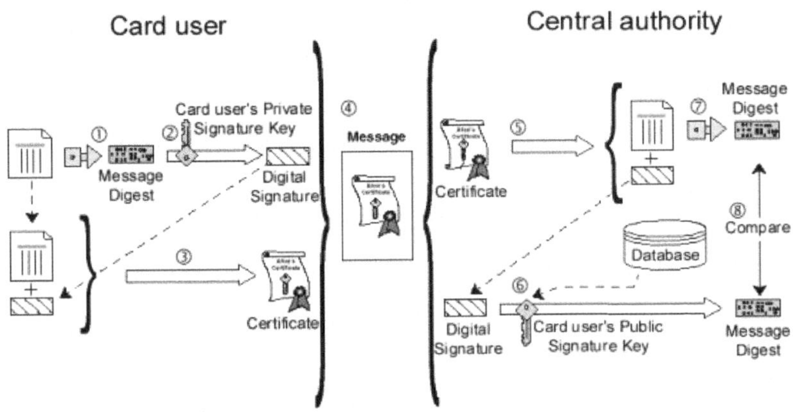

Figure 5: General Security Scheme.

- **SMART cards**

These are cards which have a chip built in. These will soon contain not just the account details of the customer, but also the thumbprint and iris pattern (eye) of the cardholder. These are unique to the card owner, and will make it much harder for the fraudulent user. Architecture of a typical smart card is shown in figure 6.

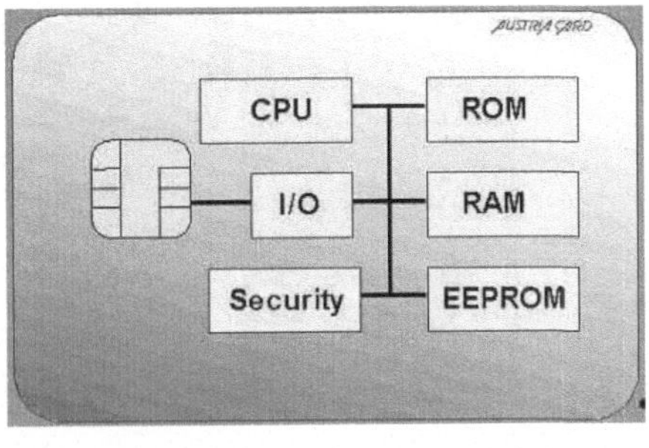

Figure 6: Architecture of a Typical Smart Card

- **Internet Banking**

Many customers now use the Internet for their banking (see Figure 7). They can access their account for performing following banking transactions:

- getting the account balance
- pay bill processing
- transfer of funds from one account to another
- manage the account

Figure 7 Internet banking

Paying in money is not so easy; cash cannot be stuffed down a phone line. The Internet is a playground for hackers and fraudsters. Security on such accounts has to be rigorous. Figure 8 shows a screen dump of a typical interface for Internet banking.

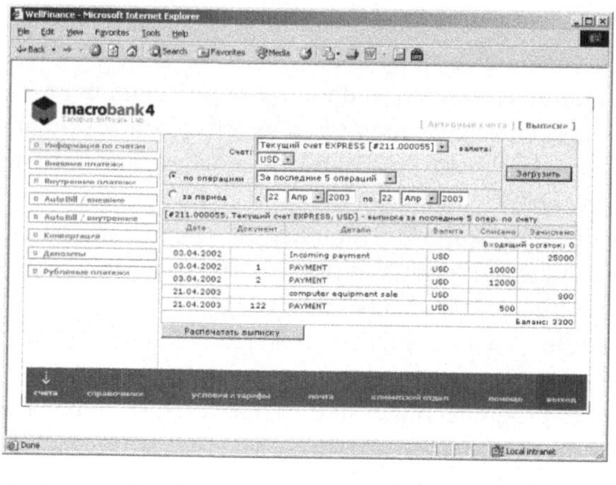

Figure 8: A typical Internet Banking Screen Dump

*** Internet Shopping**

To shop on the web you need a computer, a **web browser** (do not use the trade names *Internet Explorer* or *Netscape*), an **Internet Service Provider** (ISP), and a modem. If you are using dial-up, you will need a **56 k modem**. If you have broadband, you will have an **ADSL modem.** The advantages to the customer are:

- no need to leave house and face the heaving masses in the shopping mall;
- easy to shop around for the best price or value (not necessarily the same, as some so-called good deals may include hidden extras);
- can see a lot of goods and read details about them;
- Payment is easy.

The advantages to the retailer are:

- no need for a large premises to display the goods;
- no wastage due to shoplifting;
- not many staff needed;
- customers can access the store twenty four hours a day, seven days a week;
- retailers can use the net to check competitors' prices.

The disadvantages are:

- goods cannot be inspected or tried on;
- delivery time can be unacceptably long;
- faulty goods are hard to return;
- possibility of fraudulent trading;
- credit card details could be revealed.

Internet shopping has burgeoned over the last few years. Most major retailers have an on-line shop as well as their normal stores.

*** Expert Systems**

At their simplest expert systems are **databases** on which is stored a large amount of information that is useful for professionals in a particular specialist area. However an expert system can do more than that:

- It can be connected to data-logging sensors in an industrial plant.
- Data is constantly monitored as a live control situation.
- The system can alert the operators to the need for routine and preventative maintenance.

The system can diagnose some fault conditions. The pictures show a vast piece of machinery in an industrial plant and the expert system that is monitoring it. An expert system has three components, namely:

- **Inference engine** – a program that is used to link the questions to the database of knowledge.
- **Shell** – a set of programs rather like an operating system that coordinates the activities of the system.

- **Natural language interface** – the user types in the request in normal English, and the computer uses the inference engine to turn the request into computer language.

The help systems in some programs like those in Microsoft Office Suite have a natural language interface in which you type in the question in normal talk. The program then gives a set of options to the user.

*** ICT in Education**

The obvious area to consider is the teaching of computing and ICT, which both look at the use of computers in business. The microcomputer and the PC have been used in schools for the last twenty years or so. Earlier BBC Microcomputer (Figure 9) was very popular wit schools and other educational institutes to make students familiar with the world of digital computers. Most institutes nowadays have switched to PCs or Macs or even laptops and internetworked computer labs. BBCs are primitive, but:

- Is very simple to operate;
- Very stable; it rarely crashes.
- Is very good at data-logging.

Figure 9 An Expert System

Some schools even networked their BBCs and very proud they were too. The BBC was ousted within five to ten years by the PC which became ever more accessible both in price and operation. The school PC is a common sight; the BBCs have been consigned to prep-room shelves or the skip. The PC is a good teaching aid. It can be used for:

- Data-logging;
- Presentation Graphics to illustrate taught material;
- Mathematical modelling on spreadsheets;
- CD-ROM interactive activities;

- CD-ROM simulations;
- Use of the Internet for research;
- Virtual learning environments;
- Electronic notes.

Figure 11 shows a laptop computer being used for data logging. In addition to teaching and learning, computers can be used for administration:

- Pupil and staff database;
- Curriculum planning;
- Pupil registration;

Security of the school or college, giving pupils and staff access rights to some parts of the college and not others.

Figure 10 A BBC Microcomputer System.

Figure 11 A Laptop used in Laboratory

*** ICT in Industry**

In many industries the traditional drawing board is almost a relic. There are many **computer aided design** (CAD) packages that enable the designer to work out the designs. Drawing with a mouse is difficult, so the computer system may have a light pen and a graphics tablet (under the engineer's left hand in Figure 12 there is a graphics tablet). There are three main areas of applications of ICT, namely, Computer Aided Design (CAD), Computer Aided Manufacture (CAM), and Robotics.

Figure 12: A Graphics Tablet

CAD packages use **vector graphics**, which means that the coordinates at each end of a line are plotted. It results in smaller file sizes and changes of size can be accommodated without the distortion caused by **pixilation** (where lines appear to be stepped). The advantages of CAD are many, for example, 1) no special drawing skills are needed; 2) designs can be easily changed 3) the design can be tested using **computer modelling**.

Complex mathematical calculations are used to predict the item's behaviour under normal and extreme conditions. This makes more sense than destructive testing on prototypes, which can be highly expensive or even dangerous. The computer design, when complete, can be loaded into a **computer aided manufacturing** (CAM) machine. An example of this has been shown in figure 13.

The computer guides the machine head with a precision greater than the precision of even the finest craftsman. Such machines (figure 14) are massively expensive, but pay for themselves in terms of 1) greater productivity; 2) better precision, leading to greater reliability of the finished product; and 3) complex shapes can be machined.

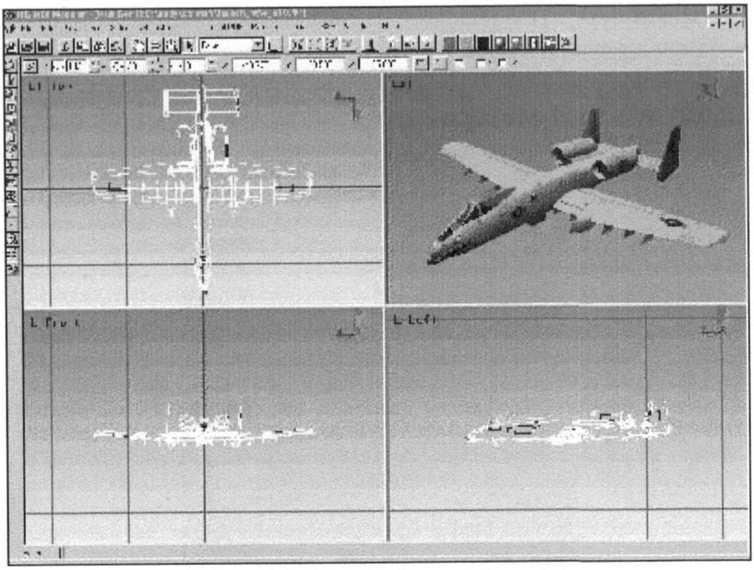

Figure 13: A Screenshot of CAD Application

Figure 14: Computer Guided High Precision Machine

Robots controlled by computers now operate many assembly lines (Figure 15). Robots are complex machines that rely on feedback to ensure that the various machine heads are positioned in exactly the right place. Although very expensive, robot assembly line machines have following advantages – 1) no need for lunch breaks and calls of nature, 2) diligence - they don't get bored, avoiding mistakes, 3) they don't go on strike, and 4) they work 24 hours a day, seven days a week. There is, however, a downside of use of robots in manufacturing line – 1) new products need complete reprogramming of the machinery, possibly with new tooling, 2) maintenance has to be carried out to a high standard, 3) computer systems failure will lead to the breakdown of the assembly line, and 4) certain processes cannot be carried out by a robot and they still need a skilled operator.

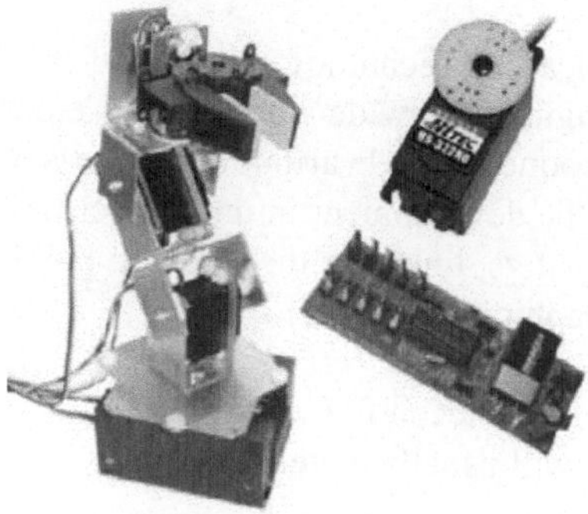

Figure 15 A robot.

*** ICT In Medicine**

The most obvious way that ICT is used in medicine is the database in each doctor's surgery in which the details of patients are kept. These would include patient's name, date of birth, address, occupation, lifestyle, and last visit to the doctor. ICT has made a massive impact in medicine beyond doctors' and hospital databases. Other areas that have seen a substantial impact from ICT include computer-controlled diagnostic equipment, computer analysis of data received from diagnostic devices. The images from the Nuclear Magnetic Resonance (NMR) scan are pretty unintelligible until computer has processed them. Following mechanisms and technologies can be of immense help to the doctor.

- Expert systems that enable doctors to access information about uncommon illnesses.
- Remote operations by specialists from other countries.
- CD-ROM material to enable junior doctors to learn new material.
- Diagnosis over the Internet.

The Internet has many sites to do with medical matters. People look up information on health, life-style, or diet. Many people use the Internet to diagnose and treat themselves for their illnesses. They often look for alternative treatments, because they are fed up with their doctors and the long waits for treatment. A little bit of knowledge is a very dangerous thing. People who do this are at one or more of following risks

- misdiagnosis; of the illness and consequent wrong treatment,
- falling for quack remedies,
- serious and lasting damage to their health, and
- in extreme cases, death

Conclusion

Information Communication Technology as one of the fast changing advanced technologies has brought worldwide impacts and emerged as a force modern agriculture and food production and various other areas over the past two decades. It owes its success to the development in microelectronics and software systems through personal computers, linked to the internet; mobile telephones and global positioning and geographic information system.

This paper concludes that a technology is guided by social change where a need is created, technology will usually develop.

References

- Adelsberger H., B. Collis, and J.M. Pawloski, (eds.), *Handbook on Information Technologies for Education and Training*, Springer-Verlag, 2002.
- Albert S., and C. Thomas, A New Approach to Computer-Aided Distance Learning: The Automated Tutor.
- Johnson B and Lundvall B, The Learning Economy, *Journal of Industry Studies"*, Vol. 1, no 2, 1994
- Cellary W., and A. Iyengar, *Internet Technologies, Applications and Societal Impact*, Kluwer Academic Publishers, 2002.

Challenges in Various Areas of AI and Neural Network

Shalini Bhartiya
Lecturer (IT), RDIAS, Delhi
Sakshi Pal Chaudhary
Lecturer, BVN, Delhi

Abstract

Artificial Intelligence is the science of creating computer applications that have the capability to exhibit human behavior. The field of neural networks is an emerging technology in the area of machine information processing and decision making. This paper will trace the challenges prevailing in the areas such as Robotics, Image processing and Expert System, thereby creating hazards or obstacles in building up techniques that can prove to very beneficial in various spheres of productivity. It will outline the difficulties resulting from the abandonment of well-known linear design methods and the subsequent advantages in terms of improved results. Finally, new challenges, such as the vector data, Digital media and Medicine will be introduced.

Introduction

The field of neural networks is an emerging technology in the area of machine information processing and decision making. The main thrusts are toward highly innovative machine and algorithmic architectures, radically different from those that have been employed in conventional digital computers. Neural networks have created an unusual amount of interest in the engineering and industrial communities by opening up new research directions and commercial and military applications. Automated information processing is achieved by means of modules that in general involve four functions: input/output (getting in and out of the machine), processing (executing prescribed specific information-handling tasks), memory (storing information), and connections between different modules providing for information flow and control.

The information-processing properties of neural networks depend mainly on two factors: the network topology (the scheme used to connect elements or nodes together), and the algorithm (the rules) employed to specify the values of the weights connecting the nodes. While the ultimate configuration and parameter values are problem-specific, it is possible to classify neural networks, on the basis of how information is stored or retrieved, in four broad categories: neural networks behaving as learning machines with a teacher; neural networks behaving as learning machines without a teacher; neural networks behaving as associative memories; and neural networks that contain analog as well as digital devices and result in hybrid-machine implementations that integrate complex continuous dynamic processing and logical functions. Within these four categories, several generic models have found important applications, and still others are under intensive investigation.

Neural-network research is developing a new conceptual framework for representing and utilizing information, which will result in a significant advance in information epistemology. Communication technology is based on the notions of coding and channel capacity (bits per second), which provide the conceptual framework for information representation appropriate to machine-based communication. Neural-network systems (biological or artificial) do not store information or process it in the way that conventional digital computers do. Specifically, the basic unit of neural-network operation is not based on the notion of the instruction but on the connection. The performance of a neural network depends directly on the number of connections per second that it effects, and thus its performance is better understood in terms of its connections-per-second (CPS) capability.

Challenges

There are significant challenges in various fields of nonlinear control. This paper will address these challenges with its focus on latest developments in theory and application of artificial intelligence and neural networks.

1. AI and Robotic Systems

a) The opacity of neural networks

In a rule-based system the rules are expressed in an artificial language with some similarity to natural languages or to symbolic logic. The basic terms and predicates, in terms of which the rules are expressed, are generally those of the problem domain. Therefore the knowledge and rules of inference used by the system are *transparent*, that is, potentially intelligible to human beings. In a neural network, in contrast, the knowledge and inferential processes are implicit in real valued connection weights among myriads of micro features. Further, representations are nonlocal and distributed. Therefore, individual micro features and connections do not usually have meanings that can be expressed in the terms of the problem domain.

Many people are troubled by the opacity of neural networks compared to the (potential) transparency of rule-based systems. With a rule-based system, they argue, you can look at the knowledge base and inferential rules, understand them, and see if they make sense. A human can, in effect, see if the system is making its decisions for the right reasons, or at least that it is not making them for the wrong reasons (e.g., on the basis of irrelevant factors). In contrast, a trained neural network might perform some task very well, but we will be unable to understand — in human-comprehensible terms — the bases on which it is doing its job. Perhaps it has found some totally irrelevant cues in the training and test data that allow it to perform well on them, but it will fail dismally when deployed.

b) Context sensitivity and embodied cognition

Much of the inflexibility and brittleness of rule-based systems — and indeed of many digital computer programs — is a consequence of their behaving the same in all contexts, whereas natural intelligence is sensitive to context and can modulate its behavior appropriately.

Due to the ability of artificial neural networks to integrate a very large number of micro features, which may be individually insignificant, they can exhibit valuable context sensitivity. However, this presents a test and evaluation challenge for connectionist systems, since we cannot test such a system in a single or simple context (e.g., in a laboratory) and assume that it will work in all contexts. Rather, it is important to identify the contexts in which the system may find itself and ensure that it operates acceptably in all of them. Since we want and expect the system to make subtle contextual discriminations, it cannot be adequately tested or evaluated in artificially constructed situations that do not demand this subtlety. Further, embodied intelligence depends crucially on the physical characteristics of the system in which it is embedded and on its physical relationships to its environment. While preliminary testing and evaluation can make use of simulations of the physical system and its environment, such simulations are always incomplete, and are more computationally expensive the more complete they are. Whereas to some extent conventional AI systems can be tested and evaluated offline, embodied AI systems cannot. Therefore physical prototypes must be integrated earlier into the development cycle.

Finally, embodied connectionist systems are to some degree opaque, that is, their *cognitive* processes are not fully transparent (intelligible) to humans.

2. AI and Expert Systems

To illustrate the sorts of issues that are known to be problematic, four examples are selected and described below: conflict; democratic decision making; argumentation; and role definition. In each case, it is argued, that adding intelligent AI systems leads to further complications, and it is concluded that recognizing these sooner, rather than later, is desirable and wise.

a) *Conflict*

First, a great deal of collaborative work involves conflict. Conflict, per se, is not a bad thing, and in many instances it is desirable and needs to be exploited if collaborations are to be successful. As well as differing in many other ways, such as in knowledge, skills, personality and ethics, different people have different agendas. This is reasonable when they have different responsibilities. Collaboration is most challenging when these conflicts fail to be resolved.
How should conflict between a human and an AI be resolved?

One could certainly imagine cases where an AI's preferences and agenda might be the desirable option. As an example, we can entertain a role for an AI to act as a mediator supporting conflict resolution between people - such an AI would always be in conflict with some of the collaborators, since mediation tends to require operations involving things such as bargaining and compromise. Would human collaborators be happy to compromise with an AI? What factors might influence their willingness to accept the AIs input, rather than overruling it?

b) *Decision Making*

Conflict may also be resolved through voting. There are arguments that voting is not actually a very good mechanism for small group decision making, with problems such as:

Empowering the largest minority and not a divided majority; Polarization of opinions; choosing the least bad option; giving undue power to floating voters; and strategic voting and bargaining so that decisions are made based on unrelated and irrelevant, and potentially even corrupt, external factors.

There are many types of voting systems and polling algorithms that lead to different group behaviors. Particular decisions may be reached because of the details of the democratic system used. Will users accept an enfranchised AI system with a vote of its own? How might those votes be weighted? How should the voting system be designed in order to support combining human and AI votes?

c) *Argumentation*

AI systems that understand language and can act on information received from other intelligences may also be open to persuasion. How will people adapt their

arguments to a non-human intelligence, on what basis will they be able to influence it? How people will work with future non-human AIs will depend to a great degree on people's beliefs about them.
Furthermore, how might AIs learn to influence their human collaborators? Successful argumentation relies on an understanding of the audience. If an agent's intelligence does not encompass a theory of mind, how can it understand its audience? Some form of prosthetic argumentation support could be considered, such as the systems described in , which can segment arguments and identify warrants and conclusions for example. But the question remains:to what degree will human collaborators accept persuasion from an artificial agent?

d) Role Definition

These three examples (conflict resolution, voting and argumentation) all rest on the answer to a fourth issue: what are appropriate roles for AIs? Roles can be official or unofficial, explicit or implicit, and fairly stable over time or rotating,evolving and ephemeral. It is not going to be easy to design roles for AIs in collaborative work systems, particularly when, in some cases, it is actually desirable for collaborators to take on poorly defined roles temporarily.

Learning is a fundamental property of artificial neural networks. There is no reason why future AI systems of this sort could not learn and evolve their own roles, as people frequently do. Task analyses, ethnographic studies or other data sources demonstrate that people have tacit understanding of their roles, and that they are not good at describing what those roles are. Why would we think an AI would be better than people at describing a role that it had evolved?

Furthermore, is it necessary for an AI to be able to describe its role, if it is performing it usefully?

As roles change, co-adaptation is likely to lead to difficulties. Collaborative AIs may also adapt to the user. Such problems will remain and there seems no reason to suppose that AIs will be any better than people at explaining what they are learning. These questions should be addressed sooner rather than later, as the answers will affect the type of intelligence we need in future generations of AI applications.

3. Challenges in Image Processing

It is clear that the methodology must be able to deal with both statistical and deterministic aspects of the problem and filters. This framework cannot be obtained by one step (leap) but it will emerge as the result of incremental steps from the joint

efforts of the signal processing community. However it is good to keep the ultimate goal in mind while solving problems for more immediate demands.
Few attempts have been made to this end. Here we consider some problems whose solutions will clearly take us forward on this path.

a) Determining Signals

We all agree that it would be important to be able to devise a feasible optimization procedure with a suitable cost function, even for a specific application, e.g. image restoration.

The unification of two or more existing filter classes will un-doubtfully increase the modeling power of the framework. Therefore, it would of great interest to determine the class of problems (signals) that can be solved (represented) by the new framework.

b) Filter Structure

A related problem is that of the filter structure, or more specifically, the filter size. An often asked question is how large should the filter size be. Most of the answers have been "try and see" type.

c) Developing New and Attracting Applications

Another equally important challenge to the nonlinear signal and image processing community is to develop new and attracting applications. Next to a mature theory (still developing), interesting applications would be the driving force to open up new frontiers in the field. Most of the current applications remain in the areas of signal (1- and M-D) restoration, enhancement, edge detection and interpolation.More such endeavors are needed in other areas such as speech analysis and processing, telecommunications and data analysis and communication.

4. New Challenging Areas

a) Vector Data

As non-linear signal processing matures it is being applied to many new applications and in new contexts. This session considers just four of these exciting fields. A key area is in the analysis of vector data. This is particular important in the processing of colour data. It is well known that colour is a three-dimensional quantity and most of us wish to view colour images. The filtering problem is that there is no natural ordering to colour data for the calculation of such features as the median.

Mathematical rigour is not sufficient in itself to solve the problem. The human 1885 visual system has a highly non-linear response to colour information and operators with the minimum MAE or MSE may give terrible pictures. It requires the inclusion of both psycho-visual properties and rigorous experimentation to achieve acceptable results in this area.

b) Cancer and Genetic Diseases

The treatment and diagnosis of cancer and other complex genetic diseases is one of the most important
challenges facing mankind today. New gene expression microarray technology allows the behaviour of thousands of genes to be monitored simultaneously over time; however modelling, prediction and eventual intervention require highly complex non-linear signal processing tools. These tools are amongst the first techniques beginning to bear fruit, in this field but require extensive study owing to the even more complex design processes required for modelling than those confronted in standard signal processing tasks.

c) Digital Media

Security and copyright of data are important issues considering the proliferation of digital media and internet file sharing mechanisms. Subsequent legal disputes regarding the authorship of material will depend on the robustness of embedded features known as 'watermarks' for authentication. Digital watermarking has been an active topic of research for several years. Watermarks must be both invisible to the viewer and resistant to attack. Non linear image processing techniques may be used to generate piecewise- linear Markov maps for both additive and multiplicative watermark embedding. The area of active noise control has been the subject of much research in recent years.

Future of AI and Neural Network

- Composite aggregation is the pattern that nature exhibits in creating open-ended novelty. They are the revolutionary foundations of a whole new approach to application development itself. A potentially infinite universe of new applications can be created by composing distributed elements fused together by ubiquitous connectivity. The new capabilities that can be created are not necessarily engineered so much as experimented with and shepherded. The force multiplier of the future will be modeling and simulation because the speed of fielding composite capabilities in virtual worlds before they are transitioned to the physical will be a key point of differentiation. This is the method by which emergent effects can be created and managed.
- Biological growth and connectivity also hint of potential new operational concepts that leverage the notion of capability equivalence. Capability

equivalence refers to the different combination of assets that can be composed to yield similar effects in particular circumstances. It is analogous to the various portfolio management and risk hedging practices used in the financial services industry. An equivalent behavioral effect can be achieved via a combination of different assets to meet the requirements of a specific transaction.

- Changing operational concepts may also trigger upstream business upheaval for suppliers in the computer industry. The philosophy of creating best-in-class systems that can do everything for everybody everywhere will have to share the stage with an emergent world view of building just-good-enough solutions that can do something for somebody somewhere. The latter will be a volume-driven game because networked constructs allow for greater breadth of reach into diverse micro markets of one.
- Scale in the future must be synonymous with mass local customization. To meet the demands of mass local customization, system development and capability delivery may have to be viewed in a different light.

Whatever future the AI world of tomorrow may bring, existing systems development, operational concepts and business models in the various industries likely will undergo considerable alteration. The prevailing models of today will have to be supplemented with biological ones to stand a better chance of successfully riding this coming tsunami of change.

Conclusion

The challenges we foresee, such as conflict and role management, require new approaches to collaborative working. These approaches must take into account the expectations that human agents will have when interacting with an artificial agent with some human-like abilities. These approaches must also take into account the limitations that the agent has, which will make it difficult to fulfill such expectations. A number of important open problems and challenges remain to be solved. The applications areas must be further developed and diversified in order to attract users as well as young researchers to devote more efforts in the field.

References

- www.neuralnetworks.ai-depot.com
- www.ebooks.com
- www.netlibrary.com
- www.wikipedia.com
- www.cs.iastate.edu

Internet Protocol Version 6 (IPv6)

Kiran Kawatra
Lecturer (IT), RDIAS, Delhi

Abstract

Internet Protocol version 6 (IPv6) is the next-generation Internet Layer protocol for packet-switched internet works and the Internet. IPv4 is currently the dominant Internet Protocol version, and was the first to receive widespread use. This paper will illustrate the comparison between the IPv4 and IPv6. It includes the detailed study of IPv6.Beside the introduction part of IPv6 the paper illustrates its design and implementation through various protocols and pictorial representation. The benefits accrued with this technology and certain limitations are also a part of this research.

Introduction IPv6

Internet Protocol version 6 (IPv6) is the next evolution in Internet Protocol. Most of the Internet currently uses IPv4, and this protocol has been reliable and resilient for over 20 years. However, IPv4 has severe limitations that are causing more problems as the Internet expands.In particular, there is a growing shortage of IPv4 addresses, which are needed for all new devices added to the Internet. The key to IPv6 enhancement is the expansion of the IP address space from 32 bits to 128 bits, enabling virtually unlimited unique IP addresses. The new IPv6 address text format is:

xxxx:xxxx:xxxx:xxxx:xxxx:xxxx:xxxx:xxxx

where each x is a hexadecimal digit representing 4 bits.

The expanded addressing capability of IPv6 provides a solution to the address depletion problem. This is especially important as more people use mobile computers, such as mobile telephones and handheld computers. The increasing demands of wireless users contribute to the depletion of IPv4 addresses. The expanded IP address capability of IPv6 solves this problem by providing enough IP addresses for the growing number of wireless devices. In addition to this addressing capability, IPv6 provides new functions that simplify the tasks of configuring and managing the addresses on the network. Configuring and maintaining networks is a labor intensive activity. IPv6 reduces some of the workload by automating several of the network administrator's tasks.

How IPV6 is different from IPv4

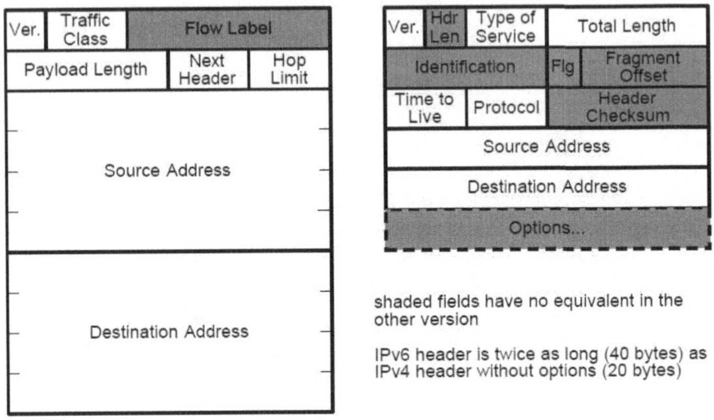

Figure 1: Packet Format of IPv4 and IPv6

To a great extent, IPv6 is a conservative extension of IPv4. Most transport- and application-layer protocols need little or no change to work over IPv6; exceptions are applications protocols that embed network-layer addresses .IPv6 specifies a new packet format, designed to minimize packet-header processing. Since the headers of IPv4 and IPv6 are significantly different, the two protocols are not interoperable. Dissimilarity between IPV4 and IPV6 are enlisted below :-

a) Larger address space

IPv6 features a larger address space than that of IPv4: addresses in IPv6 are 128 bits long versus 32 bits in IPv4. The very large IPv6 address space supports a total of 2^{128} (about 3.4×10^{38}) addresses—or approximately 5×10^{28} (roughly 2^{95}) addresses for each of the roughly 6.5 billion (6.5×10^{9}) people alive today. In a different perspective, this is 2^{52} addresses for every observable star in the known universe. While these numbers are impressive, it was not the intent of the designers of the IPv6 address space to assure geographical saturation with usable addresses. Rather, the longer addresses allow a better, systematic, hierarchical allocation of addresses and efficient route aggregation. With IPv4, complex Classless Inter-Domain Routing (CIDR) techniques were developed to make the best use of the small address space. Renumbering an existing network for a new connectivity provider with different routing prefixes is a major effort with IPv4, as discussed in RFC 2071 and RFC 2072. With IPv6, however, changing the prefix in a few routers can renumber an entire network ad hoc, because the host identifiers (the least-significant 64 bits of an address) are decoupled from the subnet identifiers and the network provider's routing prefix.

b) Stateless address auto configuration

IPv6 hosts can configure themselves automatically when connected to a routed IPv6 network using ICMPv6 router discovery messages. When first connected to a network, a host sends a link-local multicast *router solicitation* request for its configuration parameters; if configured suitably, routers respond to such a request with a *router advertisement* packet that contains network-layer configuration parameters. If IPv6 stateless address autoconfiguration (SLAAC) is unsuitable for an application, a host can use stateful configuration (DHCPv6) or be configured manually. Stateless autoconfiguration is not used by routers.

c) Multicast

Multicast provides the best attributes from both unicast and broadcast, with none of the negative aspects. Multicast provides efficient delivery of traffic in both 'one-to-many' and 'many-to-many' scenarios by sending traffic only to those interested parties that have requested the data. Routers in multicast-enabled networks build distribution trees and thus making the network responsible for replicating the data where necessary.

IPv6 does not implement broadcast, the ability to send a packet to all hosts on the attached link. The same effect can be achieved by sending a packet to the link-local *all hosts* multicast group. Most environments, however, do not currently[update] have their network infrastructures configured to route multicast packets; multicasting on single subnet will work, but global multicasting might not.

d) Mandatory network layer security

Internet Protocol Security (IPsec), the protocol for IP encryption and authentication, forms an integral part of the base protocol suite in IPv6. IPSec support is mandatory in IPv6; this is unlike IPv4, where it is optional (but usually implemented). IPsec, however, is not widely used at present except for securing traffic between IPv6 Border Gateway Protocol routers.

e) Simplified processing by routers

A number of simplifications have been made to the packet header, and the process of packet forwarding has been simplified, in order to make packet processing by routers simpler and hence more efficient. Concretely,

- The packet header in IPv6 is simpler than that used in IPv4, with many rarely-used fields moved to separate options
- IPv6 routers do not perform fragmentation. IPv6 hosts are required to either perform PMTU discovery, perform end-to-end fragmentation, or to send packets smaller than the IPv6 minimum maximum transmission unit size of 1280 bytes.
- The IPv6 header is not protected by a checksum, integrity protection is expected to be assured by a transport-layer checksum.

- The *Time-to-Live* field of IPv4 has been renamed to *Hop Limit*, reflecting the fact that routers are no longer expected to compute the time a packet has spent in a queue.

f) Mobility

Unlike mobile IPv4, Mobile IPv6 (MIPv6) avoids triangular routing and is therefore as efficient as normal IPv6. However, since neither MIPv6 nor MIPv4 are widely deployed today, this advantage is mostly theoretical.

g) Options Extensibility

IPv4 has a fixed size (40 bytes) of option parameters. In IPv6, options are implemented as additional extension headers after the IPv6 header, which limits their size only by the size of an entire packet.

Design of IPv6:

The IPv6 header format shown in Figure2 with only 6 fields and 2 addresses is in fact much simpler. Consequently the header processing is expected to be much more efficient in IPv6, thereby cutting down the processing and reducing the transit delays in internetworking devices.

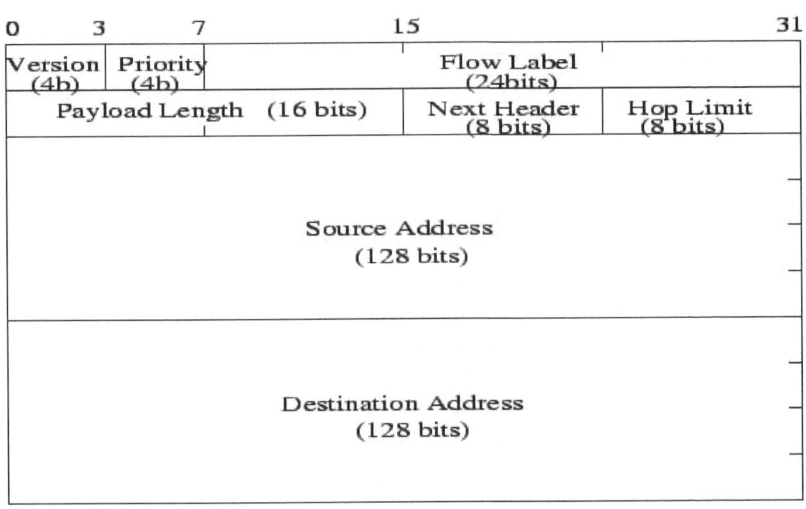

Version	4-bit Internet Protocol version number = 6.
Prio.	4-bit priority value.

Flow Label	24-bit flow label
Payload Length	16-bit unsigned integer. Length of payload, i.e., the rest of the packet following the Pv6 header, in octets. If zero, indicates that the payload length is carried in a Jumbo Payload hop-by-hop option.
Next Header	8-bit selector. Identifies the type of header mmediately following the IPv6 header.
Hop Limit	8-bit unsigned integer.Decremented by 1 by each node that forwards the packet. The packet is discarded if Hop Limit is decremented to zero.
Source Address	128-bit address of the originator of the packet.
Destination Address	128-bit address of the intended recipient of the packet (possibly not the ultimate recipient, if a Routing header is present).

Figure2: IPv6 Header Format

IPv6 address format

IPv6 addresses are 128 bits long whereas IPv4 addresses are 32 bits; where the IPv4 address space contains roughly 4 billion addresses, IPv6 has enough room for 3.4×10^{38} unique addresses.IPv6 addresses are typically composed of two logical parts: a 64-bit (sub-) network prefix, and a 64-bit host part, which is either automatically generated from the interface's MAC address or assigned sequentially. Because the globally unique MAC addresses offer an opportunity to track user equipment, and so users, across time and IPv6 address changes, RFC 3041 was developed to reduce the prospect of user identity being permanently tied to an IPv6 address, thus restoring some of the possibilities of anonymity existing at IPv4.

IPv6 address types

Unicast addresses

A unicast address identifies a single network interface. The protocol delivers packets sent to a unicast address to that specific interface. Unicast IPv6 addresses can have a scope which is reflected in more specific address names: global unicast address, link-local address, and unique local unicast address.

Anycast addresses

An anycast address is assigned to a group of interfaces, usually belonging to different nodes. A packet sent to an anycast address is delivered to just one of the member interfaces, typically the "nearest" according to the routing protocol's choice of distance. Anycast addresses cannot be identified easily: they have the structure of normal unicast addresses, and differ only by being injected into the routing protocol at multiple points in the network.

Multicast addresses

A multicast address is also assigned to a set of interfaces that typically belong to different nodes. A packet that is sent to a multicast address is delivered to all interfaces identified by that address. Multicast addresses begin with an octet of one (1) bits, i.e., they have prefix FF00::/8. The four least-significant bits of the second address octet identify the address *scope*, i.e. the span over which the multicast address is propagated.

Commonly implemented scopes are node-local (0x1), link-local (0x2), site-local (0x5), organization-local (0x8), and global (0xE). The least-significant 112 bits of a multicast address form the multicast group identifier. Only the low-order 32 bits of the group ID are commonly used, because of traditional methods of forming 32 bit identifiers from Ethernet addresses. Defined group IDs are 0x1 for all-nodes multicast addressing and 0x2 for all-routers multicast addressing. Another group of multicast addresses are *solicited-node multicast addresses* which are formed with the prefix FF02::1:FF00:0/104, and where the rest of the group ID (least significant 24 bits) is filled from the interface's unicast or anycast address. These addresses allow link-layer address resolution via Neighbor Discovery Protocol (NDP) on the link without disturbing all nodes on the local network.

Special addresses

IANA maintains the official list of the IPv6 address space. Global unicast assignments can be found at the various RIR's or at the GRH DFP pages.There are a number of addresses with special meaning in IPv6:

a) Unspecified address

::/128 — the address with all zero bits is called the unspecified address. This address must never be assigned to an interface and is to be used only in software before the application has learned its host's source address appropriate for a pending connection. Routers must not forward packets with the unspecified address.

b) Link local addresses

::1/128 — the loopback address is a unicast localhost address. If an application in a host sends packets to this address, the IPv6 stack will loop these packets back on the same virtual interface (corresponding to 127.0.0.1 in IPv4).
fe80::/10 — The link-local prefix specifies that the address is only valid in the scope of a given local link. This is analogous to the Autoconfiguration IP addresses 169.254.0.0/16 in IPv4.

c) Unique local addresses

fc00::/7 — unique local addresses (ULA) are routable only within a set of cooperating sites. They were defined in RFC 4193 as a replacement for site-local addresses (see below). The addresses include a 40-bit pseudorandom number in the routing prefix that intends to minimize the risk of conflicts if sites merge or packets are misrouted into the Internet. Despite the restricted, local usage of these addresses, they have a global address scope. This is a departure from the site-local address definition that unique local addresses replaced.

d) Multicast addresses

ff00::/8 — The multicast prefix designates multicast addresses as defined in "IP Version 6 Addressing Architecture" RFC 4291. Some of these have been assigned to specific protocols, for example ff0X::101 will reach all local NTP servers .

Benefits of IPv6

- expanded addressing capabilities
- server-less auoconfiguration (plug and play)and reconfiguration
- More efficient and robust mobility mechanisms
- built-in, strong IP-layer encryption and authentication
- streamlined header format and flow identification
- improved support for options / extensions
- Reduced Network Administration Costs
- Increased Overall Network Efficiency
- Server-less plug-and-play possible
- End-to-end, IP-layer authentication & encryption possible
- Elimination of "triangle routing" for mobile IP

Limitation of IPv6

- Quality-of-service (same QoS capabilities as IPv4)

- Flow label field in IPv6 header may enable more efficient
- flow classification by routers, but adds no new capability
- Routing (same routing protocols as IPv4)
- except larger address allows more levels of hierarchy
- except customer multi homing is defeating hierarchy

Conclusion

It is obvious that we believe scenarios must be applied on a case-by-case basis using this demonstration as a base, depending on the products that will appear in the future and the configuration of the existing environment. On the other hand, the introduction of services and products that support IPv6 revealed progress toward IPv6. The reason for this is that simply using IPv4/IPv6 dual service in the ISP meant that the network had been migrated to IPv6, due to fact that the network configuration is simple. By installing new IPv6-compliant devices and setting up the screens for managing these devices, the end user is able to begin using IPv6 without having to be aware of any changes.

References

- www.ebooks.com
- www.cisco.com
- www.netlibrary.com
- www.ipv6.org
- http://en.wikipedia.org/wiki/IPv6

Pattern Recognition Using Artificial Neural Network

Monika Aggarwal
Lecturer (IT), IITM,Delhi
Kiwi Saini
Lecturer (IT), IITM,Delhi

Abstract

Pattern recognition is the research area that studies the operation and design of systems that recognize patterns in data. Pattern recognition is the important application of artificial neural network.

In this paper we will study about Artificial Neural Network, how it works like biological neural network. It further explains the concepts of the Activation Function and Threshold Function. Artificial neurons are made to learn patterns and that is done by training them. Firing rules are applied on the summed input and output is generated according to the past training that is learnt by the neurons during training period.

Keywords: *Biological Neurons, Dendrites, Synapse, Axon Artificial Neural Network, Pattern Recognition.*

Artificial Neural Network

An artificial neural network is a system based on the operation of biological neural networks, in other words, is an emulation of biological neural system.

- **Biological Neurons**

A Biological neuron collects signals from others through a host of fine structures called *dendrites (figure 1)*. The neuron sends out spikes of electrical activity through a long, thin stand known as an *axon*, which splits into thousands of branches. At the end of each branch, a structure called a *synapse* converts the activity from the axon into electrical effects that inhibit or excite activity from the axon into electrical effects that inhibit or excite activity in the connected neurons. When a neuron receives excitatory input that is sufficiently large compared with its inhibitory input, it sends a spike of electrical activity down its axon. Learning occurs by changing the effectiveness of the synapses so that the influence of one neuron on another changes.

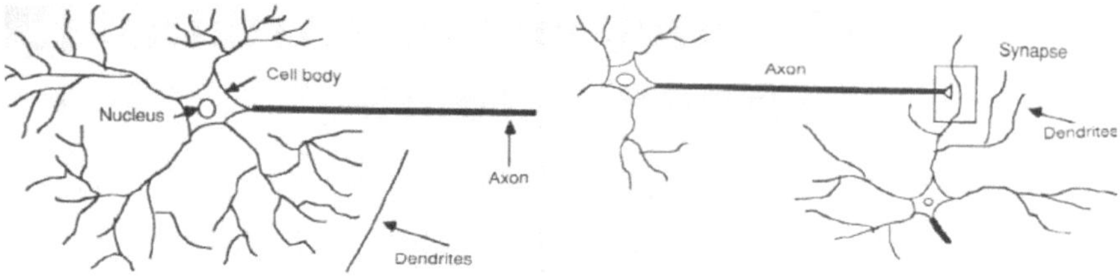

Components of a neuron The synapse

Figure 1: The Neuron Model

*** How Biological Neuron Works**

- Cell Body receives inputs from the dendrites
- All the inputs are added using summation function
- An activation function is applied on that summation
- Output is generated according to the threshold.

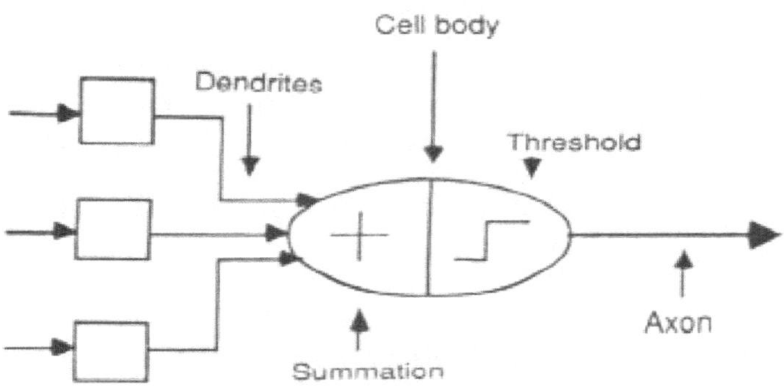

Figure 2: Working of Biological Neuron

- **Artificial Neural Network** An Artificial Neural Network is an adaptive, most often nonlinear system that learns to perform a function (an input/output map) from data. Adaptive means that the system parameters are changed during operation, normally called the training phase. After the training phase the Artificial Neural Network parameters are fixed and the system is deployed to solve the problem at hand (the testing phase). The Artificial Neural Network is built with a systematic step-by-step procedure to optimize a performance criterion or to follow some implicit internal constraint, which is commonly referred to as the learning rule. The input/output training data are fundamental in neural network technology, because they convey the necessary information to "discover" the optimal operating point.

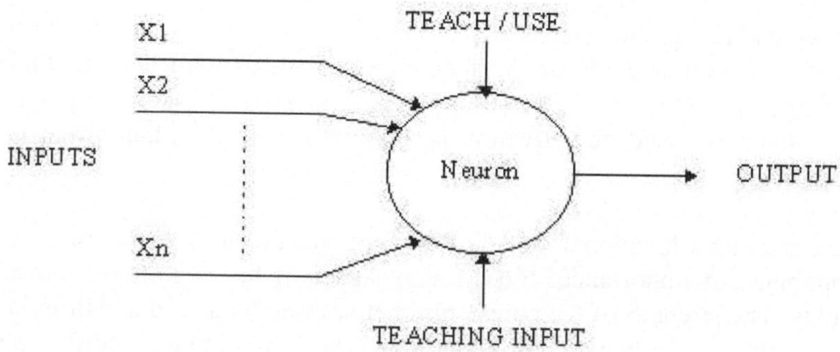

Figure 3. ASsimple Neuron

Pattern Recognition and Neural network

Human beings do not analyze the different situations of the real world as isolated facts, but they try and describe them in terms of patterns of related facts. Sometimes these relations are implicit because they all refer to the same object. Some other times, however, it is necessary to explicitly connect these characteristics in order to find a relation. It is interesting to observe the power of perception of human beings. We are very well adapted to carrying out pattern processing activities. Examples of this can be found in the recognition of hand-written characters or in image recognition. In both the cases, interpretations would be correct even if there were distortions or lack of information.

A **pattern** is an entity, vaguely defined, that could be given a name, e.g., Fingerprint Image, Handwritten word, Human Face, Speech Signal, DNA sequence.

Pattern Recognition Pattern recognition is the study of how machines can observe the environment, learn to distinguish patterns of interest, make sound and take reasonable decisions about the categories of the patterns.

In Pattern Recognition Area, one of the most important concepts is that of discriminant. In general, a discriminant is a function or operator that, when applied to a pattern, allows to obtain an output corresponding to an estimation of the class to which it belongs, or an estimation of one or more of the attributes of the pattern.The existence of discriminants constitutes the essence of pattern recognition.

The usual practice is to look for a pattern recognition system which is able to learn in an adaptive way from the experiences of several discriminants, each of them corresponding to a specific purpose. In an automatic pattern recognition system, learning and recognition stages are combined to achieve the objective desired. In this sense, neural networks are a suitable tool for the implementation of adaptive solutions solved by the computer.Using neural networks, the concept of discriminant is based on activation function that map the input space into the output space.

When creating a functional model of the biological neuron, there are three basic components of importance. First, the synapses of the neuron are modeled as weights. The strength of the connection between an input and a neuron is noted by the value of the weight. An adder sums up all the inputs modified by their respective weights. This activity is referred to as linear combination. Finally, an activation function controls the amplitude of the output of the neuron.

Mathematically, this process is described in the figure

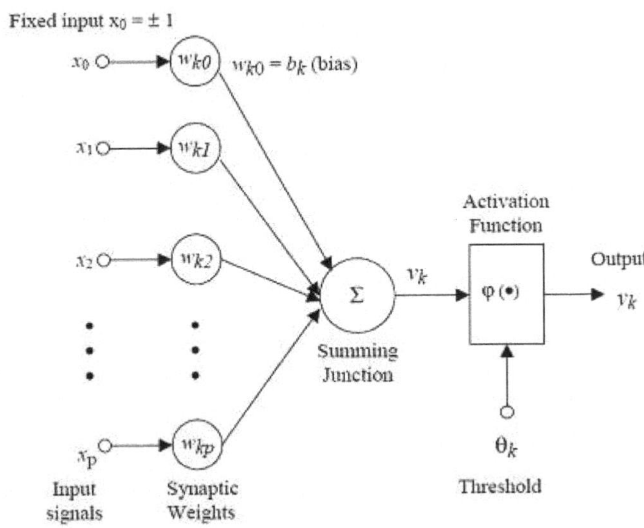

From this model the interval activity of the neuron can be shown to be:

$$v_k = \sum_{j=1}^{p} w_{kj} x_j$$

The output of the neuron, yk, would therefore be the outcome of some activation function on the value of vk.

- **Training Mode and Using Mode**

The neuron has two modes of operation; the training mode and the using mode. In the training mode, the neuron can be trained to fire (or not), for particular input patterns. In the using mode, when a taught input pattern is detected at the input, its associated output becomes the current output. If the input pattern does not belong in the taught list of input patterns, the firing rule is used to determine whether to fire or not.

*** Firing rules**

The firing rule is an important concept in neural networks and accounts for their high flexibility. A firing rule determines how one calculates whether a neuron should fire for any input pattern. It relates to all the input patterns, not only the ones on which the node was trained. A simple firing rule can be implemented by using Hamming distance technique. The rule goes as follows:

Take a collection of training patterns for a node, some of which cause it to fire (the 1-taught set of patterns) and others which prevent it from doing so (the 0-taught set). Then the patterns not in the collection cause the node to fire if, on comparison, they have more input elements in common with the 'nearest' pattern in the 1-taught set than with the 'nearest' pattern in the 0-taught set. If there is a tie, then the pattern remains in the undefined state.

For example, a 3-input neuron is taught to output 1 when the input (X1,X2 and X3) is 111 or 101 and to output 0 when the input is 000 or 001. Then, before applying the firing rule, the truth table is;

X1:	0	0	0	0	1	1	1	1
X2:	0	0	1	1	0	0	1	1
X3:	0	1	0	1	0	1	0	1
OUT:	0	0	0/1	0/1	0/1	1	0/1	1

Table1: Truth Table before applying Firing Rule

As an example of the way the firing rule is applied, take the pattern 010. It differs from 000 in 1 element, from 001 in 2 elements, from 101 in 3 elements and from 111 in 2 elements. Therefore, the 'nearest' pattern is 000 which belongs in the 0-taught set. Thus the firing rule requires that the neuron should not fire when the input is 001.

On the other hand, 011 is equally distant from two taught patterns that have different outputs and thus the output stays undefined (0/1).

By applying the firing in every column the following truth table is obtained;

X1:	0	0	0	0	1	1	1	1
X2:	0	0	1	1	0	0	1	1
X3:	0	1	0	1	0	1	0	1
OUT:	0	0	0	0/1	0/1	1	1	1

Table2: Truth Table after applying Firing Rule

The difference between the two truth tables is called the *generalisation of the neuron*. Therefore the firing rule gives the neuron a sense of similarity and enables it to respond 'sensibly' to patterns not seen during training.

- **Pattern Recognition using Neural Network**

Pattern recognition can be implemented by using a feed-forward neural network that has been trained accordingly. During training, the network is trained to associate outputs with input patterns. When the network is used, it identifies the input pattern and tries to output the associated output pattern. The power of neural networks comes to life when a pattern that has no output associated with it, is given as an input. In this case, the network gives the output that corresponds to a

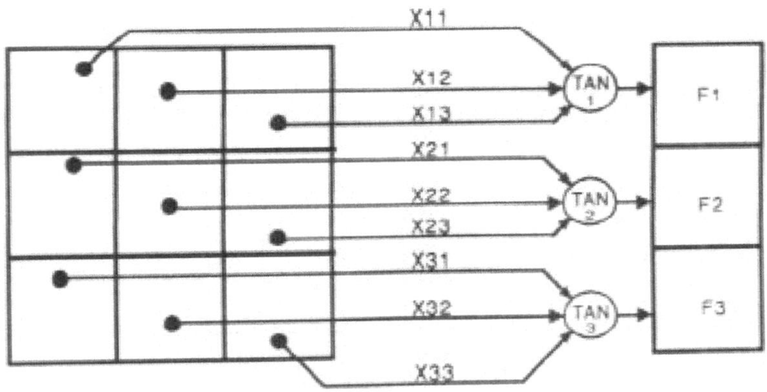

Figure 5: Pattern Recognition

For example: The network of figure 5 is trained to recognize the patterns T and H. The associated patterns are all black and all white respectively as shown below.

INPUT OUTPUT INPUT OUTPUT

If we represent black squares with 0 and white squares with 1 then the truth tables for the 3 neurons after generalization are;

Top Neuron

X11:	0	0	0	0	1	1	1	1
X12:	0	0	1	1	0	0	1	1
X13:	0	1	0	1	0	1	0	1
OUT:	0	0	1	1	0	0	1	1

Middle Neuron

X21:	0	0	0	0	1	1	1	1
X22:	0	0	1	1	0	0	1	1
X23:	0	1	0	1	0	1	0	1
OUT:	1	0/1	1	0/1	0/1	0	0/1	0

Bottom Neuron

X21:	0	0	0	0	1	1	1	1
X22:	0	0	1	1	0	0	1	1
X23:	0	1	0	1	0	1	0	1
OUT:	1	0	1	1	0	0	1	0

From the tables it can be seen the following associations can be extracted:

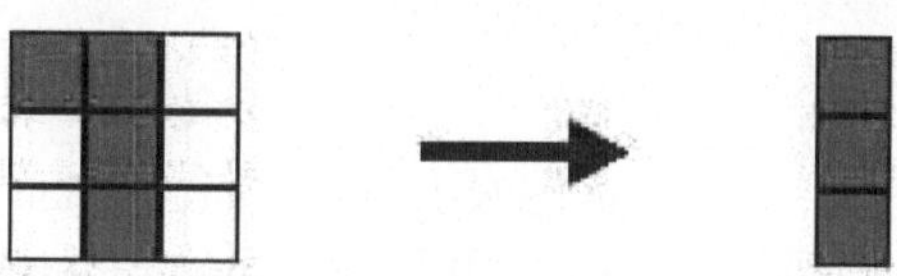

INPUT OUTPUT

In this case, it is obvious that the output should be all blacks since the input pattern is almost the same as the 'T' pattern.

INPUT OUTPUT

Here also, it is obvious that the output should be all whites since the input pattern is almost the same as the 'H' pattern.

INPUT OUTPUT

Here, the top row is 2 errors away from the T and 3 from an H. So the top output is black. The middle row is 1 error away from both T and H so the output is random. The bottom row is 1 error away from T and 2 away from H. Therefore the output is black. The total output of the network is still in favor of the T shape.

Thus the neural network generates the output according to the training provided to it. If the input matched with the trained input then respective output is generated else the input is matched with the trained inputs and related results are emitted.

Conclusion

In this paper we explained about biological neural network, how the architecture of artificial neural network is based on biological neuron. As human being uses past experiences to react to particular situation (pattern). The same feature is incorporated in machine works on ANN to recognize the pattern with the help of past training and generate output accordingly.

References

- S.N. Sivanandam, S. Sumathi and S.N. Deepa, "Introduction to Neural Networks using Mat lab 6.0". The McGraw-Hill Publishing Companies Limited, New Delhi, 2007.
- Haykin S, "Neural Networks- A Comprehensive Foundations", Prentice-Hall of India Private Limited, India, 2005.

- LiMin Fu, "Neural Network in Computer Intelligence". Tata McGraw–Hill, New Delhi, 2007.
- Christos Stergiou and Dimitrios Siganos. "Neural Networks"
- Ben Kröse & Patrick van der Smagt(1996)"An introduction to Neural Networks"
- Lic. Laura Lanzarini1, Ing. A. De Giusti2 ," Pattern Recognition in Medical Images using Neural Networks"

Data Mining & its Impact on RIM Professionals

Rama Bhatia Parihar
Lecturer (IT), RDIAS, Delhi

Abstract

Data mining, whose purpose is to extract interesting or significant information from bulk of data, has been widely used as an effective decision making tool. Records and information management (RIM) is that field within the information profession responsible for efficient and systematic control of the creation, receipt, maintenance, use, and disposition of records, including processes for capturing and maintaining evidence and information about business activities and transactions in the form of records. This paper illustrates the concept of Data mining , its issues , challenges, its interdisciplinary fields which is already been much in talk but in different dimension & will emphasize on "RIM Professionals & How RIM Professionals are getting benefits from Data Mining" in this era. This paper also emphasize on some of the queries of RIM Professionals which usually asked by them regarding Data Mining.

RIM Professionals

The field of records and information management (RIM) is defined as the systematic control of records throughout their life cycle. A "RIM Professional" is a generic term that encompasses a wide range of positions such as records managers, corporate librarians, imaging specialists, and IT managers. RIM professionals are found in a wide variety of industry, business, government, legal, healthcare, and financial settings.

Records and information management (RIM) is that field within the information profession responsible for effective and methodological repress of the creation, receipt, maintenance, use, and disposition of records, including processes for holding and sustaining evidence and information about business activities and transactions in the form of records. Records and information management (RIM) professionals exhibit particular personality traits, which should help those making hiring and career decisions. Records and information management (RIM) professionals are not much given to introspection. "Why do I like doing records-related work?" "What makes someone attracted to records management or archives management?" "What personal characteristics should one look for when interviewing applicants for a records management or archives position?" Knowing the answers to such questions could be important both to those contemplating entry into the field and those who want to establish those personality traits that suggest a successful hire. By contrast, librarians have for a long time paid a good deal of attention to the personality and image of their practitioners.

Previously RIM was basically done on physical basis but know days many computer technologies have replaced RIM work. Before time when 10 people were basically required for marinating the previous (cruscious) & current record Now a days a single computer have replaced the work of those 10 people with 1 person who will maintain that system. DATA Mining which is one of the new technologies is used now days in many small, middle & big organizations for data record purpose.

The job of the RIM professional is to enhance the quality of the information in the enterprise by enhancing the quality of the processes used in producing, storing, using, and integrating information within it. Much, not all, of this information is in the form of structured information—i.e., records—and is found in enterprise databases. Data-mining capability enables staff to enhance the quality of this information by facilitating knowledge discovery in these databases. Other capabilities, however, such as SQL and online analytical processing (OLAP), do not discover new patterns as much as they con firm patterns already thought and articulated by the investigator.

Today many universities are also offering this as a course.
Fast-forward 15 or 20 years into the future. The year is 2023. Records and information managers are now called "records and information technologists" because the primary tools of their trade—file cabinets, file folders, and paper documents—have been permanently replaced by virtual filing systems, digital storage, and electronic documents. In this future, instant messaging (IM) and e-mail have replaced phone communication, online libraries have made physical libraries all but obsolete, and electronic records have rendered paper records a mere rumor. What will the profession and your job be like in the next few decades? Only time will tell. But today, whether or not the fabled paper-less business environment ever becomes reality, the fact remains that our professional lives will he markedly different. We can safely predict that records and information management (RIM) professionals will rely much more on technology to help them do their jobs in the future—IM, the Internet, electronic storage, radio-frequency identification systems, and perhaps even eye or fingerprint-scanning security systems will be common in the workplace.

RIM Professionals: A Distinct Personality?

A study reveals that records and information management (RIM) professionals exhibit particular personality traits, which should aid those making hiring and career decisions

As a discipline, records and information management (RIM) professionals are not much given to introspection. "Why do I like doing records-related work?" "What makes someone attracted to records management or archives management?" "What personal characteristics should one look for when interviewing applicants for a records management or archives position?" Knowing the answers to such questions could be important both to those contemplating entry into the field and those who want to establish those personality traits that suggest a successful hire. By contrast, librarians have for a long time paid a good deal of attention to the personality and image of their practitioners.

In 1976, Wilmer Maedke surveyed the records management field and noted that the most important criterion in hiring was an "interest in records work." For too many years, RIM managers have characterized their entry into the field in critical terms: "I just fell into it" or "I was pushed into it." This puts the field in an unnecessarily unflattering light. There are several vocational aptitude tests (e.g., the Strong Interest Inventory) that help test takers align their interests with those who are successful in various fields.

There are also standardized tests that establish a person's ability to complete successfully an academic program in some desirable professional field (e.g., medicine, law, engineering) and, by extension, help test takers establish their "fit" with a discipline of their interest.

What, then, is already known about the personality traits of records managers? Very little. Most discussion is personal observation and anecdote. For example, in an article in The Records Management Quarterly, Robert Sanders suggests, "We records managers are known for our pessimistic point of view. We attend conferences devoted to planning for the worst imaginable contingencies. We participate in workshops on dealing with smoke and water damage ... However, without being ready to commit myself to an institution as a schizophrenic, I must admit that, alongside my usual pessimistic records management self, there lives a Wannabe Optimist."

Skills as Personality Surrogates

Until now, desirable job-related competencies (knowledge, skills, and attitudes) have been obliquely used as characteristics in lieu of personality assessments. Attempts to describe those characteristics typically needed for those in records management and library services have been published by several organizations. The UK Society of Archivists, for example, suggests that records managers must have the following characteristics.

- **Confident communication skills**. Records managers deal with colleagues from all backgrounds, from the managing director/chief executive down. They also have to contact suppliers, contractors, and outside organizations.
- **Good negotiation skills.** It is not always easy to persuade senior colleagues to hand over "their" records or to agree to a retention period/ destruction date for a record they wish to preserve forever.
- **Analytical thinking strengths**. Records managers need to understand how their organization works to be capable of constructing systems that are integrated with business processes and organizational culture.
- **Flexibility**. Records managers are often expected to turn their hand to anything remotely connected with the provision of information.
- **Comfort with new technology**. RIM managers must demonstrate the ability to use and adapt to rapidly evolving information communication technology (ICT) packages and systems.

In addition to work-related competencies, here is some "personal qualities" of successful RIM Managers :

- Alertness
- Assertiveness
- Compassion/Kindness
- Dependability
- Tenacity
- Diplomacy
- Emotional Stability
- Leadership Ability
- Imagination
- Inquisitiveness
- Need for achievement
- Flexibility
- Neatness

The things proposed by the term "data mining" is beautiful, but, unfortunately, it may not be very informative to those records and information management (RIM) professionals who need to know what data mining means for them because may be they are not from technical field but from the last 20 years they are in Record Management but now youngsters who know much about this field can replaced them. RIM managers need answers to these questions.

* What is Data Mining?
* What can Data Mining do?
* How does Data Mining work?
* What is the need to disseminate information from data mining?

* What is its significance for RIM managers?
* What is the relationship between data mining and knowledge discovery in databases (KDD)?
* What Technology Infrasture is required?
* What are the Challenges & Issues of Data Mining?
* What are its Interdisciplinary fields?

The most compelling reason for RIM managers to take an interest in data mining is simply because of data: the "data" in "data mining" are, for the most part, records created in the normal course of business of any organization. Records, then, become the structured data foundation to the data mining process.

What is Data Mining?

Data Ware house is a concept which were intended for decision support is come after the emergence of Client – Server Technology & the SQL (structured query language) (which was not sufficient to fulfill the huge & complicated requirement of client.) in 1980s This lead to the fast development of Data Warehousing & Spread new technologies for getting fruitful information. Data Mining was one of the new technology among them (some times also called Data or knowledge discovery), which is based on the thought that relevant or required information will get with in a second from huge amount of raw Data (collected day by day) in an arranged or systematic manner which will save time & money of the Client as well as of the organization & off course will increase their revenue with the help of that information.

Data Mining – the search of knowledge a term based on the idea:-

Data- Bulk of information (whether required or not)

Mine- an abundant source of something (or information)

The very large database is a "Earth" which is having a penalty of information that can be mined with the help of some tools (or software) of high technology to get the required information.

Although data mining is a relatively new term, the technology is not. Companies have used powerful computers to sift through volumes of supermarket scanner data and analyze market research reports for years. However, continuous innovations in computer processing power, disk storage, and statistical software are dramatically increasing the accuracy of analysis while driving down the cost. Data mining software is one of the analytical tools for analyzing data.

Example: Today there are many retailers who are in competition, like Big Bazar, Spencer, Big Apple and so on

For example, one of the retailers used the data mining capacity of Oracle software to analyze local buying patterns. They discovered that when men bought some soft drinks on Tuesday and Saturdays, they also tended to buy namkeen. Further analysis showed that these customers typically did their weekly grocery shopping on Saturdays. On Tuesdays, however, they only bought a few items. The retailer concluded that they purchased the namkeen to have it available for the upcoming weekend. The retailer could use this newly discovered information in various ways to increase revenue.

For example, they could move the namkeen display closer to the soft drinks display. And, they could make sure namkeen and soft drinks were sold at full price on Tuesdays.

What can data mining do?

Data mining is primarily used today by companies with a strong consumer focus - retail, financial, communication, and marketing organizations. It enables these companies to determine relationships among "internal" factors such as price, product positioning, or staff skills, and "external" factors such as economic indicators, competition, and customer demographics. And, it enables them to determine the impact on sales, customer satisfaction, and corporate profits. Finally, it enables them to "drill down" into summary information to view detail transactional data.

With data mining, a retailer could use point-of-sale records of customer purchases to send targeted promotions based on an individual's purchase history. By mining demographic data from comment or warranty cards, the retailer could develop products and promotions to appeal to specific customer segments.

How does data mining work?

It is important to have an understanding of how Data Mining works, if you want to use it. The method that is used with data mining to make predictions is called **Modeling**.

Modeling is the process of creating a model. A model can be defined as a number of examples or a mathematical relationship. The relationship or examples are created based on existing situations where an answer is already known. The purpose of data mining is to take the model and place it in a situation where the answer is unknown. While the mathematics behind data mining has existed for centuries, it is the recent increase in computer processing power and storage that has allowed data mining technology to become feasible.

To use an example of creating a model, imagine if you are the head of marketing for a telecommunications company. You have decided that you want to direct your advertising and sales towards people who are the most likely to use long distance communication services. While you may have knowledge of your own customers, it will be difficult to learn all the different attributes related to your best customers because there are too many variables to take into consideration. However, if you have a database which has information related to the income, credit history, age, sex, and occupation of your customers, you can use data mining tools to find the common attributes that are related to the customers that frequently make long distance phone calls.

The use of data mining may allow you to learn that most of your high value customers are middle aged women that are 45 years of age. You may also find that these women have an average income that is in excess of $50,000 a year. Now that you know a bit about your best customers, you can now tailor your advertising efforts to suit their needs. By doing this, you will greatly increase your chances of earning a profit. Computer algorithms are frequently used in data mining programs. However, the factors which have led to the increasing popularity of data mining technologies are the increase in both processing power and storage.

Another thing that has led to the rapid popularity of data mining technology are graphical interfaces. These interfaces have made the programs easier to use, and this has allowed them to be adapted by a larger segment of the population. Artificial neural networks are a cutting edge technology that is being used more in data mining applications. Unlike computer algorithms, neural networks are not linear, and are capable of learning. Neural networks are modeled after the human mind, and have powerful applications in data mining that have not been fully explored. In addition to this, decision trees play an important role in the development of data mining programs.

As the name implies, decision trees are structures have a number of different decisions. Each decision could be called a branch. The decisions define the rules for a given set of data. The next element that makes up an important part of data mining is called rule induction. A rule induction will pull rules from data which are based on an "if-then" scenario. The next part that makes up data mining is a genetic algorithm. The genetic algorithm will utilize techniques that are based on mutation and natural selection. The last important part of data mining tools is called the nearest neighbor. The nearest neighbor will categorize records with other records that are similar within a database.

There are a number of real-world applications of data mining programs. Generally, having information which is highly detailed will allow you to make predictions that are equally detailed. Using this detailed information to make predictions about the behavior of your customers can allow you to make large profits.
Companies can use data mining tools to get answers to complex questions. For example, a credit card company that wants to increase its revenues could use data mining to find out if reducing the minimum payments would allow them to earn more interest. If the company has detailed information related to their customers, they should be able to make accurate predictions about how customers will react to policies.

What is the need to disseminate information from data mining?

Nowadays, bulk amount of data are being accumulated. The amount of data collected is said to be almost doubled every 9 months. Seeking knowledge from massive data is one of the most desired attributes of Data Mining. Data could be large in two senses. In terms of size, e.g. for Image Data or in terms of dimensionality, e.g. for Gene expression data.

Usually there is a huge gap from the stored data to the knowledge that could be construed from the data. This transition won't occur automatically, that's where Data Mining comes into picture. In Exploratory Data Analysis, some initial knowledge is known about the data, but Data Mining could help in a more in-depth knowledge about the data.

Manual data analysis has been around for some time now, but it creates a bottleneck for large data analysis.

Fast developing computer science and engineering techniques and methodology generates new demands. Data Mining techniques are now being applied to all kinds of domains, which are rich in data, e.g. Image Mining and Gene data analysis.

What is its significance for RIM managers?

Data mining parameters include:

- Association - looking for patterns where one event is connected to another event
- Sequence or path analysis - looking for patterns where one event leads to another later event

- Classification - looking for new patterns (May result in a change in the way the data is organized but that's ok)
- Clustering - finding and visually documenting groups of facts not previously known
- Forecasting - discovering patterns in data that can lead to reasonable predictions about the future

Data mining techniques are used in a many research areas, including mathematics, cybernetics, genetics and marketing. Web Mining is a type of data mining used in customer relationship management, takes advantage of the huge amount of information gathered by a Web site to look for patterns in user behavior.

As we all know the correct and useful information is the heart or a pillar of any organization. & As the basic role of RIM Professionals is to give quality information to their client which is not possible manually in today's world where the requirement of the client as well as the organization is change day by day So, It depends on the person and his or her role and requirements. Using the results of KDD that rely on data mining can help with very routine decisions almost anywhere in the enterprise. RIM professionals basically give information used in producing, storing, and integrating information within it. All, of this information should be in arranged or structured form—i.e., records—and is found in enterprise databases. Data-mining capability enables staff to enhance the quality of this information by facilitating knowledge discovery in these databases. Other capabilities, however, such as SQL and online analytical processing do not discover new patterns as much as they confirm patterns already thought and articulated by the investigator.

RIM managers who add data mining to their information technology are enhancing the KDD process by adding an additional and powerful capability to create information that through interpretation and evaluation can lead to new knowledge—information of even greater quality and value.

During business or intelligence crises, the contribution of data mining to KDD can be very valuable for RIM managers.

The failure of the bank's marketing campaign may be resolved successfully with the aid of a RIM manager, who brings new value-added strategies. On the other hand, such situations must be approached carefully since data mining results can be misinterpreted by unskilled analysts or information workers who uncritically use data mining software without an awareness of the business problems being investigated—or of the characteristics and pitfalls of the particular data mining technologies they were using. There are many data mining software applications available, but all do not work equally well on the same type of analysis.

Part of the job of RIM managers is to specify and implement changes in formal rules and procedures for handling information in IT environments. Data mining can help RIM managers model the likely impact of these changes and measure their impact after implementation.

Though data mining can be very useful in arriving at models, an important caution for RIM managers to keep in mind is that data mining is not magic. That is, merely taking a data set, clicking an on screen icon, and expecting to solve a problem will not work. The steps of KDD surrounding data mining involve continuous interaction of humans and computers. How well those steps are performed depends on the skills and background knowledge of humans.

Today Many Companies are collaborating with each other for data mining work because it affects a lot in the growth of a particular company.
Example-
Satyam and IIIT-Hyderabad to Collaborate on Data Mining and Open Source R&D Satyam Computer Services announced , that it plans to collaborate on several critical research projects with the Centre for Date Engineering (CDE) at the International Institute of Information Technology (IIIT) in Hyderabad.

CDE will work on the 'Nurture a Research Area' programme with the IT giant. The collaboration between IIIT-Hyderabad and Satyam will focus on R&D in data mining and open source technologies apart from leveraging the expertise of IIIT to uncover business opportunities associated with social networking. "We are focusing on data mining, especially where it concerns behavioural and psychographic analysis that will give companies insights into the customers buying behaviours," said Swaminathan Srinivasan, head, BI &PM Solutions.
Example-

Big Bazaar - the lowest prices store now goes online because of this technology. So, The RIM Managers can see the benefits of Data Mining for them.

What is the relationship between data mining and knowledge discovery in databases (KDD)?

IN THE PAST FEW YEARS, A NUMBER OF research journals in library and information science have published review articles or special issues on knowledge discovery and data mining These publications have primarily discussed background, scope and terminology, methods and techniques, and tools related to the topic from orientations other than library and information science. Research publications in library and information science have been implicitly related to knowledge discovery in databases (KDD) in terms of methods and techniques, though many of them did not use the terminology "knowledge discovery in databases" explicitly. This issue is devoted to aspects of KDD that are relevant or reflective of the field of library and information science.

Knowledge discovery in databases uses a variety of methods to evaluate data for relevant relationships that could yield new knowledge. According to Fayyad et al. (1996): "KDD refers to the overall process of discovering useful knowledge from data, and data mining refers to a particular step in this process" (pg. 39). Data mining essentially focuses on identifying patterns previously not recognized and is considered only one component of the discovery process. KDD encompasses a growing collection of techniques, from a variety of disciplines, for investigating data to extract knowledge. The methods employ a broad combination and application of human expertise and information technology. "KDD comprises many steps, which involve data preparation, search for patterns, knowledge evaluation, and refinement, all repeated in multiple iterations" (Fayyad et al., 1996, pg. 41).

Data Mining term is used interchangeably with KDD. In reality, it is one of the steps in the whole process of knowledge discovery in databases. Data Mining needs a well defined business case and a diligent data preparation and has to be followed with a detailed evaluation of the discovery results.

It was recognized that information is at the heart of business operations and that decision-makers could make use of the data stored to gain valuable insight into the business. Database Management systems gave access to the data stored but this was only a small part of what could be gained from the data. Traditional OLTP systems are good at putting data into databases quickly, safely and efficiently but are not good at delivering meaningful analysis in return. Analyzing data can provide further knowledge about a business by going beyond the data explicitly stored to derive knowledge about the business. This is where Knowledge Discovery in Database (KDD) has obvious benefits for any enterprise. It involves processes like Business Case Definition, Data Preparation, Data Mining and Evaluation.

- The term data mining has been stretched beyond its limits to apply to any form of data analysis and is used interchangeably with KDD. But in true sense data mining is just a step in KDD process focusing on data analysis with minimum user intervention.

What technological infrastructure is required?

Today, data mining applications are available on all size systems for mainframe, client/server, and PC platforms. System prices range from several thousand dollars for the smallest applications up to $1 million a terabyte for the largest. Enterprise-wide applications generally range in size from 10 gigabytes to over 11 terabytes. NCR has the capacity to deliver applications exceeding 100 terabytes. There are two critical technological drivers:

- Size of the database: the more data being processed and maintained, the more powerful the system required.
- Query complexity: the more complex the queries and the greater the number of queries being processed, the more powerful the system required.

Relational database storage and management technology is adequate for many data mining applications less than 50 gigabytes. However, this infrastructure needs to be significantly enhanced to support larger applications. Some vendors have added extensive indexing capabilities to improve query performance. Others use new hardware architectures such as Massively Parallel Processors (MPP) to achieve order-of-magnitude improvements in query time. For example, MPP systems from NCR link hundreds of high-speed Pentium processors to achieve performance levels exceeding those of the largest supercomputers.

Data Mining Challenges

- Increasing data dimensionality and data size.
- Various forms of data.
- New types of data like streaming data and multimedia data.
- Efficiency in data access and information search methods.
- Intelligent upgrade and integration methods.

Data Mining as an Interdisciplinary field

- Statistics.
- Relational Databases.
- Artificial Intelligence.
- Machine Learning.
- Visualization.
- High Performance Computing:
  - Supercomputers.
  - Distributed Computing.
  - Parallel Computing.
  - Cluster Computing.

Issues

One of the key issues raised by data mining technology is not a business or technological one, but a social one. It is the issue of individual privacy. Data mining makes it possible to analyze routine business transactions and glean a significant amount of information about individuals buying habits and preferences. Another issue is that of data integrity. Clearly, data analysis can only be as good as the data that is being analyzed. A key implementation challenge is integrating conflicting or redundant data from different sources. For example, a bank may maintain credit cards accounts on several different databases. The addresses (or even the names) of a single cardholder may be different in each. Software must translate data from one system to another and select the address most recently entered.

A hotly debated technical issue is whether it is better to set up a relational database structure or a multidimensional one. In a relational structure, data is stored in tables, permitting ad hoc queries. In a multidimensional structure, on the other hand, sets of cubes are arranged in arrays, with subsets created according to category. While multidimensional structures facilitate multidimensional data mining, relational structures thus far have performed better in client/server environments. And, with the explosion of the Internet, the world is becoming one big client/ server environment.

Finally, there is the issue of cost. While system hardware costs have dropped dramatically within the past five years, data mining and data warehousing tend to be self-reinforcing. The more powerful the data mining queries, the greater the utility of the information being gleaned from the data, and the greater the pressure to increase the amount of data being collected and maintained, which increases the pressure for faster, more powerful data mining queries. This increases pressure for larger, faster systems, which are more expensive.
A new trend in data mining is its incorporation in offerings of business intelligence (BI), database, and

Conclusion

Earlier, the Management of records was done totally on manual basis. But now a day Data Base Technology has made it simple & faster. RIM is getting Beneficial after this new emerging technology. Data Mining enhance the quality work done by RIM Professionals by giving the systematic, manageable & Required Information on time.(i.e. whenever it is required). DATA Mining is one of the new technologies is used now days in many small, middle & big organizations for data record purpose. The main attribute of Data Mining is actually seeking knowledge from massive data. Data could be large in two senses. In terms of size, e.g. for Image Data or in terms of dimensionality, e.g. for Gene expression data. RIM Professionals are getting benefits from these current updated technologies, if they have knowledge to use them. It improves the Productivity of company as well as it saves the time, reduce cost & increase Revenue. With the help of Data Mining RIM professionals can do work in a fast manner as compare to the past. & also Data Mining has improves the quality work done by RIM Professionals. Now a day with the help of this technology you can get any previous or current or important record in a quick and manageable manner. Moreover, Data Mining has generates n – numbers of jobs for RIM Professionals who are having knowledge of this technology. As many companies(Retail, finance, Banking ....) are now totally depend on these technologies for their growth perspective.

References

- G.K Gupta (2006), ''Introduction to Data Mining with Case Studies", Prentice Hall of India Private Limited.
- Jiawei Han and Micheline Kamber(2001),"Data Mining Concepts and Techniques" Morgan Kaufmann publishers
- http://www.anderson.ucla.edu/faculty/jason.frand/teacher/technologies/palace/datamining.htm
- http://www.arma.org/about/overview/ethics.cfm
- http://goliath.ecnext.com/coms2/gi_0199-4724723/Mining-for-information-gold-data.html
- http://www.exforsys.com/tutorials/data-mining/how-data-mining-works.html
- http://www.hindu.com/2008/11/26/stories/2008112659230400.htm
- http://www.eas.asu.edu/~mining03/chap1/lesson_2.html
- http://findarticles.com/p/articles/mi_qa3937/is_200509/ai_n15350601
- http://www.bulletins.wayne.edu/gbk-Output/gbk-08-10-wb-08-2.html#wp21127

Predicting of Frequent Items Using Data Mining Tool - SPSS

Shubhra Saggar
Sr. Lecturer, GNIM, Delhi
Nidhi Khurana
Lecturer, GNIM, Delhi

Abstract

In today's information age, the. massive amounts of business data can be analyzed and modeled using data mining techniques Data mining involves the process of translating business needs into a problem which has to be analysed, retrieving the database with large amount of data for analysis, and applying statistical or machine leaning technique with the final aim of achieving important results for taking a strategic decision to solve the business problem. As an example, data mining is widely used in the decision-making. This paper gives an illustration of predictive modeling using SPSS. We are analyzing the sales patterns of Software Licenses of an organization so as to improve Sales Process to its Distributors, Analyze and select best strategies that reach their target customer segment. For this purpose we are applying one of the known classification or statistical model to estimate the outputs.

Keywords : *Data Warehouse, OLTP, OLAP, Custom Table, Sequence Plot*

Introduction

Earlier we have relational databases, which process the data for online analysis know as OLTP. As the business world is developing and competition is rising very high we have to plan strategies to cut the competition, thus we require a different storage that is known as Data Warehouse, Which often focus on the customer level – a useful and appropriate focus. Data Warehouse support the decision making capabilities. The data in Data Warehouse is historical in nature, which integrate all the data from various other resources including RDBMS. Dramatic advances in data capture, processing power data transmission and storage capabilities are enabling organization to integrate their various databases into Data Warehouse. As we are know filled with data and data everywhere, we need information that is meaning full data. How information and knowledge can be extracted from the huge store of data which is like we are stuffed in the room and searching a needle from it so we have to use some techniques to extract out meaningful information from this large storage of Data Warehouse .There are two major technique with the help of which we can extract knowledge and these are Data Mining and OLAP.

- **OLAP**

On-Line Analytical Processing (OLAP) is a category of software technology that enables analysts, managers and executives to gain insight into data through fast, consistent, interactive access to a wide variety of possible views of information that has been transformed from raw data to reflect the real dimensionality of the enterprise as understood by the user.
OLAP functionality is characterized by dynamic multi-dimensional analysis of consolidated enterprise data supporting end user analytical and navigational activities including:

- calculations and modeling applied across dimensions, through hierarchies and/or across members
- trend analysis over sequential time periods
- slicing subsets for on-screen viewing
- drill-down to deeper levels of consolidation
- reach-through to underlying detail data
- rotation to new dimensional comparisons in the viewing area

OLAP is implemented in a multi-user client/server mode and offers consistently rapid response to queries, regardless of database size and complexity. OLAP helps the user synthesize enterprise information through comparative, personalized viewing, as well as through analysis of historical and projected data in various "what-if" data model scenarios.[5]

- **Data Mining**

Data mining is used for searching knowledge that is interesting patterns in the data which is used for further decision making. Data mining is a powerful new technology with the great potential to help companies to focus on the most important information in there data ware house. Data mining tools predict future trends and behavior allowing business to make proactive, knowledge driven decision. Data mining can be defined as a process of analyzing data from different prospective, and summarizing into useful information that is information which can use to increase revenue and cut cost or both

The Tool: SPSS

Statically package for social Science is used Solve business and research problems using SPSS, a statistical and data management package for analysts and researchers. Compared to other data analysis packages, SPSS is easier to use, has a lower total cost of ownership, and comprehensively addresses the entire analytical process.

SPSS Base is an integral part of this process, providing functionality for data access, data management and preparation, data analysis, and reporting. It enables us to work confidently with add-on modules and other products in the SPSS Family, which provide capabilities for planning, data collection, and deployment, and add incremental functionality to areas SPSS Base also addresses.

SPSS makes it easy for you to identify duplicate cases, so you can eliminate them prior to your analysis. Use the Identify Duplicate Cases tool to set parameters and flag duplicates so that you can keep track of them for the record. Additionally, SPSS makes it easy to prepare continuous level data for analysis. The Visual Binner enables you to easily (for example, break income into "bands" of 10,000 or break ages into groups). A data pass provides a histogram that enables you to specify cut points in an intelligent manner. You can then automatically create value labels from the specified cutpoints

SPSS gives you the flexibility to complete the reverse action—you can take a data file that has a single case per subject and spread the data across multiple cases. Use the Date and Time Wizard to make calculations with dates and times, create date/time variables from strings containing date variables (such as "03/29/06"), and bring date/time data from a variety of sources into SPSS. You can also parse individual date/time units, such as year, from date/time variables to apply filters. Analyze data with comprehensive techniques Go beyond summary statistics and row-and-column. SPSS gives you a wide range of statistical procedures for basic analysis, including counts, crosstabs, cluster, descriptive, factor analysis, linear regression, cluster analysis, and ordinal regression.

Case Study

The goal here is to improve sales process to its retail analysis and select best strategies to prosper the business. The manager needs to know weather there were any significant difference in the taste and preferences. This is research is a pilot to determine weather the immense power of data mining and visualization tool.

We have a software distribution company whose last year data is taken as sample. We have used SPSS to analyze the data of this company such that the managers can take the decisions which helps him or her to compete the competition in the faster manner so some of the analysis are as follows

Stock Item:	Date	Particulars	Outwards
McAfee Managed Virus Scan ASAP Single User	28-10-2006	ADVANCE COMPUTER SHOPPE	1
McAfee Managed Virus Scan ASAP Single User	28-10-2006	COMPUTER AID	8
McAfee Managed Virus Scan ASAP Single User	28-10-2006	Trifin Information Technology Pvt.Ltd.	2
MS Office 2003 Pro- OEM	28-10-2006	Technofirm Software (PONDI)	4
MS Office 2003 Pro- OEM	30-10-2006	OCEAN INFOSOLUTIONS	1
Norton Antivirus 2007 Single User	30-10-2006	SHIVAM ASSOCIATES	50
Norton Antivirus 2007 Single User	30-10-2006	Secant Technologies	20

Table 1 : Sample data

- **Custom Tables**

This table is used to analyze the data by relating the data in terms of various variables we had applied this tool to find out the sales patterns based on date so that the manager can take the decisions to store those software which are in demand on particular dates.[9]

		Stock Item:		
		McAfee Managed Virus Scan	MS Office 2003 Pro- OEM	Norton Antivirus 2007 Single User
		Count	Count	Count
Date	21.04.06	0	1	0
	21.07.06	0	1	0
	24.07.06	0	1	0
	25.07.06	0	1	0
	19.08.06	0	1	0
	15.09.06	0	1	0

Table 2: Custom Table created using SPSS

- **Analysis**

The following table shows the total sales of three products date-wise so based on that manger can take the decision that which software should be purchased in advance so that whenever demand of that software comes it can be fulfill and this can be done based on this prediction only.

- **Sequence Plot**

One or more numeric variables are plotted. Cases are plotted in sequence. Use only when cases are sorted in meaningful order (time series data).This procedure requires that you have either time series data or other data where cases are sorted in meaningful order .Select one or more numeric variables and move them onto the Variables list. You can select a categorical variable and move it onto the Time Axis

Labels list. This variable may be numeric, string, or long string. The values of this variable are used to label the time axis.[9]

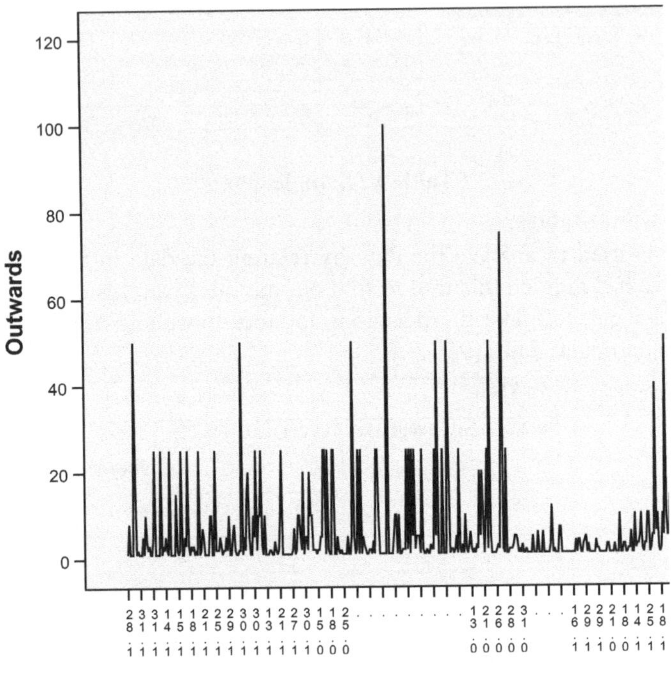

Figure 3: Sequence Plot Created in SPSS using Actual Data

Analysis

Horizontal axis shows **dates** and vertical axis shows the **quantity sold** so this sequence plot shows that which date is having maximum sales so the decision makers based on this analysis can predict that next year how the stocks should be maintained in the store which prepare the company in advance so that deal the demand which manager had predicted based on previous sales patterns.

Conclusion

This research is going to help various companies so as to find out their sales pattern and then based on that they can predict the future of their sales. They can target in advance their customers and build a lot of profit as well as be ahead than their competitors.

Future Scope

This research can be implemented in all type of organization so as to help all managers to take their decisions in advance. We can use other techniques of classification and prediction to analyze the data.

References

- Floriana Esposito," A Comparative analysis of methods for pruning Decision trees,"IEEE Transaction on pattern analysis and pattern matching Vol 19, 1997.
- Michal J A & Berry Gordon S, "Mastering Data Mining"
- http://www.sas.com
- http://www.moulton.com/olap/olap.glossary.html
- Goodwin L, Prather J, Schlitz K, Iannacchione My Hammond W, Grzymala J, "Data Mining Issues"
- Y. Zhuge, H. Garcia-Molina, J. Hammer, and J. Widom, "View maintenance in a warehousing environment", In Proceedings of the ACM SIGMOD International Conference on Management of Data, pages316{327, San Jose, California, May 1995.
- J.A. Blakeley, N. Coburn, and P.-A. Larson, "Up-dating derived relations: Detecting irrelevant and autonomously computable updates", ACM Transactions on Database Systems, 14(3):369{400, September 1989.
- http://www.spss.com

Risk Management System in NSE of India

Monika Arora
Lecturer (Finance), RDIAS, Delhi

Abstract

*The term **risk management** is applied in a number of fields. People who are in the fields of statistics, economics, psychology, social sciences, biology, engineering, toxicology, systems analysis, operations research, and decision theory, all have been addressing the field of risk management. In this regard stock exchanges were facing major challenge of managing a diverse data base. The National Stock Exchange of India (NSE) is one of the first stock exchange in the in India to use IT based system for the end to end connectivity and computer based trading. NSE has completely shifted the trade platform from the floors of stock exchange to the computer terminals at the brokerage firm and further to personal computers in the investor's home & office which has resulted in an increase in the productivity and efficiency of NSE.*

Introduction

Everybody wants to save their hard earned money and also tries to invest them in various investment opportunities. There are various financial schemes available in India. Many of them provide guaranteed returns, high interest rates, tax savings etc. In this capital market provides an opportunity to the investors to invest in various options of getting high returns on their investment. It is certain that the capital market investments have the prospects of high returns but at the same time investor should also take in to consideration the risk which they have to take in the stock market. An investor should also understand that nobody can predict the market situation and it might rise up or fall down and you might get higher returns or incur huge loss in the capital market. So there are variety of risks that market players experienced.

Capital market is the place where securities of life more than one year are traded. It can be further subdivided into:

- Primary Market: It is a market where securities are floated for the first time.
- Secondry Market: It is a place where securities which have already been issued are traded.

Investors can invest in secondry market through Securities Exchanges

National Stock Exchange of India (NSE)

National Stock Exchange of India (NSE) is India's largest Stock Exchange & World's third largest Stock Exchange in terms of transactions. Located in Mumbai, NSE was promoted by leading Financial Institutions at the behest of the Government of India, and was incorporated in November 1992 as a tax-paying company. In April 1993, NSE was recognized as a Stock exchange under the Securities Contracts (Regulation) Act-1956. NSE commenced operations in the Wholesale Debt Market (WDM) segment in June 1994. Capital Market (Equities) segment of the NSE commenced operations in November 1994, while operations in the Derivatives segment commenced in June 2000. NSE has played a catalytic role in reforming Indian securities market in terms of microstructure, market practices and trading volumes. NSE has set up its trading system as a nation-wide, fully automated screen based trading system. It has written for itself the mandate to create World-class Stock Exchange and use it as an instrument of change for the industry as a whole through competitive pressure. NSE is set up on a demutualised model wherein the ownership, management and trading rights are in the hands of three different sets of people. This has completely eliminated any conflict of interest.
NSE was set up with the objectives of:

- Establishing nationwide trading facility for all types of securities
- Ensuring equal access to investors all over the country through an appropriate telecommunication network
- Providing fair, efficient & transparent securities market using electronic trading system
- Enabling shorter settlement cycles and book entry settlements
- Meeting International benchmarks and standards

Within a very short span of time, NSE has been able to achieve its objectives for which it was set up. Indian Capital Markets are very much different from what they were 12 years back in terms of market practices, infrastructure, technology, risk management, clearing and settlement and investor service. NSE has also built up a full fledged BCP site operational for last 7 years to ensure continuity of business.

NSE's Markets

NSE provides a facility of a fully automated screen-based trading system with national reach in the following major market segments:-

- Equity OR Capital Markets
- Futures & Options OR Derivatives Market
- Wholesale Debt Market
- Mutual Funds
- Initial Public Offerings

"Over the last decade or so, there has been a paradigm shift in the Indian capital markets. The Indian markets are no longer isolated from the global economic events. We have witnessed bouts of volatility in our markets, some of which may have their origin in global events. The recent sub prime crisis and news of probable recession emerging from the US, are examples of how events which are international, can cause volatility in our markets. Inflation rates, global energy prices, exchange rate fluctuations etc. are witnessing constant changes in the recent years. These are affecting the volatility of the markets," NSE said on its website.

Risk Management and IT

What is the relationship between risk and IT, not much but in today's environment IT plays a central role in risk management in each and every field. For E.g. before the dematerialisation of shares, variety of risks were there which were being experienced by market players, that the shares which they were trading were in duplicate, reason being the signatures on the share certificates would not tally and so on. The solution to this risk was provided by IT when shares were dematerialised, and all the players started working through dematerialised accounts, with this technique, just by pressing a botton share account of selling individual gets debited and those of buying one is credited.

So, stock markets are facing a major challenge of managing a diverse data base, i.e. why it needed a data warehouse to analyse trading and payment patterns of members of the exchange, based on well defined risk classes for risk containment and maintaining market integrity. With the help of diversity in data storage technologies, data semantics, and database management techniques across multiple applications, managing and integrating information was a major issue. Hence, there was a great need for reports that required historical information to be retrieved and analyzed which required huge amount of system resources and need less to say, the associated time.

The solution to the problem lied in integrated, unified data pool that was truly subject-oriented, time-variant and nonvolatile. For this purpose Wipro team undertook the end-to-end implementation of this data warehouse from the analysis of requirement to final integration and training of user which included technical architecture design, tool selection, data extraction, metadata management, integration and training, that ultimately gave birth to the largest data warehousing project that has been implemented in India. With an initial size of more than 500 Gigabytes of data, it has the capabilities of providing following facilities:

- It has a scalable Information Architecture that will allow the information base to be extended and enhanced over time.

- It helps in the detailed analysis of member patterns, including trading, delivery and funds payment.
- Sequence of event analysis and fraud detection.
- It provides an ease of reporting on voluminous historical data
- It also provide provision for ad hoc queries and reporting facilities to enhance the efficiency of knowledge workers
- Facilitate data mining to identified the co-relation between apparently independent entities.

The successful implementation of this large and complex project has provided NSE a good satisfaction ratings from their client.

As per the believes of NSE technology shall continue to provide necessary impetus for any organisation to retain its competitive edge, ensure timeliness & satisfaction to the customer. Being fully dependant on Information Technology, NSE has also stressed on innovation and sustained investment in technology on a continual basis to ensure the satisfaction of customer, improvement in services which automatically helps in sustaining business and always remain ahead of competitors. As a policy, NSE looks to improve the quality of Services to its customers. Projects are not initiated based on a business model to reap profits but from a strategic perspective of better productivity, Value-adds & features, improving efficiency, reducing operational costs, compliance, operational transparency etc for the customers, investors and to the entire Indian Securities Industry. Some of the projects taken by NSE in last years are as under :-

1. Trading System Capacity enhancement
2. Re-engineering of Online Position Monitoring (OPMS)
3. Augmentation of Data Warehouse (DWH)
4. STP Central Hub

Trading System Capacity Enhancement

NSE's Capital Market Trading system was operational on two machine split architecture which are using Fault Tolerant mainframes and geared to handle 3 million trades. However, the CM segment had started to experience trades nearing 3 Million trades which form a threshold. On the basis of trends & expected volumes, growth in the medium term is more than thrice the current trading volume which comes out to be about 10 Million transactions per day, i.e. why 3-machine split architecture project was taken up to increase the load handling capacity of the system by introducing a 3-way split Hardware by improving existing 2-machine split architecture. it was required to improve the trading system transaction handling capacity. The, Application optimization and also by improving the processes for achieving market volume of around 6 million transactions per day.

Benefits

1. System scaled on 3 machines with distribution of users and securities with complete transparency to market participants.
2. System witnessed 3 million trades with faster response time to members at significantly lower system resource utilisation level.
3. Handling higher volume than before i.e. 6 million transactions per day from 3 million to.

Re-engineering of Online Position Monitoring (OPMS)

The system is for on-line Position Monitoring and Risk Management system for the Capital Market segment of the National Stock Exchange of India Limited. Its work is to track positions of trading members from Turnover and Exposure limits with a view of identifying and preventing potential settlement related issues. With the help of this system positions are monitored on an on-line basis and auto disablement of the violating member on the trading system.

Benefits

1 Real-time position computation and violation detection
2 Ability to handle high load of over one million client positions
3 Management of information for positions & risk values about each & every trading member
4 Information structure based on a tree of security, settlement, trading member
5 Achieve 4000 violation checks per second

Augmentation of Data Warehouse (DWH)

NSE is also having a matured data warehouse application extensively used for analysis, reporting and investigative purposes. This has helped NSE to enhance and upgrade existing data warehouse infrastructure.

Benefits

1. Response time & query performance improved dramatically by about 100%.
2. Extraction and loading time has reduced by almost 8-9 times.
3. Timely, efficient reporting. Reduced lead time in providing data to Regulator.
4. New features of Oracle 9i like Ranking, enhanced analytic functions have contributed enormously to efficiency aspect of the data warehouse usage.

Straight Through Processing (STP) Central Hub

Straight Through Processing (STP) framework seeks to provide seamless data flow both within the enterprise as well as across the market without any manual intervention using ISO 15022 messaging standards because this is a global phenomenon that an institutional fund house, details of trade confirmations executed in the day are sent out to the Custodian for effecting trade settlements. The Custodian also receives details of the executed trade from the broker of the fund house, for cross-verification of the trade data. Upon verification, if it is found that the trade details do not match the instruction documents sent across by the fund house and the broker there is a delay in effecting such settlements. Studies have shown that around 15% of global trade failures result from unmatched trade data, which in monetary terms is upwards of Billions of Dollars, a steep price pay for the lack of an efficient processing framework.

In India, of SEBI making STP mandatory. NSE has recognising that the success of the STP is crucial to make a move towards an improvement in settlement cycle for the transactions.

NSE took up the challenge of setting up a Central Hub to resolve inter-operability amongst various STP Service Providers. After developing the application software, the STP Central Hub was put for operational testing from end of March 2004 to route the messages between Service Providers.

Benefits

1. Improved efficiency, reduction of manual activities leading to higher accuracy of trade execution and settlement.
2. Reduced operational risk by automating the process from execution through to settlement.
3. Reduction in operational cost by sending data electronically.
4. Transparency & improved customer service with detailed reports about delivery and failure of messages are available instantaneously, on an on-line basis.
5. Reduced settlement cycle to facilitate T+1 settlement.

Conclusion

NSE through its strengthening technologies & innovations has made management of risk possible through immediate access of information to those who need it most and could handle check and balance on a real time basis. Thus the use of IT in NSE would continue to add more facilities to its existing products to provide more satisfaction to its customers.

References

- www.altiudirectory.com
- www.wipro.com
- www.wikipedia.com
- Brien, James AO, "Management Information System";6th ed. Tata McGraw Hill.
- Kumar Munish,"Business Information System", 2nd ed. Vikas Publication House.
- Gupta, N.K., Chopra,Monika,"Financial Markets, Institutions & Services, ane's students edition, Ane Books India.
- Varshney, P.N., Mittal, D.K.,"Indian Financial System",Eighth Ed.,Sultan chand & Sons, Educational Publisher.

Artificial Neural Network and its Uses in Present Era of Information Technology

Alok Mohan
Pursuing B.Tech, GNIT, Greater Noida

Abstract

A neural network is, in essence, an attempt to simulate the brain. Neural network theory revolves around the idea that certain key properties of biological neurons can be extracted and applied to simulations, thus creating a simulated (and very much simplified) brain. The concept of Artificial Neural Network is based on biological neurons which are an interconnection of artificial neurons which are used to process and produce information on specific areas. The purpose of this paper is to provide knowledge about this new and emerging field of the present era. The paper provides information about the working and the uses of the Artificial Neural Network.

Introduction

It is a mathematical model which is based on biological neurons. It is an interconnection of neurons (artificial) which are used to process data and produce information on specific areas.

What is an Artificial Neural Network?

An artificial neural network is a system based on the operation of biological neural networks. In other words, it is an emulation of biological neural system. A neural network is, in essence, an attempt to simulate the brain. Neural network theory revolves around the idea that certain key properties of biological neurons can be extracted and applied to simulations, thus creating a simulated (and very much simplified) brain. The first important thing to understand then is that the components of an artificial neural network are an attempt to recreate the computing potential of the brain. The second important thing to understand, however, is that no one has ever claimed to simulate anything as complex as an actual brain.

Before discussing the specifics of artificial neural nets, let us examine what makes real neural nets. Perhaps the single most important concept in neural net research is the idea of connection strength. Neuroscience has given us good evidence for the idea that connection strengths - that is, how strongly one neuron influences those neurons connected to it - are the real information holders in the brain.

Learning, repetition of a task, even exposure to a new or continuing stimulus can cause the brain's connection strengths to change, some synaptic connections becoming reinforced and new ones are being created, others weakening or in some cases disappearing altogether. The second essential element of neural connectivity is the excitation/inhibition distinction. In human brains, each neuron is either excitatory or inhibitory, which is to say that its activation will either increase the firing rates of connected neurons, or decrease the rate, respectively. The amount of excitation or inhibition produced is of course, dependent on the connection strength - a stronger connection means more inhibition or excitation, a weaker connection means less. The third important component in determining a neuron's response is called the transfer function. Without getting into more technical detail, the transfer function describes how a neuron's firing rate varies with the input it receives.

Some important features of Artificial Neural Networks

- A neural network can perform tasks that a linear program cannot.
- A neural network learns and does not need to be reprogrammed.
- It can be implemented in any application.
- It can be implemented without any problem.
- The neural network needs training to operate.
- The architecture of a neural network is different from the architecture of microprocessors therefore needs to be emulated.
- Requires high processing time for large neural networks.

Another aspect of the artificial neural networks is that there are different architectures, which consequently requires different types of algorithms, but despite to be an apparently complex system, a neural network is relatively simple.

Organization of Artificial Neural Networks

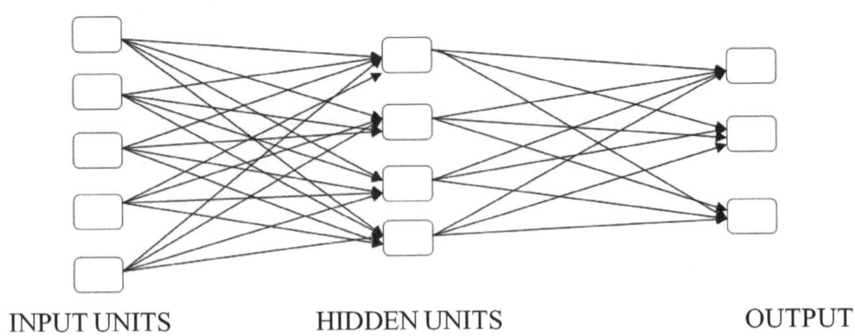

Figure 1: Organization of Artificial Neural Networks

Perhaps the most significant difference between artificial and biological neural nets is their organization. While many types of artificial neural nets exist, most are organized according to the same basic structure (FIGURE-1). There are three components to this organization: a set of input nodes, one or more layers of 'hidden' nodes, and a set of output nodes. The input nodes take in information, and are similar to sensory organs. Whether the information is in the form of a digitized picture, or a series of stock values, or just about any other form that can be numerically expressed, this is where the net gets its initial data. The information is supplied as activation values, that is, each node is given a number, higher numbers representing greater activation. This is just like human neurons except that rather than conveying their activation level by firing more frequently, as biological neurons do, artificial neurons indicate activation by passing this activation value to connected nodes. After receiving this initial activation, information is then passed through the network. Connection strengths, inhibition/excitation conditions, and transfer functions determine how much of the activation value is passed on to the next node. Each node sums the activation values it receives, arrives at its own activation value, and then passes that along to the next nodes in the network (after modifying its activation level according to its transfer function). Thus the activation flows through the net in one direction, from input nodes, through the hidden layers, until eventually the output nodes are activated. If a network is properly trained, this output should reflect the input in some meaningful way.

Training of Artifcial Neural Networks

A **neural network** has to be configured such that the application of a set of inputs produces (either 'direct' or via a relaxation process) the desired set of outputs. Various methods to set the strengths of the connections exist. One way is to set the weights explicitly, using a priori knowledge. Another way is to **'train' the neural network** by feeding it teaching patterns and letting it change its weights according to some learning rule.

The learning situations can be categorized in three distinct sorts. These are:

- **Supervised learning** or Associative learning in which the network is trained by providing it with input and matching output patterns. These input-output pairs can be provided by an external teacher, or by the system which contains the neural network (self-supervised).
- **Unsupervised learning** or Self-organization in which an (output) unit is trained to respond to clusters of pattern within the input. In this paradigm the system is supposed to discover statistically salient features of the input population. Unlike the supervised learning paradigm, there is no a priori set of categories into which the patterns are to be classified; rather the system must develop its own representation of the input stimuli.

- **Reinforcement Learning** This type of learning may be considered as an intermediate form of the above two types of learning. Here the learning machine does some action on the environment and gets a feedback response from the environment. The learning system grades its action good (rewarding) or bad (punishable) based on the environmental response and accordingly adjusts its parameters. Generally, parameter adjustment is continued until an equilibrium state occurs, following which there will be no more changes in its parameters. The self organizing neural learning may be categorized under this type of learning.

Applications of Neural Networks

Neural Networks in Practice

Given this description of neural networks and how they work, what real world applications are they suited for? Neural networks have broad applicability to real world business problems. In fact, they have already been successfully applied in many industries.

Since neural networks are best at identifying patterns or trends in data, they are well suited for prediction or forecasting needs including:

Ø Sales forecasting
Ø Industrial process control
Ø Customer research
Ø Data validation
Ø Risk management
Ø Target marketing

But to give some more specific examples; ANN are also used in the following specific paradigms: recognition of speakers in communications; diagnosis of hepatitis; recovery of telecommunications from faulty software; interpretation of multi-meaning words; undersea mine detection; texture analysis; three-dimensional object recognition; hand-written word recognition; and facial recognition.

Neural Networks in Medicine

Artificial Neural Network (ANN) is currently a 'hot' research area in medicine and it is believed that they will receive extensive application to biomedical systems in the next few years. At the moment, the research is mostly on modeling parts of the human body and recognizing diseases from various scans (e.g. cardiograms, CAT scans, ultrasonic scans, etc.).

Neural networks are ideal in recognizing diseases using scans since there is no need to provide a specific algorithm on how to identify the disease. Neural networks learn by example so the details of how to recognize the disease are not needed. What is needed is a set of examples that are representative of all the variations of the disease. The quantity of examples is not as important as the 'quantity'. The examples need to be selected very carefully if the system is to perform reliably and efficiently.

Modeling and Diagnosing the Cardiovascular System

Neural Networks are used experimentally to model the human cardiovascular system. Diagnosis can be achieved by building a model of the cardiovascular system of an individual and comparing it with the real time physiological measurements taken from the patient. If this routine is carried out regularly, potential harmful medical conditions can be detected at an early stage and thus make the process of combating the disease much easier.

Electronic Noses

ANNs are used experimentally to implement electronic noses. Electronic noses have several potential applications in telemedicine. Telemedicine is the practice of medicine over long distances via a communication link. The electronic nose would identify odors in the remote surgical environment. These identified odors would then be electronically transmitted to another site where a door generation system would recreate them. Because the sense of smell can be an important sense to the surgeon, tele-smell would enhance tele-present surgery.

Instant Physician

An application developed in the mid-1980s called the "instant physician" trained an auto associative memory neural network to store a large number of medical records, each of which includes information on symptoms, diagnosis, and treatment for a particular case. After training, the net can be presented with input consisting of a set of symptoms; it will then find the full stored pattern that represents the "best" diagnosis and treatment.

Neural Networks in Business

Business is a diverted field with several general areas of specialization such as accounting or financial analysis. Almost any neural network application would fit into one business area or financial analysis. There is some potential for using neural networks for business purposes, including resource allocation and scheduling. There is also a strong potential for using neural networks for database mining that is, searching for patterns implicit within the explicitly stored information in databases. Most of the funded work in this area is classified as proprietary. Thus, it is not possible to report on the full extent of the work going on. Most work is applying neural networks, such as the Hopfield-Tank network for optimization and scheduling.

Marketing

There is a marketing application which has been integrated with a neural network system. The Airline Marketing Tactician (a trademark abbreviated as AMT) is a computer system made of various intelligent technologies including expert systems. A feed forward neural network is integrated with the AMT and was trained using back-propagation to assist the marketing control of airline seat allocations. The adaptive neural approach was amenable to rule expression. Additionally, the application's environment changed rapidly and constantly, which required a continuously adaptive solution. The system is used to monitor and recommend booking advice for each departure. Such information has a direct impact on the profitability of an airline and can provide a technological advantage for users of the system.

While it is significant that neural networks have been applied to this problem, it is also important to see that this intelligent technology can be integrated with expert systems and other approaches to make a functional system. Neural networks were used to discover the influence of undefined interactions by the various variables. While these interactions were not defined, they were used by the neural system to develop useful conclusions. It is also noteworthy to see that neural networks can influence the bottom line.

Credit Evaluation

The HNC Company, founded by Robert Hecht-Nielsen, has developed several neural network applications. One of them is the Credit Scoring system which increases the profitability of the existing model up to 27%. The HNC neural systems were also applied to mortgage screening. A neural network automated mortgage insurance underwriting system was developed by the Nestor Company. This system was trained with 5048 applications of which 2597 were certified. The data related to property and borrower qualifications. In a conservative mode the system agreed on the underwriters on 97% of the cases. In the liberal model the system agreed 84% of the cases.

Conclusion

The computing world has a lot to gain from neural networks. Their ability to learn by example makes them very flexible and powerful. Furthermore there is no need to devise an algorithm in order to perform a specific task; i.e. there is no need to understand the internal mechanisms of that task. They are also very well suited for real time systems because of their fast response and computational times which are due to their parallel architecture.

Neural networks also contribute to other areas of research such as neurology and psychology. They are regularly used to model parts of living organisms and to investigate the internal mechanisms of the brain.

Perhaps the most exciting aspect of neural networks is the possibility that some day 'conscious' networks might be produced. There are a number of scientists arguing that consciousness is a 'mechanical' property and that 'conscious' neural networks are a realistic possibility.

The huge potential of neural network can be obtained if it is integrated with computing, AI, fuzzy logic and others related subjects.

References

- Yegnanarayana,"Artificial Neural Networks" (2003), Prentice-hall of India Pvt. Ltd.
- Oz E, "Management Information System" (2008), Vikas Publishing, (3rd Ed.)
- James A O'Brien, "Management Information System (Managing Information Technology in the E-business Enterprise)" Tata McGraw Hill (Fifth ed. 2002)
- Effy OZ, "Management Information System" Cengage Learning India Pvt. Ltd.(2006)
- J M Zurada, "Introduction to Artificial Neural Systems" Jaico publishing House(2002)
- Kishan Mehrotra, Chilukuri K Mohan, Sanjay Ranka, "Elements Of Artificial Neural Network" Pen ram International Publishing India Pvt. Ltd. (1997)